AhX 8360

FACING TWO WAYS

Ghana's Coastal Communities Under Colonial Rule

Roger S. Gocking

University Press of America,® Inc.
Lanham • New York • Oxford

Copyright © 1999 by
University Press of America,® Inc.
4720 Boston Way
Lanham, Maryland 20706

12 Hid's Copse Rd.
Cumnor Hill, Oxford OX2 9JJ

ISBN 0-7618-1354-3 (cloth: alk. ppr.)

To the memory of my father
and mother who passed away before
this work that owes so much to them
was finished

Contents

List of Photographs

List of Abbreviations

ADM	Administrative, file classification for the colonial administration
CCP	Commissioner of the Central Province
CMG	Companion of (the Order) of St.Michael and St. George
CO	Colonial Office
DC	District Commissioner
GCARPS	Gold Coast Aborigines' Rights Protection Society
HCCC	High Court Cape Coast
MBE	Member of the British Empire
NAG	National Archives of Ghana
NCBWA	National Congress of British West Africa
OBE	Order of the British Empire
PC	Provincial Commissioner
PRO	Public Record Office, London
SNA	Secretary of Native Affairs
SCT	Supreme Court, Gold Coast Colony
SOAS	School of Oriental and African Studies, London University
UAC	United Africa Company
WACA	West African Court of Appeal

Acknowledgments

In 1973, when I first arrived in Ghana to begin research on the town of Cape Coast, I had only vague ideas of how this project would unfold. Many people have played important roles in helping me to find my way and I owe them a major debt of gratitude. My advisers at Stanford University, Kennell Jackson, Paul Irwin and Richard Roberts, provided me with intellectual stimulation, and the ability to think critically about Africa's past. They set exacting standards. At times their demands seemed more designed to frustrate me than to speed the completion of my dissertation on the social and intellectual history of Cape Coast, the nucleus around which this work has evolved. Most of all, their enthusiastic response to the richness of the material that I had collected stimulated me to expand my focus beyond Cape Coast to produce this more inclusive study of Ghana's coastal towns.

Professor Morton Williams of the University of Cape Coast kindly agreed to sponsor my research when I was first in Ghana. He did much more. He and his wife very generously helped to smooth my passage through the settling-in phase that contact with a new culture invariably requires. On subsequent research trips to Ghana and mostly Accra, Dr. Kofi Baku of the Legon History Department fulfilled this role. As a fellow student of Ghana's colonial past, he could also direct me to sources of which I was not aware.

To the people of Ghana's coastal towns I owe the greatest debt of gratitude. They were invariably enthusiastic and honored that someone was deeply interested in their history. They gave generously of their time to answer questions about themselves, deceased relatives and prominent and not so prominent members of their communities. Without this information and the insights that it provided, many of the issues that I have treated would have escaped my attention. Their contribution is inadequately acknowledged in this work. Some, unfortunately, time has claimed and they are no longer alive to take some small pleasure from the completion of this project. Mr. W. S. K. (Kwesi) Johnston was both a fascinating source of information about Cape Coast's interwar political life and an important actor on this stage. His death shortly after I left Cape Coast in 1974 took from the scene one of the best-informed of local historians. I felt privileged to have known him. Messrs. J. A. Annobil and N. Forson, who were also both friends and patient informants as well as important actors on the Cape Coast stage, have also been claimed by "Time's devouring hand." In general, subsequent trips to Ghana have invariably been tinged with the sorrow of learning that many such people will not have the opportunity to see how I have used (or misused?) the information that they so generously shared with me. In the bibliography I include a full list of all my informants.

This work is also based on a great deal of archival research, much of it done in the Ghana National Archives primarily in Cape Coast and Accra. Here the extensive period of my research has paralleled the career of Mr. C. K. Gadzekpo, who, when I first meet him, was assistant archivist in Cape Coast, but is now the director of the National Archives in Accra. To him and his staff I owe a debt of gratitude for their willingness to accommodate my sometimes impatient requests for materials that were often not easy to find. Karen Fung, the curator of the Africana collection at Hoover Institution, has also provided invaluable help in locating little known reports, hard to acquire books and theses, and microfilm collections of early Ghanaian newspapers. Even after I had left Stanford University, she continued to function in this fashion, and when she herself could not deliver, she generously tapped into her far-flung network of fellow Africanist librarians.

Fieldwork in Africa and research time in the Public Record Office required funding. The Committee for the Comparative Study of Africa and the Americas at Stanford University generously funded my first foray into the field, and a subsequent Weter Foundation grant started me on the long and sometimes painful task of dissertation write-up. Mercy College, in Westchester County, New York, provided me with a base to complete this work. Grants from the college's Faculty Development Committee have helped to finance several return trips to Ghana. These later forays into the field have been invaluable in enabling me to expand the scope of this investigation of cultural interaction in the colonial setting. My Mercy College colleagues Peter Slater and Ted Rosenof also provided invaluable help with close readings of this work and invaluable suggestions on how it could be improved. John DiElsi transformed me into a "technology advocate," and with the aid of Mary Jane Chase, my WordPerfect guru, I was able to battle my way through the formatting of this monograph.

Donna Gordon-Mitchell of the Mercy College Publications Department provided invaluable help with map-making.

To Jim Gullickson, my copy editor and proof-reader, I also owe a note of special thanks. His close reading of the manuscript uncovered mistakes and inadequacies in the work of which I was unaware, and with his assistance I was able to conform to the publisher's exacting stylistic and formatting requirements.

Finally, I would like to thank my parents, who conveniently lived in London during the time that much of the research for this work was done. They provided the most comfortable base of operations. Their contribution was far more significant than this alone. They provided insights into the colonial situation derived from their own experience as colonial subjects, and also an enthusiastic interest in my many adventures and experiences while I was in Africa. Unfortunately, neither of them lived to see this work finished.

Chapter 1

Coastal Society: An Introduction

The numerous, old, weather-beaten forts and castles that "cling like leeches" to rocky promontories or steep bluffs above Ghana's surf-bound coast are vivid reminders of the long history of contact between Europe and this part of Africa.[1] Unlike their counterparts elsewhere on the West African coastline, these fortifications often stand in sight of one another. Their proximity to one another, as well as the frequency with which they have changed hands in the past, are indications of how important the wealth of this area was to the Europeans who built these imposing fortifications.[2] The Portuguese, who arrived on this coast in 1471, were the first to monopolize its trade. By the seventeenth century, however, French, Dutch, English, Swedish, Danish and Brandenburger traders were also attracted to what the Portuguese described as the Golden Coast of Guinea.[3] They, too, built fortified posts to protect themselves from one another and the suspicious Africans with whom they traded. By the eighteenth century, however, only the Danes, the Dutch and the English remained with their respective forts and castles interspersed among one another along a coastline of some three hundred miles, from the Tano River in the west to the Keta Lagoon in the east.[4]

During the initial centuries of contact, the relationship between Europe and Africa was primarily one of trade; European impact on the coast was limited. Only in the settlements directly outside the walls of the forts and castles was there substantial interaction. Nevertheless, the long-term result of this contact was to set in motion a gradual, yet inexorable refocusing of

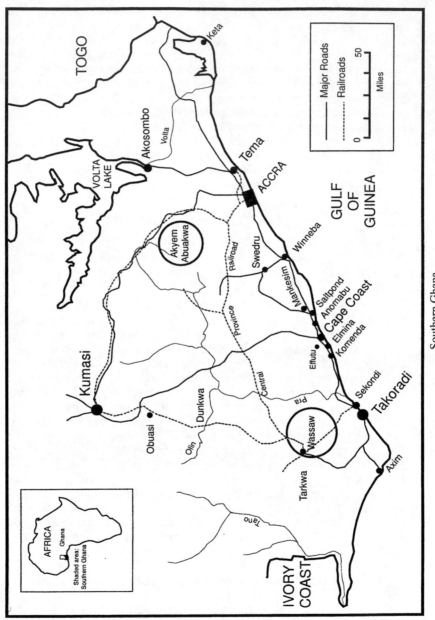

Southern Ghana

power and influence away from the interior to the coast. It was to give the relatively small and culturally heterogeneous coastal communities an importance in Ghanaian history far out of proportion to their actual size and populations. These initially tiny communities were to grow into the dominant societies around which the colonial order emerged. Already by the early nineteenth century they had come to rival in importance the larger centralized states of the interior. In the twentieth century they grew dramatically in size to become the centers of political and economic power for what was then the Colony of the Gold Coast.

At first, as centers of trade and later also as administrative, missionary and educational loci, these settlements served as both the frontier and the dispersion point for new ideas and beliefs, while in turn they borrowed customs and institutions from the interior which they incorporated into the "colonial situation."[5] Janus-like they faced two ways, and symbolized the beginning of a new order that represented a fusion of both African and European influences. In contrast to the cataclysmic encounter with colonial rule that many other areas of West Africa experienced, southern Ghana's incorporation into the colonial world was more gradual and adaptive. This process of incorporation paralleled the phases through which colonial rule in general passed. It included the arrival of missionaries and their contributions to the spread of Western education, the development of an articulate, Western-educated African elite, a flourishing newspaper and literary tradition, and an early fusion of English common law with African customary law. In the context of southern Ghana we can appreciate particularly well the complex cultural interactions of what Andrew Roberts has described as the "transforming moment" that colonial rule represented.[6] The long history of European and African cultural interaction has contributed to making this area one of the best examples in West Africa of how much absorption and adaptation there was in this transformative process.

Historians have tended to emphasize the European component of this cultural interaction and especially anglicization since by the mid-nineteenth century Great Britain had become the dominant power in this area of the West African coast. However, the interchange between indigenous cultures themselves was also of profound importance in shaping the identity of these coastal societies. The most important aspect of this cross-fertilization was the gradual "Akanization" of the southern Gold Coast which represented the other side of facing two ways. It was already underway before the establishment of formal colonial rule. Powerful inland Akan kingdoms, like those of the Akyem, the Denkyira and the Asante, had begun in the seventeenth century to influence the peoples of the coast. The more decentralized Fante, also an Akan people and culturally very similar to the Asante, had begun even earlier to affect the non-Akans they came in contact with near the coast.

The Pax Britannica, and particularly the policy of indirect rule that the colonial government adopted from the beginning of the twentieth century onward, furthered this process. As Maxwell Owusu has observed, "During the colonial period...the Akan model of statecraft, with its inherent ideology of popular rights, was adopted by or imposed, with some local modifications, on nearly all other peoples in Ghana."[7] From the colonial administration's point of view it was convenient to have one system of native government, and not surprisingly they picked that which seemed most structured. In spite of the populist pressures that Akan rulers were subject to, this system of indigenous government was more in keeping with officialdom's hierarchical conception of how colonial society should function than the more loosely organized structures of the Effutu, the Ga and the Ewe, its rivals. There was far more knowledge about Akan state-craft, and a longer history of interaction with its most important states, which were also important factors in its favor.

The partiality that the colonial government demonstrated for the Akan model of statecraft affected more than political systems. The links between social structure, customary law, language and Akan political institutions were too close for this not to be the case. Less noticed, but of vital importance for appreciating the complexity of facing two ways in the southern Gold Coast, was the extent to which Akan culture influenced the political and social institutions that developed during the colonial period. Akan norms modified succession to office within these institutions as well as membership in the extended family, inheritance of property from one generation to the next, communal ceremonies, religious beliefs and practices and finally even the customary law that regulated the behavior of communities that considered themselves to be different from their Akan neighbors. Relatively small ethnic groups, like the Effutu in Winneba, and more numerous peoples, like the Ga in and around Accra, and the Adangbe and the Ewe further eastward along the coast, came under the influence of Akanization. In general Akanization was probably most pronounced among those who lived nearer the coast and had been involved in aspects of southern Ghana's long history of contact with Europeans. This nexus tended to link them economically with their Akan neighbors, and facilitated cultural transfer. The 1948 census classified over 40 per-cent of the colony's population as Akans. However, their cultural impact on the southern Gold Coast was much higher than their percentage in the country's population would indicate.

Showing how the twin forces of Europeanization, mostly anglicization, and Akanization interacted in what an early Ghanaian lawyer and nationalist, John Mensah Sarbah, described as the "coast district" of the Gold Coast will be the main focus of this study.[8] Given the far-reaching nature of both Akan and European influences on the coast, there is a host of specific issues that could be treated within the context of facing two ways that would reflect this long history of cultural interaction. The study, however, will restrict itself to dealing with primarily political and judicial interchanges. The institution building associated with this exchange represented the most important aspect of the larger process of cultural interaction that colonial rule facilitated since it directly involved the evolution of the colonial system of government itself. It was inevitable that this would be the case because in precolonial African societies there was no real concept of the separation of judicial and political roles. Akan chiefs discharged both roles, as well as religious and ritual functions. As an indication of the need to compromise with traditional ideas about government, for most of the colonial period British political officers also acted as both administrators and judges. Expediency played a large role, but there were many who defended this anomalous situation on the grounds that otherwise "natives" would not really respect political officers as they were accustomed to seeing the same person exercise administrative and judicial responsibilities.

Nevertheless, the coming of British rule represented a fundamental challenge to the traditional link between the judicial and the political, for as Bjorn Edsman has pointed out the "far-reaching Anglicization of the whole judicial system" that followed "led indirectly to a Western-modeled restructuring of the society as a whole."[9] The gradual separation of judicial and political roles, both from Akan and British institutions, was a vital component of this restructuring. As far as the British courts were concerned, this meant creating lower courts with legally qualified magistrates who were not political officers. In the case of the chiefly courts, the Native Tribunals, this meant training educated Africans to preside over and run these courts, and gradually reducing the role of the chief in their deliberations. Ironically, however, at the same time politics and justice were becoming intertwined in new ways. The highly parochial focus of coastal political life that developed in the twentieth century linked control of Western-style municipal political affairs with controlling succession to chieftaincy. Invariably official commissions of inquiry failed to resolve these disputes and the contestants turned to the colony's High Courts. In addition to extending the boundaries of what British justice was responsible for adjudicating, these highly charged political cases could bring judicial and political officers into conflict with one another as policy considerations clashed with judicial detachment.

The interaction between politics and justice was also very evident on the level of individual lives. People who were active in the parochial political life that indirect rule promoted were also intimately involved in litigation over the possession of property, its inheritance and disposition. Interviews with a wide range of informants in Cape Coast graphically indicated how much these private and public arenas were linked. The colony's courts were the venue for both political and personal litigation, and criticisms of how these courts operated were as much the result of political convictions as of reactions to defeats in matters pertaining to private litigation. These courts did not live up to an ideal standard of British rule of law.[10] Yet they were extremely successful in institutionalizing recourse to a legal system that British judicial ideas dominated. To contemporaries it seemed as if the "restructuring" at this level of colonial society was all in favor of the latter since this was the legal tradition of the colony's High Courts. In reality, however, there was considerable adjustment on the part of English common law to customary law while the Native Tribunals that adjudicated the latter were forced into making concessions to British jurisprudence and adopting much of the procedure of the British courts.

By analyzing cultural interaction in the fashion I have outlined, this study will move beyond a focus on the form and force of protest to colonial rule which, ever since David Kimble's seminal work on the rise of Ghanaian nationalism, has been the mark and glass that fashions even recent studies of Ghana's past.[11] In the first flush of independence this preoccupation with the origins and development of resistance to colonial rule was understandable, but an excessive concern with finding the roots of mass nationalism can at best produce only a fragmented treatment of the colonial situation. The colonial situation can not be squeezed, Procrustean-like, within a rigid framework of rising nationalist consciousness. Instead, it is more realistic to see the rise of national consciousness as merely one of the many responses to the new challenges, as well as the new opportunities, that the colonial situation offered to the diverse components of colonial society. Though chronologically short in length, this "brief moment" in the continent's history "witnessed on an unprecedented scale transformations in social identities, cognitive systems and means of communication."[12]

In general, the relative importance of the interwoven themes of African and European acculturation has fluctuated in the past. During the earlier centuries, when the trade in gold and slaves dominated the relationship between the two, the European influence was clearly minimal. In a study of trade and politics in the seventeenth-century Gold Coast, Kwame Daaku pointedly describes the trading communities that developed on the coast as "Afro-European," and by juxtaposing his hyphenated terminology in this order emphasized the African component of this cultural interchange.[13] However, by the mid-nineteenth century, as a result of the expanding British administration, missionary influence and Western education, the pendulum swung far more in favor of Europe. In the early twentieth century, when this influence was reaching its apogee, the Cape Coast barrister Kobina Sekyi, who was both the product of this process and one of its harshest critics, described people like himself in a quasi-autobiographical work as "Anglo-Fantis."[14] Indeed, his early fictional works are perhaps some of the best barometers of how much anglicization the coastal societies had undergone by the early twentieth century.[15]

Taking inspiration from these insights, Ray Jenkins has described the urban communities of the Gold Coast littoral societies in the late nineteenth and twentieth centuries as "Euro-African Societies."[16] By doing so, he has sought to place greater emphasis on "ethno-cultural categories rather than sociological concepts such as 'elite' or 'class.'"[17] As late as the independence period these societies were still only in an embryonic stage of class formation.[18] The focus on social elites can easily overemphasize "corporateness, group character and exclusiveness," which S. F. Nadel has seen as essential features of such groups.[19] In addition, a rigid sociological approach neglects the important cultural trickle-down effect that characterized the colonial situation. The unevenness of this process has contributed to making it difficult to conceptualize the distinction between what was a relatively small core of "Euro-Africans," Sekyi's "Anglo-Fantis," and a much larger "Afro-European" majority. Undoubtedly, as Jenkins points out, in "attempting to differentiate between members of [these] communities" some sort of social categorization is necessary.[20] Indeed, as I shall indicate, these communities coined terminology to distinguish between what their members clearly felt were considerably different strata of coastal society. Nevertheless, by recognizing the importance of ethno-cultural interaction we can appreciate how blurred the boundaries remained between people in societies where large extended families were the norm, and which could incorporate outsiders with surprising ease.

Even where institutional membership seemed to indicate the extent of stratification in coastal society, for example, the close correspondence between economic and social standing and the Christian denomination to which one belonged, at the same time the social diversity within these denominations also indicated the extent to which Christianity had spread throughout these communities. The pervasive influence of Christian denominations also affected traditional religious beliefs and practices. The same point can be made with regard to British judicial practices. This fundamentally foreign system of jurisprudence had a tremendous impact on customary law and the operation of traditional courts. So, too, did the British colonial presence affect succession to traditional office. The disputes that developed became the lifeblood of the parochial political activity of the interwar years, and drew in a socially diverse spectrum of the local population. To varying degrees these developments were important indications of how much coastal societies in general had become Euro-African environments whose members were linked across putatively traditional and Westernized boundaries by their participation in common activities and recourse to the same institutions.

An emphasis on cultural interaction also allows us to appreciate the important links between the coastal communities of the Gold Coast and

their counterparts elsewhere on the West African littoral. In spite of their
unique beginnings and diverse historical experiences, there were substantial similarities among Saint Louis, Bathurst, Freetown, Monrovia,
Grand Bassam, Porto Novo, Lagos, and Clarence on the island of
Fernando Po, and Elmina, Cape Coast and Accra on the Gold Coast. First
of all, they functioned in a similar economic role. They were the ports
through which hinterland produce passed and where imports from the
metropole were landed. During the nineteenth century, most of these
towns became the administrative capitals of the emerging European
colonies in West Africa. As a result, there was a wide variety of positions
in the colonial bureaucracy for Africans, and up until the late nineteenth
century it seemed as if there was no limit to their advancement in the
colonial service.[21] These towns were also the "mission points" from which
Christian missionary activity radiated.[22] The mission churches, like the
colonial administration, also provided positions for Africans. The Western
education that they offered produced a stream of "educated natives" which
served to expand the ranks of Euro-African society.[23] In addition, there
was a constant movement of Euro-Africans from one community to the
next, especially between those that were part of the same colonial empires.
Some traveled for educational purposes, while others did so for job
opportunities or business. One of the important results of this inter-West
African migration was that several of the prominent families in the coastal
towns were related through marriage.[24] Members of these communities
were keenly aware of their successful counterparts (and family members)
in other West African colonies, and shared a common sense of pride in
their achievements.

Many of these communities recognized their shared uniqueness by
describing themselves as "Creole," like the racially and culturally
heterogeneous societies of the New World.[25] In the Americas, Creole
societies took many different forms. They varied from the criollo societies
of South America that won their independence from Spain in the early
nineteenth century, to the dependent, plantation-based societies of the
Caribbean. Their counterparts in West Africa were similarly diverse. As
was the case in the New World, their particular origins, the nature of the
metropolitan culture that influenced them and the cultures of their
indigenous populations were all vitally important in affecting the shape
that they took. Not all of the Euro-African communities in West Africa
described themselves as Creole, but nevertheless they were similar enough
for some to have seen them as part of a wider Pan-Atlantic, Creole
world.[26]

In describing the colonial identity of the western Atlantic Creole world,
John Elliot has pointed out that "colonial societies, like all societies, were
in a constant process of defining and redefining themselves...but found
themselves trapped in the dilemma of discovering themselves to be at once

the same, and yet not the same, as the country of their origin."[27] The Euro-African societies of West Africa, in spite of their different origins, were caught in a similar dilemma, and by recognizing this similarity we can benefit from insights derived from studies of Creole societies in the Americas, but most of all from the work done on the Creole communities of West Africa that were closest and most similar to their Gold Coast counterparts. Freetown, Sierra Leone, with its unique history, has undoubtedly attracted the most attention, and it has been in this setting that Africanists have most extensively explored the phenomenon of creolization in West Africa.[28] Many of the issues and concerns that were important to Creoles in Freetown were similarly so to Euro-Africans all over West Africa.[29] Recognizing these similarities strengthens the case for seeing Euro-African societies in West Africa as part of an even larger Creole continuum, and provides an important point of departure for analyzing those societies that have received far less attention.

Leo Spitzer's description of the collapse of the "special relationship" between Sierra Leone's Euro-African, Creole elite, and their European reference group in the late nineteenth century has obvious parallels for the Gold Coast, where at the same time European administrators and missionaries also turned against their protégés.[30] "Creolization," however, in the coastal communities of the Gold Coast in the nineteenth century was far more incomplete than it was in Sierra Leone or in the French settlements of Senegal and Dahomey. In many cases the life spans of these Gold Coast examples were much shorter. They were smaller in size. Unlike Freetown, their members were never cut off geographically from their place of origin, and neither did they achieve the same degree of separation from indigenous society. For example, in the Fante areas of the Gold Coast matrilineal ties remained strong, and males could inherit from their maternal uncles as well from their fathers.

Consequently, even the most "creolized" of families found it more difficult to preserve their wealth across generations than was the case for their counterparts in Freetown, where English common law was dominant. In general, traditional culture maintained a powerful influence that became even more pronounced, especially when the hopes that these Euro-Africans had for recognition as equals within the colonial world collapsed at the turn of the twentieth century. The "Anglo-Fanti" society that Sekyi lampooned in *The Blinkards* has left hardly any trace of itself in contemporary Cape Coast.[31] It would be far more difficult, if not impossible, to conduct a study such as Abner Cohen's analysis of contemporary elite Creole culture in Sierra Leone in a Ghanaian setting.[32] Nevertheless, recent attempts to counteract what James Thayer has criticized as the "flat, one-dimensional...and elitist" view of "Creole culture and history" in Sierra Leone, with its excessive emphasis on elites and the Europeanization of Freetown society, will help to establish an even greater congruence between this society and other Euro-African communities in West Africa.[33]

Sources and Periodization

One important shared characteristic of these West African Creole societies is the wealth of both primary and secondary material that historians can draw upon for their study. In the case of Ghana there is an almost embarrassment of riches that include the often erratic records of chiefly courts, the Native Tribunals, vast quantities of material from the colony's British courts that extend all the way from the courts of the political officers to the Privy Council in the metropole, but with the overwhelming majority of this material concentrated on the activities of the colony's Divisional Courts and its High Court. Particularly at the lower levels of the colony's court system, the illiterate, non-English speaking majority of coastal society come a little closer to taking center stage. By using these records we can appreciate the impact of facing two ways on a much wider range of social classes than the High Court records allow, and move considerably beyond the boundaries of nationalist historiography with its emphasis on politically prominent members of the Western-educated elite.

By the time colonial rule began, the main coastal towns were no longer preliterate communities. From the mid-nineteenth century Christian missionaries had made both primary and secondary education their major secular focus, and the main coastal towns, like Accra and Cape Coast, were very much centers of education with a significant proportion of their populations literate to some degree. The well-established newspaper traditions which both towns enjoyed as far back as the nineteenth century reflected the literate nature of these communities. Initially these papers lasted for only a couple of years, but by the early twentieth century weekly newspapers like the *Gold Coast Leader* in Cape Coast and the *Gold Coast Independent* in Accra appeared on a regular basis for several decades. By the 1930s there were two daily newspapers, the *Times of West Africa* and the *African Morning Post,* both of which appeared in the colony's capital, Accra.[34] Circulation varied from about five hundred for the Cape Coast fortnightly, the *Gold Coast Times,* in the 1880s to ten thousand daily for the *African Morning Post* in 1936, when it was at the height of its popularity during the Italo-Ethiopian crisis.[35] Actual readership, however, was larger than these figures suggest. Newspaper publishers were continually complaining that there was too much "lending," and not enough "subscribing," to the papers that they produced.[36]

Also indicative of the level of literacy, many of the best-educated residents of the coastal towns had quite extensive libraries that, judging from exchanges in the newspapers, they used extensively to support their contentions. Many kept their private papers, and a number of these collections are now deposited in the National Archives of Ghana. There was a well-developed obituary tradition that both newspapers and memorial services for the dead have been instrumental in creating. It has contributed to sharpening peoples' perception of their communal roles over time. On an even more systematic level, these communities produced local historians and social commentators who, in the case of the best known of them, Carl Christian Reindorf and John Mensah Sarbah, had begun, by the turn of the century, to study the histories and institutions of their societies.

Moreover, in addition to primary sources, there exists a considerable body of secondary material for the colonial period that also focuses on political and judicial matters. A significant amount of the more recent work remains in dissertation form, which is an indication of how much interest in Ghana has waned since the heady days of independence.[37] In addition, this material still continues to focus primarily on what was the original area of anglophone settlement. Studies of the British area of settlement far outnumber those on the Dutch and Danish. It is not surprising that this is so since the former areas became the most important when the Gold Coast became a British colony. Contributing to this lacunae in the country's history has also been the relative inaccessibility of the Dutch and Danish primary sources, which are in languages with which both Ghanaian and anglophone scholars, who have dominated the field of Ghanaian history, have little familiarity. In general, the Danish and Dutch settlements represented their own particular cultural configurations, but after the entire Gold Coast became a British colony in 1874, all of the coastal societies followed a basically similar path. The importance of previous European cultures declined and British culture became the paramount European influence. Consequently, drawing almost exclusively on anglophone primary and secondary sources, particularly for the twentieth century, will not pose a disadvantage for this study of the conflicts and challenges that facing two ways represented.

However, this plethora of written information has produced the more serious problem of what David Henige has described as "feedback."[38] Those who have sought to obtain accurate traditions in the colonial period have had to contend with this issue. Margaret Field, for example, while doing fieldwork among the Ga in the 1930s found that her efforts to obtain "genuine native custom" invariably ended up with "the garbled and impoverished fragments of book history" which had undermined a "richly verbal tradition."[39] It clearly upset her structural, functionalist sense of order in traditional societies, and she overlooked the important role that this "new information" played in the competition for office that indirect rule unleashed. In seeking to settle the interminable disputes over succession to chiefly "stools" during this period, colonial officials unwittingly contributed to this process by their preference for a "coherent and full account of a stool's traditional history and one that seemed to conform in broad outline to printed sources" rather than those that admitted ignorance of this past.[40]

Feedback from written sources was one way for enterprising (and educated) contestants for traditional office to take advantage of this British bias that was the "ineluctable result" of a literate tradition supplanting one that had been richly verbal.[41] This intellectual by-product of facing two ways guaranteed that Margaret Fields's search for "genuine native customs" would inevitably be chimerical. Martin Chanock, from his work on colonial Nyasaland and Northern Rhodesia, has suggested that rather than trying to establish the content of what was truly customary law, we need "to let the people hit the ground running, in all the disarray of conflict, rather than to begin with them in the stylized formations of the parade ground."[42] This undoubtedly has to be the approach we must take in dealing with traditional society in general, and particularly in politically and socially highly volatile environments where no static, traditional society ever really existed.

If "feedback" from literary sources has undermined "genuine tradition," feedback from nationalist historiography has influenced how individuals remember their own pasts. The "highlights-focus" of this tradition has affected most of all the educated, in that they tend to see their lives, or those of their parents, somehow intimately linked to events like the Lands Bill controversy of 1897, the establishment of the National Council of British West Africa in 1920s, and most importantly, the Nkrumahist phase of the independence struggle. This was forcefully brought to my attention when I was conducting interviews in Cape Coast in 1974. Older people who I knew from newspapers and government correspondence had played important roles in their communities during the 1930s and 1940s had distressingly confused memories of what they had done. They would rapidly skip from their youth to events of the Nkrumah era, and then become hopelessly entangled chronologically when, as a result of my prompting, they would try to fill in obvious gaps with events that belonged to the Nkrumah period.

The rush to independence in the fifties clearly played a role in promoting this collective amnesia. The pace of change was rapid and the promises so great that this era overwhelmed in perceived importance the much more ambiguous period that came before. In addition, Nkrumah and the politicians that led Ghana to independence in 1957 dismissed this earlier period as "collaborationist," and those who were part of it seem to have consciously and unconsciously suppressed memories of their involvement in this politically discredited past. The value of oral history, under these circumstances, is limited to helping establish family connections, educational backgrounds and career positions: important social information but hardly enough to reconstruct the complex political and social environment of the coastal towns.

One obvious way to counteract this tendency to telescope the colonial past is to deal with the entire colonial period, and the richness of the documentary sources makes this possible. Also, to escape the selectiveness of nationalist historiography, we need to see the colonial period as possessing its own internal dynamics that run deeper than either reactions to world events or the highlights of the nationalist struggle would suggest. Instead, I prefer to see this past as distinguished by two interconnected phases. The first consisted of European cultural assimilation which, as was the case in Sierra Leone, reached its apogee in the late nineteenth century. The second phase was a reaction to this Europeanization of coastal society which gave rise to a revival of traditional culture and its institutions. It began in the late nineteenth century, but really had its major effect on the intellectual, political and social life of the coastal communities in the twentieth century.

The colonial government's formal implementation of indirect rule for the colony at the turn of the century played a major role in stimulating and directing the nature of this revival. It was inevitable that colonial rule and the new cultural norms that it sought to impose on African society would have sparked an antithetical reaction. I argue, however, that while the colonial government's policies heavily influenced the form and shape that this reaction took, it also meant that Africans were often able to manipulate these new conditions to their own advantage. African reaction to colonial rule was not simply one of resistance or collaboration, as some have seen it, nor was there a clear-cut dichotomy between traditional and Westernized society as many modernization theorists of the 1960s tended to assume.[43] Those who have accepted these assumptions and have stressed the irreconcilable and destructive tensions between radically different cultures have failed to notice the emergence of new societies, especially those of the coast.

More recent scholarship has sought instead to emphasize the ambiguous nature of this process of emergence, characterized by what Terence Ranger described in 1983 as the "invention of tradition." He has argued that "customary law, customary land-rights and customary political structures...were in fact *all* invented by colonial codification...[as part of] a conscious determination on the part of colonial authorities to 'reestablish' order and security and a sense of community by means of defining and enforcing 'tradition.'"[44] Colonial officials, he acknowledges, could not have done this "without a great deal of African participation."[45] More importantly, "codified" and "reified custom" allowed those who were in positions of dominance to increase their control.[46] However, Ranger and others who have emphasized the role of invented tradition as a tool of control in the colonial order initially focused primarily on areas where

Europeans rapidly imposed colonial rule, and which at the time were in a state of profound upheaval due to slave raiding and wars of conquest. Social disorganization provided opportunities to "invent traditions" that enabled colonial administrators to create order that suited imperial needs.

In contrast, in the Gold Coast "state crystallization" was much further advanced at the time the British were imposing colonial rule. The Asante empire in the interior was one indication of this, and as James Sanders has indicated, so too were Fante states "crystallizing" in the littoral, which also contributed to the far-ranging process of Akanization of this area.[47] There was neither political nor social homeostasis. Nevertheless, a much greater degree of cultural homogeneity existed than was the case, for example, in Nyasaland and Northern Rhodesia, for which Martin Chanock has taken Ranger's insights furthest with his investigations of the invention of customary law in these British colonies.[48] It meant that Africans in the Gold Coast could take advantage of their links to their own societies to manipulate and modify its institutions to suit individual purposes. As I shall show in this study, no one person, group of persons or administrators monopolized the invention of tradition.

Not surprisingly, in recently "revisiting" the role of the invention of tradition in colonial societies, Ranger has modified his earlier emphasis on "cleavage" and "coercion" to capture the ambiguity and "relative autonomy" of the colonial period by speaking instead of "contested imaginings" of tradition.[49] Contributing to this climate of invented tradition or contested imaginings was the example that the mother country herself offered. The late nineteenth and the first half of the twentieth century were, as David Cannadine has shown, extremely fruitful periods for the invention of monarchical traditions that first served to assert national grandeur, and later emphasized continuity in a period of change.[50] They served to link the metropole to her colonies and gave rise to a host of empire celebrations which rapidly acquired sanction as tradition. The King's Birthday List of Honors, with its eagerly awaited award of knighthoods, CMG's, OBE's and MBE's, became an integral part of the colonial calendar, as did Empire Day with its parades and patriotic speeches, the governor's ceremonial durbars, a "tradition" borrowed from the Indian Empire, and finally even a "unique" royal visit that in the words of the editor of the *Gold Coast Leader* "[would] surely go down in our local history."[51] In the metropole much of the invented tradition of this period was fashioned out of material that was genuinely venerable, as was also the case in the Gold Coast. The result was (and remains) considerable confusion between "custom" and "tradition," as is evidenced by the interchangeable fashion in which the two terms were (and still are) used in the African context. Custom, however, as Eric Hobsbawm has argued, "does not preclude innovation and change to a point," while "the object and characteristic of 'traditions,' including invented ones, is invariance."[52] The colonial government, which on one hand argued for change to prevent institutional "atrophy [and] decay," and on the other wanted to uphold "genuine native tradition," was caught on the horns of a dilemma.[53] It was a situation that competitors for office could easily exploit, for in the period of rapid transformation that characterized colonial rule both flexibility and invariance seemed necessary to provide stability in a society where old social patterns were in a state of flux and often no longer applied.

In *The Eighteenth Brumaire of Louis Bonaparte,* Karl Marx scathingly describes "the tradition of all the dead generations" as

> weigh[ing] like a nightmare on the brain of the living. And just when they seem engaged in revolutionizing themselves and things, in creating something that has never existed, precisely in such periods of revolutionary crisis they anxiously conjure up the spirits of the past to their service and borrow from them names, battle cries and costumes in order to present the new scene of world history in this time-honored disguise and this borrowed language.[54]

In the Gold Coast there was clearly much "conjur[ing] up of the spirits of the past," and where so much importance came to be attached to tradition, or custom, it meant that the cast of players that the "revolutionary crisis" of colonialism threw up could exploit the customarily loose and flexible rules of the "traditional state" and its institutions by using new skills and stratagems to pursue what in essence were new political and social spoils.

Appreciating the full implications of the contested imaginings of tradition, whether they were in the realm of political institution building, or in the emergence of a legal system, provides an added reason for treating the entire span of colonial history. Just as we have to see the reaction to European ideas and institutions as linked phases of colonial rule, so too do we have to investigate the invention of tradition over the entire span of colonial history. Changing colonial policies intimately influenced the way in which "invented" political traditions developed. Equally important, it was not only policy decisions that affected this process. As I shall seek to show, it was also the changing social composition of coastal society that played a vital role in stimulating contests for traditional office, the functioning of "traditional" institutions, and their interaction with the larger colonial order. Consequently, this study will pay far more attention than has been customary to the backgrounds and careers of the broad range of people who were the participants in the highly contested political life of the coastal communities, as well as often also the litigants in court cases in which the colony's common law tradition was to emerge. As Lawrence Stone has pointed out, prosopography has contributed to disproving earlier ideologically based interpretations of the Puritan Revolution in England. By using biographical information both about the better-and the lesser-known actors on the colonial stage, we can similarly "sift truth from falsehood" for a period in Ghana's past where ideological considerations still predominate.[55] From biographical details we can get a far more realistic picture of "the new scene of world history" than the explosive highlights of the nationalist struggle allow.

In his recent genealogical study of Cape Coast stool families, Augustus Casely-Hayford points out that "given the importance of family and genealogy in West Africa...many scholars have employed a proso-pographical approach at some level of their research."[56] He argues that in the case of the Gold Coast this is evident in the works of Reindorf, Ward and Priestley since they seek to "place biographical and genealogical data into a chronological and critical framework."[57] He suggests that even "the indigenous Fante historical method could be viewed as a form of oral prosopography. Collective biography and genealogy are the essence of the greater part of Akan indigenous history," and it was this tradition that influenced the development of the "eulologic pocket biographies" that are an enduring feature of Ghanaian popular history.[58] Echoing Thomas Carlyle, one of the first of historical popularizers, Magnus Sampson, argued that "history is indeed biography 'writ large'."[59]

The result, however, has been a conventionalized format that stresses the achievements of the country's "great men" without whom "there can be no history."[60] Not surprisingly, the well-established obituary tradition of the Gold Coast press that extends back to the nineteenth century reflects a similar focus, but with the important advantage of including a much wider and diverse collection of subjects than the "distinguished" sons and daughters of the country. When used with the even more widely diverse biographic tradition that is an integral part of memorial services, it is possible to broaden considerably the picture of coastal society beyond the rather exclusive elite society with which nationalist historiography has dealt.[61] I have already pointed out that there are important limitations to this material, but in conjunction with contemporary information from the press, administrative files and court cases, "information that [is] un-impressive in isolation" can become extremely revealing of important social trends in coastal society.[62]

Notes

1. Brodie Cruickshank, *Eighteen Years on the Gold Coast of Africa* (1853; reprint, New York, 1966), 1:27.

2. Altogether in this area there existed roughly one hundred castles, forts and lesser posts (called lodges) "at one time or another, and most of them contemporaneously." Arnold W. Lawrence, *Trade Castles and Forts of West*

Africa (Stanford, Calif., 1964), 42. In contrast, the rest of the vast West African coastline contained only eleven other significant coastal fortifications.

3. For an extensive description of this period of early European exploration and settlement on this coast, see John W. Blake, *West Africa: Quest for God and Gold, 1454-1578* (1937; orig. publ. as *European Beginnings in West Africa, 1454-1578;* reprint, London, 1977).

4. Europeans called this section of the Guinea coast the Gold Coast since it was from here that most of the gold from West Africa came.

5. This terminology comes from Georges Balandier, *The Sociology of Black Africa: Social Dynamics in Central Africa* (1955: reprint, New York, 1970), 21-22.

6. Andrew D. Roberts, ed., *The Colonial Moment in Africa: Essays in the Movement of Minds and Materials, 1890-1940* (Cambridge, U.K., 1990), 1.

7. Maxwell Owusu, "Rebellion, Revolution, and Tradition: Reinterpreting Coups in Ghana," *Comparative Studies in Society and History* 31, no. 2 (April 1989):377.

8. John Mensah Sarbah, *Fanti National Constitution* (1906; reprint, London, 1968), 15.

9. Bjorn Edsman, *Lawyers in Gold Coast Politics, c.1900-1945: From Mensah Sarbah to J. B. Danquah* (Uppsala, 1979), 214.

10. Political officers presiding over courts was one of the most important departures from the ideal.

11. David Kimble, *A Political History of Ghana, 1850-1928* (Oxford, 1963). For a more recent example of this approach see Kofi Awoonor, *Ghana: A Political History from Pre-European to Modern Times* (Accra, 1990).

12. Roberts, *The Colonial Moment in Africa*, 1.

13. Kwame Daaku, *Trade and Politics on the Gold Coast, 1600-1720* (Oxford, 1970), 5.

14. The hero of this fictional work is a young "Anglo-Fanti" who is educated in England and unsuccessfully tries to remain true to his Fante roots. The story closely parallels Sekyi's own youthful years. The London-based weekly newsmagazine *West Africa* serialized this work, "The Anglo-Fanti," from 25 May to 18 September 1918. Also, Nancy Cunard included extracts from this work in her book, *Negro Anthology* (London, 1934), 774-779.

15. His other important work in this genre is *The Blinkards,* a "light comedy of the Shavian type" in which the author lampoons the "anglomaniacs" in Cape Coast in the early twentieth century. J. Ayo Langley, introduction to *The Blinkards* (London, 1974), 11. Sekyi wrote this play in 1915-1916 when he returned to Cape Coast after completing his first degree at London University. It was performed in Cape Coast in 1916. Ray Jenkins, "Sekyi's Formative Years," *West Africa*, 6 September 1982.

16. Ray Jenkins, "Gold Coast Historians and Their Pursuit of the Gold Coast Pasts: 1892-1917" (Ph.D. diss., University of Birmingham, 1985), 43-50, and "Gold Coasters Overseas, 1880-1919: With Specific Reference to Their Activities in Britain," *Immigrants and Minorities* 4, no. 3 (1985):7.

17. Jenkins, "Gold Coasters Overseas," 7.

18. Richard Jeffries, *Class, Power and Ideology in Ghana: The Railwaymen of Sekondi* (Cambridge, U.K., 1978), 184.

19. S. F. Nadel. "The Concept of Social Elites," *International Social Sciences Bulletin* 8, no. 3 (1956):415.

20. Jenkins, "Gold Coasters Overseas," 7.

21. For example, in 1894 Dr. John Farrell Easmon, a Sierra Leonian, became the chief medical officer for the Gold Coast colony. At the turn of the century these expectations came to an end with the rise of a virulent pseudoscientific racism. Dr. Easmon's career well reflected these changes. For a description of his confrontation with Governor William Maxwell see Adell Patton, "Dr. John Farrell Easmon: Medical Professionalism and Colonial Racism in the Gold Coast, 1856-1900," *International Journal of African Historical Studies* 22, no. 4 (1989):601-636, and *Physicians, Colonial Racism, and Diaspora in West Africa* (Gainesville, Fla., 1996), 93-122.

22. This was how the editor (Francis Fitzgerald) of the London-based monthly newsmagazine *African Times* described them in 1866. *African Times,* 23 June 1866.

23. During the nineteenth century both colonial administrators and Euro-Africans referred to the educated African coastal elite in this fashion.

24. Kristin Mann, in her pioneering study of marriage and family among the Lagos elite at the turn of the twentieth century, describes some of these alliances. Kristin Mann, *Marrying Well: Marriage, Status and Social Change Among the Educated Elite in Colonial Lagos* (Cambridge, U.K., 1985). The most extensive study of one of these families with Gold Coast connections is Adelaide Cromwell's *An African Victorian Feminist: The Life and Times of Adelaide Smith Casely Hayford, 1868-1960* (London, 1986).

25. See Leo Spitzer, *The Creoles of Sierra Leone: Responses to Colonialism, 1870-1945* (Madison, Wis., 1974), 12. The term was also in use in Dahomey in the 1880s to refer to the several thousand returned Brazilians and other Westernized West Africans who gave such towns as Ouidah, Agoue and Grand-Popo their special character. Dov Ronen, "The Colonial Elite in Dahomey," *African Studies Review* 17, no. 1 (April 1974):57-58.

26. For example, Kenneth Little and P. C. Lloyd have both recognized the Creole similarities of such societies: K. Little, "The Significance of The West African Creole for Africanist and Afro-American Studies," *African Affairs* 49, no. 197 (October 1950):309-319, and P. C. Lloyd, *Africa in Social Change: Changing Traditional Societies in the Modern World* (Harmondsworth,U.K., 1967), 128-130. More recently, Ulf Hannerz has suggested an even wider application for the

"creolist point of view" by suggesting that "a macro-anthropology of culture which takes into account the world system and its center-periphery relation" would be well served by a perspective that "identifies diversity itself as a source of cultural vitality." "The World in Creolization," *Africa* 57, no.4 (1987):556.

27. John H. Elliot, "Introduction: Colonial Identity in the Atlantic World " in *Colonial Identity in the Atlantic World, 1500-1800,* eds. Nicholas Canny and Anthony Pagden (Princeton, N.J., 1987), 9.

28. Some of the better-known works are: Christopher Fyfe, *A History of Sierra Leone* (London,1962); Arthur T. Porter, *Creoledom* (London, 1963); J. E. Peterson, *Province of Freedom: A History of Sierra Leone* (Evanston, Ill., 1969); Leo Spitzer, *The Creoles of Sierra Leone* (Madison, Wis., 1974); A. P. Kup, *Sierra Leone: A Concise History* (Newton Abbot, U.K., 1975); Barbara E. Harrell-Bond, Allen M. Howard and David E. Skinner, *Community Leadership and the Transformation of Freetown, 1801-1976* (The Hague, 1978); and Akintola Wyse, *The Krio of Sierra Leone: An Interpretive History* (Madison, Wis., 1989).

29. Evelyn Rowand identifies a number of these concerns that ranged form personal matters like Christian marriage and inheritance of property to policies of colonial expansion. "Press and Opinion in British West Africa, 1855-1900" (Ph.D. diss., University of Birmingham, 1972). As a further indication of this commonality of interests, there have been a substantial number of works with an anglophone, pan-West-African focus that have dealt in considerable detail with these issues. For example: J. A. Langley, "West African Aspects of the Pan-African Movement " (Ph.D. diss., University of Edinburgh, 1968); Lamin A. Mbye, "Senior African Civil Servants in British West Africa, 1808-1895 " (Ph.D. diss., University of Birmingham, 1969); T. S. Gayle, "Official Medical Policy in British West Africa, 1870-1930 " (Ph.D. diss., University of London, 1972-1973); Rina Okonkwo, "The Emergence of Nationalism in British West Africa, 1912-1940 " (Ph.D. diss., City University of New York, 1979); and Joy Williams, "The Educated and Professional Elite in the Gold Coast and Sierra Leone, 1885-1914" (Ph.D. diss., UCLA, 1980).

30. Spitzer, *The Creoles of Sierra Leone,* 39-69.

31. Many of the buildings and places that are mentioned in the play are still there, but their dilapidated appearance is graphic testimony to how much this town is now a backwater. Its eminent sons and daughters have left for more vibrant urban areas like Accra and Sekondi/Takoradi.

32. A. Cohen, *The Politics of Elite Culture: Explorations in the Dramaturgy of Power in a Modern Society* (Berkeley, 1981).

33. James S. Thayer, "A Dissenting View of Creole Culture in Sierra Leone," *Cahiers d'Etudes Africaines* 121-122, XXXI-1-2 (1991):216. Indeed, there has been a lively debate over the applicability of the term "Creole" even in the Freetown context. See Skinner and B. Harrell-Bond, "Misunderstandings Arising from the Use of the Term 'Creole' in the Literature on Sierra Leone," *Africa* 47, no. 3 (1977):305; Christopher Fyfe, "The Term Creole: A Footnote to a

Footnote," *Africa* 50, no. 4 (1980):422; and A. Wyse, "On Misunderstandings Arising from the Use of the Term 'Creole' in the Literature on Sierra Leone: A Rejoinder," *Africa* 49, no. 4 (1979):409-417. Indicative of this new focus is B. Harrell-Bond, Allen Howard and David Skinner's *Community Leadership and the Transformation of Freetown,* which is the most extensive description of the non-Creole society of Freetown. While Akintola Wyse's *The Krio of Sierra Leone* seeks even more directly to show the "two-faced character" of "Kriodom," his terminology to describe this society (derived from Yoruba rather than the West Indian experience) is itself an indication of his emphasis on how "the European veneer merely marked a basic African culture whose features were no different from those of unacculturated Africans" (8). And most recently on the question of "krio" identity, see Odile Goerg, "Sierra Leonias, Créoles, Krio: La Dialectique de l'identité," *Africa* 65, no. 1 (1995):114-132.

34. For a history of this press see K. A. B. Jones-Quartey, *History, Politics and the Early Press in Ghana* (Accra, 1975), and Clement E. Asante, *The Press in Ghana: Problems and Prospects* (Lanhan, Md., 1996).

35. *Gold Coast Colony Blue Book,* 1882, and Nnamdi Azikiwe, *My Odyssey: An Autobiography* (London, 1970), 259.

36. *Gold Coast Leader,* 16 June 1923.

37. Only recently has this "frozen frontier" begun to "thaw." Ray Jenkins, "North American Scholarship and the Thaw in the Historiography of Ghanaian Coastal Communities," *Ghana Studies Bulletin* 3 (December 1985):20.

38. David P. Henige, "Kingship in Elmina Before 1869: A Study in 'Feedback' and the Traditional Idealization of the Past," *Cahiers d'Etudes Africaines* 55, XIV-3 (1974):499-520.

39. Margaret J. Field, *Social Organization of the Ga People* (London, 1940), 196.

40. Henige, "Kingship in Elmina Before 1869," 519.

41. Ibid.

42. Martin Chanock, *Law, Custom and Social Order: The Colonial Experience in Malawi and Zambia* (Cambridge, U.K., 1985), 10.

43. For example, David Apter, *Ghana in Transition* (New York, 1963).

44. Terence Ranger, "The Invention of Tradition in Colonial Africa," in *The Invention of Tradition,* ed. Eric Hobsbawm and Terence Ranger (Cambridge, U.K., 1983), 249-250.

45. Ibid., 252.

46. Ibid., 255.

47. James Sanders, "The Political Development of the Fante in the Eighteenth and Nineteenth centuries: A Study of a West African Merchant Society" (Ph.D. diss., Northwestern University, 1980), 280.

48. Chanock, *Law, Custom and Social Order.*

49. Terence Ranger, "The Invention of Tradition Revisited: The Case of Colonial Africa," in T. Ranger and O. Vaughan, eds., *Legitimacy and the State in Twentieth Century Africa: Essays in Honour of H. M. Kirk-Greene* (London, 1993), 106.

50. David Cannadine, "The Context, Performance and Meaning of Ritual: The British Monarchy and the 'Invention of Tradition,' c. 1820-1977," in *The Invention of Tradition*, 101-164.

51. This was on the occasion of the visit of His Royal Highness the Prince of Wales to the Gold Coast in 1925. *Gold Coast Leader,* 18 April 1925.

52. Eric Hobsbawm, "Introduction: Inventing Traditions," in *The Invention of Tradition*, 2.

53. Acting Governor Northcote cited in *Gold Coast Independent,* 6 August 1932.

54. Karl Marx, *The Eighteenth Brumaire of Louis Bonaparte* (1852; reprint, New York, 1969), 15.

55. Lawrence Stone, "Prosopography," *Daedalus* (Winter 1971):68.

56. Augustus L. Casely-Hayford, "A Genealogical Study of Cape Coast Stool Families" (Ph.D. diss., School of Oriental and African Studies, London University, 1992), 26.

57. Ibid. Carl Reindorf, *History of the Gold Coast and Ashanti;* William E. F. Ward, *A History of the Gold Coast* (London, 1948); and Margaret Priestley, *West African Trade and Coast Society* (London, 1969).

58. Ibid.

59. Magnus Sampson, *Makers of Modern Ghana: Volume One* (1937; reprint, Accra, 1969), 13.

60. Ibid.

61. These biographies are contained in the printed programs for these services. People keep them as remembrances, but even when they are not available local biographers are remarkably good at remembering the information that goes into making up these short, conventionalized biographies.

62. Casely-Hayford, "A Genealogical Study of Cape Coast Stool Families," 29.

Chapter 2

The Making of Coastal Society

The ease with which Europeans erected castles and established themselves along the Golden Coast of Guinea was largely attributable to the sparsity of population and the lack of powerful kingdoms in this region. African peoples were themselves relative newcomers to this area.[1] Oral traditions indicate that the coastal settlements that they established only antedate by a few generations the arrival of Europeans in the mid-fifteenth century.[2] The Portuguese, who were the first Europeans to come in contact with this coast, took advantage of the links that existed between the small coastal communities and their parent states inland to trade for gold and other products from the interior such as ivory, elephant teeth, skins, dyewoods, beeswax and small numbers of slaves.

These newcomers soon decided that they needed to erect fortifications beside the coastal settlements from where they conducted their trade to protect themselves from fellow European rivals as well as potentially hostile African populations.[3] It was during the seventeenth century, however, as the trade in slaves to the New World became the dominant economic activity on the coast, that fort and castle building reached its peak. The profits that this trade promised served to attract many more Europeans who, to protect their interests, built forts and castles like the Portuguese before them. This expansion of trade served to elevate insignificant fishing settlements to the status of coastal entrepôts, with the size of the fortification in their midst an indication of the settlement's trading importance.

The most important of these settlements were located where the various European trading companies established their headquarters.[4] The largest was the castle of Elmina, which the Dutch seized from the Portuguese in 1637. As the founders of the first European settlement on the coast, the Portuguese had been able to pick a choice site for its location.[5] It was near the most productive gold mines, and the mouth of the Benya River on which it stood offered the only really natural harbor on the coast. The second most important settlement, although not in size, was Cape Coast Castle, eight miles to the east, which English merchants made their headquarters on the coast from 1664.[6] In comparison with Elmina its landing facilities were much poorer. The rocky promontory on which it stood offered limited protection from the heavy surf. Even poorer were the landing facilities for Accra, the third most important area of European settlement, roughly ninety miles to the east of Cape Coast. In this location, however, the grassy coastal plains extended inland for almost twenty miles and allowed easy access into the interior. The result was that several European trading companies built fortifications in this area, but by the eighteenth century only the Dutch, the British and the Danes remained.[7]

Around many of these settlements there developed what a Dutch slave trader, William Bosman, described for Elmina in the early eighteenth century as "very populous negroe towns."[8] As trade began to increase with Europeans, the African settlements around the forts and castles became more wealthy and important. The result was that they began to challenge the inland states to which they had initially been subordinate. In the case of Elmina, the original town seems to have been a "village of two parts...a bowshot one from the other."[9] The commonly accepted view, Harvey Feinberg maintains, is that the two larger inland, neighboring states, Eguafo and Fetu, controlled these two sections of the village with the Benya River, which flows through this area, probably being the boundary between them.[10] Sometime around 1514, with the assistance and support of the Portuguese, Elmina achieved its independence from Eguafo and Fetu.[11] Clearly Elmina's independence as a separate "republic" must have been advantageous to the Portuguese. It allowed them to eliminate the control that the rulers of the inland kingdoms exercised over the coast, and instead, as an anonymous Dutch cartographer maintained in 1629, the Elminians lived "as a republic on their own and mostly governed by the Portuguese Governador."[12]

After the Dutch captured Elmina in 1637, they sought even more control over the town, particularly over its fighting forces, which they involved in their wars to control the coast's trade. Around 1724 they formally organized the seven wards that made up the town into an established military formation. According to local tradition, the Dutch gave them flags and awarded them numbers that signified their importance in the overall battle order.[13] Seven of what are presently known as the ten

The British bombardment of the town of Elmina in 1873. From the *Illustrated London News*, 19 July 1873.

asafos in Elmina still retain these numbers, and it seems as though these primarily military institutions, referred to in English as companies, did develop out of this need on the part of the Dutch for African military support. Ansu Datta and R. Porter have argued that the *asafo* was "indigenous to various Akan peoples."[14] The Elmina situation, however, best indicates how much these institutions in the coastal towns were "influenced by the situations created through contact with Europeans."[15]

In a similar fashion to other coastal towns, European intervention inadvertently also contributed to enhancing the political significance of the *asafos*. From the eighteenth century onward the leaders of these military units, whom the Dutch called ensigns, became some of the dominant figures in Elmina's political life. As the power and effectiveness of the Dutch West India Company declined in the eighteenth century, these men "replaced other elders and key men as important persons, because these new leaders gave a voice to the young men, who were the core of the wards, and to the common man in general."[16] As an indication of their importance, the Dutch paid them monthly stipends with the great ensign, the overall leader of the seven wards, receiving the most impressive *kostgeld*.[17]

In addition, the *asafos* played a major role in installing the first of what the Dutch described as the town's "kings." This must have happened sometime before 1732, since in that year, for the first time, the company records describe the "First King," Codja Comma, signing an agreement with the Dutch along with Ando, the "Second King," and Enduama Esenam, the "Third King."[18] Feinberg has speculated that Elmina's participation in the Dutch campaign against the African trader John Konny in 1724 may have contributed to enhancing the town's importance and its determination to have a ruler similar to those of its neighbors.[19] The fact that there were three kings, as David Henige has suggested, may also have been a reflection of the original "tripartite division of the town."[20] Toward the end of the century, however, what the Dutch described as the "Upper King" became the dominant figure in this triumvirate, and they indicated this from 1781 by paying him a stipend equal to that which they paid other monarchs in the Gold Coast.[21]

As was the case among other coastal communities, the important inland states exerted considerable influence over the direction these political changes took in Elmina. Even though the town was basically independent, inland states were still more powerful than any of the coastal offshoots to which they had given rise. The most successful of these "Kingdoms," as Bosman described them, had also profited from the expanded trade with Europeans as well as benefited from the introduction of new food crops. One of the indications of this was a significant increase in urbanization beginning in the seventeenth century.[22] It meant that the largest towns were still in the subcoastal and forest regions, and their political administration offered what Bosman described as the "confused and perplexed...hardly to be comprehended" coastal communities important models to follow.[23] In conjunction with the European influences that were affecting these coastal peoples, their extensive borrowing from the indigenous peoples of the interior was to contribute to the dual nature of the "coast district's" cultural heritage. By the late seventeenth century, seven of the "countries" that were located along the coast were kingdoms and were "governed by their respective Kings," while the rest "seemed to approach nearer to common-wealths."[24]

In describing these political units, Bosman considered the kingdoms to be "monarchical," since "power and jurisdiction [was] vested in a single person."[25] On the other hand he considered the commonwealths to be more "republican in structure," and intermediate between the more centralized kingdoms inland and the more disorganized conditions on the coast.[26] In the late seventeenth century, Elmina's system must have bordered on the anarchic, and significantly, though Bosman lived there off and on for fourteen years (1688-1702), he made no attempt to describe it.[27] Under these circumstances, installing a king, similar to those in the inland monarchies, may very likely have represented a desire to replace the "tyrannical government" that the town had suffered from "some of their generals" with more stability[28]

In Cape Coast there were also important European influences on the development of the town, but in contrast to Elmina the European presence came later, and until the end of the seventeenth century was far more contested and peripheral. It was not until 1610 that the Portuguese established a lodge on the seashore beside what at the time was a collection of villages.[29] It was later abandoned and it was only in the 1650s that Swedish, English and Danish companies began building forts in this area to control the increasingly valuable trade. Eventually, in 1664, the English took control of Cape Coast, and in the 1680s the Royal African Company, which had acquired a monopoly on the West African trade from the English Crown, began to transform the main fortification into the second largest castle on the coast.[30]

Nevertheless, the company's control over the town remained weak, and there was a significantly wider range of opportunities for enterprising Africans to exploit than was the case in Elmina. One of the earliest representatives of this "new class" in Cape Coast was the "mulatto" Edward Barter, who according to Bosman built a house "not unlike a small fort" under the English castle.[31] At the time that Bosman described him, he had "greater power on the coast than all the three English agents together."[32] Putatively he was pro-English, but this did not prevent him from taking advantage of his position to further his own interests by trading with other Europeans. Conflict with the company inevitably came to a head when the energetic and irascible Sir Dalby Thomas became captain-general in 1703,

Cape Coast from Macarthy Hill. From the *Illustrated London News*, 11 April 1874.

and Barter had to escape to Elmina where he died soon after.[33] Barter, like his counterparts John Konny of Princess Town and John Kabes of Komenda, was both an entrepreneur and an early "state builder."[34] In Cape Coast there was less room for maneuver than there was in the smaller settlements where European rule was even more marginal, but nevertheless Barter at the zenith of his power could "raise a large number of armed men" and was "very much respected, honoured and served by the principal people about him."[35] However, like many of these early state builders not much seems to have survived his downfall.[36]

The kingdom of Fetu straddled one of the most important trade routes into the interior and the area was very much on the path of migration to the coast. From as early as the fifteenth century there were significant Fante, Abra and Asebu settlements around Cape Coast (or Oguaa, to give this location its indigenous name).[37] It also meant that Fetu always had to fear the possibility of invasion by its more powerful neighbors. For example, in 1693 the Asebu and the Twifus threatened Fetu's precarious existence when they invaded and forced its king to flee to Cape Coast.[38] According to one local tradition, it was out of this forced retreat that the military and political system of Cape Coast emerged.[39] The king's bodyguard established the town's first *asafo*, Nkum, and his drummers established the second *asafo*, Bentsir. The artisans, who had remained after they built the castle, and were very likely slaves imported from the slave coast, were sometime after 1693 attached as "camp followers" to Nkum.[40] Later on, perhaps as early as the eighteenth century, they established their own *asafo*, appropriately known as Brofumba, which in Fante means "white men's servants" and signified their origin.

The kingdom of Fetu survived the invasion of 1693, as well as that by the Fante in 1707-1708. Sometime in the 1740s Kwadwo or Kojo Egyir, who was probably the brother-in-law of the king or *dey* of Fetu, established himself as a major slave trader in Cape Coast and became extremely wealthy.[41] He claimed that many of the slaves he was supposed to have sold to Europeans had died, and instead he settled them on lands near Cape Coast. They became his "domestics," and according to Cape Coast traditions became the "rural" section of his bodyguard which sometime later became Ntsin Asafo.[42] It was, however, the Seven Years War (1756-1763) that enabled him to go from being merely Brempong (wealthy) Kojo to the most powerful man in Cape Coast. During the long blockade to which the French and their Fante allies subjected the English, he became the castle's main purveyor, and when the war was over he decided to take advantage of his increased status to create for himself his own stool.[43] Whether he actually became king of Cape Coast seems unlikely. The company records do not describe him as such.[44] Nevertheless, later on in Cape Coast's history his descendants claimed that he had indeed been king, or *omanhen*, and, even more implausibly, "founder" of Cape Coast.[45]

It is unlikely that we will ever be able to settle the former question definitively since the numerous stool succession inquiries of the colonial period have already failed to do so.[46] However, Brempong Kojo's career does seem to have represented an important step in Cape Coast's achievement of independence from Fetu. Until the 1820s the African Company continued to pay "ground rent" to the *dey* or king of Fetu, but his jurisdiction over the town seems to have been declining.[47] For example, in 1681, when trouble broke out in Cape Coast between the company's agent and the inhabitants of the town over escaped slaves, the *dey* of Fetu had hurried to Cape Coast to "mediate" this dispute.[48] In contrast, in 1803 there was once again a major riot in the town that pitted the company against the townspeople, but on this occasion it was purely through the actions of local leaders that the dispute was resolved.[49] Indeed, sometime in the late eighteenth century, as conditions in the hinterland began to deteriorate due to Asante expansion into this area, most of what was left of the Fetu kingdom seems to have collapsed, and its *dey* retreated to Cape Coast where he and his successors competed with Brempong Kojo and his successors for recognition as the king of Cape Coast.[50]

Contributing to this confusion, as Augustus Casely-Hayford has suggested, was that Brempong Kojo had both Effutu and Fante descendants who adhered to patrilineal and matrilineal principles of descent respectively and consequently recognized different people as his successors.[51] The Fante descendants also had claims to the Fetu stool and very likely conflated its stool history to strengthen their position. Indeed, he suggests, from looking at the investigations carried out in the colonial period in which the government sought to untangle the conflicting claims to what had then become the Oguaa paramountcy, by the end of the eighteenth century there may well have been three competing stools in this area: the original stool of Fetu, a similarly patrilineal stool that had been established in Cape Coast, and the matrilineal Brempong Kojo stool that laid claims to what by the middle of the nineteenth became one position.[52]

Apart from initiating the end of Cape Coast's subservience to an inland state, Brempong Kojo's enstoolment also seems to have represented the introduction of Fante succession principles into the town's political life. Up until this time succession to office in Cape Coast seems to have been patrilineally determined, and as Margaret Priestley has suggested for Anomabu, perhaps closely connected with *asafo* membership.[53] Some kind of patrilineal succession may have been the original Effutu custom which seems to have been common to the Guan-speaking peoples of whom the Effutu were a subgroup. But even this is not clear since the information that does exist is conflicting. According to the Lutheran pastor Wilhelm

Johann Müller, who spent seven years in the service of the Danish African Company from 1662-1669, and visited the Fetu Kingdom:

> When a king of Fetu dies, he is succeeded not by his eldest son or another son, but by his brother, nephew, uncle or whoever is closest among the collaterals of royal blood. This person is chosen and elected by the estates and leading men of the country while the king is still alive.[54]

This would seem to indicate matrilineal succession which in general, as George Hagan has pointed out, was the case among the Effutu.[55] In Winneba, however, where some of the survivors from the Fante destruction of Effutu in 1708 possibly relocated, patrilineal and matrilineal succession alternate, but this is a mid-nineteenth century development, and the town's king list seems to indicate that the original system was patrilineal. Even in this situation choice was wide. There was no primogeniture and any son of a previous *odefey* could conceivably succeed to office.[56] In general, succession whether patrilineally or matrilineally determined was imprecise, and in spite of the rules that exist in theory, far more often than John Mensah Sarbah suggests, the "people" probably exercised their "right to select some person not a member of the heritable blood."[57]

However, the general trend by the nineteenth century seemed to be in the direction of matrilineal succession, the system that applied in the most important states in this coastal area. In the seventeenth century, these were undoubtedly the loosely aligned Fante states which were extending their control over weaker neighbors like the Etsi to the north and to the south, and in the early eighteenth century had continued to absorb weaker peoples to the east and west like the Gomas, Asebus and Effutus.[58] More important than the actual size of Fanteland was the political and cultural influence that these dynamic peoples exerted on their neighbors. Apart from spreading their language, they also intermarried and the Akan matrilineal family system diffused throughout the coastal region. Like their fellow Akan, the Asante, the political system that the Fante evolved was also based on matrilineal succession to office, and this too became one of their important contributions to the coastal settlements where succession had perhaps been much more ill defined and haphazard.

The link between Cape Coast and Fanteland is well exemplified in the case of Brempong Kojo, since both of his parents were from the town of Ekumfi Adansi in the Fante state of Ekumfi.[59] Anomabu, however, is an even better example than Cape Coast of the role of Fante culture in influencing the development of the important coastal settlements, most of all because its link to the Fante interior was much closer. According to local traditions, the town's founders were Fantes from Mankessim who defeated the Etsi peoples who were already in this area and engaged in fishing and salt making.[60] Judging from the earliest European accounts of this coastal area, which do not mention a Fante presence on the coast, James Sanders has concluded that this migration and the establishment of Anomabu must have taken place sometime in the late sixteenth or early seventeenth century.[61] However, with the development of trade with Europeans, Anomabu rapidly became one of the most important entrepôts on the coast. It was the major outlet for trade passing through Fanteland to the coast. Up until the disastrous Asante invasion of 1807 and the abolition of the slave trade in 1808, it continued to enjoy this position.

Nevertheless, Sanders has argued that the actual "crystallization of the Anomabu paramountcy occurred mainly in the nineteenth century." Up until the enstoolment of Amonu Kuma (1740-1801), Anomabu's rulers were little more than military leaders, known to Europeans as "captains," or "principal *caboceers*," and not really until after the disruptions of the Asante coastal invasions in the first decades of the nineteenth century did the Amonu "dynasty" become truly established.[62] Significantly, it was with the Amonus that what is now considered the typical Fante system of matrilineal succession replaced the patrilineal system that was associated with the *asafos* out of which the "pre-dynastic" leadership in Anomabu seems to have come.[63] No detailed historical studies for inland Fante states have yet been undertaken, but what seems most likely, given the fairly normative nature of Anomabu, is that state crystallization was going on all over the Fante world by the late eighteenth century, and Anomabu's attempt to give more structure to its political institutions was part of a larger process.

State crystallization influenced by Fante political ideas did not necessarily bring stability to the coastal towns in the eighteenth or nineteenth centuries. The entire region was far too disturbed for this to have been the case. In addition, the struggle between the adherents of matrilineal versus patrilineal succession, which tended to pit matrilineages against *asafos*, contributed yet another dimension to the politically "confused and perplexed" nature of these communities. In Elmina, for example, according to disputed traditions, patrilineal succession supposedly replaced the earlier matrilineal selection of the town's *omanhen* at the death of Ampon Dziedur.[64] Whether this reversal from the norm actually happened has been as difficult to establish as Brempong Kojo's claims to be the first *omanhen* of Cape Coast.[65] Numerous stool succession inquiries during the colonial period have also failed to untangle Elmina's "confused and perplexed" stool history.[66] Instead, what we can best conclude from the existence of the town's conflicting traditions is that regardless of which principle ruled, there were undoubtedly those with a vested interest in upholding its opposite.[67]

In addition to establishing two competing principles of succession to the position of *omanhen*, Fante matrilineal succession also came to affect positions in the *asafos*. It is difficult to know when this began. There does not seem to be any evidence of this in the eighteenth century, which may indicate that patrilineal succession among the *asafos* was still too entrenched to be affected by the spreading influence of the maternal family. For example, the company records for Cape Coast seem to indicate that "Captain Aggrey" succeeded his father, Brempong Kojo, as the *tufuhen*, or commander of the Cape Coast *asafos*, sometime around 1780.[68] As late as 1853 patrilineal succession was still the case in Cape Coast. In that year when the town's *tufuhen* died, his son, James Robert Thompson, was "appointed" to be his father's successor.[69] Brodie Cruick-shank, in describing the *asafos* in the coastal towns in the 1850s, seems to indicate that all *asafo* offices descended in this way.[70] By the end of the century, however, the situation was obviously changing. William Zacheus Coker, who succeeded Thompson in 1888, was the latter's maternal nephew.

We might argue that Cape Coast, where this took place in 1888, had been so affected by what John Mensah Sarbah described as "frequent intercourse with European traders" as to be aberrant.[71] In Anomabu, however, according to the Cape Coast lawyer Kobina Sekyi, who collected oral histories in the town in the 1930s, the position was "transferred" from one "house" to another in the early nineteenth century.[72] More than likely this represented a switch in the principle of succession since today the *tufuhen* of Anomabu is a stool holder who has succeeded to his office matrilineally. It seems fair to surmise that in keeping with what Sanders has indicated was the emergence of matrilineally selected divisional chiefs in the early nineteenth century, succession to the position of *tufuhen* also came under the influence of Akan principles. In a number of inland states such as Denkyira and Abura the position of *tufuhen* is also matrilineally inherited, and as Robert Stone has also pointed out, in some Akan areas (Ekunfi) even the office of *supi* is matrilineally inherited.[73] It is hard to determine how recent a development this might be.

The "double descent" that James Christensen considered characteristic of Fante society, in which *asafo* membership and succession to office were patrilineally determined and chiefly positions were matrilineally inherited, is really only a rough guide to understanding succession to office even in the Fante fishing communities that he studied in the 1950s.[74] Succession principles in all of these coastal Fante communities have been affected by a long history of competition between matriliny and patriliny. On the other hand, those who have challenged the accuracy of double descent characterizing Fante succession practice, and have tended to pick one principle over the other as truly normative, clearly assume far too much precision in social customs. In a more recent study, for example, I. Chukwukere has argued that it was the "intensive interaction with European traders, priests, educators and administrators...[which was responsible for bringing] about the apparent cracks in the walls of Fante matriliny."[75] From the perspective of the coastal settlements, it seems just as likely that Fante matriliny brought about "cracks" in what originally might have been a stricter succession to office in the *asafos* based on patriliny.

Accra, which was to become the most important town during the colonial period, also began as an offshoot of an inland kingdom. However, in this case geography and history served to make the break between parent and offspring more complete than was the case elsewhere. The Ga peoples, who were to emerge as the dominant group within this town, had begun moving into the area of grassy plains south of the Akwapem escarpment by the sixteenth century.[76] By this time they were well on their way to absorbing the original Guan peoples, and by the seventeenth century they had begun to leave the low hills that arise out of this plain and were moving towards the coast. Archaeological evidence dates the founding of what Europeans described as Great Accra to the late sixteenth century.

The opportunity to trade with Europeans who had recently begun to arrive in this area influenced this movement coastward. Initially "the Ga appear to have been reluctant to allow Europeans to build permanent establishments," and in 1576 they destroyed the fort that the Portuguese built on the coast.[77] However, by the middle of they seventeenth century they had put aside this earlier reluctance and in 1649 the Dutch West India Company constructed Fort Crèvecoeur at "Little Accra," the first European fortification in this area of the coast.[78] The Danes replaced what had been a tenuous Swedish presence and in 1661 began to construct what was to become Christiansborg Castle at the settlement of Osu, two miles to the east of the Dutch fort. In 1672-1673 the English company, the Royal African Company, began construction of "James Fort at the village of Tsoco, a mere half a mile to the west—within cannon-shot—of Fort Crèvecoeur."[79] The result was three important European fortifications in less than three miles of coast, which meant that unlike Cape Coast or Elmina no one European power was able to become dominant in this area. Three distinct *majii*, or towns, developed: Kinka, Nleshi and Osu, with Kinka and Nleshi also known by the names of the forts in their midst: Ussher Town and James Town.[80]

According to Ga traditions, Accra was settled sometime during the reign of Okai Koi (1610-1660), but this most likely is a conflation of the process of coastal migration, which more likely took place as a series of migrations of extended family groups headed by priests. As was the case in the Fante areas, the inland capital lost control over its coastal offshoot, but for Accra this was a much more rapid and catastrophic development. Between 1677 and 1681 the aggressively expansionist Akan kingdom of Akwamu decided to control the lucrative trade of the Accra plains and invaded and destroyed Great Accra. Many Ga sought refuge on the coast under the protection of the European forts, but in 1680-1681 the Akwamu conquered even these sanctuaries and subjected the entire area to their overrule. In 1730 the Akwamu were themselves defeated by other Akan people, the Akyem chiefdoms, and for a while the Ga were able to regain a measure of independence. However, this did not last long; in 1742 the Asante defeated the Akyem and incorporated Accra into the southern provinces of the Asante empire.[81]

As a result of these invasions and conquests, state crystallization was more embryonic than it was in the Fante areas of the coast. Even in the nineteenth century Accra remained divided into distinct towns, which in turn were divided into different quarters, or *akutsei*. Kinka, or Ussher Town, consisted of four *akutsei*—Asere, Abola, Gbese and Otublohum; Nleshi, or James Town, consisted of three—Alata, Sempe and Akanmaji; while Osu consisted of four *akutsei*—Kinkawe, Asante Blohum, Alata and Aneho. Reflective of the relatively decentralized nature of the Ga social formation was the manner in which authority was shared. *Wulomei*, or priests, exercised both religious and judicial roles. The *asfoatsemei*, or fathers of the *asafo*, were responsible for military affairs, while the *mantsemei*, or fathers of the town, had as their most important function presiding over local adjudication. Sometime in the late eighteenth or early nineteenth century, as the powers of the *mantsemei* in general increased, the *mantse* of the Abola *akutso* emerged as *primus inter pares*. But this was little more than symbolic, and in the early colonial period this ordering was to become a fiercely contested issue that was to remain one of the central issues of twentieth century political life.[82]

The presence of three competing European trading companies with castles in close proximity to one another also added to the "confused and perplexed" nature of Accra's political life. On one hand the close connection between these trading castles and the towns around them worked against the crystallization of a centralized state since these towns were able to retain their separate identities well into the nineteenth century. It was not until 1850 that the British bought Christiansborg Castle from the Danes, and seventeen years later acquired Ussher Fort from the Dutch. Within these towns, however, one of the results of European patronage seems to have been to elevate the *mantse* of the various *akutsei* into more prominent figures than they had been formerly. According to Margaret Field, who conducted the first systematic study of the Ga peoples of Accra in the 1930s, before the arrival of Europeans the *mantse* had actually become "a vestigial survival without function," as they had already lost both their priestly and military roles.[83] By mistakenly assuming that these *mantsemei* were royalty because they sat on stools, and were surrounded by the pomp associated with royalty, Europeans awarded them recognition that invariably created tension between *mantsemei* and their elders as the former tried to exercise powers that the latter felt were not theirs.[84]

Also contributing to these tensions was the long history of invasion and conquest that made Accra particularly culturally heterogenous. As the names of the many *akutsei* indicated, Accra was a potpourri of ethnic groups. Apart from the *Ga mashi,* the original Ga settlers, there were Adangme, Alladas and a range of Akan peoples who included Akwamus, Akyems, Fantes and Asantes. People from what was to become Nigeria and freed slaves from Brazil continued this influx of outsiders in the nineteenth century. Undoubtedly, however, it was the Akan element that was most important and was to contribute to a substantial Akanization of Accra, or as John Parker has perhaps more accurately expressed it, "the Gaisation of Akan institutions."[85] Over time there was considerable borrowing of Akan cultural artifacts that included the regalia of political office, titles, festivals, the *asafo* military organization, music, religious practices, and, with the most complex results of all, important aspects of matriliny.[86]

At least as much as in other coastal communities, this resulted in considerable tension between two very different systems of succession and inheritance. For example, in the seventeenth century the Ankama chief (an Akan) who had "ruled over the whole country as the Head Chief," had tried to enstool a matrilineal successor, but had been prevented from doing so by the Gas, who had sided with the "lineal male descendent."[87] Nevertheless, the disappointed contestant for this office established his own stool, and founded what is known today as the Gbese quarter in Ussher Town. On the other hand, in some cases it was possible and advantageous to combine patrilineal and matrilineal principles of succession. In 1681, when the Akwamus conquered Accra, they appointed Otu, a member of an Akwamu divisional chief's stool family, to be the governor of their new province. He was useful to the new rulers because of his trading contacts with the Dutch, who had elevated him to the position of chief broker. However, to maintain his loyalty and that of his descendants, Otu had to enter into a cross-cousin marriage arrangement that was to result in sharing the governorship between both his *abusua* and that of the Akwamu royal family.[88] Indicative of how intertwined Ga and Akan customs were regarding inheritance was the struggle in the eighteenth century involving the Ga *akwashon mantse,* one of the *mantse* of Ussher Town, and his maternal uncle's sons who claimed their dead father's property. Even though Kwatei Kojo, the *akwashon mantse,* had succeeded to his position patrilineally, he forcefully claimed his uncle's property on the grounds that inheritance to it had already been "tainted...with the Twi (Akan) custom."[89]

From this brief look at the background to coastal society, we can conclude that by the nineteenth century nearly all of the important communities on the littoral had emerged as independent polities.[90] Apart from the role that trade with Europeans had played in effecting this change, there were other developments that served to further increase the importance of the coast relative to the immediate hinterland. The rise of powerful, expansionist states, like the Akwamu, Denkyira, Fante and the Asante, resulted in breaking up what Ray Kea has described as the "mosaic of sovereign, independent polities" that had existed close to the coast as late as the early eighteenth century.[91] Apart from creating political instability, this also affected urbanization in this area. For the new states that emerged, the towns close to the coast tended to become little more than staging areas along the trade routes into the interior, or at best centers of administration rather than being also the loci of craft industries as they had been formally. The Asante expansion toward the coast in the nineteenth century accentuated this process. In many instances their forces actually destroyed important towns in the hinterland and contributed directly to the area's declining urban population.[92]

Unlike the Fante, they sought tighter control over those areas they incorporated into their empire, which made them even less likely to encourage the emergence of powerful urban centers in this region. In addition, as they pushed closer towards the coast, they threatened the trading interests of the British, who by the nineteenth century had become the most important Europeans on the coast. British trade depended on the existence of independent coastal peoples like the Fante and the Ga who acted as their middlemen, and as Asante pressure mounted the coastal peoples came to rely increasingly on the British for help. It meant that in addition to being important centers of trade, towns directly on the coast, like Accra, Winneba, Anomabu and most of all Cape Coast, began to acquire a new function as military centers that further enhanced their importance vis-à-vis their urban rivals inland.

However, this enhancement of the importance of coastal towns coincided with the expansion of British power on the coast that was to set in motion a competing force. The abolition of the slave trade in 1808 put pressure on the British government to control the activities of its merchants on the coast, with the result that in 1821 the crown decided to assume the direct administration of the forts and settlements on the Gold Coast. Governor, Sir Charles Macarthy's disastrous expedition against the Asante in 1821 temporarily ended this undertaking, but in 1843, once again under pressure from the antislavery lobby in Britain, Parliament resumed control over the British settlements on the coast. Indicative of increasing British control was Governor Hill's signing of what came to be known as the Bond of 1844, which gave "the Queen's judicial officers," in conjunction with "the chiefs of the district," the right "to try and inquire into murders, robberies and other crimes."[93] The era of legitimate trade that followed the abolition of the monopolistic control that slave trading companies had enjoyed gradually resulted in increasing the number of independent British merchants. In 1838 the Wesleyan Methodists established the first Christian mission in Cape Coast, and this also contributed to increasing the numbers of Europeans and European influence on the coast.

Initially, however, the almost constant state of war, or threats of war, in the first half of the nineteenth century contributed to enhancing the importance of indigenous leaders in the coastal towns. Macarthy had only small numbers of British troops at his disposal, and the bulk of his forces were local, most of whom came from the coastal towns and their subcoastal allies. As an indication of this, the center of gravity in Fanteland passed from the inland towns of Mankessim and Abora, which had been the traditional assembly points for the Fante peoples, to Anomabu, and it was the coastal chiefs rather than those from inland who took over the task of organizing Fante participation in this campaign.[94]

Not surprisingly, the *asafos* were affected by these developments, and most likely it was at this time that they attained the number and designation in the battle order that they presently have in coastal towns like Cape Coast and Anomabu. To further strengthen the effectiveness of local military forces, chiefs who were primarily territorial in their authority were incorporated into the military hierarchy as wing chiefs in a fashion similar to what existed in Asante. James Sanders has shown in his investigation of the stool histories of the divisional chiefs of the present-day Anomabu paramountcy that few of these positions can be traced back before the early nineteenth century.[95] He has also indicated that it was at this time that many of the town's outlying villages were incorporated into the paramountcy, and their chiefs elevated to positions in the state's military hierarchy.[96] Untangling the available evidence to get a clear picture of how this happened is not easy since this process of incorporating new chiefly positions and villages into the Anomabu paramountcy has been an ongoing one. It does seem fair to conclude, however, that the Asante wars of the early nineteenth century, which enhanced the significance of Anomabu and emphasized the need for a military command structure, for a while contributed to significant state crystallization in this town.

There were similar forces at work among the decentralized Ga in Accra that propelled that community in the direction of more state crystallization. According to the Reverend Carl Reindorf in his *History of the Gold Coast and Ashanti,* Accra evolved from what he described as an "absolute fetishcracy" to a "patriarchal" form of government.[97] When this actually happened is hard to determine, but by the battle of Katamanso in 1826, when the Gas joined together with other coastal peoples to defeat the Asante, they took the field under the military and religious leadership of Taki Komi, who was the *mantse* of the Asere *akutso.*[98] Like other coastal communities, state crystallization in Accra in the nineteenth century was a continuing process. Around 1840, for example, supposedly at the suggestion of the Fante who once again needed allies against the Asante, the people of Accra again came together under the leadership of a single *mantse,* the Asere *mantse,* who became the leader of the Ga people, or the Ga *mantse.*[99] As Ray Kea has pointed out, the introduction of large quantities of firearms into the Gold Coast radically altered the nature of military organization.[100] The distribution of this weaponry became an important responsibility of the *mantsemei,* which served to enhance their position as fathers of the town.

Even in Elmina, which was an Asante ally, there were contingent forces at work promoting state crystallization. The town's long-standing relationship with the Asante had made it a natural target for the Fante and their allies, while the Dutch as a declining power on the coast were unable to provide much protection.[101] Consequently, after the victorious Asante campaign of 1806-1807, the Elminians had sought a protectorate relationship with the *asantehene,* but after the defeat of his armies in 1826, this was modified to be more a friendly alliance. Larry Yarak has suggested that by being able to use the *asantehene*'s support as well as that of the Dutch, Kwadwo Dsiewu, who became *omanhen* of Elmina in 1831, was able to strengthen his predecessors "relatively weak position in the political order."[102] His uncommonly long reign, from 1834 to 1867, was one indication of this. In contrast to previous *amanhen,* he died in office rather than being destooled. And finally the expansion of the *besonfu,* the *omanhen*'s body of councillors, from seven in 1833 to fourteen sometime afterward also seems to be evidence of his strengthened powers vis-à-vis the *asafos.*[103]

At the same time, however, particularly where there was the greatest British administrative and adjudicative presence, as was the case in Cape Coast, chiefly powers were in the long run in decline, even if their military role temporarily increased. Brodie Cruickshank, who for eighteen years was a merchant resident on the coast and served as one of the area's judges, recognized how much this increasing "supervision...[had] tended to lessen the consequence of the chiefs."[104] In the coastal towns chiefs found that the increasing popularity of these "British" courts undermined their own judicial institutions since they were cheaper and provided "equal distribution of justice to rich and poor."[105] According to another of these British merchants cum-judge, Francis Swanzy, the people had so much appreciated this alternative system of justice that "they had forced it on us."[106]

Undoubtedly the most important contributor to this expansion of British control was the extremely able Lieutenant George Maclean, who became chief administrator of the Gold Coast settlements in 1827. To maintain peace on the coast, he sought to prevent the outbreak of serious disputes

as well as adjudicating even simple issues that he felt had the potential for
unleashing major conflicts. By 1843, when Parliament took over control
of the settlements, his court's activities extended far beyond the
boundaries of the coastal towns. The judicial activity clearly affected local
rulers. As King Aggrey of Cape Coast remarked bitterly in 1865,
"Maclean...in a very peculiar, unpredictable and unheard of manner
wrested from the hands of the local kings, chiefs and head men their
power to govern their own subjects."[107]

It was a contradictory situation since until 1874, when the Gold Coast
finally became a colony, the British attitude towards the coastal settlements
vacillated, with the opponents of official control seemingly in the
ascendancy. Nevertheless, local officials with or without the permission
of Parliament sought to extend British control even to the point of
abolishing traditional positions that they considered "a source of potential
trouble."[108] This was what Administrator Conran did in the case of King
Aggrey of Cape Coast in 1866. The latter's attempt to imprison his subjects without appeal to the British court and his intention to raise a "small
police force" would have represented an encroachment on what had
become a British monopoly of criminal adjudication in Cape Coast. The
governor then took advantage of the long-standing rivalry between the
Aggrey and Brempong Kojo stool families to recognize Kwesi Atta, a
matrilineal descendant of Brempong Kojo, but demoted him to the position
of "headman" of Cape Coast.[109] In a similar fashion to King Aggrey, for
his opposition to the British acquisition of Elmina in 1872, King Kobina
Gyan met the same fate as his Cape Coast counterpart, as the British also
deported him to Sierra Leone.

In conjunction with such direct attacks on their administrative and
adjudicative role, the shift from slave trading to the "legitimate trade" in
palm oil from the 1830s onward also undermined the economic power of
chiefs on the coast. The production and sale of palm oil required little if
any capital, since palm trees grew wild, and almost anyone could produce
and sell palm oil in small quantities. According to Brodie Cruickshank,
one of the results of this changed economy had been a much more
"extensive diffusion of property throughout every class of society."[110] It
had been reflected in an "indiscriminate" expansion in the ranks of petty
traders to the point where it was hard "to conceive where there was any
room for buyers among such a nation of peddlers."[111] Not surprisingly,
coastal towns such as Cape Coast, Anomabu and Accra continued to retain
their "republican" and "egalitarian" quality. Unlike the "bush chiefs" in the
towns of the interior who could "claim...the services of the inhabitants as
vassals," Cruickshank pointed out that coastal chiefs were little different
from other "private individuals."[112]

In addition to political, judicial and economic changes, from the 1830s
onward expanding missionary activity also played a major role in under-

mining chiefly authority.[113] Up until this time the impact of Christianity had been restricted primarily to mulattoes who were closely connected to the major coastal castles. Very rapidly, however, the Basel and Methodist missionaries, who initiated this new phase of Christianity in the Gold Coast, focused their proselytizing efforts on the general population. Particularly in the case of the Methodists, they also came to realize that there was a close correlation between their success in converting Africans to Christianity and providing Western education. As a reflection of this, by 1858 membership in the church's seven circuits stood at 2,000 with 6,000 attending public worship, while roughly 1,250 boys and girls were receiving education in some thirty-one schools.[114] Clearly, more than an astute linkage of religion and education was responsible for this rapid success.

As Mary McCarthy has suggested, "The cataclysmic changes which had occurred since 1807...had...thrown Fante society into a general state of disequilibrium, providing a receptive field for the planting of new ideas."[115] It had been a testing time for local deities who had failed to provide protection during the Asante invasions, and as an indication of how much on the defensive their priestly representatives felt, they had tried to stop the new religion. But rather than arresting this process, confrontations with Christians only resulted in humiliating indications of how little power they had to punish those who offended local beliefs. Though the priests were the immediate losers, chiefs, who were intimately part of local religious ritual and derived much of their authority from this association, were also affected. It was an indication, however, of how much the coastal chiefs had lost power that they were far more inclined than those inland to accept the governor's judicial supremacy in settling what were potentially explosive matters.[116]

In addition to demonstrating how much judicial independence coastal chiefs had lost and the declining influence of traditional religious beliefs, missionary success served to expand the size of the educated community in the coastal settlements. Recruitment into the ranks of this Euro-African community no longer depended on birth. Christianity, and the concomitant Western education that it offered, provided entry into a society whose members saw themselves as both distinct and entrusted with a vital role in spreading "civilization" to their heathen brethren. There was also a close link between this community and the settlements' trading economy. Its leading members were invariably merchants who had benefited from the more laissez-faire postwar conditions, and by the middle of the nineteenth century they were replacing the European traders who had either been independent merchants or representatives of the London firms that traded on the coast.[117] In addition, these wealthy merchants, often lay leaders in the Methodist Church, were sometimes, like their European counterparts, appointed to positions in the administration.

It was not surprising that they came to see themselves as the leaders of the African community as well. The vacuum that was developing in what came to be known as the "native order" created considerable opportunities for them to function in this capacity by straddling both the traditional and the Western world. They could appeal to British officials both in the Gold Coast and in the metropole, and when this failed they could also turn to traditional institutions to challenge British policies that ran counter to their interests. In 1853, for example, the four most important "mulatto" merchants in Cape Coast "rehabilitated" the "Kings Court," to challenge the British court's policy of dealing with "hopeless debtors."[118] Three years later they were involved in destooling the king, who they felt had become too "faithful to the British government."[119] In 1865, when it seemed that the British Parliament was contemplating whether to "transfer to the [natives] the administration of all the governments" on the coast, once again "educated natives" became very active in supporting King Aggrey of Cape Coast.[120] Finally, they were instrumental in the attempt to form a Fante Confederation between 1868 and 1871 which would have united the native states of the interior at a time when it seemed as if the British were going to abandon them to Asante conquest.

Ironically, their involvement with the native order served in the long run to weaken it further. Governors used this new challenge that the native order offered to deport its leaders, and demote those who took their place. The native rulers of the three most populous and important coastal towns—Elmina, Cape Coast and Accra—all suffered periods of deportation between 1866 and 1894.[121] It was hardly surprising that by the end of the nineteenth century this section of coastal society was at the nadir of its influence. Particularly in the large coastal towns, it seemed as if district commissioners were at the point of totally replacing the "tottering and uncertain power of the chiefs."[122] The process of state crystallization that had been one of the most important by-products of independence from inland kingdoms seemed to be in danger of being upstaged in the coastal towns by "direct rule."

Eventually, however, around the turn of the century the colonial administration came to realize that it could not do without some local authority figures even in the large, "civilized" towns of the coast. They needed such people to help implement the modest sanitary reforms they introduced to improve public health. Wars in the interior required large numbers of porters, and obtaining them also required "native authorities." In addition, a new generation of colonial governors, who were increasingly in favor of indirect rule as the most suitable policy for governing subject peoples, gradually began the long process of incorporating the chiefly order into the machinery of colonial government. That traditional culture, and the native order specifically, had not disappeared, even if "perplexed and confused," was largely due to its deep roots," even in the most "creolized" of coastal communities. On the surface it seemed obvious that these societies were deeply divided, as I shall show in the next chapter. Religious beliefs, occupations and education underscored these considerable differences, but as I shall also show in the following chapter there remained important structural features in the most creolized of coastal societies that linked the "educated classes" with their "illiterate brethren." The interaction of all these factors were what distinguished this "coast district" from the interior and gave its towns their unique Euro-African character.[123]

Notes

1. For a discussion of this early period of migrations into this area and its settlement, see James Anquandah, *Rediscovering Ghana's Past* (London, 1982).

2. An excellent indication of this can be found in the twenty-nine "Legends and Traditions of [Our] Native Land" which were serialized in forty-five episodes in the Cape Coast newspaper *Western Echo* between November 1885 and December 1887. Cited in R. Jenkins, "Subverting 'Law Imperialism': The Journalist–Historians of the Gold Coast–Ghana 1882-1888," a paper presented at the Thirty-third Meeting of the African Studies Association, 1-4 November 1990, 21.

3. During this long history of contact as many as seven European countries, or their national chartered companies, kept fortified stations on the Gold Coast. They were the Portuguese, the Dutch, the Danes, the Swedes, the French, the English and the Brandenburgers. For the most extensive treatment of the history of these forts and castles, see A. L. Lawrence, *Trade Castles and Forts of West Africa* (London, 1963).

4. The Portuguese forts belonged to that nations's crown, while other European forts were built by private chartered companies whose home governments gave them monopolies of the trade in this area. Invariably, these companies received a grant from their government to offset the cost of maintaining these expensive fortifications. Ibid., 26.

5. The Portuguese had begun building this castle in 1482, nine years after their discovery of gold in this region. Ibid., 98.

6. For a history of the English trading companies on the coast, see K. G. Davies, *The Royal African Company* (London, 1957).

7. The British and the Dutch monopolized the best trading areas with their forts and castles interspersed among one another. The Danes, who were later arrivals, were relegated to the initially less attractive eastern portion of the coast.

8. William Bosman, *A New and Accurate Description of the Coast of Guinea* (1704; reprint, London, 1967), 43. Bosman was an employee of the Dutch West India company from 1688 to 1702. He had risen during this long period of service

to the position of factor, the most important position among the company's officials after the governor.

9. "Abstract from the 'Voyage' of Eustache de la Fosse to Mina, 1479-80," in *Europeans in West Africa*, J. W. Blake, ed. and trans. (London, 1942) 1:240. Eustache de la Fosse was a Flemish merchant who visited this area in the fifteenth century.

10. Harvey Feinberg, *Africans and Europeans in West Africa: Elminans and Dutchmen on the Gold Coast During the Eighteenth Century* (Philadelphia, 1989), 77.

11. John Vogt, *Portuguese Rule on the Gold Coast, 1469-1682* (Athens, Ga., 1979), 85-86.

12. Cited in Kwame Daaku and Albert van Dantzig, "An Annotated Dutch Map of 1629," *Ghana Notes and Queries* 9 (November 1966):15.

13. Witness before the 1934 Commission of Inquiry into the Elmina Stool Dispute, ADM 11/1692, NAG, Accra. Cited in Harvey Feinberg, "Who Are the Elmina?" *Ghana Notes and Queries* 11 (June 1970):25.

14. Ansu Datta and R. Porter, "The Asafo System in Historical Perspective: An Inquiry into the Origin and Development of a Ghanaian Institution," *Journal of African History* 12, no.2 (1971):297.

15. Ibid.

16. Feinberg, *Africans and Europeans*, 111.

17. His *kostgeld*, or stipend, was one ounce of gold or its equivalent value in trade goods per month. Feinberg, *Africans and Europeans*, 107. In the nineteenth century this individual was described in government records as the *tufuhen*, the Akan term.

18. Ibid., 100.

19. Harvey Feinberg, "The Nature of Elmina Political Development in the Eighteenth Century," a paper presented at the Connecticut Valley African Colloquium, 6 March 1971, 22, cited in D. Henige, "Kingship in Elmina Before 1869: A Study in Feedback and the Traditional Idealization of the Past," *Cahiers d'Etudes Africaines* 55, XIV-3:507.

20. Ibid., 506.

21. Feinberg, *Africans and Europeans*, 102.

22. Ray Kea, *Settlements, Trade, and Polities in the Seventeenth-Century Gold Coast* (Baltimore, 1982), 12-13.

23. Bosman, *A New and Accurate Description*, 164.

24. Ibid., 5.

25. Ibid., 165.

26. Ibid.

27. Instead, he chose to describe Axim, which he felt to be one of the most "regular" of the coastal "Republicks." Ibid., 164.

28. Ibid., 43.

29. Apart from fishing, the gathering of crabs and market activities, from which the name Oguaa (market) probably derived, there was also iron smelting in this area of the coast. D. A. Penfold, "Excavation of an Iron Smelting Site at Cape Coast," *Transactions of the Historical Society of Ghana* 12 (1971):1-15.

30. Albert van Dantzig, *Forts and Castles of Ghana* (Accra, 1980), 40.

31. Bosman, *A New and Accurate Description*, 51. This is how Kwame Daaku has described people like Barter. *Trade and Politics on the Gold Coast, 1600-1720* (Oxford, 1970), 104.

32. Ibid., 51. The Royal African Company had sent Barter to England to be educated in 1690-1691. In 1693 he was one of the company's agents at an annual salary of thirty pounds. Ibid., 98.

33. Davies, *The Royal African Company*, 280-281.

34. For a discussion of this role as "state builder" see Henige, "John Kabes of Komenda: An Early African Entrepreneur and State Builder," 1-19.

35. Bosman, *A New and Accurate Description*, 51.

36. However, tradition in Cape Coast attributes to him the founding of the mulatto *asafo*, Akrampa, which in the early nineteenth century seems to have functioned as the English governor's bodyguard company. K. W. S. Johnston, "The Asafu in Cape Coast History," a paper presented at the University College of Cape Coast before the Historical Society of Ghana, 19 December 1963, NAG, Cape Coast, Acc 90/64, and J. C. de Graft Johnson, "The Fanti Asafu," *Africa* 5, no. 3 (July 1932):310.

37. For a description of this process of early settlement, see Casely-Hayford, "A Genealogical Study of Cape Coast Stool Families," 36-38.

38. Sometime afterward he returned to Fetu, for either he or his successor was taken prisoner by the Fante when they conquered this kingdom in 1707. PRO, Treasury Records of the African Companies, T. 70/5, 15 January 1707/8, cited in James Sanders, "The Expansion of the Fante and the Emergence of the Asante in the Eighteenth Century," *Journal of African History* 20, 3 (1979):352.

39. Johnston, "The Asafo in Cape Coast History." However, the Cape Coast barrister E. J. P. Brown has suggested a much earlier origin dating back to the mid-fifteenth century, when the original Fante migrants descended into the valley that contained the Effutu village of Oguaa. *Gold Coast and Ashanti Reader* (London, 1929), 1:139. Johnston's explanation, however, has more plausibility since it accounts much better for the present-day loyalties of the town's *asafos*.

40. The origins of Number Seven *Asafo*, Amanfur, seem also to have been similar to Brofumba's. Originally, they too were slave artisans whom the English brought to work on the castle. They settled at Amanfur, which in Fante means "new town." De Graft Johnson, "The Fanti Asafu," 311.

41. Brown, *Gold Coast and Ashanti Reader*, 2:122. Brown spells his name Kwadwo, but in stool succession inquiries of the colonial period his name was spelled Kojo. I shall use the colonial spelling since this is how he was referred to in the colonial period. There is disagreement over what his relation was to the *dey*

of Fetu. The prominent Cape Coast lawyer E. J. P. Brown has maintained that he was the *dey's* step-son. Ibid. The Crowther Enquiry, the most extensive investigation of Brempong Kojo's identity in the colonial period, indicated that he was married to Akwaaba Abba, the wife of a former *dey* of Fetu. Casely-Hayford, "A Genealogical Study of Cape Coast Stool Families," 64.

42. Brown, *Gold Coast and Ashanti Reader*, 2:122.

43. As reward for his services, the Committee of the Company of Merchants Trading to Africa presented him in 1774 with two silver goblets. They became an important part of his stool regalia. Brown, *Gold Coast and Ashanti Reader*, 2:125. The stool is the symbol of Akan rulership, and is similar to the throne in European culture.

44. D. Henige has investigated these records. See *The Chronology of Oral Tradition: Quest for a Chimera* (Oxford, 1974), 154-155.

45. For example, see the Crowther Cape Coast Stool Succession Inquiry, 1916, ADM 11/629, NAG, Cape Coast. *Omanhen* is the Fante/Akan term for the paramount chief that Europeans used to refer to as king. The plural is *amanhen*.

46. D. Henige has dealt at length with the difficulties of establishing historical accuracy in dealing with the traditions of the Fante coastal states. Participants in the innumerable stool disputes of the twentieth century introduced so much feedback from written sources into these traditions as to make it impossible to distinguish fact from fiction. He has discussed these issues in: *The Chronology of Oral Tradition;* "Kingship in Elmina Before 1869"; "The Problem of Feedback in Oral Tradition: Four Examples from the Fante Coastlands," *Journal of African History* 14 (1973):223-235; "Seniority and Succession in the Krobo Stools," *International Journal of African Historical Studies* 7, no. 2 (1974):203-226; and "Akan Stool Succession Under Colonial Rule-continuity or Change?," *Journal of African History* 16 (1975):285-301.

47. Payment of this "ground rent" is mentioned in J. J. Crooks, *Records Relating to the Gold Coast Settlements from 1750-1874* (1923; reprint, London, 1973), 128. The payment amounted to forty-eight pounds. It may have lapsed in the past and represented an attempt to rally local kings to the British side at a time when the Asante were a major threat to the coast. This king's African title, *dey*, is an indication of the Guan as opposed to Fante background to the Fetu kingdom. However, by the end of the eighteenth century the Fante had emerged as the dominant cultural force in the area, and not surprisingly Cape Coast kings came to reflect this by styling themselves *amanhen*, the Fante title for paramount rulers. In the nineteenth century this seems also to have become the case in Elmina.

48. W. Claridge, *History of the Gold Coast and Ashanti* (1915; reprint, London, 1964), 1:122-123.

49. There is a detailed description of the 1803 conflict in R. Porter, "The Cape Coast Conflict of 1803: A Crisis in Relations Between the African and European Communities," *Transactions of the Historical Society of Ghana* 11 (1970):27-82.

50. The evidence for this comes from the succession list for the Aggrey family, which became the rival stool family, as it goes back to the 1780s.

51. Casely-Hayford, "A Genealogical Study of Cape Coast Stool Families," 71. There was also considerable confusion over who his legitimate successor was since apart from his relationships with his wife, he supposedly had relationships with his "domestics" (slaves), and there developed five divisions of his family. For diagrams of these relationships see ibid., 62-63.

52. Ibid., 70.

53. Margaret Priestley, *West African Trade and Coast Society* (London, 1969), 15.

54. "Wilhelm Johann Müller's Description of the Fetu Country, 1662-1669," in *German Sources for African History, 1599-1669*, ed. Adam Jones (Wiesbaden, 1983), 184.

55. George P. Hagan, "Aspects of Social Change Among the Effutu of Winneba" (Ph.D. diss., Oxford University, 1975), 34. Nevertheless, many other commentators have assumed that it was patrilineal. For example: Brown, *Gold Coast and Ashanti Reader*, 1:196; Otutu Bagyire VI, *Abiriwhene*, "The Guans: A Preliminary Note," *Ghana Notes and Queries* 7 (January 1965):21-23; and D. Birmingham, "A Note on the Kingdom of Fetu," *Ghana Notes and Queries* 9 (November 1966):30-33.

56. *Odefey* is the Effutu term for paramount ruler. In Winneba they still speak Effutu, but Fante is increasingly becoming the most widely spoken language, and Fante/Akan terminology is becoming more common.

57. Sarbah, *Fanti National Constitution*, 20. Indeed, David Henige has gone so far as to suggest that "matrilineal succession within a particular *abusua* may have been customary in the sense that it represented a kind of vague notional ideal...but alternative *procedures* as well as alternative *candidates* were always available." "Akan Stool Succession Under Colonial Rule: Continuity or Change?" 300. There is no reason why the same "notional ideal" could not also apply to patrilineal succession.

58. For a description of these wars of conquest see James Sanders, "The Political Development of the Fante in the Eighteenth and Nineteenth Centuries: A Study of a West African Merchant Society" (Ph.D. diss., Northwestern University, 1980), 109-119.

59. Brown, *Gold Coast and Ashanti Reader*, 2:122. Ekumfi Adansi is a small village in the Ekumfi paramountcy. It is about seven miles to the east of Mankessim.

60. Sanders, "The Political Development of the Fante," 163. According to these traditions it was the Etsis who taught the Fantes how to fish and make salt.

61. Ibid., 165-168.

62. This was really with Kofi Aferi, who became Amonu II in 1857 and was on the stool until 1865. Sanders, "The Political Development of the Fante," 280.

63. Ibid., 279.

64. According to J. Sylvanus Wartemberg, an Elminian historian, he was enstooled from 1660 to 1680, which would have been before the town acquired a king according to the Dutch records. *Sao Jorge d'El Mina: Premier West African European Settlement, Its Traditions and Customs* (Ilfracombe, U.K., 1950?), 87-88. Unfortunately, Wartemberg gives no indication of what his sources are for this dating. Like most other Elminians, he was deeply involved in the town's politics and how objective he was is moot.

65. In addition to Elmina, some of the other larger Akan coastal towns still practice patrilineal succession, such as Shama and Winneba, where succession alternates.

66. The main reason for this is that the various contenders for positions in the traditional state were responsible for substantial feedback from written sources into the town's oral tradition as they sought to advance their own claims. For a discussion of this issue see Henige, "Kingship in Elmina Before 1869," 499-520.

67. One tradition maintains that Ampon Dziedur was suspected of mishandling the town's finances and the *oman* (the *omanhen*'s councillors) decided to destool and execute him. No one from his maternal family warned him, but two of his three sons did, and as reward for this loyalty he decreed that from thenceforth only sons could succeed to the town's stool. The opponents of changing from patrilineal to matrilineal succession argued that the system had always been in the male line, because Amankwaa, the town's supposed founder, came to Elmina alone. According to them, Ampon Dziedur merely limited the right of succession to the families of the two sons who had proven loyal. Cited in Harvey Feinberg, "Elmina, Ghana: A History of its Development and Relationship with the Dutch in the Eighteenth Century" (Ph.D. diss., Boston University, 1969), 73-74. Unfortunately, the extensive Dutch records give no indication of when this switchover might have taken place.

68. Cited in Datta and Porter, "The Asafo System in Historical Perspective," 284. If this was indeed so it must have added even more tension to the already "confused and perplexed " political life of the town.

69. Obituary for James Robert Thompson, *Western Echo*, 6 March 1886. As an indication of how "custom" had changed, in 1929, when E. J. P. Brown described this succession, he maintained that Thompson had "followed his paternal uncle." *Gold Coast and Ashanti Reader*, 2:153.

70. Cruickshank, *Eighteen Years on the Gold Coast of Africa*, 1:250.

71. Sarbah, *Fanti National Constitution*, 24.

72. W. E. G. Sekyi, "Traditional History of Various Tribes, 'Anamabu,'" 9. 554/64, NAG, Cape Coast, cited in Sanders, "The Political Development of the Fante," 285.

73. Robert Stone, "Colonial Administration and Rural Politics in South Central Ghana, 1919-1951" (Ph.D. diss., Cambridge University, 1975), 29. This is also the case in Cape Coast today. I attended an installation of a maternal nephew as a *supi* when I was doing fieldwork in the town in 1974.

74. James Christensen, *Double Descent Among the Fanti* (New Haven, Conn., 1954).

75. I. Chukwukere, "Akan Theory of Conception: Are the Fante Really Aberrant?" *Africa* 48, no. 2 (1978):137-147.

76. The origin of the Ga-Adangbe peoples of whom the Ga are a subgroup is still unresolved. Oral tradition says that they migrated into Ghana from the east with Egypt, Nubia and Mesopotamia often cited as the original homeland. Anquandah, *Rediscovering Ghana's Past,* 114. It is hard, however, to discount the role of feedback from particularly religious sources (the Bible) in shaping this tradition. Neither has linguistic nor archaeological evidence been able to resolve this question. See also Paul Ozanne, "Notes on the Early Historic Archaeology of Accra," *Transactions of the Historical Society of Ghana* 6 (1962) and "Notes on the Later Prehistory of Accra," *Journal of the Historical Society of Nigeria* 3 (1964).

77. John Parker, "Ga State and Society in Early Colonial Accra, 1860's-1920's" (Ph.D. diss., London University, 1995), 15.

78. Irene Quaye, "The Ga and Their Neighbors, 1600-1742" (Ph.D. diss., University of Ghana, 1972), 42-70.

79. Parker, "Ga State and Society," 16.

80. Fort Crèvecoeur became Ussher Fort in 1868 when the Dutch gave it to the British as part of a general exchange of coastal forts to rationalize European holdings on the coast. It was then named after the British administrator who was instrumental in carrying out this exchange. Albert van Danzig, *Forts and Castles of Ghana* (Accra, 1980), 63.

81. Parker, "Ga State and Society," 44-45.

82. Ibid., 27.

83. Margaret Field, *Social Organization of the Ga People* (London, 1940), 74.

84. Ibid. Field's highly critical view of indirect rule as having affected Ga political life for the worst may have led her to exaggerate how impotent *mantsemei* actually had been before the establishment of European rule. She felt that "every stool palaver [had] been brewed by European patronage," and that colonial ordinances had continued this disruptive situation by trying to impose Akan political institutions on the Gas. Ibid., 76-79.

85. Parker, "Ga State and Society," 25.

86. Anquandah, *Rediscovering Ghana's Past,* 124.

87. A. B. Quartey-Papafio, "Law of Succession Among the Akras or Ga Tribes Proper of the Gold Coast," *Journal of the African Society* 10, no. 37 (October 1910):66.

88. For a description of this arrangement and how it worked see Ivor Wilks, "Akwamu and Otublohum: An Eighteenth Century Akan Marriage Arrangement," *Africa* 29, no. 4 (October 1959):391-404.

89. Ibid., 68.

90. Not all of them were equally independent. Shama and Winneba were still not entirely free from the control of the inland states of Ahanta and Goma Assin, respectably.

91. Kea, *Settlements, Trade, and Polities*, 324.

92. This is what happened to the important Fante towns of Abora and Mankessim as a result of the campaigns of 1806 and 1807. Claridge, *A History of the Gold Coast and the Ashanti*, 241. The population decline in this area was so obvious as to be noted by a number of Europeans who traveled from Cape Coast to Kumasi in the second decade of the nineteenth century. For example: Thomas Bowditch, *Mission from Cape Coast Castle to Ashanti* (1819; reprint, London, 1966), 15, 19, 156-157; Joseph Dupris, *Journal of Residence in Ashantee* (1824; reprint, London, 1966), 4-6, 44; and William Hutton, *Voyage to Africa* (London, 1821), 1140-1146.

93. Crooks, *Records Relating to the Gold Coast Settlements from 1750-1874*, 296.

94. Macarthy to Bathurst, 16 May 1823, CO 267/58, PRO. Cited in *Social Change and the Growth of British Power in the Gold Coast: The Fante States, 1807-1874*, by Mary McCarthy (New York, 1983), 96.

95. Sanders, "The Political Development of the Fante," 307.

96. James Sanders, "Village Settlement Among the Fante: A Study of the Anomabo Paramountcy," *Africa* 55, no. 2 (1985):181-182.

97. Carl Reindorf, *The History of the Gold Coast and Asante* (1889; reprint, Accra, 1966), 105.

98. Field, *Social Organization of the Ga People*, 157. She uses the legend that she recounts that describes this to claim that *mantsemei* were only "minor priests," but John Parker has pointed out that not only is her chronology of this event faulty, but after this war "Taki Kome continued to wield extensive secular authority in Accra...[which included] the power to impose capital punishment." Parker, "Ga State and Society," 75.

99. Field, *Social Organization of the Ga People*, 160.

100. Kea, *Settlements, Trade and Polities*, 158-167.

101. One indication of the limited power of the Dutch was their inability to punish the Elminians who were responsible for the murder of the Dutch governor in 1808. Claridge, *A History of the Gold Coast and Ashanti*, 1:267. On the other hand, it was the threat of the arrival of an Asante army that was responsible for the Fantes and their allies abandoning the blockade they had subjected the Elminians to from 1809 to 1811. Henry Meredith, *An Account of the Gold Coast of Africa* (London, 1812), 90-91.

102. Larry Yarak, "Elmina and Greater Asante in the Nineteenth Century," *Africa* 56, no.1 (1986):34.

103. Rene Baesjou, ed., *An Asante Embassy on the Gold Coast: The Mission of Akyempon Yaw to Elmina, 1869-1972* (Leiden, 1979), 19.

104. Cruickshank, *Eighteen Years on the Gold Coast of Africa*, 2:11.

105. Ibid.

106. *Parliamentary Papers*. Report of the Select Committee appointed to inquire into the state of the British Possessions on the West Coast of Africa, 1842. Evidence of Francis Swanzy. Cited in Macarthy, *Social Change and the Growth of British Power,* 147.

107. King Aggrey to Governor Pine, 16 March 1865, CO 96/67, PRO. The most extensive description of Maclean's career on the coast is G. E. Metcalfe's *Maclean of the Gold Coast* (London, 1972).

108. Governor Conran to the Secretary of State, 15 April 1867, CO 96/74, PRO.

109. In 1867 the British and the Dutch exchanged their forts and settlements to rationalize their possessions on the coast. However, this exchange upset local alliances and war broke out between the people of Cape Coast and the Elminians. Kwesi Atta led his people in this conflict, and, as punishment, Governor Ussher formally "banished and outlawed" him. *African Times,* 23 May 1869. From this point onward there was no formally recognized traditional ruler in Cape Coast until 1911. Augustus Casely-Hayford has argued that in 1856 Kweku Atta "united" the two Cape Coast stools, but clearly this was not a "unification" that eliminated conflicting matrilineal and patrilineal claims to the paramountcy of the town. "A Genealogical Study of Cape Coast Stool Families," 61.

110. Cruickshank, *Eighteen Years on the Gold Coast of Africa,* 2:37.

111. Ibid.

112. Ibid., 1:242.

113. The Basel Mission Society was the first to arrive in 1828. But all of the first contingent of missionaries died and it was not really until 1832 that continuous mission work began. Methodist missionaries arrived in 1835, and in contrast to the Basel missionaries, who moved inland to the Akwapim Hills, these later arrivals began their activities in the coastal towns with Cape Coast their headquarters. F. L. Bartels, *The Roots of Ghana Methodism* (Cambridge, U.K., 1965), 12-19.

114. Ibid., 76.

115. McCarthy, *Social Change and the Growth of British Power,* 109.

116. The best example of this was the confrontation between Chief Adoo of Mankessim and British judicial authorities in 1851. King Adoo had punished a group of particularly zealous Christians who had desecrated the most sacred fetish grove of the Fante peoples at Mankessim. The British, however, intervened and fined him for destroying Christian property. Brodie Cruickshank, who was the assessor in this case, tried to be evenhanded by awarding the king and the fetish men he was supporting damages for the sacrilege committed, but it was only after threats of a military expedition against Adoo and pressure on him by the *amanhin* and chiefs of Anomabu and Cape Coast that he submitted to this decision. Cruickshank, *Eighteen Years on the Gold Coast of Africa,* 2:299-335. We might note that the effect of this experience on Adoo was so profound that soon after he

sent his children to the Methodist school in Mankessim and he himself started attending church.

117. Governor Hill to the Secretary of State, 20 April 1852, CO 96/25, PRO. Edward Reynolds has dated the emergence of this African merchant class in the Gold Coast to the 1830s. "The Rise and Fall of an African Merchant Class on the Gold Coast, 1870-74," *Cahiers d'Etudes Africaines* XIV-2 (54):253-264.

118. Merchants and others of Cape Coast to Governor Fitzpatrick, 25 August 1853, CO 96/28, PRO.

119. Governor Connor to the Secretary of State, 18 December 1854, CO 96/31, PRO.

120. Resolution number three of the Select Committee of the House of Commons appointed to consider the state of the British Establishments on the Western Coast of Africa. This was to exclude Sierra Leone. Cited in Crooks, *Records Relating to the Gold Coast Settlements from 1750-1874*, 369.

121. King Aggrey (1866-1869), King Kobina Gyan (1873-1894) and King Taki Tawia (1880-1883).

122. William Brandford Griffith Junior, Acting Queen's Advocate, to the Governor, William Brandford Griffith (his father), enclosed in the latter's "Memorandum on Native Prisons," a dispatch to the Secretary of State, 7 April 1888, CO 96/191, PRO.

123. Sarbah, *Fanti National Constitution*, 15.

Chapter 3

Nineteenth-Century Coastal Society:
The Limits of Creolization

To contemporary observers nineteenth-century coastal society in the Gold Coast possessed clearly perceived social divisions that went far beyond what they were familiar with in their own societies. They assumed that this was evidence of a society marked by fundamentally servile relationships. To Governor Richard Pine, the whole social fabric of the coast, "woof and warp," was based on "slavery."[1] Even Africans who were far more sympathetic to their own society could share similar sentiments. E. Casely Hayford, the Cape Coast lawyer, felt that before the passage of the Emancipation Ordinance and the Slave Dealing Abolition Ordinance in 1874 "the Gold Coast [could] be divided into two classes, freemen and slaves and pawns."[2] The 1874 legislation eliminated what were the most obvious and embarrassing aspects of servility in the new colony, but ironically the social divisions that developed under crown colony rule were potentially greater than between free born and slaves. In the past there had often been considerable economic differentiation between the free born and slaves, but in the new colony other criteria reinforced economic divisions, and underscored the differences between what the colony's press referred to synonymously as the "better" and the "poorer classes," or as the "literate" and the "illiterate classes."[3]

Dress styles were the most obvious distinguishing characteristic that set these "classes" apart. The "native gentlemen" of the "better classes" dressed in the singularly unsuitable woolen jackets and trousers that were fashionable in Great Britain, while men of the "poorer classes" could wear as little as breechclouts, or for more formal occasions, bundles of robes known locally as "cloths." "Native ladies," under the influence of the missionaries, wore frocks and blouses which set them off very distinctively from their illiterate or "heathen" sisters who scandalized the better classes by not covering their bosoms.[4] In the well-established towns, like Elmina, Cape Coast and Accra, residential segregation played an important role in spatially dividing "classes." Europeans and the better classes of Africans lived in quarters that were distinct from those of the poorer classes.[5] Membership in religious and secular organizations was an important indication of social differentiation on an institutional level. Invariably the better classes were Christian and the poorer classes were pagans. By the end of the nineteenth century most of the prominent coastal families were either Anglican or Methodist. Catholic proselytizing from the 1880s added an important challenge to this norm and in general contributed to the expansion of the colony's Christian population. Membership in an array of fraternal and improvement organizations coincided roughly with religious affiliation and added an even more subtle dimension to the divisions within coastal society.[6]

Marriage patterns between members of the better classes demonstrated considerable group endogamy which also cemented social boundaries. By the late nineteenth century, originally Dutch Euro-African families like the Bartels, the Pietersens and the Van Heins were as much Cape Coast families as they were Elminian. Likewise in Accra, with its several Euro-African communities, there was extensive intermarriage between originally Dutch and Danish Euro-African families like the Vanderpuijes, the Lutterodts and the Reindorfs with their Anglo-African counterparts, the Bruces, the Bannermans and the Hansens, as well as with such prominent Cape Coast families as the Hutchisons, the de Grafts and the Grants. Apart from fusing together families with different European backgrounds, these marriage patterns helped to break down the boundaries between people who were also part of Ga or Akan cultural environments, and served to make this elite more culturally homogenous. As Samuel Tenkorang has observed, intermarriage among the elite of the educated classes contributed to making this section of coastal society "one large extended family of blood and affinal relations."[7] Families like the Coles, the Cokers and the Hutchinsons were a pan-West African network of blood and affinal relations which served also to promote an additional sense of distinctiveness among this Euro-African elite. Ray Jenkins has pointed out that these "lateral ties" served to reinforce a "shared cultural experience."[8]

The success of the mission churches and the education that they brought with them played a vitally important role in underscoring the sense of difference between the "better" and the "poorer classes since these changes affected life styles." On a more subtle level, it also stimulated group identity based on the belief in being part of the momentous work of converting Africa to Christianity. It was a time when Africans seemed destined to play an increasingly important role in this proselytizing mission. Bishop Samuel Ajayi Crowther's consecration in 1864 as the first bishop of the territories of West Africa beyond the British Dominions was one of the most important indications of this. For Gold Coast Christians the exploits of their own Thomas Birch Freeman in taking Christianity to the Asante was a more immediate indication of the role of the native ministry in the great work of Christian salvation. Not just ordained ministers were the heroes of this mission. Appropriately enough, two leading Cape Coast merchants, F. C. Grant and John Sarbah, were important members of the committee that organized the 1885 Methodist Jubilee celebrations in Cape Coast.[9] On a more humble level, small-scale traders in up-country areas were often instrumental in establishing Christian communities.

Freetown, Sierra Leone, where the dual thrust of Christian proselytizing and the spread of Western education had gone furthest, represented what James Hutton Brew, the editor of the Cape Coast newspaper *Gold Coast Times*, described as a "loftier order of Christian civilization."[10] He was continually exhorting his readership to follow more the example of their more advanced "fellow colonists."[11] To the editor of the London-based monthly *African Times*, "Bathurst, Freetown, Monrovia, Cape Coast and Lagos were the luminous points from which Christian civilization [would] radiate."[12] Helping in the spread of Christianity to those "just emerging from the shade of barbarism" was only part of this mission.[13] Brew's "loftier order" also embraced the social milieu of the metropole. In his various newspapers he faithfully reported events like weddings, funerals, concerts, conversaziones, at homes, teas and dinner parties which he held up as "gatherings...that tend to cultivate relations whose very existence [were] essential to the well being of a place."[14] The unsettling newness of this social environment provided fertile ground for the many different improvement societies and social clubs that came into existence in the late-nineteenth century. Some were only short-lived, but others, like the fraternal societies, have survived until the present.

The raison d'être for much of this activity was mastering the social mores of Victorian Britain. The unparalleled degree of social equality with which women mixed with men was one indication of the need for a new social etiquette, and a considerable amount of the improvement effort was directed to the uplift of the "fairer sex." For example, in 1885 James Hutton Brew, the editor and proprietor of the newspaper *Western Echo*, called for "ladies" in Cape Coast to form an "organization" patterned after one existing in Sierra Leone that would provide both social uplift and political education.[15] Clearly men also needed models, and Brew was equally adamant in stressing the Gold Coast's need for "men like Samuel Lewis, Mr. Sawyerr and Independent Grant," the leading African politicians in Freetown, who could "speak up" for the colony's interests.[16] In general improvement was, as Leo Spitzer has argued for the Creoles of Freetown, a way of "display[ing] material wealth—especially of possessions like 'English' furniture, knick-knacks, and clothing—which were concrete proof of an individual's status within a society whose top standards were set in Europe."[17] For their counterparts in the Gold Coast it was very much a dual competition to catch up with both the metropole and their more advanced "fellow colonists" in Sierra Leone.

Missionary expansion and the Europeanization associated with it also coincided with considerable commercial expansion, and here also the "colonists" of West Africa saw a "mission" role for themselves. In the Gold Coast, the coming of crown colony rule in 1874 coincided with a major expansion in trade between a rapidly industrializing Europe and West Africa. The increase in the Gold Coast's imports and exports from around three hundred thousand pounds in 1872 to a little over one million pounds in 1899 was a graphic indication of this.[18] The expanding variety of the products that the colony exported and imported contributed to this growth in trade.[19] Greatly facilitating these changes were the steamships which beginning in the 1870s provided faster service and larger cargo capacities than the sailing ships of the past. By the middle of the 1880s steamships had almost entirely replaced sailing vessels. Initially this made it much easier for African merchants to participate in the trading economy than had been the case earlier in the century, when a few London firms monopolized the area's export and import trade.[20] As Raymond Dumett has pointed out, "localized economies" were drawn "more fully into the currents of the capitalist system."[21] In 1868 the editor of the *African Times* had anticipated a "race of native capitalists."[22] By the end of the nineteenth century his prophecy seemed to be unfolding.

The successful African merchants who were to become "commercial kings" in this expanding capitalist system could move beyond the "principle of barter" that Brodie Cruickshank felt, in the 1840s, characterized much of the petty trade of this "nation of peddlers."[23] Like their counterparts in Freetown and Lagos, they were often the entrepreneurs who penetrated into the hinterlands pursuing new economic opportunities. The Cape Coast merchants Francis C. Grant and John Sarbah played a dynamic role in the development of the Gold Coast rubber trade in the 1880s.[24] A fellow Cape Coaster, C. Barnes, was a pioneer "of the timber industry in the Western Province," while Magnus Sampson claims that King Ghartey of Winneba, during his merchant days, was the first "to introduce palm-nut cracking on the Gold Coast."[25] It was hardly surprising, as Evelyn Rowand has shown from her study of the press and its opinions in British West Africa, that in the late nineteenth century the mercantile elite all over this area were in favor of colonial expansion into the hinterland.[26] Opening up trade routes into the interior was a high priority for them as was promoting peace through imperial government, if necessary. John Sarbah, for example, while he was one of the few African members of the colony's Legislative Council, demonstrated this concern with "the need for improving conditions for carrying on trade" in his speeches in the council.[27]

In Sierra Leone there was a similar expansion of trading opportunities which played a critical role in the upward mobility and rapid creolization of the Liberated African population. Indicative of this, "by the 1870s the term [Creole] had come to mean Settlers, Liberated Africans and their descendants."[28] In a similar fashion expanded trade in the Gold Coast enabled a much more diverse population to take advantage of the opportunities it offered. Earlier in the century, when independent African merchants had been few in number, the most important had been the sons and daughters of European traders. By the 1880s, however, such people no longer dominated the ranks of the African commercial class. For example, at this time the two wealthiest men in Cape Coast were John Sarbah and Jacob Wilson Sey, neither of whom were mulattoes. The former was from the nearby town of Anomabu, a member of the royal family of the Anomabu state and of "pure African descent."[29] Sey seems to have been less privileged. His parents were illiterate, and he had begun life as a farmer, palm wine seller and coffin maker in Cape Coast. Somehow he seems to have made a valuable gold strike which elevated him from being a "poor illiterate" to "Jacob Wilson Sey Esq."[30]

Reflective of the importance of trade and the opportunities that it promised, "the preferred Euro-African occupation was that of 'self-employed' businessman."[31] Even ministers and teachers very often "abandoned" these high status "callings" in "preference" for trade, as was the case of the successful Accra merchant, George Frank Cleland.[32] He had begun as a Wesleyan Methodist school teacher in Accra, but he was later transferred to Prampram. In this busy entrepôt he was able to master "the science of his new vocation."[33] However, the ranks of the colony's "commercial kings," as Susan Kaplow has indicated, "were effectively closed to all but a few."[34] The limited availability of credit and fierce competition with metropolitan trading houses guaranteed that the number of commercial kings would be small in number. Larger in number were those whose "emporium[s]" were "homogeneously stocked with tin pans, loud-patterned basins, iron pots, a few rolls of cloth and bottles of American rum."[35] Even more numerous were the "petty traders" who hawked their wares in the market place or along the roads of the colony's busy towns. A step above these capitalists who made up the majority of the colony's trading population were the agents who worked either for the commercial kings, or, in larger numbers, for the various metropolitan trading houses that began to proliferate on the coast in the 1880s. Here, also, there was considerable difference between the earnings of branch managers, trading agents and clerks.

The extent to which trade and commerce dominated the economies of the main coastal towns of West Africa by the last decades of the century is graphically indicated by the occupational statistics that exist. In 1891 Dr. James F. Easmon, in a draft report on the census of the Gold Coast Colony, estimated that of the "acquired occupations" (excluding agriculture and fishing), 30.29 percent of the working population of Cape Coast were involved in trading and 24.04 percent in Accra.[36] Similarly the percentage of traders in the overall working populations of the colony's other busy port towns was uniformly high, but it clearly came as no surprise to Dr. Easmon that Cape Coast, "the oldest civilized town," should be in the forefront of this development. Both Freetown and Lagos, with around 30 percent of their populations engaged in commerce in the 1880s, had almost the same percentages as Cape Coast, which is indicative of the similarity of their economic culture.[37] Trade, rather than the agricultural industry that Sierra Leone's humanitarian founders had envisaged, became the main spring of that colony's existence, and brought it into line with other, older coastal entrepôts on the West African coast like those of the Gold Coast. Economic congruence served to reduce the importance of the specific origins of these coastal societies. As A. P. Kup has observed for Sierra Leone, "trade provided the key whereby Liberated Africans entered Creoledom."[38]

It was this deep involvement in the capitalist system which contributed to the importation of the class distinctions associated with the metropole, "a nation of shopkeepers." More than just economic specialization was involved. Increasingly, as trading activities became more complex, entry into the more lucrative levels of the capitalist system depended on mastering some degree of Western education. One had to keep books, and as responsibilities increased, be able to communicate in writing with one's superiors either in the colony or in the metropole. It was this link between Western education and West Africa's expanding trading economies that was one of the main reasons for the success of the Christian missions. Early in the century missionaries had hoped that the "Bible and the plough" would civilize Africa.[39] Instead, on the West African coast the far more important link that developed was between the schoolbook and the store. Missionary success was intimately linked to the spread of Western education, which provided the link between the "Three Cs"—Christianity, civilization and commerce. Indicative of this in the Gold Coast, the expansion of church membership and the number of denominational schools kept pace with one another.[40]

The result was also considerable differentiation within the ranks of the "better classes" based both on economic as well as educational standing.[41]

The press in the Gold Coast distinguished between the "scholar class" and "native gentlemen" whose wives and daughters were "native ladies." Many of these "ladies" and "gentlemen" measured up to the exacting standards of Europeanization that Victorian Britain held up as the civilized ideal. The explorer Richard Burton, who could be viciously critical of "educated natives" in general, nevertheless grudgingly recognized that there were some "mulattoes" as well as "natives" in the Gold Coast who he thought were "palpably superior in intellect" to many of the Europeans residing on the coast.[42] Invariably such people had received a secondary education outside of the colony either in Freetown or Great Britain, with the latter the preferred destination. In a similar fashion to what Michael Echeruo has described for Lagos, there were advertisements in the Gold Coast press for boarding schools in the metropole.[43] Between 1880 and the end of the century, Ray Jenkins has identified thirty-three Gold Coast Africans who went on for advanced training in Great Britain. Almost half of them (sixteen) returned to the colony as lawyers, while a substantial number also qualified as engineers and a few in business and medicine.[44]

Not until 1876, when the Methodists established Wesleyan High School in Cape Coast, was secondary education available in the Gold Coast, as it had been in Sierra Leone since 1845.[45] For the much larger percentage of the educated classes that the press usually referred to as "scholars," standard seven, the end of primary school, represented the limit of their formal Western education. Attaining this educational level was considerably more of an achievement than it would be today, but nevertheless Europeans invariably disliked these "half-educated natives," the products of primarily mission schools. To the West African traveler Mary Kingsley, they "displayed [a] second hand, rubbishy white culture."[46] To others they were lazy and inept.[47] Even Africans could be bitterly critical of their "sycophancy," and their "aping of European manners and customs."[48] In reality, however, they played a vital role in the functioning of colonial society by filling a wide range of lesser positions. They were clerks and storekeepers for the large trading firms. As the lowest grades of clerks in the colonial civil service, they were indispensable for the proper functioning of the colony's administration. As catechists and primary school teachers for the mission churches, they played a vital role in the spread of Christianity and Western education. There was a great deal of underemployment and unemployment among their ranks, since even before the government's entry into the field of education the mission schools produced far more scholars than there were positions for in the colony's economy.

It was a measure of how important education became as an avenue for upward mobility that successful merchants tried to provide the best schooling possible, particularly for their sons. For example, John Sarbah sent three of his children (including one daughter) to England for education, and his eldest son, John Mensah Sarbah, returned home in 1887 as the first Gold Coast African to qualify for the bar.[49] Even more impressive was John Sarbah's contemporary, the Cape Coast merchant F. C. Grant, who educated all of his nine boys in England.[50] As was the case in Sierra Leone, such education promised entry into the professions, and the far greater security that this offered than the unpredictable world of commerce. The result was, as Spitzer has pointed out for Freetown, that "professional men—doctors, lawyers, churchmen, newspaper editors, upper-level civil servants—along with wealthy merchants and businessmen...[came to occupy] the top level of Creole society."[51] In addition to the security that the professions offered, they were clearly lucrative—especially law. In 1866 Governor Conran estimated that the most successful of the "advocates" in the Gold Coast were making over one thousand pounds per annum.[52] As competition with European trading houses increased in the late nineteenth century, and the future of the colony's commercial kings became more uncertain, professional education, along with investments in property, seemed the best way for the educated classes to ensure the good life for their children.[53]

Apart from professional positions, crown colony status resulted in a dramatic increase in positions for Africans in the colony's administration that also offered far more security than commerce. In 1867 the civil staff consisted of only 85 people, but three decades later this number had increased more than tenfold to 863.[54] Europeans occupied the majority of the senior positions, but there was a significant sprinkling of Africans both from the Gold Coast, other West African colonies (mostly Sierra Leone), and the West Indies in positions of importance in the judiciary and the medical, customs, postal, treasury and political departments, as well as in the military and the police force. However, Gold Coast Africans made up the overwhelming majority of the employees in the colony's admin- istration. Clearly, within this overall group there was considerable difference in rank and income. In 1894 the highest-paid African in the colonial service was a Sierra Leonian puisne judge, Justice Francis Smith. His base annual salary was one thousand pounds, while the colony's chief justice was making fifteen hundred pounds.[55] At the same time J. L. Minnow from Cape Coast, a first-class officer in the Customs Department, received an annual salary of two hundred pounds. A fifth-class clerk, one of the lowest-paid positions in the civil service, received an annual salary of thirty-six pounds. Between such people there was considerable social distance.

In addition to accentuating social divisions, expanding opportunities for Africans in the civil service contributed to the sense of mission that characterized late-nineteenth-century coastal society. In conjunction with their role in spreading Christianity and commerce, the better classes could envisage an increasingly important role for themselves in administering the colony. Ironically, it seemed that they would implement the stymied vision of the Fante Confederation from within the ranks of the civil service. David Kimble has pointed out that "in 1883, of the forty-three 'higher posts' in the Gold Coast, nine were filled by Africans."[56] They were undoubtedly cheaper to employ than Europeans, and also their ability to survive in the tropics made them likely to serve for much longer periods of time than the latter. Longevity in the colonial service inevitably resulted in their rising in the ranks. No where was this better exhibited than in the Medical Service, where up until the end of the century blacks and whites served on basically the same terms. Reflective of this, in 1894 three of the top five positions in the Gold Coast Medical Service were filled by Africans, with the chief medical officer an African from Sierra Leone.[57] They were recognized as some of the most able of the colony's doctors. The governor, Sir William Brandford Griffith, felt that Dr. Easmon, the chief medical officer, was the most capable medical man in the colony.[58]

In the latter part of the nineteenth century the social tensions that resulted from migration from up-country also served to exacerbate the social divisions that underscored the unique nature of these societies. In Freetown the most important divide was between Creoles, or Sierra Leoneans, as they also called themselves, and the "aborigines" from up-country. Both hostility and a patronizing sense of themselves as "civilizing agents" characterized the attitudes of the former to the latter.[59] There was also considerable migration to important coastal towns in the Gold Coast, like Cape Coast and later on Accra, from up-country. Between 1891 and 1901, when the colonial government conducted the first official censuses, Cape Coast more than doubled in size from 11,614 to 28,984.[60] In a similar fashion to its Sierra Leonean counterpart, there was considerable ethnic variety in this population of newcomers. By the end of the nineteenth century, when Cape Coast was enjoying boom conditions, one could see on its busy Commercial Street brightly dressed Fante market women, their menfolk in more somber robes, coastal peoples like the Ewe and the Ga, Asantes and other Akans with their distinctive facial scarification, Krumen from Liberia with their filed front teeth and magnificent physiques, Hausas with their Koranic skullcaps and other Muslims, people from the north like Dagombas, Grunshis and Wangaras.

In addition, Lieutenant Governor George Straham's "peremptory" abolition of slave trading and slavery in 1874 created a great deal of lasting turmoil.[61] It resulted in the creation of a class of ex-slaves who had either left their masters in 1874 or subsequently had come as carriers to the coast and had escaped from those who had brought them. In Cape Coast they had settled in their own community, on the east bank of the Fosu Lagoon, appropriately called Freetown. There was a great deal of resentment on the part of the better classes towards this community, a number of whom may very likely have been previously the former's property. According to James Hutton Brew, "in nine out of ten cases [they were] homeless and pillars of a system of terrorism."[62] Between them and people he referred to as "Hausas," they accounted for what he felt was the increasing number of brutal robberies, housebreakings, shootings and murders, which he lost no opportunity to report on in his newspaper.[63] Gerald McSheffery has argued that after the abolition of slavery there was a continuing stream of ex-slaves to the coast who would have contributed to this "system of terrorism."[64] Raymond Dumett and Marion Johnson have questioned how large this migration was, but at the same time they argue that "the inability of local labor markets to absorb many ex-slaves during the period 1875-1895 led to the emergence of an embryonic *lumpenproletariat* rather than a genuine working class."[65] Many of these people would have gravitated to towns like Cape Coast with disturbing social consequences.

Those who stress the geographical and hence the cultural connections between the coastal societies of Gold Coast and the interior as a major difference between these communities and those of Sierra Leone pay too little attention to how ethnically diverse the former were. Both in Sierra Leone and in the Gold Coast the poorer classes who comprised indigenous society displayed considerable heterogeneity in their composition. Even the fishing communities in the Gold Coast, perhaps the oldest communities on the coast, reflected this. By the end of the nineteenth century the Pax Britannica had stimulated a regular movement back and forth of "stranger fishermen" looking for better beaches or more building space for their villages. They could be Akans as well as members of different ethnic groups like Ewes from the Volta region. The largest portion of the poorer classes who were engaged in farming on the outskirts of the coastal towns were equally ethnically heterogeneous. The plethora of land cases in the colony's courts involving trespass and illegal cultivation indicate that their position in coastal society was often as equally insecure as that of the stranger fishermen. Both groups could easily win the enmity of established communities that felt threatened by their presence.[66] For the latter this could be the *asafos,* with their membership primarily consisting of the poorer classes, while for the former this would more likely cut across class lines to pit members of the poorer classes against landowners who were members of the better classes.

The Matrilineal Family: The Challenge to Creolization

The sense of mission on many levels and the perceived sense of class distinctions based on economic educational and religious factors establish a prima facie case for seeing the littoral societies of West Africa as part of a wider phenomenon of creolization. Nevertheless, most contemporary scholars have preferred to stress the differences between the coastal communities of the Gold Coast and the Creole society of Sierra Leone. For Christopher Fyfe, "the European educated elite of the coastal communities of the Gold Coast remained part of Fante or Ga society—unlike the Sierra Leone Creoles who had been cut off geographically from their homelands."[67] More recently, Ray Jenkins has criticized the "utility" of applying the concept of "creole" or "creolized groups" to members of "communities [who] were not expatriates, repatriates or returnees."[68] Like Fyfe, he sees even "families [who] acknowledged an expatriate paternal ancestor" as being "indigenised to a remarkable degree."[69] As evidence of the latter, Augustus Casely-Hayford in his genealogical study of Cape Coast stool families has argued that in spite of "reinforc[ing] the differences between lineages [Westernization] did not affect the basic affiliation of the Fante to the stool."[70]

Undoubtedly, the coastal societies of the Gold Coast had considerable ability to absorb outsiders at many social levels, and the underlying structure of these communities played an important role in bridging the gaps between their different social strata. Most important was the matrilineal family which is common to all Akan peoples of the Gold Coast. As Fyfe has indicated, "even the children of Europeans, in these matrilineal societies, usually identified with the families of their African mothers."[71] It is facile, however, to see this as simply indigenization. Inevitably there was considerable tension between the matrilineage and the nuclear family that the Christian missionaries upheld as the "civilized" ideal. The rigidity of the latter contrasted with the flexibility of the former, which allowed for considerable "inventiveness" when it came to determining membership and status in the matrilineage. Best of all, the active tension that resulted from these very different family systems reflected both the "pull" of Westernization and the "push" of Akanization that underscored the attractions and the limits of creolization in this setting.

The eight exogamous martriclans, or *mmusa* (singular, *abusua*), around which Akan societies are structured, "cut across both tribal and political boundaries."[72] Members of these clans are expected to share certain responsibilities such as providing hospitality and the sharing of funeral expenses for *abusua* members even from different states. James Boyd Christensen, who was the first to systematically study the coastal Fante, observed that though the Fante themselves usually make no distinction between the larger totemic clan (the *abusuakuw*) and the localized *abusua*, there is indeed a local *abusua* as well as segments within this local *abusua* which he described as the extended family. The latter in turn segments into individual households which, depending on the wealth and importance of the household head (the *fie panyin*), could include his own siblings and their uterine offspring, his wife or wives and their children, his sisters and their offspring as well as grandchildren and great-grandchildren in the maternal line, and finally male and female slaves (domestics) and their offspring who would all be incorporated into the local *abusua*.[73]

What this extremely complex web of social relationships meant was that the Akan matrilineage was both generationally and socially inclusive, and reflected within its ranks the diversity of the larger society outside.[74] It was an inclusiveness that went considerably beyond the "ward system," or "fostering," in Sierra Leone where up-country children were sent to live with "better-to-do Creoles for whom they would perform household chores in return for the opportunity to go to school."[75] It was a system, as Spitzer has pointed out, that did work as a "powerful vehicle for the integration of hinterland Africans into creole society. The exposure of up-countrymen to colony households often led them to imitate Creole manners and to adopt Creole standards in clothing, house-building, furnishing, and religion."[76] Incorporation into the Akan matrilineage undoubtedly had a similar impact in the coastal societies of the Gold Coast, but it also meant much more than cultural assimilation. The result could be the formal incorporation of outsiders who were entitled to succeed to family (*abusua*) positions as well as inherit property. This was true for the families of the better classes as it was for the poorer classes, but with the important complication that within the extended families of the former there would also be smaller, Christian-style nuclear families which would be in competition with matrilineages in the matter of inheritance.

The family of Jacob Wilson Sey, the wealthiest man in Cape Coast in the 1890s, was an excellent example of how this incorporation could take place, and the tensions that could result. He "had a household of some two to three hundred people."[77] Many of these people were of slave origin and had entered Sey's household as young children, but over the years he had incorporated them into his family.[78] In addition, even though Sey was a "very staunch Methodist," this did not stop him from having several (dozen?) children by some of his female domestics.[79] It was hardly an unusual situation for people of his standing in Cape Coast, though the number of his children may have been well above average. In a similar fashion to people of his standing, he also contracted a church marriage, and this union produced a few sons and daughters. Sey seems to have intended to have the one surviving son of this church marriage succeed European style to the bulk of his property. However, father and son had a bitter quarrel in 1897, and Sey altered his will to benefit instead twenty-four of his domestic children.[80]

In 1898 the Methodist clergyman Reverend A. W. Parker managed to arrange a reconciliation between father and son, and Sey added a codicil to his will that entitled his remaining son and daughter by his church marriage to small portions of his fortune.[81] When the father died in 1902, the son was extremely disappointed to discover how small his share was, and he unsuccessfully challenged the validity of the will in the Cape Coast

Divisional Court. Instead, the judge placed the bulk of the fortune in the hands of an administrator whose task it was to carry out the complex terms of the will. In keeping with Sey's interest in education, the will favored the brightest of his domestic sons by providing for their education in England, and promising them five hundred pounds on their obtaining professional qualifications within twenty-one years of Sey's death in 1902.[82] Only one was able to meet these terms (Annan Sey, who became a deacon in the Church of England), with the result that the remaining shares passed to Sey's surviving daughters (domestics) as the will stipulated.

Even when there was a more favored and competent male to succeed than there was in the case of the Sey family, the redistributing of family wealth among a wide and diverse group was inevitable. It was graphic evidence of how linked the different strata of coastal society could be even if the family in question had a long Euro-African connection. For example, after the death of Samuel Collins Brew in 1881, there were disputes over the sharing of his property among his children as well as between his children and his matrilineage.[83] James Hutton Brew, the fourth generation descendant of the European trader Richard Brew, who was originally from the Isle of Man and established this well-known example of a Gold Coast, Euro-African family, successfully challenged his father's testamentary intention to leave his assets to fund the education of his youngest son.[84] At that time the elder brother, James Hutton Brew, was practicing as a "country advocate" in the law courts of the colony, and was able to use his legal knowledge to his own advantage.[85] He did so by maintaining that "native law prevented his father from excluding as beneficiaries all members of his family save one...and succeeded in establishing himself as the administrator of his father's estate."[86]

However, the illiterate members of his father's matrilineage immediately challenged Brew's right to function in this position. They got the king of Anomabu, where Samuel Collins Brew had been a trader and owned important properties, to arbitrate the division of this property. He suggested that the matrilineage take half the property and allow the children the other half, which would be returned to the family upon their deaths. To Brew, it was an unacceptable compromise since he had potential heirs who did not belong to his maternal family, and the matter finally ended up in the Cape Coast High Court. On this occasion, however, Brew reversed his arguments to take advantage of the greater sympathy that the court then had for the interests of wives and surviving children than for the rights of matrilineages, but he was not as successful as he had been in his earlier court battles.[87] The court recognized the matrilineal family's right to "certain old family lands" while "other lands purchased by the defendant (except one)" were to pass to Brew, who was also claiming to be the head of the family. The balance of the estate, after court expenses had been subtracted, was to be "equally divided between the plaintiff and the defendant."[88] However, this also generated contention, since Brew's claims to be head of the family were also challenged, but the court considered this issue to be beyond its competence and refused to rule.[89] In addition, given the nature of the property in question, lands and immovable property, an acceptable division was impossible and this contained the seeds of bitter disputes in the future.[90]

The superimposition of European cultural norms on an underlying Akan social structure clearly contributed to the contentiousness of the intrafamilial relations in both the Sey and Brew families. Apart, however, from indicating how much the divisions within the larger society were reproduced within individual households, these court cases also graphically demonstrate how difficult it was to preserve generational continuity among even the most Europeanized of coastal families. Doing so was greatly dependent upon maintaining the integrity of both fixed and real property, which clashed with the "reabsorptive" emphasis in Akan principles of inheritance. The study of this aspect of the Akan matrilineal system has received far less attention than the matrilineage's ability to survive being "whittled down" as the colony's economy became more commercialized.[91] It was particularly important in the Akanized coastal areas of the Gold Coast where both the concept of the nuclear family and the alienation of land and fixed property in English common law clashed with customary ideas about the family and, most of all, the possession of landed property.

Neither of the court cases that I have described were unique as the court records of the period indicate, and such litigation provides evidence of important differences between Sierra Leone Creoledom and the Euro-African society of the Gold Coast. There was much more tension between African and European legal norms in the littoral societies of the Gold Coast than there was in Freetown, where the legal distinction between "Creoles" and "Up-countrymen" was legally precise, and reflected in what H. M. Joko Smart has described as a much more "watertight" distinction between English common law and native law.[92] For the " 'non-native[s]' (Creoles) the law governing wills [was] English law before 1st January 1880, i.e. the Wills Act, 1837; that governing their death intestate [was] the Local Administration of Estates Ordinance, cap 45, which [drew] copiously upon English Law."[93] And since "non-natives" were not allowed to obtain freehold property in the provinces, any attempt to dispose of such property was null and void.[94] As a result the kinds of conflict between different legal systems that was the hallmark of Gold Coast land litigation were largely eliminated. Restrictions on property ownership for Creoles outside of the settlement removed a very lucrative avenue of litigation that Gold Coast lawyers enjoyed.

There were also other important differences between these societies.

The loose structure and incorporative nature of the *abusua*, apart from benefiting domestics and their children, also made it easy to absorb outsiders from significantly different cultures. European cases of this absorption are relatively well known primarily through the work of Margaret Priestley and, more recently, Mary McCarthy. With few exceptions, however, those interested in immigrants from Sierra Leone and particularly from the Americas have been "preoccupied with examining the inflows and influences of groups of pioneer repatriates rather than attempting to estimate the contributions of the first or second generations of their descendants."[95] Undoubtedly, part of the reason for this lies in the narrower cultural gap between the first and second generations of such immigrants and indigenous society. They clearly shared much more of a common background, and their continued absorption into the host society was increasingly easier.[96] Not surprisingly, such people have tended to escape the notice of historians.

The case of William Zacheus Coker, whose father originally came from Sierra Leone in 1857 to work in the Gold Coast civil service, is a particularly good example of how rapidly the Akan *abusua* could absorb foreign outsiders as well as incorporate them into the highest ranks of traditional society. Coker senior married a Cape Coast woman who was a royal member of the Anona *abusua*.[97] In the same year Coker junior was born. As an indication of the close ties that still existed between his father and Sierra Leone, he was sent to that colony for his education. Upon completion of his high school education, he returned to the Gold Coast and entered government service in 1879 as the clerk to the Queens Advocate. He clearly had ability, and by 1882 he had become the registrar of the Supreme Court.[98] In 1886, however, when James Robert Thompson, the *tufuhen* of Cape Coast, died, Coker sought to succeed to what was the second most important traditional position in the town. His mother was Thompson's brother, and Coker claimed the right to succeed to his maternal uncle's position. Succession to *asafo* positions is supposedly patrilineal in Akan communities, and Thompson had been "appointed" his father's "successor" in 1853 when the latter had died. Nevertheless, Coker, the first-generation descendant of a Sierra Leonean outsider, was able to outmaneuver whatever competition there was for this position, and was installed as the *tufuhen* of Cape Coast in 1888.[99]

His success in doing this was dependent on his ability to take advantage of the conflict that already existed in Cape Coast between matrilineal and patrilineal principles of succession. According to the Cape Coast newspaper *Western Echo,* the office of *tufuhen* "had been hereditary in Coker's maternal] family until the appointment of the late Chief Thompson."[100] Whether or not this was indeed so is hard to determine. James Hutton Brew, the editor of the paper, clearly had a vested interest

William Zacheus Coker, c.1920s. Source: T. R. Coker (son).

in supporting someone like Coker since he could help with Brew's larger project of bringing order to the "frothy and ebullient" poorer classes.[101] Undoubtedly, Coker's ability to parlay his standing in colonial society to his own advantage also helped him to win installment in this traditional office. Initially, he tried to retain his position of registrar of the Supreme Court, but must have realized that in the face of Governor Brandford Griffith's unrelenting opposition to him "mixing...in any activities which would prejudicially affect the holding of his government appointment," he would have to make a choice.[102] Before he could do this, the colonial treasurer discovered that he had been embezzling monies entrusted to him in his capacity as court registrar. He was tried, convicted, fired from his position and sentenced to seven years penal servitude.

In spite of this setback, he was still able to remain *tufuhen*, and when he got out of prison in 1896 he established himself in Cape Coast by rapidly demonstrating to the colonial authorities how indispensable he was.[103] This phase of Coker's career, which was to last over thirty years, demonstrates how much the demands of traditional office could also serve to bridge the gap between the better and the poorer classes. As *tufuhen*, he had to be intimately involved in the day-to-day affairs of the town's seven *asafos*, which entailed arbitrating disputes over the use of flags and emblems, securing the right to passage for one *asafo* through the quarter of another, officiating at important *asafo* ceremonies, settling disputes over fishing rights and preventing, when all else failed, this ever "turbulent" section of coastal society from erupting into violent conflict. It required a continual juggling act made even more difficult by his belonging, like all males in Cape Coast, to his own *asafo*.[104] One way "to prevent strife" was to have numerous children "out of wedlock" by women who lived in the different *asafo* quarters of the town.[105] Apart from demonstrating his impartiality, this also meant that he had to accept the responsibility for supporting and educating children whose mothers were from the poorer classes of Cape Coast society.[106] Consequently, Coker's family, like Jacob Wilson Sey's, extended considerably beyond the boundaries of his two church-married wives and their many children.

The Gas, the other important ethnic group to be affected by European settlement on the coast, also possessed a diverse and socially flexible family system that could span several social strata and relatively easily incorporate new members. Margaret Field characterized their society as little more than a collection of family compounds which had been "forced by slaving to form towns."[107] She described their political system as a "democratic gerontocracy" possessing far less political structure than existed among the Akan.[108] As a result, "like eddies in a fluid" they had a long history of absorbing "new ideas" and persons from their neighbors.[109] Undoubtedly the most important of these contributors were the Akan. For example, even though the Ga were traditionally patrilineal, which did not favor the sons of Akan men who married Ga women, under Akan influence they had modified their principles of succession so that the "son of a daughter of a stool family was often allowed to succeed even when the father was a total stranger."[110] There was a long and complex history to this adjustment to Akan concepts of succession, as Ivor Wilks has shown in the case of the eighteenth-century marriage arrangement between Akwamu (Akan) and Otublohum (Ga). In this case succession alternated "between...two matrilineal groups, but the candidates for office [had to] be sons of the previous occupant."[111]

The history of the various waves of Brazilian emigrants who settled in the Accra area beginning in the 1830s is a good case study of how absorptive Ga society could be in practice. The first of these groups which arrived some time in 1836 were Bahaian males (Muslims) fleeing from Brazil after the uprising of 1835.[112] One of the chiefs of Ussher Town gave them land, and they settled down as farmers and as craftsmen. As Accra began to develop after 1878, the land that they had received increased in value and desirability, and descendants of the original settlers sought to sell portions of it. Invariably there were disputes, and typically they ended up in the British court. Most of these Brazilians were Muslims, and the defendants in the first of these actions to come before the court tried to argue that inheritance in their community was governed by Muslim rather than Ga customary law.[113] Chief Justice John Marshall, who heard the case, refused to accept this argument on the grounds that the members of this community had married Ga women, spoke Ga, used native courts and to all intents and purposes had been absorbed into Ga society. Indeed, absorption had gone even further than intermarriage. Judging from the names of the descendants of the chief who had originally granted land to the Brazilians, later generations had also been incorporated into his chiefly lineage.[114]

The second wave of Brazilians who came in the 1840s and 1860s were from a more privileged strata of Brazilian society. Most of them were Christians, and they entered Accra society primarily as merchants. The more successful of them, like the Ribeiros and the Perigrinos, rapidly established themselves in the upper echelons of the better classes. They intermarried with other members of this elite, and their children branched out into occupations other than trading. For example, by the 1890s two of the sons of Francisco Ribeiro held important positions in the secretarial staff of the civil service.[115] One of them, M. F. Ribeiro, went to the Inns of Court and returned to the Gold Coast as a qualified barrister in 1898.[116] His other brother, H. F. Ribeiro, also qualified as a lawyer.[117] The Ribeiros married into the Cleland family, a prominent Accra family, and also into the family of the famous Methodist missionary Thomas Birch Freeman.[118] Apart from their marriage connections, like so many other members of the better classes the schools that they attended in Accra also

The Ribeiro family, c. 1920s. Source: George Cleland Francisco Ribeiro.

helped to determine whether they ended up as Anglicans or Methodists.[119] Whatever the denominational affiliation, by the beginning of the twentieth century the family had obviously been incorporated into the upper levels of Euro-African society in Accra.

Culturally the Gold Coast was not a tabula rasa nor was it so culturally diverse that one cultural orientation could bring it together, as Martin Lynn suggests was the case for "Creole society" in Clarence in the island of Fernando Po.[120] The "loftier order of Christian civilization" that Brew held up in the 1880s as the ideal for the better classes of coastal society in the Gold Coast was still very much in competition with indigenous cultures. Geographical linkage as well as the size of the Euro-African society in these locations contributed to this important difference between even such a "luminous point" as Cape Coast and Freetown, the "Athens of West Africa." Both absolutely and proportionately the size of the former's creolized population was considerably smaller than that of Freetown. Sixty-six percent of the latter's population of 21,931 in 1881 was officially listed as "settler."[121] Given the extensiveness of mission education, a high percentage of the latter would have been literate to some degree and would have been part of that society's better classes. In Cape Coast, the town most affected by missionary activity in the Gold Coast, according to the 1891 census, 30.34 percent of the town's population of 11,614 was Christian. According to the same census, 23 percent of Cape Coast's population could read and write; this group would have comprised its better classes.[122] Accra at that time had a proportionately smaller population of "educated natives," since the missions had set up schools in that town later than had been the case in Cape Coast. However, with a population of 16,267 in 1891 the absolute number of educated natives was probably greater.[123]

As a result of the relatively smaller size of its better classes and the active tension between them and indigenous social structures, Euro-African society in the Gold Coast responded in significantly different ways to the collapse of the "special relationship" between its elite and their European mentors at the end of the nineteenth century.[124] The Europeanization of the upper positions in the civil service, the mission churches and the metropolitan monopolization of the trading economy were the most visible aspects of this "deteriorating relationship."[125] In Sierra Leone, as Spitzer has pointed out, it resulted in a belief that Creole society was "bordering on degeneracy."[126] The Euro-African elite in the Gold Coast were equally pessimistic. By the end of the nineteenth century the careers of such shining examples of African advancement in the civil service as those of Dr. John Farrell Easmon and Hendrik Vroom had ended in disgrace, even though they had both received promotions and citations for meritorious service.[127] Abrasive young missionaries, such as the Reverend Dennis Kemp, publicly castigated fellow African ministers for not "living the Christian life in Africa."[128] And finally, indicative of the decline of the commercial princes, of the nineteen merchants who signed a petition to the secretary of state in 1894 requesting the annexation of Asante, only five were African.[129] It was hardly surprising that by this time newspaper reports of African advancement in the civil service were invariably tempered with a fatalism that somehow the recipients of these honors would not prove a credit to their race.

Sierra Leone Creoles responded to these disappointments with explanations that varied from blaming overindulgent lifestyles and punishment "by an 'offended Creator' for 'misused and abused advantages'" to more secular explanations that their "decrepitude" stemmed from too much Europeanization.[130] Edward Wilmot Blyden became the most articulate spokesman for the latter position, and his ideas found a warm reception particularly among his fellow English-speaking Euro-Africans. In Sierra Leone his celebration of what he described as the "Negro Personality" played an important role in stimulating a number of Creoles to reassert what they saw as their true African identity. For a while, name and dress "reform" were among the most immediate ways of indicating this new cultural identity, but as Spitzer has shown there was also considerable interest on the part of these cultural nationalists in healing "battered race pride by restoring their heritage to a place of honor."[131] In the Gold Coast there were similar expressions of cultural assertion. The Dress Reform Society that some of the most socially prominent Creoles established in Freetown in 1887 had its counterpart in the Mfantsi Amanbuhu Fékuw that a number of prominent "native gentlemen" established in Cape Coast two years later. John Mensah Sarbah, one of the founders of the Fékuw, maintained that this organization had come about due to their "dissatisf[action] with the demoralising effects of certain European influences" and the "determin[ation] to stop further encroachments into their nationality."[132]

However, "it was a measure of how deeply rooted these European encroachments had become in Cape Coast that few of the Fékuw's members actually followed their society's ideals."[133] Instead, faced with the practical difficulties of getting rid of what were well-established family names and the limited opportunities to dress in "native cloths," or speak Fante on public occasions in a town where there were many non-Fante speakers, the Fékuw's activities became more literary in scope. Initially this consisted of "collect[ing], discuss[ing] and compiling a record of native sayings, customs, laws and institutions."[134] Rapidly, however, the focus became primarily legal and institutional, as John Mensah Sarbah's two main works, the by-product of this inspiration, indicate.[135] What Ray Jenkins has aptly described as the "literary exuberance" of the late nineteenth and early twentieth century went beyond a preoccupation with the "Negro in Ancient History," which was more typically the focus that

the literary efforts of this period took in Sierra Leone.[136] Even historical
works like Carl Christian Reindorf's *History of the Gold Coast and Asante*
(1895), Jacob Anaman's *Gold Coast Guide for the Year 1895-6* and John
Mensah Sarbah's *Fanti National Constitution* (1906) were far more
focused on the Gold Coast past than on establishing links to the
civilizations of classical antiquity which was the case, for example, with
the Sierra Leonean A. B. C. Merriman-Labor's *Epitome of a Series of
Lectures on the Negro Race* (1900).

Even more important and reflective of the differences between the Gold
Coast and Creoledom in Sierra Leone was the increasingly legalistic focus
that the "literary exuberance" took in the former colony. One of the most
important indications of this was the series of articles that Sarbah wrote
which were based on his study of the Cape Coast judicial records and
published in 1897 as *Fanti Customary Laws*. In the preface to this work
he described his task as being "to reduce into writing the Customary Laws
and Usages of the Fanti, Asanti, and other Akan inhabitants of the Gold
Coast."[137] He was particularly concerned with providing "the first correct
idea on Customary Laws to newly arrived European officials, who, having
no intelligent person to explain things to them, would fain say there were
no Customary Laws."[138] As the Sey and Brew cases indicated, most of all
in the case of inheritance, customary law and English common law were
very much in competition with one another in the Gold Coast, which, as
I have already described, was not the case for Creoledom in Sierra Leone.

Initially the British government had tried to separate African and
European legal affairs in the Gold Coast by creating two courts: a Judicial
Assessor's Court and a Magistrate's Court. It was a hard distinction to
maintain particularly since the same person presided over both institutions.
Captain George Maclean, who was first appointed to these positions in
1843, sat with "native assessors" when he officiated as the judicial
assessor, but with the passage of time this practice waned and the
demarcation between these courts began to fade. The Supreme Court
Ordinance of 1876 (passed two years after the Gold Coast became a British
colony) created one court system, and finally in 1878 the Judicial
Assessor's Court was abolished.[139] From this time onward judicial matters
that might have been heard in the Judicial Assessor's Court were heard in
the colony's Supreme Court. However, there was considerable carryover.
Many of the cases that Sarbah mentions in his *Fanti Customary Laws* had
been litigated in the Judicial Assessor's Court, and these judgments
became the written corpus of the colony's customary law. In a legal
tradition based on stare decisis it was inevitable that these decided cases
would have a profound effect on the development of an indigenous
common law. Significantly, most of this material deals with property and
inheritance, which were contentious issues in a society where there were
competing notions about the family and the ownership of its assets.

The other precedent that Sarbah's work established was to give an important advantage to Akan customary law over other forms of customary law. As Mary Kingsley noticed in her commentary on his *Fanti Customary Laws,* he was attempting to make Fante customary law the basis for customary law in the colony.[140] It was not surprising that this was so. Most of the legal matters that came before the British courts concerning customary law involved natives who were Fante or at least Akans. The result was a "codified customary law in the Colony that came to be dominated by a tradition that was strongly matrilineal."[141] It meant that the interaction between Akanization and Anglicization was to be most apparent in the colony's judicial system. The collapse of the "special relationship" between Britain and her Creole protégés in West Africa undermined the attractiveness of Freetown as a "loftier order of Christian civilization," and at the same time gave rise to a cultural revival in the Gold Coast in which Akan customary law was one of the main components. In the next chapter I will focus on how this took place. It involved the colonial government, the mission churches, the colony's small but articulate group of African lawyers and the men and women who were affected by these changes. It reflected the class divisions as well as the differing interests between men and women in colonial society. In the competition to take advantage of the different legal systems that emerged, women were both winners and losers.

Notes

1. Cited in Richard Burton, *Wanderings in West Africa from Liverpool to Fernando Po* (London, 1863), 2:97. The widely practiced system of pawning, which until midcentury European as well as African merchants relied on to ensure the repayment of debts owed them, did much to promote this belief. According to Brodie Cruickshank, this practice allowed an "acknowledged head of a family...the unquestionable right to depose of his descendants and collateral relations in any way he might think fit." Cruickshank, *Eighteen Years on the Gold Coast of Africa,* 1:313.

2. J. E. Casely Hayford, *Gold Coast Native Institutions with Thoughts Upon a Healthy Imperial Policy for the Gold Coast and Ashanti* (London, 1903), 81. However, he did believe that it was a much more "humane and considerate" form of slavery than that of "ancient Rome" or "that of Afro-American history."

3. For examples of the use of this terminology see *Western Echo,* 24 August 1886.

4. The issue was serious enough for the editor of the Cape Coast newspaper *Western Echo* to suggest that there should be "compulsory wearing of gowns by the poorer classes...and the authorities should compel the natives to do away with their cloths." Without this official intervention, he felt that the people of the Gold

Coast were going "to be kept at the first stage of civilization." *Western Echo,* 28
November 1885.

5. For example, in Cape Coast there was a main street that ran northward
from the castle and divided the "town into two nearly equal parts." The houses of
Europeans and successful African merchants were on the west side of this main
street, while those of the "natives" lay to the east "huddled together in the most
crowded manner, and without the slightest regard to light or air, or the
convenience of approach." Cruickshank, *Eighteen Years on the Gold Coast of
Africa,* 1:23-24. Richard Burton considered that Gothic House, one of the largest
and most impressive in the western half of the town, would have been "a
handsome residence even near London." Burton, *Wanderings in West Africa,*
2:93.

6. Among the fraternal organizations there was a distinct hierarchy with the
"craftsmen" of the English and Scottish Order of Freemasons the most exclusive.
In the 1870s and 1880s less-exclusive organizations like the Good Templars
(instituted on 25 September 1887–*Gold Coast Times,* 17 November 1877), and the
Oddfellows (instituted on August 1880–*Gold Coast Times,* 12 August 1882), and
temperance societies like the Gold Coast Temperance Society (Methodist) and the
Knights of Marshall (Catholic) also emerged at this time and widened the base of
membership in these organizations. Undoubtedly with considerable exaggeration,
in 1900 the Cape Coast newspaper *Gold Coast Aborigines* "suggested that nearly
every young person" in the Gold Coast was a member of a friendly society. *Gold
Coast Aborigines,* 3 March 1900.

7. Samuel Tenkorang, "John Mensah Sarbah, 1864-1910," *Transactions of the
Historical Society of Ghana* 14, no. 2 (1973):73.

8. Jenkins, "Immigrants and Minorities," 10.

9. F. L. Bartels, *The Roots of Ghana Methodism* (Cambridge, U.K., 1965),
104.

10. *Gold Coast Times,* 24 December 1884.

11. Ibid.

12. *African Times,* 23 June 1866. The African-Aid Society established this
monthly publication in 1861. The secretary of the Society, F. Fitzgerald, was its
editor and a fervent supporter of African initiative. According to one of the
permanent secretaries in the Colonial Office, the "educated natives" of the West
Coast of Africa were "almost the sole subscribers and contributors" to the
publication. Memorandum of 9 March 1869, CO 96/79, PRO, cited in Kimble,
A Political History of Ghana, 89.

13. *Western Echo,* 29 July 1886.

14. *Western Echo,* 18 November 1885. Brew's first paper was the *Gold Coast
Times,* which ran with some breaks from 1874 to 1885. His second paper was the
Western Echo, which ran from 1885 to 1887. K. A. B. Jones-Quartey, *History,
Politics and Early Press in Ghana: The Fictions and the Facts* (Accra, 1975), 93-
94.

15. *Western Echo,* 28 November 1885.

16. Samuel Lewis, the first West African to be knighted (1893), and Alfred Sawyerr (later Shorunkeh Sawyerr) were both barristers. William "Independent" Grant was a successful merchant.

17. Spitzer, *The Creoles of Sierra Leone,* 36.

18. The colony's imports in 1872 were valued at £260,101. Exports were valued at £385,281. Similar figures for 1899 were £1,323,217 and £1,111,738. *Gold Coast Colony Blue Book,* 1872 and 1899.

19. In midcentury it was gold dust and palm oil that dominated the export trade from the Gold Coast. For a description of this trade see Martin Lynn, "Change and Continuity in the British Palm Oil Trade with West Africa, 1830-55," *Journal of African History* 22 (1981):331-348. By the 1880s new exports like rubber, kola nuts and lumber had also become important exports. For a description of the rubber trade see Raymond Dumett, "The Rubber Trade of the Gold Coast and Asante in the Nineteenth Century: African Innovation and Market Responsiveness," *Journal of African History* 12, no. 1 (1971):79-101.

20. In 1886, for example, 251 steam vessels and only 21 sailing vessels called at Gold Coast ports. *Gold Coast Colony Blue Book,* 1886.

21. Raymond E. Dumett, "African Merchants of the Gold Coast, 1860-1905: Dynamics of Indigenous Entrepreneurship," *Comparative Studies in Society and History* 25 (1983):667.

22. *African Times,* 22 February 1868.

23. Cruickshank, *Eighteen Years on the Gold Coast of Africa,* 2:36. The sobriquet "commercial king" comes from Magnus Sampson, *Makers of Modern Ghana, vol. 1, From Philip Quarcoo to Aggrey* (Accra, 1969), 1:45.

24. For a description of these activities see Raymond E. Dumett, "John Sarbah the Elder and African Mercantile Entrepreneurship in the Gold Coast in the Nineteenth Century." *Journal of African History* 14, no. 4 (1973):653-679.

25. Sampson, *Makers of Modern Ghana,* 1:58. When the Gold Coast became a colony in 1874, it was divided into three provinces: the Eastern Province, the Central Province and the Western Province.

26. Evelyn Rowand, "Press and Opinion in British West Africa, 1885-1900" (Ph.D. diss., University of Birmingham, 1972), 60.

27. Minutes of the Gold Coast Legislative Council, 27 September 1890, CO 98/6, cited in Dumett, "John Sarbah the Elder," 677.

28. Porter, *Creoledom,* 52. It also allowed for greater trading penetration into the hinterland. Akintola Wyse, *The Krio of Sierra Leone: An Interpretive History* (London, 1989), 5.

29. Isaac Ephson, *Gallery of Gold Coast Celebrities* (Accra, 1969), 59-60.

30. Ibid., 53-55. Dumett maintains that he did have connections with a royal *abusua.* If this was indeed so it would help to explain his otherwise rather improbable rise from near rags to riches in Cape Coast. Dumett, "African Merchants of the Gold Coast," 672.

31. Jenkins, "Gold Coast Historians," 77.

32. Sampson, *Makers of Modern Ghana,* 1:166.

33. Ibid.

34. Kaplow, "African Merchants of the Nineteenth Century Gold Coast," 236.

35. Mary Kingsley, *Travels in West Africa: Congo Français, Corisco and Cameroons* (1897; reprint, London, 1965), 31.

36. Enclosed in Sir William Brandford Griffith's dispatch to the Secretary of State, 11 November 1892, CO 96/226, PRO.

37. According to the 1881 *Gold Coast Colony Blue Book,* 30.5 percent of Lagos's population were involved in commerce.

38. A. P. Kup, *Sierra Leone: A Concise History* (Newton Abbot, Devon, 1975), 156.

39. J. B. Webster, "The Bible and the Plough," *Journal of the Historical Society of Nigeria* 2 (1963):418-434.

40. In 1874 the Wesleyan Methodists, the most successful of the Christian denominations in the Gold Coast, had 3,500 church members and 11,000 attending service (Bartels, *The Roots of Ghana Methodism,* 98). By 1899, they had 4,378 church members and over 16,000 attending service (Minutes of the European Synod, 1899, Methodist Missionary Archives, SOAS). From 1880 Catholic missionaries were also active in the colony, and by the turn of the century they had almost 5,000 converts (Helene Pfann, *A Short History of the Catholic Church in Ghana,* Cape Coast, 1965, 52). The number of students went from around 5,000 in 1881 to over 12,000 by the end of the century (Kimble, *A Political History of Ghana,* 73-74).

41. This was also so in Sierra Leone. "Creoles did perceive differences among themselves and between themselves and other people." Spitzer, *The Creoles of Sierra Leone,* 14. The "'aristos'—professional men and wealthy merchants occupied the top of the social and economic pyramid in Freetown." Wyse, *The Krio of Sierra Leone,* 42. They "looked down on the Krio poor," while in the middle there "was a petty bourgeoisie of retailers, craftsmen and artisans, and below them the Krio manual workers who shared with incomers from inland the manual employment provided by private employers and by the government and the armed forces." Christopher Fyfe, "1787-1887-1987 Reflections on a Sierra Leone Bicentenary," *Africa* 57, no. 4 (1987):413. The boundaries of this society also extended beyond Freetown to include, as James Thayer has pointed out, Creole village life where the original settlers had begun "on a more or less equal footing, [but] different social classes soon emerged among them." J. S. Thayer, "A Dissenting View of Creole Culture in Sierra Leone," *Cahiers d'Etudes Africaines* 121-122, XXXI-1-2 (1991):219.

42. Burton, *Wanderings in West Africa,* 2:73.

43. Michael J. C. Echeruo, *Victorian Lagos: Aspects of Nineteenth Century Lagos Life* (London, 1977), 53. Indicative of how important this practice was, there were also debates in the Gold Coast press over the advantages and

disadvantages of sending young children off to boarding school in England. See, for example, *Western Echo,* 23 October 1886.

44. Ray Jenkins, "Gold Coasters, 1880-1919: With Specific Reference to Their Activities in Britain," *Immigrants and Minorities* 4, no. 3 (1985):46-47. In this period gold mining seemed to have a golden future. This accounts for the large number of mining engineers.

45. This was the Christian Missionary Society (CMS) Grammar School.

46. Mary Kingsley, *West African Studies* (London, 1899), 17.

47. R. Burton, *To the Gold Coast for Gold* (London, 1883), 2:98.

48. *Western Echo,* 16-23 December 1886, and *Gold Coast Echo,* 22 October 1888.

49. Tenkorang, "John Mensah Sarbah," 66.

50. Obituary for F. C. Grant, *Gold Coast Chronicle,* 19 November 1894.

51. Spitzer, *The Creoles of Sierra Leone,* 15.

52. Governor Conran to the Governor General, 20 November 1866, CO 96/72, PRO. The governor's salary at that time was £1,200 per annum.

53. Sey and Sarbah built elegant residences for themselves and added to the ranks of stately homes in towns like Cape Coast and Accra. Doing so was one secure investment "outlet" for "wealthy Africans." Kaplow, "African Merchants of the Nineteenth Century Gold Coast," 236.

54. *Gold Coast Colony Blue Book,* 1867 and 1898.

55. The two highest-paid administrative officials were the governor of the colony, who had a base annual salary of £4,000, and the colonial secretary, who received £1,250. *Gold Coast Colony Blue Book,* 1894.

56. Kimble, *A Political History of Ghana,* 94. Five of them were district commissioners in the Gold Coast. At this time Lagos and the Gold Coast were administratively joined.

57. There were four Africans out of twenty-two, one of whom was from the Gold Coast. He was Dr. W. B. Quartey-Papafio, the fifth-most senior member of the service. *Gold Coast Colony Blue Book,* 1894. Africans received the same pay but were not entitled to the same leave allowances.

58. Governor Brandford Griffith to the Secretary of State, 25 June 1892, CO 96/224, PRO. Easmon was the first to clinically describe hemoglobinuric fever, known locally as blackwater fever. He published these findings in *Blackwater Fever* (London, 1884). For a description of his career see Adell Patton Jr., "Dr. John Farrell Easmon: Medical Professionalism and Colonial Racism in the Gold Coast, 1856-1900," *International Journal of African Historical Studies* 22, no. 4 (1989):601-636.

59. Spitzer, *The Creoles of Sierra Leone,* 76.

60. Cited in Kimble, *A Political History of Ghana,* 144. At the beginning of the twentieth century it was only slightly smaller than Freetown with a population of 34,149. R. R. Kuczynski, *Demographic Survey of the British Colonial Empire* (1948: reprint, Fairfield, N.J., 1977), 1:26.

61. He had taken "advantage" of the turmoil that the war with Asante in 1873-1874 had resulted in to abolish these practices without any compensation to owners. The secretary of state was concerned with the speed with which Straham had moved, but he was obviously satisfied that this thorny issue had been resolved. Straham argued that there was no need to pay compensation to owners as had been done to slave owners in the British Empire in 1834, since Britain had discharged this responsibility by coming to the defense of the coast people. Straham to the Secretary of State, 19 September 1874, CO 96/112, PRO. There was no Parliamentary protest and without such support the protest from the educated natives in the colony, who were invariably slave owners, was ineffective. As an indication of how far-reaching support in Britain was for abolition, Francis Fitzgerald, the editor of the London monthly *African Times,* who in the past had championed the causes of the educated natives, enthusiastically supported Straham and his decision not to pay compensation. *African Times,* 29 August 1874.

62. *Western Echo,* 19 December 1885.

63. Many of the Hausas probably were from northern Nigeria. The British had used such troops in their wars against the Asante in 1873-1874, and some had remained in the colony after the war was over. David Killingray, "Bald Biographies of the Barely Reclaimable: Native Officers of the Gold Coast Constabulary, 1874-1901," *Ghana Studies Bulletin* 3 (December 1985):11.

64. Gerald M. McSheffrey, "Slavery, Indentured Servitude, Legitimate Trade and the Impact of Abolition in the Gold Coast, 1874-1901: A Reappraisal," *Journal of African History* 24 (1983):359.

65. Raymond E. Dumett and Marion Johnson, "Britain and the Suppression of Slavery in the Gold Coast Colony, Ashanti, and the Northern Territories," in *The End of Slavery in Africa,* ed. Suzanne Miers and Richard Roberts (Madison, Wis., 1988), 93.

66. In the fishing community there was the potential for major friction, especially if these strangers introduced new and more efficient fishing nets, and could catch and sell fish cheaper than their competition. The chiefs who benefited from the fees would find themselves under tremendous pressure to ban such nets and the fishermen that used them.

67. Christopher Fyfe, *Africanus Horton: West African Scientist and Patriot* (New York, 1972), 15.

68. Ray G. Jenkins, "North American Scholarship and the 'Thaw' in the Historiography of Ghanaian Coastal Communities," *Ghana Studies Bulletin* 3 (December 1985):26.

69. Ibid.

70. Casely-Hayford, "A Genealogical Study of Cape Coast Stool Families," 17, 22.

71. Fyfe, *Africanus Horton,* 15.

72. Adu Boahen, "The Origins of the Akan," *Ghana Notes and Queries* 9 (November 1966):4.

73. James B. Christensen, *Double Descent Among the Fanti* (New Haven, Conn., 1954), 19-20.

74. Christensen's observations on Fante family structure can in general be extended to other Akan people.

75. Spitzer, *The Creoles of Sierra Leone,* 80.

76. Ibid.

77. The Governor to the Secretary of State, 28 May 1891, CO 96/216, PRO.

78. This is clear from the evidence submitted by Henry F. Amissah, clerk to Sey from 1898 to 1902, in the Cape Coast Divisional Court in the case of *Elizabeth Ferguson v. Others* and *Abba Appusafua v. Others,* 2 January 1926. Cape Coast Judgment Book, SCT 5/6/2, NAG, Accra. Sey's home in the center of Cape Coast was one of the town's large stately homes, but it is unlikely that all these people lived in it. He also owned numerous other properties, some of which he rented to the government and private firms, but others no doubt were inhabited by his large retinue of "people."

79. Ephson, *Gallery of Gold Coast Celebrities,* 54.

80. "It is alleged that [his son] taunted him for his ugliness." Ibid., 55.

81. Reverend Parker was the superintendent minister of the Methodist Church in Cape Coast and very active in the Gold Coast Aborigines Rights Protection Society. Information on this aspect of Sey's life comes from the Cape Coast Divisional Court case *In the Matter of the Estate of Jacob Wilson Sey,* 1 August 1902. Cape Coast Judgment Book, SCT 5/6/1, NAG, Accra.

82. This information comes from the Cape Coast Divisional Court case *Estate of J. W. Sey and K. E. Sey and Others v. Henry Van Hein,* 9 October 1925. Cape Coast Judgment Book, SCT 5/6/2, NAG, Accra.

83. The dispute between his children came before the Cape Coast High Court on 26 May 1881 as the case of *James H. Brew v. Francis Williams and John Ogoe,* and was appealed on 10 April 1882. H.C.C.C. 287/52, cited in Priestley, *West African Trade and Coast Society,* 186. The dispute between the matrilineage and Brew's children came before the Cape Coast High Court on 7 February 1883 as *Assafuah v. Brew.* Cape Coast Record Book Civil and Criminal, SCT 5/4/103, NAG, Accra.

84. For the history of this family see Priestley, *West African Trade and Coast Society,* and Casely-Hayford, "A Genealogical Study of Cape Coast Stool Families," 77-79.

85. He had not been formally called to the bar. These early attorneys existed in a precarious relationship with the colony's British judges. For a description of their "trials" see Kimble, *A Political History of Ghana,* 68-70.

86. Priestley, *West African Trade and Coast Society,* 186.

87. It is hard to know why this was so from the spare judicial records of the case. Brew may very likely have come up against a judge who particularly disliked him. As a result of his often intemperate outbursts, Brew had many enemies in the relatively small, introverted world of Euro-African coastal society.

88. *Assafuah v. Brew.*

89. The family refused to recognize James Hutton Brew as its head in spite of his standing in coastal society, and imputed that he belonged to the "domestic" branch of this family and consequently was not entitled to this position. They were suggesting that his mother had been one of Samuel Collins Brew's female slaves.

90. For example, in 1905 there was another bitter court battle when Brew tried to sell the "family" house in Anomabu. Case in the Cape Coast Divisional Court: *T. B. F. Sam v. Albert Brew,* 5 October 1905, Cape Coast Judgment Book, SCT 5/6/1, NAG, Accra. In 1909 the matrilineage was once again in court seeking to win possession of property not far from Cape Coast known as Bradadzi land which had been acquired by Sam Kanto Brew, a second-generation descendant of Richard Brew. Case in the Cape Coast Divisional Court: *Sarah Wood v. Maud Thompson,* 18 December 1909, Cape Coast Judgment Book, SCT 5/6/2, NAG, Accra.

91. Polly Hill, *The Migrant Cocoa Farmers of Southern Ghana: A Study in Rural Capitalism* (Cambridge, U.K., 1963), 123.

92. H. M. Joko Smart, "The Local Court System in Sierra Leone," *Sierra Leone Studies: New Series* 22 (January 1968):37.

93. H. M. Joko Smart, "Inheritance to Property in Sierra Leone: An Analysis of the Law and Problems Involved," *Sierra Leone Studies: New Series* 24 (January 1969):4.

94. Ibid., 5.

95. Ray G. Jenkins, "'West Indian' and 'Brazilian' Influences in the Gold Coast-Ghana; c.1807-1914: A Review and Reappraisal of Continuities in the Post-Abolition Links Between West Africa and the Caribbean and Brazil," paper presented to the Twelfth Annual Conference of the Society for Caribbean Studies, 12-14 July 1988.

96. Christopher Fyfe's work *Africanus Horton: West African Scientist and Patriot* stands somewhere between these two extremes. There are also a number of less well-known works that deal with aspects of intercolonial migration. For example: K. A. B. Jones-Quartey, "Sierra Leone's Role in the Development of Ghana, 1820-1930," *Sierra Leone Studies: New Series* 9 (1957):73-84, and Jeffrey Green, "Caribbean Influences in the Gold Coast Administration in the 1900s," *Ghana Studies Bulletin* 2 (December 1984):10-16.

97. Interview with T. R. Coker, W. Z. Coker's son, Cape Coast, 31 July 1974.

98. *Gold Coast Colony Blue Book,* 1879. His salary was sixty pounds per annum. At this time his father was dead. He had drowned in the notorious Accra

surf in 1867. Obituary for Emma Coker, W. Z. Coker's mother, *Gold Coast Leader,* 14 November 1928.

99. "Coker *Tufuhen?*" file, SNA 11/1109, NAG, Accra.

100. *Western Echo,* 14-28 February 1887.

101. There is no mention of competitors in the records of the times. In 1929, however, when Coker was nearing the end of his career as *tufuhen* of Cape Coast and was under bitter attack from other members of the educated elite, his opponents claimed that Thompson's son had been absent from Cape Coast when his father died. He had been offered the "stool" when he returned, but had "refused it." The Thomas Enquiry, 1929, SNA 11/1109, NAG, Accra.

102. "Coker *Tufuhen?*" file.

103. He took advantage of the outbreak of war with the Asante and used his *asafo* connections to supply the military with badly needed carriers.

104. Coker belonged to Benstir *asafo,* the largest of the town's *asafos.*

105. Coker interview.

106. My informant, T. R. Coker, was a son by one of Coker's non-church wives. Coker also had more than one church wife. His first wife died and he remarried. Coker interview.

107. Field, *Social Organization of the Ga People,* 72.

108. Ibid., 74.

109. Ibid., 76.

110. Ibid., 51. Theoretically, these sons would inherit neither from their mother's brothers nor from their father. However, sons of a Ga man and an Akan woman would be doubly advantaged. They would inherit from their father and from their mother's brothers.

111. Ivor Wilks, "Akwamu and Otoblohum: An Eighteenth Century Akan Marriage Arrangement," *Africa* 29, no. 4 (October 1959):394.

112. Jenkins, "'West Indian' and 'Brazilian' Influences in the Gold Coast," 4.

113. This case is referred to in the Supreme Court case of *Jemina Nassu and Others v. the Basel Mission,* 10 July 1915. Judgment Record Book, SCT 2/6/5, NAG, Accra. Unfortunately, I was not able to find a record of the original case.

114. This was Chief Ankrah of the stool family of the Dadeban section of the Otublohum quarter of Dutch Accra. His successors were Chief Pedro the Brave (d.1888) and Chief Antonio (d.1897).

115. *Gold Coast Colony Blue Book,* 1894.

116. Jenkins, "Immigrants and Minorities," 49.

117. Interview with George Cleland Francisco Ribeiro, great-grandson of the original Ribeiro, Francisco Ribeiro, a Brazilian trader (via Portugal?), 24 July 1994, Accra.

118. Ibid.

119. Interview with Miguel Ribeiro, another great-grandson of Francisco Ribeiro, 31 July 1994, Accra.

120. Martin Lynn, "Commerce, Christianity and the Origins of the 'Creoles' of Fernando Po," *Journal of African History* 25 (1984):262.

121. CO 267/344, PRO, cited in Barbara E. Harrell-Bond, Allen Howard and David Skinner, *Community Leadership and the Transformation of Freetown, 1801-1976* (The Hague, 1978), 34.

122. *Report on the Census for the Gold Coast Colony for the Year 1891* (Accra, 1891).

123. Reflective of this, in the 1890s the colony's capital and largest town was able to support more newspapers than Cape Coast. It is difficult to estimate the size of the educated classes from newspaper circulation since there was a great deal of borrowing. Indicative, however, of the larger educated population in Accra, its important newspapers like the *Gold Coast Chronicle* and the *Gold Coast Express* had larger circulations than their Cape Coast counterparts, the *Western Echo* and the *Gold Coast Aborigine*. In the 1896 there was even talk of a daily newspaper, the *Gold Coast Observer,* but only one issue seems to have been published. *Gold Coast Chronicle,* 9 July 1896, and K. A. B. Jones-Quartey, *History, Politics and Early Press in Ghana: The Fictions and the Facts* (Accra, 1975), 95.

124. "Pseudo-scientific racial beliefs were partially responsible for this, as well as developments in tropical medicine which made it possible for Europeans to live in the tropics with some degree of safety. The improved economic performance of the West African colonies made it possible to employ larger numbers of Europeans. They were far more expensive than Africans, but in the racist atmosphere of that period the superior efficiency, and greater sense of responsibility that European officers allegedly offered justified this increased expense as far as colonial administrators were concerned." Roger S. Gocking, "Creole Society and the Revival of Traditional Culture in Cape Coast During the Colonial Period," *International Journal of African Historical Studies* 17, no. 4 (1984):605-606.

125. For a discussion of these changes see Spitzer, "The Mosquito and Segregation in Sierra Leone," *Canadian Journal of African Studies* 2, no. 1 (Spring 1968):49-61, and Raymond E. Dumett, "The Expansion of Scientific Medical and Sanitary Services in British West Africa," *African Historical Studies* 1, no. 2 (1968):153-197.

126. Spitzer, *The Creoles of Sierra Leone,* 109.

127. Governor Maxwell, in a classic example of the virulent racism of the late nineteenth century, removed Easmon from his position as chief medical officer of the Gold Coast and then forced him to resign entirely from the Colonial Medical Service. For a description of this case see Patton, "Dr. John Farrell Easmon," 601-636. Vroom began his career working in the Dutch administration but later, in 1876, he joined the British administration as a district commissioner. In 1901 Governor Maxwell reduced his salary by almost half on the grounds that he was a native of the Gold Coast. He was shunted away to areas of lesser importance far

from the coast, where his family was, and when he finally tried to retire Governor Nathan offered him the choice between a real hardship post or a pittance of a pension even after twenty-nine years of service! Governor Nathan to the Secretary of State, 1 May 1901, CO 96/379, PRO. Vroom died in 1902 before the matter could be resolved. As a supreme piece of hypocrisy, "for his meritorious services, he was graciously awarded the Companionship of the Distinguished Order of St. Michael and St. George in 1900 (CMG)." Ephson, *Gallery of Gold Coast Celebrities,* 66.

128. Bartels, *Roots of Ghana Methodism,* 139. Kemp made this claim while he was on leave in England, but it rapidly became public knowledge in the Gold Coast.

129. Cited in Kaplow, "African Merchants of the Nineteenth Century Gold Coast," 183.

130. Spitzer, *The Creoles of Sierra Leone,* 110.

131. Ibid., 120.

132. John Mensah Sarbah, *Fanti National Constitution* (1906; reprint, London, 1968), xvii.

133. Gocking, "Creole Society and the Revival of Traditional Culture," 607.

134. Sarbah, *Fanti National Constitution,* xvii.

135. *Fanti Customary Laws* and *Fanti National Constitution.*

136. Jenkins, "Gold Coast Historians," 160.

137. John Mensah Sarbah, *Fanti Customary Laws* (1897; reprint, London, 1968), ix.

138. Ibid.

139. T. O. Elias, "A Note on the Supreme Court Ordinance, 1876," in *Essays in Ghanaian Law, 1876-1976,* ed. Ekow Daniels and R. R. Woodman (Legon, 1976), 32-37.

140. For Kingsley's views on Sarbah see S. Gwynn, *The Life of Mary Kingsley* (London, 1932), 177.

141. Roger S. Gocking, "Competing Systems of Inheritance Before the British Courts of the Gold Coast Colony," *International Journal of African Historical Studies* 23, no. 4 (1990):616.

Chapter 4

Marriage and Inheritance: Facing Difficult Choices

Initially, the Christian missions did little to challenge African marriage practices so as not to upset their still fragile communities. It meant tolerating the polygynous features of African society in the Gold Coast, but it was inevitable that as these fledgling communities became better established there was increased sentiment to do something about what the missionaries considered the moral dilemma of Christian converts living in polygynous relationships. According to the Methodist Synod of 1871, polygyny was "the prevailing sin of Africa...the great obstacle in the way of many giving thanks to God."[1] In 1875 the Synod publicly took up the closely related question of women's status in native marriage, and decided to "discountenance the payment of bridewealth or any practice out of harmony with a true Christian spirit and deportment."[2] Especially unacceptable was the way in which they considered native custom sanctioned the dismissal of a wife who failed to live up to her what her husband considered her responsibilities. The grounds for divorce in native marriage reinforced their opinion that women in African society "were little better than a purchased article."[3]

The immediate outcome of this campaign was that the Methodists created two levels of membership in their church. The small number who could live up to the ideal of Christian monogamy were accepted into full membership, while those who for whatever reason could not put an end to their polygynous marriages were consigned to the lesser category of "trial members." They could not hold positions in the church's hierarchy, and neither could they participate in religious ceremonies like taking communion.[4] In 1885 the Methodist Synod formally recognized the existence of these two categories of membership and officially approved what had been emerging as church policy in the previous decade.[5] To a large extent this division in the ranks of church membership reflected the division in the society at large, since full members were much more likely to be members of the better classes than trial members who were more likely to be illiterate. For many it was even more difficult to move up than it was to overcome illiteracy, since choosing between wives already married was an all but impossible task.

The legislation that the government introduced in the 1880s to regulate marriage in the colony added an important legal dimension to what had already become an important division within the ranks of coastal society. Up until 1884 the actual contracting of a Christian marriage had been left entirely to the mission churches and the marriage certificates that they issued the colony's courts recognized as legally binding documents.[6] However, in 1878, due to some changes in German marriage law, the Basel Missionaries found that they were unable to contract a marriage in the colony which would be valid in Germany. Upon investigating the situation, the Queen's advocate discovered that it was really only possible to contract a legal Christian marriage in the colony if one was a British subject and the clergyman either an Anglican or a Roman Catholic.[7] As Shirley Zabel has pointed out, "at that time there was no local legislation on marriage...and it was far from clear that English law would apply especially where German nationals were involved."[8] It was a measure of how contentious the issue of marriage already was that it was not until November 1884, after several drafts, that the colony's Legislative Council finally passed a bill, based on the Hong Kong and Ceylon ordinances.

The Marriage Ordinance of 1884 created marriage districts, gave the governor the power to appoint registrars of marriages, the power to license any place of worship for the celebration of marriages, indicated what the preliminary procedure should be, how the marriage should be registered and the fees to be paid. Ministers of religion were allowed to continue as marriage officers, but the state asserted secular authority over the institution to accommodate all religions and persons without any religious affiliation. It was hardly surprising that this was so since this was the precedent that had been established in Hong Kong and Ceylon. More contentious was the question of what should be the relationship between ordinance marriage and customary or native marriage, as well as what rules should govern inheritance for those who contracted an ordinance marriage. In stipulating what would make an ordinance marriage invalid, the ordinance went well beyond the restrictions based on consanguinity then in force in England to exclude anyone already married "by native law or custom to any person other than the person with whom such marriage is had."[9] Those contravening this regulation were guilty of bigamy, but what this also meant was that inadvertently the Marriage Ordinance granted formal recognition to customary marriage. However, most controversial of all, the ordinance stipulated that in cases of intestacy all personal property would be inherited in accordance with the laws of England in existence in 1884, customary law notwithstanding.[10]

To the government's legal officers issues involving the devolution of property were at least as important as maintaining monogamy and making contract and native marriage exclusive of one another.[11] They felt that "in their zeal to promote Christian marriage," many missionaries "could not be trusted" to emphasize the legal ramifications of a contract marriage. As a result, the government tried initially to make district commissioners marriage registrars, and severely limited the number of places where marriage ceremonies could actually take place. However, there was so much opposition to this that the final bill included ministers of religion as marriage officers and allowed marriages to be "celebrated in any licensed place of worship by any recognized minister of the church."[12]

Nevertheless, the missionaries were highly critical of the ordinance, which they had initially hoped would strengthen their hands in the struggle against polygynous marriage. They were most critical of the way in which the ordinance placed both contract and native marriage on an equal legal footing. In addition, they felt that the complicated procedures required to contract an ordinance marriage would contribute to making these basically Christian marriages even less attractive than they had been previously. The government's marriage statistics did indeed show this to be the case.[13] Between 1877 and 1883 Christian marriages for the colony had averaged over 180 per annum, but from 1886 to 1889 they plummeted to only 72 per annum.[14] The Methodists, the largest Christian denomination in the colony, kept up a constant pressure on the government to amend the ordinance. In 1890 they were at least successful in getting the number of registrars increased, the number of places licensed to perform marriages expanded, and in keeping down the cost of licenses. On the issue, however, of government registration, there was no compromise, and Christian marriage in the colony remained first and foremost a civil contract subject to the common law of England.

The missionaries and the government obviously had very different concerns about marriage, but both were introducing new ideals that were destined to challenge the status quo. Conflict between the demands of monogamous, Christian marriage and what was known as country marriage or native marriage became an important reflection of the larger conflict between what I have described as creolization and Akanization in the coastal communities of the Gold Coast. The ambiguous protest from the educated classes to the 1884 Marriage Ordinance was an indication of how difficult it was to bring together these competing cultural poles. James Hutton Brew, the fiery editor of the Cape Coast paper *Gold Coast Times*, had initially called upon the government to enact legislation that would license dissenting bodies to perform marriages, and to reform the colony's laws on English lines.[15] However, when the Marriage Ordinance was enacted in 1884, he accused the government of being the "licensee of polygamy and the upholder of heathenism."[16] Shortly after, reflecting the basic ambiguity on the part of the educated classes to Christian marriage practice in general, he attacked what he saw as the ordinance's attempt to extend monogamy to native marriage. In contrast to what he saw the ordinance demanding, he maintained that it was "not native law that a man have one wife." In a native marriage the "first wife had privileges accorded her by usage," but the ordinance now made it possible for each wife to "enter a caveat."[17] Under these circumstances, even a native wife would be able to prevent her husband from taking another mate.

This was not what the ordinance stipulated. It was bigamous to be married in native fashion and then contract a church marriage and vice versa, but the ordinance said nothing about how many native marriages a man could make if he married only in native style. As Brew recognized, however, the ordinance did give new legal power to "native" wives as well as "church" wives since the former could now legally prevent their husbands from abandoning them in favor of a more socially prestigious church wife. It was not merely a hypothetical right. Native wives were able to use this power to challenge their husband's marriage plans. For example, in 1893, when Joseph A. Boham, a dispenser at the Colonial Hospital in Accra, tried to marry Mary Helen Hayford, the daughter of a Wesleyan Methodist minister, his native wife was successfully able to prevent this by causing a caveat to be entered with the court registrar.[18]

However, neither did the missionaries want to preserve polygyny in native marriage, and Brew's concern with this issue was one indication of how different and ambiguous attitudes on the part of the better classes to Christian marriage could be in general. The long, rambling, inconclusive, fictional serial entitled "Marita: On the Folly of Love" that appeared in the *Western Echo* soon after the passage of the 1884 ordinance provides graphic insight into what some of these differences were. The author of this serial, who was very likely the young J. E. Casely Hayford, holds Christian marriage responsible for upsetting the man's traditional position as head of the household in the African family.[19] The permanence of the relationship makes it impossible to discipline a wayward spouse by sending her back to her family.[20] Consequently, Christian wives are no longer willing to obey their husbands, which exposes them to the immoral designs of unprincipled men.[21] The conclusion, not surprisingly, is that women in the Gold Coast are still too "ignorant" to "understand" the complex role of the spouse in a Christian marriage.[22]

Even though it is a caricature of Christian marriage that the serial presents, the author's melodramatic excesses do give some indication of how disquieting men found the new status that Christian marriage conferred on women. Miss Wissah, the uneducated woman in the story who had lived contentedly for eight years with Quaibu, her highly educated, "country" husband, displays a spirited independence immediately after she converts to Methodism and forces him to marry her in Christian style.[23] Her "demands," and those of other women similarly married, that the serial digresses to treat are obviously intended to appall the reader, and show why these unions are unworkable.[24] Quaibu's mournful prophecy that Christian marriage is tantamount to "placing a sharp instrument...[in the hands] of people just emerging from the shade of barbarism" turns out to be all too true.[25] Nevertheless, his plea for "pure monogamy without the oath" as a substitute for Christian marriage is disingenuous and a considerable concession to missionary demands. It was evidence of how much Christian values had become an integral part of coastal society.

By stereotyping women in this fashion and making them responsible for the inappropriateness of Christian marriage, the author conveniently ignores the appeal of such unions to them. In a number of important ways Christian marriage scaled down the many advantages that men enjoyed in native marriage. According to John Mensah Sarbah, in the latter

> the wife could not declare her marriage void, nor could her family give her permission to remarry in the absence of the consent of her husband, signified by his releasing her from her conjugal obligation, either by chalking her, or by saying so in the presence of competent witnesses.[26]

The grounds for divorce also favored husbands. A man could divorce his wife for adultery or witchcraft, but the wife could not "enforce or discontinue marriage on the grounds of her husband's adultery or his marrying more wives."[27] *He* could divorce her also if *he* was "impotent, or neglect[ed] his wife or grossly ill-treat[ed] her, or absent[ed] himself for a long period, so that she committ[ed] adultery."[28] In this instance, he could not recover his *consawment* (bridewealth) as he could in the case where his wife was deemed at fault. In general, however, the obligation to return the *consawment,* if the marriage collapsed, made the woman's family very hesitant to support a divorce that was judged the fault of the woman. Not surprisingly, as a result, a woman could not appear on her own behalf in divorce cases before traditional courts. This was the responsibility of the head of her family, whose role it was to balance her interests against those of the family.

Christian marriage, on the other hand, was an agreement between individuals and not matrilineages, and this potentially benefited women and their children. According to the long-term European resident Brodie

"A Belle of Cape Coast Castle." From the *Illustrated London News*,
17 January 1874.

Cruickshank, the wife was "entitled to the undivided addresses of her husband." He had to provide "more carefully for the wants of the family...and contrary to the native law affecting heathens, [Christian marriage] [left] them entitled to his property. With advantages of this description, the institution of Christian marriage became very popular with the sex."[29] Even if Cruickshank's uplifting picture of Christian marriage and its attractiveness may have been considerably overdrawn, divorce actions before the colony's law courts indicated that it did give women a legal standing they did not enjoy in customary law. They did not have to rely on their families to initiate actions in the British courts, but could bring such actions themselves. In general, as Susan Kaplow has indicated, women already had considerable access to the British courts and were active litigants in cases that ranged as far afield as debt collection and ownership of property.[30] Christian marriage expanded the range of issues that they could litigate, and was destined to increase as statutory enactments in the metropole and in the colony expanded the legal rights of women.

From as early as 1859, women could bring actions for divorce before the colony's courts on their own behalf.[31] To obtain a decree nisi was not easy. They had to prove both adultery and cruelty, with the latter amounting to "personal injury" that placed the woman's "safety at stake."[32] Once this was proven, she could obtain a decree nisi and her husband had to pay costs. Even if a woman only won the right to a legal separation, she could expect the court to award her financial support for herself and her children, as was the result of the 1874 case of *Elizabeth Brown v. Charles Brown, Augustus Rhule Corespondent.*[33] Such victories for women seem to have been the exception rather than the rule, but nevertheless what was perhaps more unsettling to men was their requests for divorce stood far less chance of being granted than would have been the case in a traditional court. For example, in the 1874 case of *Thomas Penny v. Mary Penny* for dissolution of marriage, the judge decided that the charges of drunkenness and adultery that the plaintiff alleged had not been proved and the petition was dismissed.[34] Nevertheless, men still enjoyed considerable advantages in these courts of law. They could, for example, sue corespondents for damages while women did not have this option. However, in contrast to traditional courts that allowed an aggrieved husband to reclaim the full value of his *consawment,* the awards in such actions tended to be little more than symbolic.

The Marriage Ordinance of 1884 did improve the status of women both as plaintiffs or respondents in divorce proceedings by unequivocally bringing ordinance marriages under the application of English common law.[35] Not surprisingly, there was a significant number of educated and even partially Western-educated women, like the fictional Miss Wissah, who wanted Christian marriage. The divorce proceedings that came before the colony's courts indicated that these women appreciated the marital fidelity as well as the financial support that Christian marriage was supposed to guarantee wives.[36] The parents from the better classes also wanted their daughters to make Christian matches, and in a similar fashion to what Kristin Mann has described for their counterparts in Lagos, parents were willing to provide expensive education, even in England, to make this more likely.[37] Even Brew himself wanted to see female improvement, and soon after he established the *Western Echo* he introduced a "Ladies Column," which was to stimulate women in the colony to be "not a wit behind [their] sisters on the other side of the Atlantic."[38] He encouraged them to "improve" local "manners" by holding "tea parties" and encouraging "singing groups." He wanted them to "stop ladies of the lower class from frequenting houses of ill fame," and to have them adopt more "decent" standards of dress. Rapidly his major interest became encouraging the formation of a Ladies Association patterned after the one recently established in Sierra Leone.[39] It was hardly conceivable that the membership of this association would have been "contented" being country wives. Nor would their Western-educated husbands have wanted this. The elaborate Christian weddings that the colony's press described in great detail were one indication of this. They invariably linked prominent coastal families, with successful sons marrying eligible daughters, and the ideal was clearly the monogamous Christian family.

Even Casely Hayford followed this path. In 1897, while still in England after being called to the bar, he married Beatrice Madeline Pinnock, the daughter of a prominent Accra family. Two years after her death in 1901, he married again, this time to Adelaide Smith, the daughter of a prominent Sierra Leonean Creole family, also in England and by the same Anglican clergyman who had married him to his first wife.[40] Twenty-five years after producing his bitter criticisms of Christian marriage in "Marita: On the Folly of Love," Casely Hayford described his own marriages in his semiautobiographical and allegorical novel *Ethiopia Unbound*.[41] The main character in this story, Kwamankra, who is a mixture of Casely Hayford and his hero, Edward Wilmot Blyden, acts as a staunch defender of African culture.[42] Apart from advocating wearing Fante clothing and speaking Fante, he defends Fante religious beliefs, marriage systems and home life.[43] Yet Kwamankra's own marriage, which, as Adelaide Cromwell has observed, incorporates experiences from Casely Hayford's two marriages, is uncompromisingly European.[44] From the courtship in London to his wife's death in childbirth in the Gold Coast, Kwamankra is clearly the devoted monogamous husband. In real life, Casely Hayford's first marriage was undoubtedly very much like this. His second marriage to Adelaide Smith also began in this fashion, but eventually was to break down partially due to long periods of separation

"A Bush Woman." From the *Illustrated London News*, 17 January 1874.

between them, and as a result of personality conflicts which as Cromwell suggests were exacerbated by their different backgrounds.[45]

With this kind of strain it was not surprising that his earlier ambiguity toward monogamous, Christian marriage resurfaced. By the time he finally separated from his wife in 1914, Casely Hayford had already fathered several children by his various country wives.[46] Like his fictional character Bonsu Penins in "Marita: On the Folly of Love," also a successful lawyer, Casely Hayford came to "follow the fashion of his country."[47] They had both begun with church marriages to the daughters of prominent coastal families, but in the face of the demands that these unions posed they had opted for the more flexible relationships that characterized country or native marriage. Coastal society in the Gold Coast had long offered this option. As a concession to Christian sensibilities in the Gold Coast, only the church wife had the honor of being referred to as "Mrs."; those women married only in native fashion were known simply as "wives." In microcosm Casely Hayford's married life reflected the difference between Freetown Creole society and its partially creolized counterpart in the Gold Coast. In Sierra Leone, Edward Blyden had defended polygyny as a "practical eugenics" whose "operation...over centuries [had produced] continuously a vigorous and prolific race of men and women."[48] It was, however, little more than an assertion of his own iconoclastic vision of the "African Personality." Particularly for the elite, Christian marriage remained the uncontested social ideal, and even its dissolution was frowned upon.[49] It is significant in this regard that Adelaide Smith Casely Hayford, when she returned to Sierra Leone in 1914, did not seek a divorce and never married again.

It was, however, much easier for a well-established lawyer like Casely Hayford to take advantage of the various marriage options that Gold Coast society offered than for members of the scholar class. For young men from this strata of coastal society who lacked financial resources, getting married native style was not easy, and ironically Christian marriage offered a way of escaping the heavy bridewealth payments that the woman's family demanded. The missionaries had attacked what they considered to be this buying of women in native marriage, and had offered their converts Christian marriage as an alternative. Judging from the reaction in the press, more than just bridewealth was at stake. The anomalous nature of Christian marriage could threaten the control that families in general exercised over their daughters to the benefit of young men. As "Voltiguer," a contributor to the *Western Echo* recognized, in reaction "some parents" had gone "to...dangerous extremes hedging their children round" with "insuperable barriers."[50] Partly as a means of preserving what another contributor to this debate considered "class" or "caste" endogamy in coastal society, Christian weddings became extremely expensive.[51] According to European practice the woman's father was to pay for this, but in reality contributing to the suitably extravagant wedding celebrations became very much part of the groom's responsibility.

Effectively this meant that only people of similar social standing could afford to marry. Particularly for the social elite these "nuptial ceremonies" replaced in importance the exchange of *consawment* with its attendant implications of wife buying. Their cost, however, was to become a source of constant complaint in the press.[52] Christian marriage clearly provided new opportunities for both men and women in coastal society, but at the same time it created its own restraints that were designed to maintain the new class boundaries and limit the independence of women. Christian marriage "created a discrete unit over which [men] established patriarchal authority."[53] Contrary to the fears of both Bonsu Penins and Quaibu in "Marita: On the Folly of Love," the Victorian ideal of Christian marriage that the missionaries upheld was in important respects more patriarchal than country marriage. An arrangement in which husbands were to be the "economic providers and wives [to be] mothers and homemakers" placed in jeopardy the traditional economic independence of African women.[54] As Kristin Mann has shown for elite Christian women in Lagos, this could leave women dependent on their fathers or their husbands far beyond what was normal in country marriage.[55]

More contentious than control over the marriage union were issues regarding the ownership and devolution of property that the 1884 Marriage Ordinance sought to regulate. Here Euro-African society exhibited even more ambiguity than was the case regarding rights in marriage and its termination. The conflicts that this gave rise to were to have important consequences for how the colony's legal system developed, primarily because Christian marriage had important economic implications. During the latter half of the nineteenth century, when merchants were still the most important component of Euro-African society, Christian marriage made it possible for successful members of this group to escape the demands of the extended family. Traditional kin ties, as Susan Kaplow has pointed out, were inimical to this stage of

> primitive accumulation. The merchants' needs—to concentrate wealth in their own hands, to control it for their own ends, to dispose or divide it as they saw fit—ran counter to the working principles of Akan society.[56]

Equally important, by willing their personal property to their wives and children, husbands could preserve it intact from one generation to the next. The hostility that this could precipitate was well demonstrated in a particularly bitter exchange in the *Western Echo* between someone who appropriately signed himself "Vanderbilt" and various "Young Men." Vanderbilt, whose "stores [were] filled with all sorts of merchandise," attributes his success to having "scrupulously shut up [his] heart against

the distress of the needy, the orphans and the widow; and solely minded
[his] own P's and Q's."[57] As far as recognizing any responsibility to help
others who had failed in business, he maintains that his only obligation is
to his "own sons and daughters," who he intends "to make the most
prominent in the country." Finally, he feels that he is "impregnable" to the
traditional social pressure on wealthy individuals like himself to help
others less successful. Instead, he justifies his conduct by arguing that "if
every one had done as they [the rich] we would all be rich."[58]

Vanderbilt's rugged individualism may have been a somewhat extreme
case, as the slew of hostile letters to the editor that followed his column
indicated.[59] More typical was John Sarbah's refusal to accept responsibility
for the debts of his extended family.[60] The scaling down of obligations to
the larger extended family in this fashion were all part of what Sarbah's
son, John Mensah Sarbah, recognized as "the advance of civilization
tend[ing] to break up the unity of the family."[61] Of more long-term
significance, successful merchants like John Sarbah sought to make sure
that their Christian wives, or children from these unions, inherited their
property. They drew up elaborate wills to ensure that this would be so.
For example, William Godson Bruce, a wealthy Accra merchant, in his
will specifically barred "any of his Brothers, Sisters, Uncles, Aunts,
Cousins, or any other branch of the family" from inheriting his "houses
situated in James Town," which he left to his children.[62] As an indication
of how much importance they attached to making sure that such property
remained in the possession of their immediate family, few of the
prominent merchants of this period died intestate.[63]

However, there was considerable potential for tension between this
nuclear family and the *abusua*. The latter offered important resources of
its own, and merchants, as members of such extended families, were not
at all adverse to using them. Family lands, fixed property and even
accumulated wealth, such as gold dust, could be used by enterprising
family members with the assumption that any increase in wealth that
accrued they would return to benefit the extended family itself.[64] The
extended family also became a source of labor which gave African
merchants an important advantage vis-à-vis their European competitors.
The British merchant A. W. Swanzy recognized how much this was so
particularly after the abolition of slavery, when labor was in short
supply.[65] It meant that both "blood" relatives and "domestics" could be
counted on to act as factors, storekeepers, produce buyers and even
carriers. They were more likely to be reliable and honest than strangers,
since their actions could be subjected to much "closer scrutiny."[66]

Raymond Dumett has also noted that many of the more successful
merchants of the late nineteenth century "were either members of royal
lineages or otherwise closely related to the paramount chiefs of their home

districts."[67] Apart from enhancing their social prominence, Dumett has argued that

> this would have given them access to the resources that the royal *abusua* commanded. Merchants, consequently, took advantage of a web of traditional family relationships that could stretch all the way from their several country wives to links with the important coastal royal lineages. Polygyny in such a context offered much more than the opportunity to have large numbers of children or male sexual gratification.[68]

Wives were invariably a man's immediate agents and even such "respected" figures like "Father" J. P. Brown, a "pillar" of the Methodist Church in Cape Coast and F. and A. Swanzy's general agent, had at least one "concubine" in addition to the "church" wives that he married during his long career.[69] Through his numerous wives, a merchant could also establish links with other important matrilineages. For example, James Hutton Brew's father, Samuel Collins Brew, married into the royal lineage of the town of Dunkwa, which was strategically important as far as trade with Asante was concerned.[70]

Membership in two radically different family systems gave prominent members of coastal society important legal benefits as well. The British court considered them British subjects and entitled to the protection of English common law. It meant that in land and property disputes, title deeds, actual possession of land or buildings and a single individual claiming ownership were much more important to the judges before whom this litigation came than the unfamiliar and confusing principles of customary law.[71] The division of the court system between the High Court and the Judicial Assessor's Court reinforced this bias. Up until 1878, cases involving customary law came before the judicial assessor, who sat with native assessors who advised him on principles of customary law. The result was that the colony's High Courts tended to be seen as an English common law preserve. Litigants who wanted the standards of this legal system applied in their cases were at a distinct advantage over those who wanted customary law to apply, and who, to make matters worse for them, were usually illiterate.

On the other hand, taking advantage of customary law in cases that involved indebtedness to either Europeans or Africans could be distinctly advantageous for any one who was in debt. By having a family member claim that mortgaged property was family rather than individually owned, debtors could avoid having to surrender it. With distressing regularity for creditors, actions to collect debts through foreclosure were invariably challenged by interpleader actions. There were both administrative and judicial rulings that tried to prevent particularly educated natives from taking advantage of both of these legal systems, but there was considerable disagreement over maintaining this standard, and it was even harder to maintain it in practice.[72] Instead, the colony's legal system was forced to rely on the obsolete common law practice of imprisonment for debt that in 1869 had finally been replaced by the Bankruptcy Act in Britain. It was an indication of how intractable this problem of debt enforcement was in the colony that even though there was universal condemnation of imprisonment for debt as helping neither the creditor nor the debtor, it remained in force without substantive changes until 1934.[73]

One of the unexpected results of the Marriage Ordinance of 1884 was that by inadvertently recognizing the legal status of native marriage, it also strengthened the legal standing of the "native family" and the customary law which regulated its affairs. After 1884, claimants in interpleader actions could also expect more sympathy from the British court when they maintained that the property in question was family rather than individually owned. As the colony's chief justice, William Brandford Griffith, was to recognize after many years of practice in the colony, "the English Courts [would] not allow family property to be seized in execution of a debt, unless in exceptional circumstances."[74] Ever since the days of the Judicial Assessor's Court, the British courts had recognized the existence of both family and self-acquired individual property. The former was subject to customary laws of inheritance, which meant that it remained in the possession of the matrilineage. With regard to individual property, however, the manner of its disposition in cases of dispute often came to revolve around the type of marriage that a deceased person had contracted.

In the case of *Re Isaac Anaman* in 1892, Judge Francis Smith established what was to remain the court's official position on this issue until 1959.[75] At issue in this case was whether a dying declaration of property overrode the intestacy provisions of the Marriage Ordinance. John Mensah Sarbah, who defended the caveator in this case, Jacob Anaman, argued that marriage under the Marriage Ordinance did not affect an African's personal law, which allowed him to make a *samansiw*, a nuncupative will. Isaac Anaman, on his deathbed, had conformed to all the customary requirements for such declarations, and consequently he could not be considered to have died intestate, as his wife claimed. The judge, however, disagreed with this "clever argument," and ruled that only a written will drawn up in compliance with English common law was valid for someone married under the 1884 Marriage Ordinance; therefore, Isaac Anaman's wife, Amelia Anaman, was entitled to be the administrator of his estate.[76] The ruling in the case of *Cole v. Cole* that came before the Full Court in Lagos in 1898 established the legal precedent in the Gold Coast with regard to children.[77] In this case the court ruled that the legitimate children of an ordinance marriage, regardless of their mental competence, were to inherit from their father if he died intestate.

Sarbah's challenge to the primacy of English common law was not necessarily in favor of the matrilineage, but it did assert the claims of native law and custom which in the long run were to the advantage of the *abusua*. However, he recognized that *samansiw* was probably a product of what he described as "later customary law." He was only able to trace it back to Brodie Cruickshank's description "of death-bed declarations made in the presence of responsible witnesses."[78] Instead, he argued that "the only disposition of property known to the Early Customary Law was a transfer followed by immediate possession," and he suggested that it was "contact with British rule in the old settlements [that] gave rise to the practice of reducing into writing such transactions."[79] What Sarbah indicated was that the long history of trade with Europeans, and the "accumulation of wealth by means of lucrative trade" that followed, created new ideas about property that overrode earlier claims of "kindred in blood."[80]

If this was indeed so, the development of the customary ceremony of *samansiw* was very much the result of what Martin Chanock has described as "changes in material relations."[81] There was nothing unusual about this since, as Eric Hobsbawm has pointed out, "'custom' cannot afford to be invariant, because even in 'traditional' societies life is not so. Customary...law...shows [a] combination of flexibility in substance and the formal adherence to precedent." It "does not preclude innovation and change."[82] On the surface stare decisis and statutory enactments during the colonial period promised considerably less flexibility than what had come before, but there were contingent forces at work that were to force seemingly "invariant" legal traditions to adjust to new circumstances.[83]

The cultural renaissance that the collapse of the "special relationship" between Europeans and their Euro-African protégées at the end of the nineteenth century contributed to was guaranteed to increase the number and complexity of these challenges. Judge Smith's determination to assert the primacy of English common law must be seen as a reaction to the increasing assertiveness of customary law in general. His ruling coincided with what the editor of the Accra paper *Gold Coast Chronicle* noticed had been a "revival of the silly, unnatural and iniquitous native law of inheritance" among the Gas.[84] He attributed this to the unpopularity of Christian marriage in which "divorce was beyond the reach of 99 percent."[85] Indeed, there had been a slight downturn in the number of Christian marriages between 1894 and 1895, but this was not the trend; by the end of the century the number increased.[86] More important in helping to explain this revival in the native law of inheritance was the role of the colony's lawyers in challenging the application of common law in property disputes, and the willingness on the part of the British courts to rule in favor of the matrilineage. For example, in the case of *Ameko v. Amevor*

that came before the High Court in Accra in 1892, the chief justice, J. T.
Hutchinson, ruled that the largest share of the estate in dispute should
devolve in accordance with native law. Brothers, sisters and children were
entitled to get "something" only as "a moral duty," and the court took it
upon itself to distribute a small portion of the estate to brothers and sisters
"the defendant [was] at variance with."[87]

This resurgence can also be seen as representing a reaction on the part
of males who felt threatened by the new legal rights that the introduction
of English common law seemed to offer women. Reasserting the legal
rights of the matrilineage weakened the power of individual women and
their children in the colony's courts of law. In general the matrilineage
could already command far more resources to defend its interests. Many
of its members were likely to be of the same generation as the deceased.
When it came to hiring a lawyer to undertake litigation they could rely on
the resources of the matrilineage itself. The wife, on the other hand, was
much more isolated and financially dependent. This was particularly so if
her marriage had conformed to the Christian ideal of the woman as home
maker and child raiser. Instead, she had to rely on her kin, who would
have to pay the legal fees if they lost the case. Neither could she expect
help from her children if they were young; instead, as in the Nigerian case
of *Cole v. Cole*, it was the mother who had to bring suit for a minor child
who the court also considered to be a "lunatic." In a very similar fashion
to the situation that Kristin Mann describes for elite women in Lagos,
colonial courts in the Gold Coast were expensive and unpredictable venues
with the added disadvantage of being embarrassingly open to the public.[88]
Compounding the problems of the bereaved spouse, as the Accra
newspaper *Gold Coast Chronicle* expressed it, was the "ruthless
indifference" of the matrilineage "to [her] sorrow" and the interests of the
children.[89]

On the other hand, the resurgence of customary law could also work
against the interests of husbands who were seeking to "concentrate wealth
in their own hands." There was a long history to this conflict in coastal
society, but, ironically, as the "halcyon days" of the African merchant
drew to a close at the end of the nineteenth century, the climate of rugged
individualism that Vanderbilt had exhibited began to wane.[90] As Susan
McRory has shown, the scale of operations of this new generation of
African merchants was much smaller than that of their predecessors, and
the gap between them and European firms much greater.[91] It meant that the
gap between the *abusua* and a successful family member was
commensurably smaller than it had been when African merchants were
seeking to make their sons and daughters "the most prominent [people] in
the country."[92] Under these circumstances the *abusua* could much more
easily exert its "reabsorptive" capacity. It was much harder for African
businesses to survive the death of a founder, and court cases increasingly

resulted, as Raymond Dumett has observed, in the division of property among multiple heirs.[93] Complicating the litigation that inevitably followed were the claims of "domestics" who also were incorporated into the *abusua* with ill-defined and often contested rights to share in the inheritance of family property.

It was hardly surprising that in this new order lawyers replaced merchants as the leaders of African society.[94] It was easier for prominent coastal families to preserve status by educating their sons for professional careers in general, but this also helps to explain the resurgence in customary law. The existence of two competing legal systems was a lawyer's paradise. This was particularly so since many of the judges before whom litigation in the colony's British courts came were not very familiar with customary law. It gave experts like John Mensah Sarbah a considerable advantage. His appointment to the Legislative Council in 1900 enabled him to pursue the battle for recognition of customary law on two fronts. He had represented the caveator in *Re Isaac Anaman*, but in spite of his defeat, he was able to keep up a constant attack against the "outrageous" aspects of the Marriage Ordinance in the colony's Legislative Council, and finally, in 1909, he was able to win an important modification of intestacy procedure.[95] The Marriage Ordinance was amended so that both the wife and the family were to be given a share of an intestate man's property.[96]

Both to Sarbah and Casely Hayford, the manner of inheritance was more than just a theoretical legal point. In the case of Sarbah, like other members of the "Gone Fantee" movement, he was willing to use his own family affairs to challenge the primacy of English common law.[97] When he made his will in 1903, he appointed his mother and two sisters his executrices.[98] In 1904 he married an ordinance wife, but he only added a minor codicil to the original will which gave this wife and her children only £250 and three hundred shares in an Asante gold mining company. In 1910 he died suddenly, and his wife unsuccessfully sought to challenge the validity of her husband's will. Compounding her problems, the gold mining shares turned out to be worthless, and she was reduced to importuning the government to pay for her children's education.[99]

In contrast, Casely Hayford's will of 1913 was more complex than Sarbah's and reflected the variety of child-producing liaisons he entered into by this point in his life. The will recognized a clear distinction between "inherited family wealth and the wealth he had personally accumulated...[as well as making] a distinction between his matrilineal and patrilineal responsibilities."[100] He requested that most of his personal wealth be divided among the "progeny of the two Christian marriages that he had by 1913 (he allegedly had others subsequently), and that his family wealth be redistributed among his extended family."[101] He also wanted to preserve a distinction between children he produced from casual relationships as opposed to those who were the result of marriages by indigenous or European custom by requiring that the latter bear the name "Casely" immediately before the surname "Hayford."

It is unlikely that Sarbah conceived of his arrangements working out quite so badly for his wife and her children. Instead, he probably wanted the same treatment for them that he describes in *Fanti Customary Laws* as the practice that had developed "in the early days of the missionaries...[in which at her husband's death] his children and widow took half of his moveable property, while his own family took the other half."[102] Perhaps he was seeking to build up his nuclear family's half, and the gold mining shares were part of this plan. His early and fairly sudden death (at forty-six) robbed him of the time needed to complete this project. Nevertheless, the priority that he gave to his matrilineage is an indication of how attitudes to marriage and customary notions of inheritance were being rethought even among staunch Christians.[103] Sarbah's father, for example, had willed the bulk of his personal property to his nuclear family, and in contrast to his son had made relatively small bequests to his matrikin. Like members of his generation, he wanted to ensure that the bulk of his property passed to his nuclear family when he died in 1892.[104] As the court records of the early twentieth century indicate, John Mensah Sarbah's deviation from his father's behavior was not unique. In a similar fashion for other members of the Euro-African elite, balancing the interests of the nuclear family against those of their *abusua*'s proved difficult and contentious.[105]

Undoubtedly the deteriorating relationship between Europeans and their Euro-African protégés provided the intellectual climate of opinion for this reversal of ideals. Yet it was ironic that missionary and administrative attempts to structure marriage on the coast provided one of the most important contexts in which this cultural revival expressed itself. More than just conformity to a Christian lifestyle was involved since the emergence of two very different family structures also meant competing systems of inheritance. The colony's British courts became the main venue for litigating such conflicts, which brought English common law into conflict with predominantly Akan customary conceptions of inheritance. As such it represented a reversal from an earlier, more "socially realistic" phase in the colony's jurisprudential tradition which was best exemplified in the opinions of the long-serving chief justice, Sir William Brandford Griffith (1895-1909).[106] He had continued the tradition of "judicial activism" established by Captain George Maclean, the Gold Coast's first judicial assessor, who had "looked upon the judiciary as a sub-division of the executive" and as a "major instrument for promoting civil change."[107]

The emergence of the policy of indirect rule in the early twentieth century also played an important role in the recognition of customary law. The new approach to incorporating the native state into the machinery of colonial government in the early twentieth century also meant enhancing the status of customary law before the colony's courts. Indirect rule also meant awarding the chiefs administrative roles and the political power that went with this. Invariably what this meant was that the cultural revival that was the reaction to the deteriorating relationship between the Euro-African community and their European reference group also developed a political dimension. It was more than just the beginnings of a protonationalist movement, as scholars have tended to see. It also represented an important linking between what the colonial administration called the "native order" and what came to be known as the "intelligentsia." Here once again colonial legislation was designed to keep these two sections of Gold Coast coastal society separate, but it was no more successful in achieving this than the Marriage Ordinance was in establishing a clear legal distinction between the rights of the nuclear as opposed to the extended family. In both cases European institutional norms were in competition with African institutions, specifically those of Akan society. Likewise, a wide range of social classes were involved, which ensured that there would be substantial invention of tradition to accommodate all those who wanted to participate in what was supposed to be the native order.

Notes

1. Minutes of the Gold Coast District Synod, 1871, Methodist Archives, SOAS.

2. Cited in Dennis Kemp, *Nine Years at the Gold Coast* (London, 1898), 49. Reverend Dennis Kemp was chairman of the Gold Coast district from 1892 to his retirement in 1897. He had initially come to the colony in 1888. Bartels, *The Roots of Ghana Methodism*, 126.

3. Kemp, *Nine Years at the Gold Coast*, 49.

4. Ibid.

5. Ibid.

6. For example, they were recognized as proof of marriage in divorce cases before the colony's courts: *Elizabeth Brown v. Charles Brown, Augustus Rhule Corespondent*, 10 March 1874, and *John H. Fletcher v. Ellen Fletcher and R. Harrison*, 16 December 1874. SCT 5/4/99, NAG, Accra.

7. The Queens Advocate to the Governor on the history of the Marriage Ordinance of 1884, 5 February 1887. Enclosed in the Governor's dispatch to the Secretary of State 3 November 1890, CO 96/212, PRO. In 1883 the question of the legality of marriage in the colony itself had also become moot. A petition for divorce had been denied in the Cape Coast High Court on the grounds that the marriage was legal since it had been performed by a dissenting clergyman (a Methodist). The plaintiff's counsel had tried to take advantage of the legal

uncertainty in the colony about which ministers could perform legal marriages. It underscored to the administration how much legislation was needed in this matter.

8. Shirley Zabel, "Legislative History of the Gold Coast and Lagos Marriage Ordinance: III," *Journal of African Law* 23, no. 1 (1979):11.

9. *An Ordinance for Regulating the Law of Marriage,* chapter 41. However, in an important concession to customary practice a man could marry his deceased wife's sister or niece.

10. Ibid., chapter 48.

11. The Queens Advocate to the Governor, 5 February 1887, CO 96/188, PRO.

12. *An Ordinance for Regulating the Law of Marriage,* chapter 29.

13. The chairman and general superintendent of the Methodist District, Reverend W. T. Coppin, formally protested to the colonial secretary that the ordinance's "complicated character" would serve to "discourage Christian marriage and increase polygamy." Instead, he wanted to see the "simple procedure" in existence in Lagos and Sierra Leone introduced to the Gold Coast "where all marriages were legal when performed by a duly accredited clergyman." Reverend Coppin to the Colonial Secretary, 4 January 1886. Enclosed in the Governor's dispatch to the Secretary of State, 3 November 1890, CO 96/212, PRO.

14. *Gold Coast Colony Blue Book,* 1877-1883. In 1884 and 1885 the *Blue Book* reported no marriage statistics. For the second average see the Governor's dispatch to the Secretary of State, 3 November 1890, CO 96/212, PRO. It is worth noting, however, that even before 1884 the number of church marriages was declining dramatically. From a high of 351 in 1878, they had dropped to 104 in 1883. Understandably, missionaries were concerned with the declining popularity of Christian marriage, but undoubtedly their own stricter standards must have contributed to this decline.

15. *Gold Coast Times,* 7 October 1882.

16. *Western Echo,* 9 January 1885.

17. *Western Echo,* 9 January 1886.

18. Acting Chief Justice to the Colonial Secretary, 13 May 1893, CO 96/233, PRO.

19. It is often difficult to be sure of the authorship of articles in the Gold Coast press because they were either unnamed or their authors used a variety of colorful noms de plume. Ray Jenkins, however, concludes from his "familiarity with the intellectual biographies of Brew and his nephew, Casely Hayford, that the latter was the author [of "Marita: On the Folly of Love"]." Jenkins, "North American Scholarship," 27. Circumstantial evidence also seems to support this claim. After Brew left the colony early in 1888, there was one further installment of the serial in the *Gold Coast Echo,* the successor paper to the *Western Echo,* and Casely Hayford was the editor.

20. *Western Echo,* 24 March 1886.

21. *Western Echo,* 8 May 1886.

22. *Western Echo,* 29 July 1886.

23. In another indication of role reversal, she also pressures him into becoming a class member in the Methodist Church.

24. Apart from telling the story of Miss Wissah's and Quaibu's courtship and unhappy marriage, the serial also digresses on several occasions to present other fictional accounts of unfortunate church marriages. They include a wide range of educated natives such as doctors, merchants and even ministers! The message is always the same. The wife's excesses undermine the traditional position of the husband as the head of the household, and they are responsible for the tensions that result.

25. *Western Echo,* 29 July 1886.

26. Sarbah, *Fanti Customary Laws,* 52.

27. Ibid.

28. Ibid.

29. Cruickshank, *Eighteen Years on the Gold Coast of Africa,* 2:97-98.

30. Susan B. Kaplow, "African Merchants of the Nineteenth Century Gold Coast" (Ph.D. diss., Columbia University, 1975), 132-134.

31. The Legislative Council enacted an ordinance to this effect in 1859. It brought divorce law in the settlements into line with the recently passed Matrimonial Causes Act of 1857 in the metropole. In this legislation a man could petition for a dissolution of marriage (divorce *a vinculo matrimonii*) on the grounds of his wife's adultery. She, however, had to prove (1) incestuous adultery, (2) bigamy with adultery, (3) rape, (4) sodomy, (5) bestiality, or (6) adultery, coupled either with desertion for two years or more, or with cruelty. See B. H. Lee, *Divorce Law Reform in England* (London, 1974), 14.

32. For example *Elizabeth Brown v. Charles Brown, Augustus Rhule Corespondent,* 10 March 1874. High Court Cape Coast Record Book, SCT 5/4/99, NAG, Accra.

33. 10 March 1874. High Court Cape Coast Record Book, SCT 5/4/99, NAG, Accra.

34. 9 March 1874. High Court Cape Coast Record Book, SCT 5/4/99, NAG, Accra.

35. For example, in the case of *Des Bordes v. Des Bordes and Mensah,* which came before Chief Justice Hector Macleod just before the passage of the 1884 Marriage Ordinance, the judge was in considerable doubt as to whether English common law should apply. The marriage in question was not recognized under the Marriage Acts of England, but he decided that it was in the interests of the "young" colony to treat such marriages as "indissoluble" and under "the operation of the divorce law of England." Since adultery and cruelty had been established, he granted the petition. Cited in Sarbah, *Fanti Customary Laws* 267-270.

36. In addition to the cases I have already mentioned there were the cases of *Charlotte Davis v. Samuel Davis*, 21 September 1874, High Court Cape Coast Record Book, SCT 5/4/99, NAG, Accra; *Mercy Ridley Kuofi v. Robert Kuofi*, 10 June 1881, Cape Coast Registrars Minute Book, SCT 5/9/1, NAG, Accra; *Davis v. Davis*, 28 March 1883, High Court Cape Coast Record Book, SCT 5/4/1035, NAG, Accra; and *Dougan v. Dougan*, 10 December 1885, Cape Coast Registrars Minute Book, SCT 5/9/1, NAG, Accra.

37. Mann, *Marrying Well*, 77. For example, John Sarbah sent his daughter, Evangeline, to school in England. Kaplow, "African Merchants of the Nineteenth Century Gold Coast," 158.

38. *Western Echo*, 9 January 1886.

39. *Western Echo*, 6 March 1886.

40. Adelaide M. Cromwell, *An African Victorian Feminist: The Life and Times of Adelaide Smith Casely Hayford, 1868-1960* (London, 1986), 68. It is not clear why he selected an Anglican minister since both he and his wife were practicing Methodists. According to his wife, their minister at the chapel where they worshiped in London was so furious that he "practically denounced [them] from the pulpit." We can speculate that perhaps Hayford was seeking the greater social recognition that came from being married in the Established Church.

41. *Ethiopia Unbound: Studies in Race Emancipation* (London, 1911).

42. In the 1870s, Blyden had publicly advocated polygyny as best suited to Africans. At that time the young Casely Hayford was a student at the Wesleyan Boy's High School in Freetown, where Blyden was the editor of the newspaper, the *Negro*. He "had made a profound impression on Hayford who became his life-long follower and probably his most devoted disciple." Hollis R. Lynch, *Edward Wilmot Blyden: Pan-Negro Patriot, 1832-1912* (London, 1967), 240.

43. Casely Hayford, *Ethiopia Unbound*, 71-75, 136.

44. Cromwell, *An African Victorian Feminist*, 67.

45. Ibid., 89. Their first daughter, Gladys, was born with a slight deformity, and Mrs. Casely Hayford took her to England to seek medical attention. She spent several years there hoping that her husband would be able to join her. Even when she returned to the Gold Coast they did not live together. Casely Hayford lived and worked in Sekondi and his wife lived in the more cosmopolitan town of Cape Coast.

46. Ibid. Mrs. Adelaide Smith Casely Hayford returned to Freetown, Sierra Leone, where she established a vocational school for girls. For a history of her life see Cromwell, *An African Victorian Feminist*.

47. *Western Echo*, 24 February 1886. Bonsu Penins is Quaibu's friend and confidant. In the story, he advises Quaibu not to contract a church marriage with Miss Wissah. He prophesies from his own experience that a church marriage will "rouse up defects in her" that in country marriage lie dormant, and eventually she will become a "roaring lion to devour him."

48. Edward Blyden, *African Life and Customs* (London, 1908), 25.

49. There were obviously couples who lived together "out of wedlock, sometimes for years," but as Spitzer has indicated "the ideal...was that a wedding take place in a church as soon as there was enough money for all preparations." *The Creoles of Sierra Leone,* 30.

50. *Western Echo,* 24 August 1886.

51. "Canocamid's" response, ibid.

52. For example, *Gold Coast Chronicle,* 18 January 1896; *Gold Coast Express,* 22 November 1897 and 11 September 1899 (letter from "Marita").

53. Susan B. Kaplow, "Primitive Accumulation and Traditional Social Relations on the Nineteenth Century Gold Coast," *Canadian Journal of African Studies* 12, no. 1 (1978):25.

54. Mann, *Marrying Well,* 45.

55. Ibid., 81.

56. Kaplow, "Primitive Accumulation," 25.

57. *Western Echo,* 10 February 1886.

58. Ibid.

59. *Western Echo,* 24 February 1886. "Tom, Dick and Harry" accused him of "living among us just like medals without prizes."

60. John Sarbah to John Duker, 1 December 1876, Sarbah Collection 6/4, NAG, Accra. Cited in Kaplow, "Primitive Accumulation," 26.

61. Sarbah, *Fanti Customary Laws,* 61.

62. W. C. Bruce, 26 March 1876, Deeds Registry, Accra. Cited in Kaplow, "Primitive Accumulation," 25. It was hardly surprising that he went to such pains to exclude matrilineal inheritors since only eight years before he died there had been the important decision in the appeal case of *Akosua v. Orbodie* that had come before Judicial Assessor W. A. Parker. In conjunction with the chiefs of Christiansborg, Ussher Town and James Town, he had overturned a lower court decision in favor of patrilineal inheritance being customary among the Ga. Instead, the Assessors's Court had ruled "that the nephew is the lawful heir according to the custom of the country." Cited in A. B. Quartey-Papafio, "Law of Succession Among the Akras or the Ga Tribes Proper of the Gold Coast," *Journal of the African Society* 10, no. 27 (1910):70.

63. This included even important Asantes who lived in coastal towns, like Prince John Ossoo Ansah. Ansah was the son of a former *asantehene* who had been handed over under the terms of the treaty between the British and the Asante in 1831 to be educated in Britain. On his return to the coast, he had settled in Cape Coast where he engaged in trade. He had become a Methodist and married a Fante woman in a Methodist ceremony. In his will he left his "property, house and land to his legitimate children...to be divided amongst them when the youngest reached twenty-one." His wife, Sarah, was "to enjoy and use his house and other properties so long as she remained a widow." *Re. John Ansah,* 21 March 1885, Cape Coast Registrars Minute Book, SCT 5/9/1, NAG, Accra.

64. Gocking, "Competing Systems of Inheritance," 605-606.

65. It was one reason why European merchants were unwilling to penetrate into the interior. See, for example, Albert Swanzy, "Civilisation and Progress on the Gold Coast of Africa," *Journal of the Royal Society of Arts*, 23 (1875):422.

66. Gocking, "Competing Systems of Inheritance," 606.

67. Raymond E. Dumett, "African Merchants of the Gold Coast, 1860-1905: Dynamics of Indigenous Entrepreneurship," *Comparative Studies in Society and History* 25 (1983):680.

68. Gocking, "Competing Systems of Inheritance," 606.

69. Information from the Cape Coast Divisional Court case of *George Fynn v. Arabah Iyinah and Arabella Brown,* 8 October 1926. Cape Coast Judgment Book, SCT 5/6/3, NAG, Accra.

70. Governor Maxwell to the Secretary of State, 3 August 1895, CO 96/259, PRO.

71. For example, *Yamike v. Adako* (1853), cited in J. M. Sarbah, *Fanti Law Review of Decided Cases on Fanti Customary Law* (London, 1904), 3; *Jonfia v. Inkatsia* (1892), cited in ibid., 71; and *Bokitsi Case* (1902), cited in ibid., 154.

72. In 1885, William Brandford Griffith, who was then one of the colony's pusine judges, tried to solve this dilemma by ruling "that an educated native could not claim the benefit of native laws and customs" when it came to matters pertaining to debt. Shortly before, however, his fellow judge H. W. Macleod had ruled just the opposite. *Western Echo,* 10 February 1886.

73. For example, the Cape Coast newspaper *Gold Coast Aborigines* was "puzzled" by how this practice that had been abolished in England and "not known in Sierra Leone or Lagos" continued to exist in the Gold Coast, particularly since creditors did not get their money back. *Gold Coast Aborigines,* 22 July 1897. The practice was abolished in Sierra Leone in 1883 with the passage of An Ordinance for the Abolition of Imprisonment for Debt and for the Punishment of Fraudulent Debtors. In spite of what the editor of the *Gold Coast Aborigines* thought, imprisonment for debt was "known" in Lagos. However, in the twentieth century judges acquired far more discretion in allowing creditors to imprison debtors. The Gold Coast reforms of 1934 basically brought the latter colony into line with what pertained in Nigeria. It was indicative of the similarities between the two. For the history of these changes see "Imprisonment for Debt," CSO/4, NAG, Accra.

74. *A. F. Lokho v. Konklofi,* 20 March 1907. Judgment Book, Accra, SCT 2/6/3, NAG, Accra.

75. Smith was from a well-established Sierra Leonean family, and in 1871 he became the first Creole to qualify for the bar. Cromwell, *An African Victorian Feminist,* 32. With his background he was not likely to support customary law over English common law.

76. This decision was handed down on 13 March 1894. For this ruling, see Sarbah, *Fanti Customary Laws,* 221-227.

77. *Cole v. Cole,* I *Nigerian Law Review,* 15-23. The decision is also cited in the Cape Coast Judgment Book, SCT 5/6/1, NAG, Accra.

78. Cruickshank, *Eighteen Years on the Gold Coast* of Africa, 2:214.

79. Sarbah, *Fanti Customary Laws*, 97.

80. Sarbah, *Fanti National Constitution*, 25, and *Fanti Customary Laws*, 96.

81. Martin Chanock, "A Peculiar Sharpness: An Essay on Property in the History of Customary Law in Colonial Africa," *Journal of African History* 32 (1991):65.

82. Hobsbawm, "Introduction: Inventing Traditions," in *The Invention of Tradition*, 2.

83 Ibid.

84. *Gold Coast Chronicle*, 29 July 1896.

85. Ibid. His argument was that since people could not get divorced easily if they were married as Christians, they were selecting native marriage, in which divorce was easier. Apart from resulting in a return to native laws of inheritance, he considered this "highly productive of immorality." This was a way of embarrassing the missionaries who argued that Christian marriage promoted morality.

86. In 1894 there were 159 Christian marriages, in 1895 there were 124, but in 1900 the number was up to 174. *Gold Coast Colony Blue Book*.

87. *Amekoo v. Amevor*. Cited in Sarbah, *Fanti Customary Laws*, 220-221.

88. Mann, *Marrying Well*, 86.

89. *Gold Coast Chronicle*, 18 January 1896.

90. This is how the Accra newspaper *Vox Populi* described this period on 23 November 1932.

91. Susan T. McRory, "The Competition for the Merchandise Trade in the Gold Coast, 1900-1939" (Ph.D. diss., Columbia University, 1980), 85.

92. *Western Echo*, 10 February 1886.

93. Dumett, "African Merchants of the Gold Coast," 691.

94. Indicative of this change, in 1898 the governor appointed T. Hutton Mills, an Accra barrister, to be one of the two unofficial members on the colony's Legislative Council, positions that until then "merchant princes" had monopolized.

95. S. Azu Crabbe, *John Mensah Sarbah, 1864-1912* (Accra, 1971), 34-35.

96. The law stipulated that a man who had made a contract marriage and died intestate should have his personal property divided between his matrilineage and his wife. If there were children, then the property would be divided in three equal parts with family, wife and children each receiving an equal share.

97. Reverend Attoh Ahuma popularized the term "Gone Fantee." See Tenkorang, "John Mensah Sarbah," 77-78.

98. *J. M. Sarbah deceased Ekua Marian Sarbah Cavetrix*, 23 March 1911. Cape Coast Registrars Minute Book, SCT 5/9/22, NAG, Accra. Information about his will, which he made on 16 July 1903, comes from the records of this case.

99. The government did not entertain her plea. Neither could the widow agree to her mother-in-law's offer to educate the children provided that they lived with her. Crabbe, *John Mensah Sarbah*, 10.

100. Casely-Hayford, "A Genealogical Study of Cape Coast Stool Families," 292.

101. Ibid.

102. Sarbah, *Fanti Customary Laws*, 44.

103. J. M. Sarbah was a staunch Wesleyan Methodist. He was an active member of the Cape Coast circuit, and in 1900 he presented to Wesley Chapel in Cape Coast "a magnificent Pipe-Organ in memory of his lamented father (d. 1892) and brother (d. 1892)." Sampson, *Makers of Modern Ghana*, 125.

104. John Sarbah's will, 31 August 1889. Cited in Kaplow, "Primitive Accumulation," 25.

105. Not unlike other Euro-African families, a long and bitter set of legal battles followed between the widow, her children and the mother and her successors. In 1944 litigation over what was left of the estate finally ended up before the Privy Council. "Hon. John Mensah Sarbah, C. M. G. deceased–estate of," CSO 4/8/146, NAG, Accra.

106. S. K. B. Asante, "Interests in Land in the Customary Law of Ghana–A New Appraisal," *Yale Law Journal* 74 (April 1965):865.

107. Edsman, *Lawyers in Gold Coast Politics*, 23.

Chapter 5

Indirect Rule Versus Municipal Government

Initially, Crown Colony rule was marked by a concerted effort to replace what the colony's acting Queens advocate, William Brandford Griffith Jr., described as the "tottering and uncertain power of the chiefs."[1] This was particularly the case in the coastal towns where British courts had taken over the administration of justice, and the most recalcitrant of local rulers had been deported or demoted. However, officials rapidly realized that the "Protected Territories," the large and relatively unknown territory outside the immediate area around the seaboard settlements that made up the colony, could not be administered directly, and there would have to be some "exercise of native authority by the chiefs."[2] In 1878 the government proposed its first Native Jurisdiction Ordinance, which was an attempt to define what these powers would be. Uncertainty about the reaction from the chiefs, as well as doubts about the wisdom of the ordinance on the part of the colony's new governor, resulted in its never being implemented.[3]

It was not until 1883 that Governor Rowe, who was a strong supporter of recognizing chiefly rule, finally enacted a Native Administration Bill. This new bill differed from its predecessor with only one significant modification: it defined more precisely the method of appeal from the chief's tribunal to the British courts. Initially, the government applied the ordinance to only six "head chiefs," and as an indication of how limited officials considered its applicability it was not until 1898 that it began to be applied much more generally.[4] As far as the colony, and particularly the coastal settlements, were concerned, there was no intention to apply it in such locations. As the bill's preamble stated, its purpose was "to facilitate and regulate the exercise in the Protected Territories of certain powers and jurisdiction by native authorities."[5] Indeed, to the chief justice the ordinance was "a matter of expediency" until such time as the government would be able to extend direct rule, "as on the coast," to the interior.[6] It was hardly surprising that he lost no opportunity to attack the chiefly "tribunals [that he felt had become] intolerable to the natives that had tasted of the comparative civilization of the coast."[7]

In reality, however, even in the "civilized coast" district commissioners could not avoid relying on local chiefs to perform a number of functions that varied from providing carriers to implementing ordinances designed to improve the sanitation of the coastal towns. Even modest success in such matters as discouraging people from burying family members in their homes, clearing bush from public roads and cemeteries, filling up stagnant pools and preventing outbreaks of violence depended on the cooperation of local authority figures. Not even in the large towns like Accra, Cape Coast and Elmina were there enough government personnel to discharge such duties. Rapidly, however, officials on the spot came to realize that they could not expect any cooperation from local rulers who had no authority. As a quid pro quo they had to allow them courts and even wink at their maintaining prisons. It was partially due to this inconsistent attitude that King Taki Tawia I was able to maintain his court and prison until 1890, when on the advice of the chief medical officer his *kpabu* was finally closed.[8]

In the 1880s the British courts also exhibited contradictory positions with regard to the legitimacy of native courts. In 1881 the Divisional Court of the Central Province had ordered Quamin Fori, the king of Aquapim, to pay damages to one of his subjects in compensation for illegal arrest. The king's officers had apparently used so much violence in securing this man's arrest that it was this issue that had influenced the British court in its decision. Along with inhuman conditions of imprisonment, corrupt judges and excessive fines, British officials felt that this was typical of how native courts functioned.[9] Nevertheless, the Full Court had overturned the judgment on the grounds that the king had "acted within the powers which had always been recognized and allowed to the Native Court." Indeed, the court felt that the king's only "fault" was that he had not proceeded further with the case itself.[10]

A similar case arose in 1886-1887 which resulted in a much more complete investigation of the legal standing of native courts. In this instance the district commissioner of Saltpond had ruled that King Ackinie of Aikunfie had illegally imprisoned one of his subjects on the grounds that the "Supreme Court Ordinance of 1876 had swept away the previously existing judicial powers of native kings and chiefs."[11] On appeal the Divisional Court of the Western Province had affirmed this judgment, but on final appeal to the Full Court these earlier judgments were overturned. This court, in a far-reaching decision, ruled that the Supreme Court Ordinance of 1876 had "in no way impaired the judicial powers of native kings and chiefs, and that...[no] other Ordinance [had] taken them away."[12]

The case dealt specifically with chiefly jurisdiction in the Protected Territories, but, as Chief Justice William Brandford Griffith was later to recognize, by this time the legal distinction between the colony and the Protected Territories was breaking down. In 1886, for example, when the Gold Coast was separated from Lagos, the "Gold Coast Colony" was defined as comprising "all places, settlements, and territories belonging to us [the Crown] on the Gold Coast."[13] Significantly, this area was geographically located only in terms of longitude. Also reflective of this development, the colony's Legislative Council was beginning to enact ordinances that applied without distinction throughout this area. Undoubtedly, however, one of the most ironic results of this de jure establishment of the colony was that the legislation regulating native jurisdiction that had initially been enacted to apply to the Protected Territories increasingly came to apply also in what had originally been considered the colony.

The eventual result was to bring the functioning of all native courts under review. A few months before he retired in 1895, the governor, Sir William Brandford Griffith, appointed a commission headed by Sir James Hutchinson, the colony's chief justice, and assisted by one of the colony's puisne judges, the colonial secretary as well as the two Africans on the Legislative Council, to investigate the operations of native courts.[14] The commission had publicly taken evidence in Elmina, Cape Coast, Victoriaborg and Aburi, "examining nearly 50 witnesses."[15] It determined who "constituted" such courts, the limitations on their jurisdiction, the mode of procedure, remuneration for members of the court and the fines and fees these courts levied. Not surprisingly, since it treated the chiefly courts in the coastal towns as legitimate sources of judicial authority, the commission in its recommendations called for the passage of a new Native Jurisdiction Ordinance that would make "no distinction...between native courts in the interior and those in the coast towns where an English court is held also."[16]

Sir William Maxwell, who succeeded Sir William Brandford Griffith as governor in 1895, was far more committed to indirect rule and was much more enthusiastic about the commission's recommendations than his predecessor.[17] He had come from the Straits Settlement, where an indirect rule form of government was already well developed, and along with his many other projects he wanted to introduce a similar system in the Gold Coast.[18] As an indication of this, he brought Hendrik Vroom, the most

senior and experienced of the African district commissioners, to Accra to
be the provisional secretary of native affairs. The new governor abolished
Brandford Griffith's fledgling Roads Department, and instead he wanted
to have the chiefs and the district commissioners work together to build
roads, while he felt that the Compulsory Labor Ordinance that his
government had enacted would "strengthen the hands of chiefs."[19] The
expedition to Asante at the end of 1895 and into early 1896 temporarily
interrupted these plans, but as soon as it was over he was seeking an even
more comprehensive reorganization of the native order through the passage
of a new Native Jurisdiction Bill.[20]

By this bill he wanted to "improve the position of native headmen,
while at the same time making them more responsible to the government
for the proper performance of the functions assigned to them."[21] He was
willing to give these chiefs both judicial and police authority by
registering their courts and prisons, specifying how the former would
proceed and by having the district commissioners work with the chiefs to
maintain law and order.[22] These native courts were to remain part of the
colony's overall judicial system. Appeal from their decisions was to lie
first with the district commissioner's court and then with the superior
courts of the Supreme Court. Apart from defining more precisely how
native courts were to function, this new Native Jurisdiction Bill also
emphasized more strongly the derived nature of the power of chiefly
jurisdiction. The governor reserved the right to "suspend" native courts
that did not discharge their functions in accordance with British standards
of justice.[23]

Undoubtedly, the most innovative aspect of this new attempt to define
indirect rule in the colony was the governor's recognition that it had to be
extended to the coastal communities as well. He included among the
colony's "class one" chiefs, or *omanhene* (*amanhin* in current terminology), both Taki Tawia of Accra and Kobina Gyan of Elmina.[24] At the
same time, however, in keeping with his antagonism to Western-educated
Africans, he adamantly refused to recognize people of this "class" who
claimed chiefly status. He rejected George Eminsang's claim to be *tufuhen*
of Elmina.[25] Similarly he refused to recognize Kojo Mbra, the "*so-disant
King of Cape Coast*," who he felt was too close to native lawyers.[26] When
W. Z. Coker sought to accompany Colonel Sir Francis Scott's expedition
to Kumasi, the governor had him peremptorily sent back to Cape Coast
even though he had been very helpful in obtaining carriers.[27] In 1897,
King Taki lost his stipend by joining the protest led by the educated
natives against the Town Council Bill.[28]

In general, Governor Maxwell's promotion of what came to be defined
as indirect rule, though cut short by his early death, stimulated a spiraling
interest in the chiefly order that colonial officials clearly had not
anticipated.[29] Conveniently for such office seekers, the government's need

for carriers for the expedition to Asante at the end of 1895 provided them with an opportunity to promote themselves as legitimate members of the chiefly order. Even Kobina Gyan of Elmina, who had recently returned from exile in Sierra Leone, and had initially tried to distance himself from the unpopular business of recruiting carriers for military service, quickly realized that noncompliance with this order could undermine his standing with the government. This was so particularly since his rivals George Eminsang, who considered himself to be the *tufuhen* of Elmina, and Chief Quacoe Andoh, who had replaced Gyan as "king" of Elmina when the latter was in exile, were cooperating.[30] Neither on their own could supply as many carriers as the government required, and significantly the district commissioner was soon suggesting that they should all be recognized as legitimate chiefs.[31] He was more than willing to recognize their judicial power since they were using their courts to punish deserters.

On the other hand, W. Z. Coker, who had recently been released from prison, tried to use the government's need for carriers as an opportunity to supplant his much weaker rival, Kojo Mbra. By using his connections to the *asafos,* he was able to raise two thousand carriers for military service.[32] He was determined to regain government favor by demonstrating how indispensable he was, and obviously hoped that he would be able to win government recognition for his court as well as the right to operate his own prison. Kojo Mbra, who had become "an inveterate hater of government," rapidly acquired a reputation for being an obstructionist, and eventually ended up being prosecuted in the district commissioner's court for failure to comply with the Compulsory Labor Ordinance.[33] Much to the disgrace of the stool family, he was found guilty and fined one hundred pounds with the option of three months in jail.[34]

The prosecution, however, miscarried, for on appeal in the Cape Coast Divisional Court the original verdict was overturned on the grounds that since the government did not recognize Kojo Mbra as a chief of Cape Coast it could not hold him legally bound to comply with its orders![35] The implications of this verdict were obvious as it represented for the Cape Coast native order the culmination of the process that *Oppon v. Ackinie* had begun for the chiefly order in general. In the official confusion that followed, Kojo Mbra, who had been illegally operating a court and a prison for several years, got permission to operate his prison in exchange for agreeing to supply carriers.[36] Ironically, he was still not officially recognized as king or *omanhen* of Cape Coast, and a year later the colonial secretary was describing the decision to allow him a prison "an egregious blunder."[37] From here onward, however, it was too late to challenge his de facto standing as *omanhen* of Cape Coast.[38]

Undoubtedly there had been competition in the past to control the chiefly hierarchy, but what was new about this surge in interest was that many of the contenders for office were people from the ranks of the educated classes. W. Z. Coker and George Eminsang were among the first in Cape Coast and Elmina to establish this trend, but as time went by they were clearly not alone. On one hand this development could exacerbate the well-established sense of stratification that existed in coastal societies, particularly where the "educated" and the "illiterate" were seen as distinct "classes" in these societies. But on a more subtle level it was to serve in yet another way to bridge the gap between what in the early twentieth century became known as the "intelligentsia," or "scholars," and the "people." Ironically, it did so by fostering a competition for office and government recognition that often pitted members of the intelligentsia against illiterate or at best semiliterate opponents, but at the same time brought them together to compete in the same political arena.

This was clearly the case in Elmina, where European-educated George Eminsang was in competition with the illiterate Kobina Gyan and Quacoe Andoh for government recognition.[39] Between 1896 and 1899 all three of these men died, but significantly the competition between Western-educated and illiterate chiefly officeholders continued.[40] Kobina Condua, who succeeded Gyan, had been a trader and was literate enough to sign his letters to the district commissioner. Equally significant, he was surrounded by fellow scholars who had also been employed by European firms and seem to have been even more literate. They soon fell out with one another over the issue of the rights of "stranger" fishermen to fish in Elmina waters. Condua lost the vital support of the *asafos* and was destooled in 1899.[41] Reflective of the tensions this issue had exacerbated, his successor, Kwesi Mensah, was an illiterate fisherman himself, and by the time of his destoolment in 1912 the town had become "divided into two opposing camps: one known as 'the Progressives' and the other as 'the Unprogressives' or 'Conservatives.'"[42] According to the *Gold Coast Leader* there was significant correlation between the degree of Western education and the composition of these factions.[43]

Western education also played an important role in determining who would succeed King Ghartey IV of Winneba after he died in 1897. The candidates from the two rival stool families, the Ghartey and the Acquah, were both members of the scholar class. However, according to a local historian, George Acquah Robertson of the Acquah Anona family "was recommended...purely on merit of his training and wide business experience accumulated in England."[44] Clearly there were other reasons why James Robert Ghartey, the ex-king's son, was not selected. One of the town's two *asafos*, Dentsifu or Number Two *Asafo*, was extremely hostile to the Ghartey family, and this played an important role in determining the outcome of this succession struggle. But significantly, in a similar fashion to his counterparts in Elmina, Robertson, whose stool name was Acquah II, also ran afoul of his illiterate councillors. According to the local district commissioner, it was his failure to follow their advice that, after much contentiousness, resulted in his destoolment in 1907.[45]

Even in Accra, where there had been a much more extensive history of educated natives being involved in the native order, the coming of indirect rule stimulated competition between illiterate chiefs and those with different levels of Western education. For example, soon after Kojo Ababio IV was enstooled in 1891 as the king of James Town, he was refusing to be under King Taki Tawia of Ussher Town on the grounds that James Town was British while Ussher Town was Dutch.[46] Part of this conflict revolved around Kojo Ababio IV asserting judicial independence by seeking his own court and prison, as well as over conflicting ideas "of collective identity, status and authority."[47] But in addition, the rivalry between these two chiefs was compounded by their different educational levels. Taki Tawia was illiterate, while Kojo Ababio IV had attended one of the Wesleyan Methodist schools in Accra and had also spent time as a seaman.[48] Probably best of all in the coastal communities, he came to represent what officials considered the colony's "progressive" chiefs. In contrast to Taki Tawia, who was distinctly uncooperative during the Asante Expedition of 1895-1896, Kojo Ababio IV provided 1,400 carriers.[49] As an indication of his official reputation, even though he was actively involved in leading the opposition to the Lands Bill and the Town Council Ordinance, Governor Hodgson nominated him to sit on the first Accra Town Council in 1898.[50]

Appropriately enough, however, it was in Cape Coast, the educational capital of the colony, that the advantage of a Western education was most pronounced. This was best seen in the way that the struggle to control chiefly adjudication developed in the early twentieth century. Initially there were three contesting courts. W. Z. Coker presided over one, his archrival, Kojo Mbra, another, and Kofi Sackey, one of the town's hereditary chiefs, over the third.[51] The colonial government's decision to recognize only one prison effectively forced these three rivals to come together to form one court. By the end of the nineteenth century, however, Coker had definitely emerged as the central figure of this triumvirate. As the only literate person on what was officially known as the Native Tribunal, he kept a written record of its proceedings, collected the monies paid in fees and fines, and for a while even seems to have moved the operation to his own home.[52]

Apart from being attracted by the income that the exercise of adjudication promised, traditional office offered other attractions for the educated elite. There were immediate political advantages to controlling local native courts that became apparent, especially in Cape Coast, during the anti-Lands Bill agitation in 1897.[53] The court could be used to threaten with imprisonment those who refused to contribute to the Gold Coast Aborigines' Rights Protection Society (GCARPS) delegation to England to protest this legislation. Native Tribunals also provided merchants with an important instrument for enforcing the repayment of debts owed them by the mostly illiterate women who retailed their merchandise. Constant attacks in the press regarding the unworkable nature of the obsolete English common law practice of imprisonment for debt were a direct indication of how important this issue was. One editor, for example, felt that there should be a special "Debtors and Creditors Court as an intermediate court between the District Commissioner's and the Divisional Court."[54] Instead, it was the Native Tribunals that took over much of this work. As an indication of how active they were in dealing with small-scale indebtedness, it was invariably scandals over the excessively long periods of incarceration for such debtors (often women) that brought the "illegal" activity of these courts to the district commissioner's attention.[55]

In addition, Native Tribunals were much more willing to recognize the practice of pawning, which was the traditional means of enforcing debt repayment.[56] Ironically, in spite of the government's attempts to stamp out all forms of forced servitude, this practice seems to have increased in the 1880s and 1890s. Missionaries and educated Africans observed this to be the case on the part of even "well-to-do merchants, heads of farming families, and kings and chiefs [who] turned to pawnage as a way of continuing to add domestic servants and dependents to their households as a substitute for 'slavery.'"[57] In general the increase in this practice, as Raymond Dumett and Marion Johnson have argued, was closely linked to the spread of commercial capitalism. Acquiring imported consumer goods and paying for expensive litigation that the increased commercialization of land stimulated required capital.[58] Pawning relatives or dependents was one way to acquire this, but could easily produce disputes that could not be resolved in the British courts. Indeed, in 1892, as an indication of how much it was against this practice, the government made pawning a felony under the Gold Coast Criminal Code.[59]

Also, the colony's numerous moneylenders took advantage of these Native Tribunals. Securing bank loans was all but impossible for the majority of the population, and this served to spawn a host of moneylenders who made loans at what officials considered to be blatantly usurious rates. The result was that once again the British courts were highly unsympathetic to moneylenders who tried to use them as a means of enforcing delinquent debtors to discharge their obligations. In 1918, as an indication of this, the government passed an ordinance (Recovery of Money Loans Ordinance) that allowed British courts in cases involving debt to investigate the terms of the loan transaction itself. In cases where the court decided that terms of repayment were onerous, it could order new conditions, and even force the creditor to repay to the debtor monies already paid and deemed excessive. Native Tribunals, on the other hand, were hardly likely to do this since, as John Mensah Sarbah indicates, an interest rate of 50 percent was quite traditional.[60]

Undoubtedly the best indication of how important the debt enforcement role of Native Tribunals was comes from the records they kept of their activities. The earliest extant records for the coastal area date back to 1909, the records of the proceedings in the Cape Coast Native Tribunal. Here, recorded in W. Z. Coker's elegant copperplate, it is quite clear how frequent debt cases were before this court.[61] Many of them involved members of the better classes seeking repayment on debts owed them by illiterates who must have been their retail agents. There is a pro forma quality to these prosecutions since they invariably end with verdicts in favor of the creditor. Justice apparently seemed biased enough for "Scrutineer," writing in the *Gold Coast Leader,* to criticize the "two sets of justice, one for the rich and the other for the poor," that seemed to obtain in the town's Native Tribunal.[62]

In addition to "scholars," "merchant princes" and moneylenders who wanted control over the various institutions of the native order, the "frothy and ebullient" members of the local *asafos* also became involved in the struggle to control traditional society that de facto recognition of the native order in the coastal towns precipitated. Indeed, administrators came to single them out as the primary "instigators of disturbance and the sources of non-cooperation."[63] Undoubtedly these organizations had a long history of violent action in the past, but in contrast to the chiefly order they had survived the imposition of colonial rule in the Akan coastal towns far better. A. B. Ellis, a British army officer who spent eight years in the Gold Coast, most of them in Cape Coast, observed that

> the colonial government, while destroying the power of the chiefs, ha[d] left the company organization intact; and the captains of the companies [were arrogating] to themselves an independence and freedom from restraint which formed no part of the original scheme.[64]

It was hardly premeditated. In the militarily volatile climate of the nineteenth century that the ever-present threat of war with the Asante created, native forces had invariably played vital roles in British campaigns against this enemy. Even after the British replaced local forces with European and West Indian troops later in the century, *asafo* leaders continued to have important tasks such as recruiting carriers, protecting telegraph wires and acting as guides and interpreters. Participation in the expanding colonial world in this fashion ensured that the officeholders in these organizations would continue to play an important role in local affairs.

W. Z. Coker, as I have described, was able to win his way back into favor with the administration in Cape Coast by providing carriers for the 1895-1896 Asante expedition. Chief Andoh's rise in Elmina was closely linked to his participation in the Sixth Asante War (1873-1874) and subsequent threats of war against this kingdom in the 1880s. It was on the basis of the government support he claimed for such services "rendered" that he had sought to "deprive Prince Attah of kingship" in 1884.[65] Like Coker, his father was not from Elmina, but a fisherman from Sekondi, while his mother had been "a slave woman of the Dutch government."[66] He had been able to make himself popular in number four *asafo* (Wombir), and though he had no claim to hereditary office, he was apparently able to use his "wealth" to have himself "made one of the stool holders in court."[67]

Similar in many respects was the career of Captain Kojo, one of the senior Ussher Town *asafoatse*. He, too, had taken advantage of his *asafo* connections to provide the British with carriers at the time of the Sixth Asante War, and ever since 1878 had been the recipient of a government stipend of thirty shillings a month "as an act of grace."[68] He had further improved his position with the administration when King Taki Tawia had either been unwilling or unable to supply carriers for the Asante expedition of 1895-1896. In return for his services, he had received a present (a watch) from Governor Nathan, and with this recognition he had tried to establish himself as the main representative of the native order in Ussher Town when King Taki Tawia died in 1902.[69] The intense rivalry that existed between the four *akutsei* that made up Ussher Town, or Kinka, made this a difficult task, particularly since Captain Kojo's standing in the *asafos* was under attack.[70] In contrast to Coker, who also had to fend off competitors, he was illiterate, and in conjunction with his declining faculties, due to his age, more aggressive rivals were able to eclipse him.[71]

In addition to their military contributions, the *asafos* also played an important role in the economies of the coastal surf ports. As George Hagan has pointed out for Winneba, "without learning any new skills," the fishermen who primarily made up their membership "became an essential arm of the modern economy."[72] They were the people who manned the surfboats that brought cargo to and from the oceangoing ships that anchored as much as a mile off shore. Fishing chiefs, who were closely linked to particular *asafos*, entered into contracts with the European firms that needed surfboat men, and stood to gain financially from this. It also meant that at times they had to reconcile the opposing interests of the fishing community and the merchants. For example, in 1899 the merchants in Cape Coast pressured the government into preventing fishermen from using the town's main landing beach so that there would be more space for surfboats. Eventually the fishing community retained a lawyer and secured a victory in the Cape Coast Divisional Court.[73] The government retaliated by passing a Beach Obstruction Ordinance, but to prevent continuing friction between the large and vociferous fishing community and the merchants the government had to undertake extensive blasting of the rocky landing beach so that there would be sufficient room for both fishing canoes and surfboats.[74]

By continuing to play an important role in the affairs of their societies the *asafos* were able to maintain and even strengthen their sense of corporate identity. In describing the Cape Coast *asafos* in 1908, the district commissioner, Arthur ffoulkes, emphasized what he considered to be the "strong *esprit de corps* that [existed] regarding their customs and emblems."[75] It meant that to prevent what the editor of the *Western Echo* had disdainfully described in 1886 as "their frothy ebullitions of valor," which inevitably ended up in bloody inter-*asafo* rioting, in 1892 the government passed the Native Customs Ordinance to give the district commissioners power to prohibit all *asafo* customs, the celebration of which invariably seemed to result in bloody rioting between *asafos*. On the few occasions for which permission was given for *asafo* celebrations, local district commissioners demanded that the *asafo*'s leadership post a bond to guarantee good conduct. Whether there had been less rioting of this nature in the past is hard to determine. Terence Johnson, however, has indicated that between 1890 and 1909 there was a significant increase in the number of such disorders in the southern Gold Coast.[76] In 1914 this development reached its apogee with a particularly bloody riot in the small fishing village of Berreku in which between ninety and a hundred people lost their lives.[77]

Apart from their "frothy" ebullience, the *asafos* also became an important source of opposition to chiefly powers in the native state. Here once again it is difficult to know how much of a new development this was. Brodie Cruickshank makes no mention of this role in describing the "companies" in the 1840s.[78] However, by the time Assistant Secretary of Native Affairs J. C. de Graft Johnson, a Cape Coast native, did the first systematic study of the Fante coastal *asafos* in 1932, he considered that the *asafos* "definitely constitute[d] the third estate without which no native form of government [was] possible in the colony." He was convinced that these organizations had "a voice in putting a chief on and in removing him from a public as distinct from a family stool."[79] Clearly this was very much the case by the turn of the century as the *omanhen* of Komenda Kobina Yewan discovered. Between 1899 and 1902 there were five attempts to destool him. His main local opponent was the town's *tufuhen*, who was able to use his position as leader of this small fishing village's *asafos* to challenge effectively his paramount chief. In this conflict, local dissatisfaction with the paramount ruler was combined with Lands Bill protest, and finally with the help of the GCARPS, the *asafos* were able to depose the *omanhen* in 1902.[80]

The increasing number of destoolments and succession disputes that these *asafo*-initiated challenges generated often needed rapid government attention, and it seemed as though some thoroughgoing evaluation of the native order's place in the colony was necessary. The annexation of Asante and the Orders in Council that defined the boundaries of the Northern

Territories, Asante and the Gold Coast Colony in 1902, which placed on a much firmer legal foundation the government's powers of legislation, provided the opportunity to do this.[81] The governor could then claim that the ambiguous relationship with the chiefs that the Bond of 1844 had defined had been superseded by a new arrangement which signified that chiefly powers were not inherent, but derived from the Crown. This was the argument that Governor Nathan used in approving the deposition of Kwamina Faibiu, the *ohen* of Awudwa and Tarkwa, in 1901.[82] He claimed that Governor Brandford Griffith's destoolment of King Quamin Enimil of Eastern Wassaw in 1889 had already established the precedent. But unlike this earlier destoolment, which had been based on Enimil's violation of treaties with the Gold Coast chiefs prohibiting human sacrifice, in the case of Faibiu the governor had introduced a novel twist in the argument over the source of chiefly power by maintaining that chiefs in the Gold Coast held office "by the wish of the people and at the will of the Governor."[83]

Control of rich auriferous lands were also at stake, which ensured that the destoolment would be bitterly contested. Indeed, even after the governor declared Kwamina Faibiu destooled, he refused to hand over the stool paraphernalia, which effectively blocked the enstoolment of a successor. It was on account of the protracted litigation that this case and other contested destoolments around this time produced that the government passed the Chiefs Ordinance and the associated Stool Property Detention Ordinance in 1904. This legislation made the governor's decision in contested enstoolments or destoolments final, and compelled an ex-chief to hand over to the district commissioner the stool and all other symbolic paraphernalia.[84]

Governor Nathan, however, was careful to point out that this legislation was "not to impose in any way on the rights of natives, but merely to provide for the effective exercise of those rights."[85] Indeed, during his administration the government did begin to adopt a more formal relationship with the colony's native order that was symbolized by the adoption of indigenous terminology to describe officeholders. For example, he solicited the help of the GCARPS to obtain the correct Akan terminology to describe officeholders in this area of the colony, and *omanhin, ohin, tufuhin and safuhin* replaced chief, subchief, field marshal and captain as the official titles for these positions.[86] In the Ga area a similar transformation took place with *manche* or *mantse, mankralo* and *asafoatse* taking the place of head chief or king, subchief and captain.[87] And in 1904 the governor and his staff were all present at the installation ceremony for the new *mantse*, Taki Obili.[88] This was much in contrast with the installation of the Alata *mantse*, Kojo Ababio IV, a mere twelve years before, when the colonial secretary had come upon the ceremony purely by happenstance.[89]

Even more indicative of this changing attitude to the chiefly order was the government's creation in 1902 of a new department known as the Secretariat of Native Affairs "to secure greater consistency in the administration of native affairs and to collect more complete records with regards to them than has previously been possible."[90] In contrast to the one-man operation that Hendik Vroom's brief tenure as secretary of native affairs in 1895-1896 had represented, this department consisted of a secretary of native affairs and three traveling commissioners. In keeping with the determination to Europeanize all senior positions in the administration, these four appointments were held by Europeans. The department was to take over many of the functions that district commissioners had discharged in the past, like supervising the sale of gunpowder (very important in the celebration of customs), preventing smuggling, maintenance of native roads and ferries and preventing riots and disturbances.

In addition, there were new tasks that reflected the government's de facto recognition of the increasing importance of traditional society. Arbitrating "tribal land disputes" was one such task.[91] The major expansion of the colony's gold mining and timber exporting industries had contributed to a rapid rise in concession granting on the part of such communities, with often bitter disputes over who really "owned" the land in question. Also in dispute at this time were the colony's boundaries. Helping to establish the frontiers between German territory on the east and French territory on the west were part of the department's responsibilities. However, it was an indication of how vague was officialdom's understanding of the role the chiefly order would fill in the unfolding colonial order that many of these tasks did not prove to be the main focus of the department's activities.

The Concessions Court the government established in 1900 in the wake of the defeated Lands Bill took over the task of arbitrating land disputes. There had never been much of a role for chiefs in determining where the colony's boundaries would be, and anyway they were already close to being finally established in 1902. District commissioners, as stationary appointees, were the more logical officers to carry out functions like supervising road maintenance, issuing gunpowder permits and preventing riots and disturbances. Instead, as an important indication of how intense competition for traditional office was becoming, the main role of the secretary of native affairs became arbitrating disputes over enstoolment and destoolment that by the second decade of the twentieth century had begun to reach epidemic proportions.

However, it was not until 1904, when Sir John Rodger became the governor of the colony, that the debate over restructuring the native order began in earnest. Like his earlier predecessor, Sir William Maxwell, he, too, had come from a long period of service in the Straits Settlements, and

brought with him a well-established commitment to indirect rule.[92] From
his first tour of inspection, he concluded that the "whole question of the
rights and duties of native chiefs in [the] Colony was not in a satisfactory
condition."[93] Rapidly he drafted new legislation to define the jurisdiction
of native courts, but when he applied for guidance from the secretary of
state and the Colonial Office's law officers, he was told that since the Gold
Coast was "now a Colony" this was a matter for its own Legislative
Council to decide.[94] What came to be known as indirect rule was to
develop in a highly *sui generis* fashion though the question of chiefly
jurisdictional rights was central to this process, as it was in all of Britain's
African colonies where variants of this system emerged in the early
twentieth century.[95]

    With the important exception of the colony's chief justice, Sir William
Brandford Griffith, nearly all senior administrative officers had come to
recognize that there were limits to how many European judges there could
be, and the need to "strengthen the hands of the chiefs by whom a large
part of the Colony [was] necessarily governed."[96] Governor Rodger was
even willing to see native courts exist in "perfect harmony" with those of
the district commissioners. The latter would adjudicate "all the civil work
of the European community," while the former would "deal with suits
between natives involving questions of native law and criminal matters of
minor import." In the Straits Settlements, he pointed out that a similar
arrangement was "fully recognized."[97] Particularly contentious was the
issue of which arm of government should actually supervise and regulate
these native courts. If these courts were indeed to exist, the chief justice
wanted to see them under the supervision of the Supreme Court, which
was impractical given the small size of the colony's judicial staff. Instead,
it was far more practical to make district commissioners, who were widely
distributed throughout the colony, responsible for overseeing how native
courts functioned.

    The third important group of participants in this debate were the
colony's small but articulate group of qualified African barristers, who
were an integral part of the judicial system. On one hand they supported
the administration's willingness to recognize the existence of native courts,
but at the same time they supported the chief justice's demand that these
courts should be under the judiciary's control. On the related issue of
codification of customary law they were also strongly in favor of this
being under strict judicial control. They differed, however, over whether
customary usage became native law only after it had been noticed in a suit
or was attested to by experts.[98] Largely as a result of this concern, John
Mensah Sarbah had "reduced into writing the Customary Laws and usages
of the Fanti, Asanti, and other Akan inhabitants of the Gold Coast."[99] The
number of other works that followed on customary law and indigenous
political systems in the early part of the twentieth century by himself and

others demonstrated how important this issue was, and the critical role that African barristers played in the codification of customary law in general.[100]

Also, in contrast to both the judiciary and the executive, they wanted to see a formal role for "natives" of "good character and intelligence" in assisting the chiefs in the dispensation of justice.[101] Apart from acting as an "incentive to the rising generation," they saw this as a way of improving the admittedly often poor quality of justice in chiefly courts. It was their vision of "molding the customs of the country to the general principles of British law," and an updated expression of the Western-educated elite's desire to be an important participant in the unfolding colonial order. Both the expense and the opportunity this would have given African lawyers to have the run of the chiefly courts ensured that the suggestion would not receive official favor. If there was anything that both the judiciary and the executive were agreed on, it was that all lawyers should be excluded from the chiefly courts so as to keep the cost of justice in them as cheap as possible.

Indicative of how deep the divisions were between the colony's executive and the judiciary, the governor resorted to amending aspects of the Native Jurisdiction Bill of 1883 so that every clause of the new bill would not be open to discussion.[102] The most important of these amendments was the extension of chiefly courts to the entire colony. The bill also defined the jurisdiction of native courts, established the fees and fines that they could charge, provided machinery for enforcing their judgments and made it obligatory that these courts would keep a written record of their judgments. More controversial was the procedure for appeal, which was to lie with the district commissioner's court rather than with the divisional courts which African lawyers would have preferred.[103] Most controversial, however, was the power the bill gave to the governor to "suspend for a stated time, or [to] depose any chief, who shall appear to him to have abused his power, or be unworthy, or incapable of exercising the same justly."[104] John Mensah Sarbah and Hutton Mills managed to get the original word "dismiss" replaced with "depose," but even so the bill was a fundamental challenge to the chiefs' position that their power was inherent and not derived from the authority of the Crown.[105]

Nevertheless, the attractiveness of government recognition was a powerful incentive for chiefs to seek inclusion under the terms of the new Native Jurisdiction Bill. Neither did the government resort to its powers of "destoolment"; instead, as contested destoolments and enstoolments became more frequent, it sought to resolve these disputes by conducting "inquires." However, in deference to the prerogatives of the judiciary, the secretary of native affairs who conducted these investigations had no legal machinery to enforce his findings, and they resulted in being little more followed in destoolments and who the government should recognize.

Robert Stone has characterized this phase of indirect rule in the Gold Coast as "non-interventionist" in scope.[106] The central government was primarily interested in the smooth functioning of the traditional state's judicial machinery and the resolution of disputes, but little else. Like the original bill of 1883, the amended 1910 ordinance gave chiefs the power to make bylaws that would promote "the peace, good order, and welfare of the people of [their] division."[107] Up until 1927, however, when indirect rule became much more interventionist and designed to incorporate the chiefly order into the machinery of colonial government, there was never any significant exercise of this power to make bylaws.[108] In contrast, however, to the Northern Nigerian Emirates, where noninterventionist indirect rule tended to produce political homeostasis, in the southern Gold Coast it served to stimulate an even more intense competition for traditional office.[109] This was hardly what administrators had anticipated, and their response was an ever more interventionist policy to create the elusive political stability that they sought.[110]

Municipal Government for the "Detribalized" Coast

Noninterventionist indirect rule was part of a larger policy of creating separate and distinct spheres of political activity for what the colonial government felt were radically different sections of colonial society which ironically contributed to the political instability in the colony. While this reevaluation of the chief's position in colonial society was going on, the government was also introducing an even more controversial system of municipal government for the colony's major coastal towns. The aim behind this policy was to create Western-style institutions for what the colonial government came to consider the largely "detribalized and even denationalized" coastal population.[111] In spite of the concessions to chiefs in such communities, the central government felt that there should be different political arenas for those they felt belonged to Westernized as opposed to traditional society. Undoubtedly there had developed major differences between these sections of colonial society, which were symbolized by the contrast between the coastal towns and the interior. The boundaries, however, between these hypothetical poles of colonial society, even in the towns, were far more blurred than colonial administrators were willing to recognize. Ironically, the struggle that developed to control municipal politics served to bring them even more together.

The first Draft Municipal Ordinance, published in 1888, offered Africans an elected majority, but in exchange for this the municipality was to finance its activities out of local taxation.[112] It was enough to doom any voluntary acceptance of this ordinance, and not until 1894 did the government attempt once again to pass a Town Councils Bill. On this occasion it more realistically recognized that local property taxes would not be enough to enable these councils to discharge all of their many responsibilities, and there would have to be some subvention from the general revenue. Greater financial dependence inevitably meant less political power for African elected members, which anyway coincided with the increasing distrust of educated Africans holding senior positions in government. The new bill gave the official members a majority, which ensured that this proposed municipality would be even less popular than its predecessor. As a result, when the government finally established a town council in Accra in 1898, it was in the face of considerable opposition.

There was, however, an underlying tension between the better classes and the traditional order that publicly came to light when, to prevent the government from seizing King Taki Tawia's houses, the town's three most important barristers paid his tax. A mob actually threatened Quartey-Papafio when this became known, and one of Taki's war captains, Charles Kwamin, tried to challenge this tax payment in the district commissioner's court.[113] The larger significance of this conflict was that it indicated how different the attitudes of the coastal intelligentsia and the chiefly order were to the existence of a town council. In principle the better classes supported the idea. In 1887 their counterparts in Cape Coast had held local elections at the time of Kojo Mbra's enstoolment as part of their own "humble effort to train up [their] people in the art of self-government."[114] Even earlier, in 1865 and 1854, they had elected mayors and sought to introduce municipal government in the town. These institutions had soon won the enmity of the chiefs, who saw them as competitors for judicial authority and claimants for dwindling sources of local revenue.

It was hardly surprising that to a chief like King Taki Tawia, whose "power had practically disappeared," an official town council represented yet another challenge to what little authority he still possessed.[115] Significantly, when the government finally did decide to appoint African members to the Town Council, one of the appointees was Kojo Ababio IV of James Town (Nleshi), who had taken no part in the boisterous opposition to the collection of house taxes in 1897.[116] Two years later, when the first council's legislative term expired, the government continued with this attempt to diffuse chiefly antagonism to the Town Council by appointing Chief John Vanderpuije, who was a hereditary chief of Ussher Town.[117] He had been a successful trader in Ada who on his return to Accra had been elected in 1888 by members of his *we,* or lineage, to succeed his father as *wetse.* He had been able to take "advantage of both new trading opportunities and established family status to rise to a position of wealth and authority."[118] Like many of such chiefs, he was literate and "lived comfortably in European style."[119] To European officials he represented progressive African opinion that could be expected to support their initiatives.

In 1904, when the government applied the bill to Sekondi, there was a noticeably less-spirited opposition to this ordinance partly because the native order was bitterly divided at that time. Conflict over the distribution of monies that the government had paid for the compulsory acquisition of land for new harbor works, a railroad terminal, government bungalows and building sites for the European firms that had moved to Sekondi as it had become the center of the mining boom in the Western Province resulted in the destoolment of Chief Kwau Johnfia in 1903.[120] He had refused to surrender the stool paraphernalia and accept his destoolment. His family had retained the barrister P. Awooner Renner and the case had gone to the Divisional Court, where Johnfia's opponents had won.[121] Like many of these cases that were to become a regular feature in the political affairs of coastal communities as urban lands became more valuable, this decision had not resolved the dispute, and two factions had emerged that competed bitterly with one another to enstool their candidate as the town's *ohene*.

Consequently, most of the opposition to the bill came from the town's Western-educated Africans who, in contrast to their counterparts in Accra and Cape Coast, were often not originally from Sekondi.[122] In general the links that existed between this community and the illiterate classes were weaker, and as a reflection of this much of the protest against the bill was actually directed from Cape Coast.[123] Sekondi, which had only very recently emerged from being an unimportant coastal town, lacked a history of opposition to colonial policies. It meant that the tensions between the better classes and the chiefly order were far less developed than they were in Accra or Cape Coast, but at the same time there was little experience in opposing unpopular colonial policies. As a graphic indication of how different this town was, when elections were finally held for the four unofficial positions on the Town Council in 1905, four Europeans were returned unopposed.

Hardly surprisingly, it was in Cape Coast, with the longest history of opposition to colonial polices, where implementing the Town Councils Bill proved most contentious. Not until 1906 did the government seek to apply it to this town. Compounding the hostility to direct taxation was the sense of betrayal that Cape Coasters harbored towards the colonial government as a result of the recent downturn in the town's fortunes. At the turn of the century Cape Coast had experienced boom conditions as a result of the expansion of the colony's gold mining and logging industries. However, railway construction from Sekondi and Accra into the interior affected Cape Coast disastrously. In 1901 the town officially had a population of 28,948, but ten years later this had dramatically declined to 11,269.[124] Shipping had also decreased, many of the major European firms had relocated to Sekondi, and there were even rumors that the government was about to close the town as a port.[125]

Nevertheless, in spite of the shared feeling of betrayal on the part of the colonial government, in a similar fashion to Accra, there was a strong undercurrent of tension between the town's "intelligentsia," as they had come to describe themselves, and the traditional elite that stemmed from their basically different attitudes to the existence of a town council. In principle the intelligentsia welcomed the opportunity to participate in local government. To them the objectionable aspects of the Town Council Bill were the "hated house tax" and official domination of the council. They felt that the council should be funded from a government grant, and only later, when it was well established and had demonstrated its effectiveness, should the government introduce local taxation.[126] The Freetown Municipal Council (established in 1893), which had both an African mayor and an African majority, was an example of what they thought should obtain in the Gold Coast.[127]

On the other hand there was no position on the Town Council for representatives of the native order. John Mensah Sarbah had tried to resolve this threat to the *omanhen*'s authority by suggesting that he should be an ex officio member, and also that work services be accepted in lieu of taxes for those who lacked means. This latter suggestion would have served the double purpose of also involving the *asafos* in the affairs of the Town Council, and would have provided an alternative to the "hated house tax." The government, however, considered these suggestions unworkable. The difficulty that the provincial commissioner experienced in getting the town's *asafos* to drain the evil-smelling Fosu Lagoon on the western outskirts of Cape Coast was one good reason for opposing this suggestion. From the government's perspective, the town councils were designed to move the large towns away from such inefficient voluntary arrangements that had the added disadvantage of providing an occasion for inter-*asafo* rioting.[128]

With so much general opposition to the bill, it was hardly surprising that initially the GCARPS worked closely with Kojo Mbra as they had during the Lands Bill protest. The possibility, however, for friction existed especially since there was also substantial disunity among the intelligentsia themselves. A younger, more radical segment of the GCARPS had already been agitating for more action on the society's part, and was critical of the way in which it seemed to be resting on its laurels.[129] The Reverend Egyir Asaam, who had left the *Gold Coast Methodist Times* in 1897 to be the editor of the GCARPS's newly established newspaper, the *Gold Coast Aborigine,* had fallen out with the society over the issue of editorial freedom, and sometime around 1902 he had gotten together with J. P. H. Brown to establish another newspaper, the *Gold Coast Leader.*[130] Also, the situation offered a more calculating individual like *Tufuhen* Coker an opportunity to strengthen his position in the town by claiming that he was "representing the whole companys [sic]

Cape Coast from Lighthouse Hill, 1997. The town has changed relatively little: the castle is on the coast, beside it to the west is Christ Church (1865; Anglican), in the center is Wesley Chapel (1837; Methodist) and directly to the west is the old District and Provincial Commissioner's Office. Author's photograph.

in the town, and [that] nobody else was to speak for the companys."[131]

When it became obvious that the government was going to apply this bill to Cape Coast in 1906, it was the Egyir Asaam faction that took the initiative in opposing it, and Reverend Asaam himself went to Britain to protest to the king.[132] Soon, however, there was friction over who should actually address the government. By 1906 the disagreement over this was serious enough to require outside arbitration and the Union Club of Axim was called in.[133] The club decided in favor of the *omanhen* and levied a fine on the society. The tension, however, continued as Kojo Mbra refused to allow the GCARPS to see correspondence between himself and his solicitors in London.[134] It continued after Reverend Asaam returned, as the secretary of the society was soon complaining to Kojo Mbra that "though Asaam had been in the town for more than a week, he had not deigned to communicate with the Society."[135]

By this time it was obvious that it was only a matter of time before the bill was going to come into force in Cape Coast, but apparently to enhance his standing in the town vis-à-vis his GCARPS opponents, the *omanhen* announced that he had been able to have the bill repealed. At this point the division between Kojo Mbra and the GCARPS became even more hostile as the society's president, E. J. P. Brown, irately warned him "not to arrogate to himself the representation of the country...[and demanded that] he should place his expressed loyalty beyond question."[136] In contrast, the society was able to point to a number of achievements on its part in getting the government to compromise on some of the more objectionable features of the bill. On account of the "depressed condition" of the town, the government agreed to consider lowering the original 5 percent assessment on houses to 3 percent, and also appointed a popular African physician, Dr. R. A. Savage, as the Town Council's medical officer of health.[137]

In 1905 the government had tried to provide an even larger measure of African participation by trying to appoint two local Africans to official positions. They had tried to win the *omanhen*'s permission, but after they had been "attacked" by the townspeople they had declined.[138] A year later, when the alliance between the *omanhen* and the GCARPS was no longer functioning, Dr. Savage obviously felt that he was free to accept a position on the Town Council as its health officer. However, feelings were still far too high in the town for any Africans to stand for election. Nor did the four Africans the governor "nominated" take their seats on the council, and for the first two years of its existence it was indeed little more than a government department.[139]

Even as an arm of government it worked imperfectly, for its members had no real authority to act on important issues. All of its major decisions had to be referred to the provincial commissioner, who was the senior political officer in the town.[140] It also lacked legislative power and the means of enforcing whatever regulations it actually passed. The decline in the town's economy, which was most severe around 1906, placed serious limitations on its attempts at generating revenue, and instead the government had to subsidize it so that it could carry out even the modest tasks that the Public Works Department and the Sanitary Committee had taken care of before.

In general, this was the predicament that all of the colony's town councils found themselves in. They were underfinanced, lacked authority and were hardly training Africans in self-government. In 1908 the Cape Coast council became somewhat more representative of African interests when, to counter the threat that "certain whitemen" were going to run for its four unofficial seats, and on account of the "neglected condition into which the town had sunk," the GCARPS "delegated" four of its members to stand for election.[141] Clearly the society still held out some hopes for transforming this organization into something that represented African aspirations. They were to be frustrated once again, however, as public health issues determined that these organizations did not become truly representative municipalities, but remained little more than an arm of colonial government.

An outbreak of plague in Accra in January 1908 caused enough of a scare to stir all of the colony's town councils into heightened activity exterminating rodents, erecting quarantine stations and preventing the movement of people into and out of the affected area. To remedy this, as soon as the scare was over the government amended the Town Council Bill to make the provincial commissioner president of the council. To the Cape Coast intelligentsia this came as a serious disappointment since it obviously strengthened the official presence on this body. The editor of the *Gold Coast Leader* suggested that "the government should make the necessary sanitary improvements in the town and then the responsibility for maintaining them should be handed over to the Town Council."[142] Once again, the Freetown Municipal Council with its elected African majority and its African mayor was the model after which he thought the Cape Coast Town Council should be patterned.

Instead, official representation on the town councils in the Gold Coast increased, and once again public health issues were responsible. In 1910 there was a serious outbreak of yellow fever that took the lives of ten Europeans and two Africans in Sekondi.[143] The metropolitan government was so disturbed by this that they sent Sir Rupert Boyce, the leading British expert on the disease, to advise on preventative measures.[144] Of critical importance to the future of the town councils, he maintained that the *Aedes aegypti* mosquito, the carrier of the yellow fever virus, was a "domestic mosquito," in contrast to the *Anopheles*, the carrier of the malaria protozoa. It bred in household water containers and in improperly disposed garbage, so that unlike the Anopheles, which bred in a much wider variety of places and anyway ranged further afield, it was possible to think in terms of eradicating the *A. aegypti* in the large towns where Europeans, the most vulnerable population, were concentrated.[145]

It seemed possible to achieve this by imposing stricter controls on urban sanitation, and the town councils were the obvious agencies to undertake this job. To make them more capable of this task they were once again reorganized. The most important change was to make the medical officer of health a government appointee, and the council lost the power of appointing its own health officer.[146] In contrast to the merely advisory position of his predecessor, he was to be a full voting member. He was in charge of the council's expanded staff of sanitary inspectors and workers. Finally, the government introduced a system of tests to determine the "mosquito levels" in the urban areas.[147] It was the medical officer's responsibility to make sure that they were carried out regularly and accurately.

In the climate of fear that the 1910 yellow fever outbreak created, the medical officer dictated a great deal of the town council's activities. In Cape Coast, for example, the first appointee, Dr. F. Berringer, who replaced Dr. Savage, was particularly zealous, and rapidly tried to enforce a strict adherence to the regulations governing water storage that the town council passed. According to the *Gold Coast Leader,* he had "become the uncrowned king of Cape Coast."[148] There were complaints in the press over what were described as "the rude and unfeeling manner in which his sanitary inspectors entered people's homes, broke their water jars suspected of being mosquito breeding sources, poured kerosene into drinking wells and even cut down banana trees that were suspect also."[149] The unofficial members of the town council tried to prevent this, but their protests were invariably overruled by the officials who were in the majority.[150]

Not surprisingly, with the government so radically undermining their conception of how the town council should function, the GCARPS decided in 1912 to protest by refusing to contest the elections scheduled for that year in Cape Coast.[151] Two years later, after the society had staged an elaborate reconciliation dinner with the new Governor, Sir Hugh Clifford, they were optimistic enough about his conciliatory attitude towards the society to renew their interest in the town council, which resulted in the first contested election.[152] Their optimism, however, was short-lived. Closely allied with public health was the question of regulating building construction and eliminating congestion, and this concern soon began to dominate the town council's activities once again to the detriment of African aspirations. The public works engineer, who had always been a voting member of the council, began to rival in importance the medical officer, as his permission was necessary before any building permits could be issued. It meant that by the end of the second decade of the council's life, African councillors found themselves challenging (with little success) unpopular decisions.

It was impossible for the African councillors to hide their disappointment with how the council functioned and their role in its affairs. According to E. J. P. Brown, the most important African councillor on the Cape Coast body, "the duty of the councilors was simply to meet monthly for the purpose of passing vouchers and other warrants for payments to the laborers and staff."[153] Indeed, the way in which the Town Council had evolved created a major dilemma for the upper echelons of the Western-educated elite. They had almost no influence in framing its policy. All they could do was ineffectually oppose its most unpopular decisions. However, at the same time they did not feel that they could boycott this institution and acquire the reputation of being noncooperators. This fear was particularly acute in Cape Coast, where it seemed that the town's reputation for opposition to government policy was already vindictively held against it when it came to expenditure on improvements.[154] It was a dilemma that was to precipitate yet another split within the ranks of coastal society. As I shall show, it came to separate those who continued to favor cooperation and those who came to be known as the noncooperators.

At the same time the unpopularity of these councils did put an end to the struggle between the chiefly order and the intelligentsia over who should control African representation on them. *Asafoatse* C. B. Nettey, who was the representative of the Ga *mantse* in Accra, was the last to hold such a position, and from 1911 onward, when his term expired, no other traditional officeholders were to sit on a town council until George Moore won election to the Cape Coast Town Council in 1938.[155] The foreignness as much as the unpopularity of these institutions ensured that only professionals and the most Western-educated of African merchants felt capable of challenging the colonial officials who conducted the council's affairs. It meant that the lower echelons of the educated classes, people who were usually referred to as "scholars," were also effectively excluded from participation in the affairs of the town councils. As a result, even in Cape Coast, the colony's educational center, "the proceedings of the council were a mystery" to the public.[156]

Governor Rodger's conception of how "the government of native races should be carried out" had been based on his assumption that the colony's population could be divided into three separate and distinct classes: the uneducated, the educated and the chiefly order.[157] Ironically, rather then helping to demarcate the political boundaries between these sections of colonial society, as the governor expected, the elite-dominated town councils had the unanticipated effect of sending increasing numbers of the scholars the colony's schools were producing out into the chiefly order to satisfy their political ambitions. One indication of this was the flood of destoolments and succession disputes that came to characterize affairs in the chiefly order by the second decade of the twentieth century. It was especially so in the coastal communities where the power of traditional rulers had suffered most and scholars were most numerous.

The competition on the part of a relatively small number of Western-educated Africans to control chiefly courts in the nineteenth century expanded dramatically in the early twentieth century to include those who in the past would have turned their backs on such positions. The Accra barrister A. B. Quartey-Papafio, in discussing this earlier period, had pointed out that due to there then being "practically no source of revenue left to native authorities...[there had been great] difficulty getting men to occupy the stools of their ancestors."[158] By the end of the second decade of the twentieth century, when the native order had become an officially recognized component of colonial administration, this distaste for enstoolment had been superseded by an entirely different mood. Instead, as an editorial in the Accra newspaper, *Gold Coast Independent* described it:

> As soon as a stool was empty contending parties disturbed the peace for possession, moving heaven and earth to assist and accelerate their claims...even if [they were] secondary in consideration...[and making] a show of their own unfitness.[159]

What was particularly significant about this competition to hold traditional office was the number of "educated" men who were contenders. In eulogizing *Tufuhen* Coker on the occasion of his death in 1932, the *Gold Coast Independent* described him as "about the first [among the educated classes] to identify himself thoroughly with native administration." He had done so at a time when educated or Christianized "eligibles" for chiefly positions had

> turned their backs on their rightful heritage and fled as if for their lives from their native town or states when vacancies occurred on stools, rather than assume or succeed to the dignities of such positions.[160]

The increasingly important native order would no doubt have attracted scholars even if municipal institutions had offered them more opportunity for participation. Neither could they all be absorbed, as was much more easily the case in the nineteenth century, into positions in government or mercantile employment. Clearly, however, the special advantage of the weak and unstable native order was that it offered these newcomers unparalleled opportunities to manipulate and exploit its often ill-defined and highly flexible customary practices to their own advantage.

The often bitter and enduring struggles that followed imparted a highly parochial quality to the political affairs of these coastal communities. Robert Stone has described this as the politics of "transactional factionalism."[161] It involved groups that could be as small as sections of extended families or as large as the residents of wards or quarters in a town. Primarily "materialistic transactional" considerations linked members of these factions together, rather than a common ideology. They struggled to control tribunal revenue, money from the renting or sale of stool lands, tolls from ferries or fishing beach usage, the possession of permits for purchasing gunpowder which was an integral part of local celebrations, and as symbolic of their right to do this, the stools, paraphernalia and *ahenfies* of chiefly office.[162] In the following chapter I shall give examples of how this developed in a number of the colony's coastal communities.

Notes

1. "Memorandum on Native Prisons," enclosed in his father's (governor of the colony) dispatch to the Secretary of State, 7 April 1888, CO 96/191, PRO.

2. Chief Justice Sir David Chalmers to Governor Freeling, included in the Governor's dispatch to the Secretary of State, 10 April 1877, CO 96/120, PRO.

3. Kimble, *A Political History of Ghana*, 460-461. This was Governor H. T. Ussher (1879-1880).

4. In 1889 the government applied it to one more "head chief," but by 1909 it had been extended to over forty. Kimble, *A Political History of Ghana*, 462. The bill, by referring to paramount rulers as "Head Chiefs" rather than as "Kings," reduced them in importance, and not so subtly indicated that their authority was derivative (from the British Crown) rather than inherent.

5. *The Native Jurisdiction Ordinance*. Cited in G. E. Metcalfe, *Great Britain and Ghana: Documents of Ghana History, 1807-1957* (London, 1964), 390.

6. The Chief Justice to the Colonial Secretary, in the Governor's dispatch to the Secretary of State, 7 November 1883, CO 96/153, PRO.

7. William Brandford Griffith to the Secretary of State, 7 April 1888, CO 96/190, PRO.

8. Minute by H. M. Hull, 6 February 1890, ADM 11/1/1086, NAG, Accra, cited in Parker, "Ga State and Society," 210.

9. It should be noted that at that time the British prisons were hardly models of penal progressiveness. For example, in December of 1883 C. H. Bartels, a former African district commissioner who had been convicted of embezzlement six months before, died under scandalous circumstances in the James Fort prison in Accra. Governor Rowe to the Secretary of State, 7 December 1883, CO 96/153, PRO. Prison conditions were so bad in the colony that officials recognized that Europeans were not likely to survive even a short period of

imprisonment and the policy was to send such felons to the metropole. Governor Rowe to the Secretary of State, 25 May 1882, CO 96/149, PRO.

10. *Bruce v. Quamin Fori,* c.1881. Cited in *Oppon v. Ackinie,* 24 October 1887. In Sarbah, *Fanti Customary Laws,* 236.

11. Cited in *Oppon v. Ackinie,* 24 October 1887. Sarbah, *Fanti Customary Laws,* 233.

12. Ibid., 237.

13. Cited in William Brandford Griffith, "The Status of Native Courts in the Gold Coast Colony," *Journal of the Society of Comparative Legislation* 9, no. 1 (1908):172.

14. "Report of the Commission appointed by the Governor on the Ist of August 1894, to enquire into various matters relating to Native Courts." Enclosed in the Governor's dispatch to the Secretary of State, 15 April 1896, CO 96/272, PRO.

15. Ibid.

16. Ibid. There was one dissenting voice. The colonial secretary, A. Sharood, held to the older opinion "that no king or chief should be allowed to exercise any jurisdiction in a town where a district commissioner held court."

17. He forwarded the commission's report to the secretary of state.

18. Sir William Maxwell had entered the service of the Straits government in 1865. He had served in various capacities until becoming governor in 1893. Obituary for Governor William Maxwell, *Times,* 14 December 1897.

19. Governor Maxwell to the Secretary of State, 14 December 1895, CO 96/263, PRO.

20. Governor Maxwell to the Secretary of State, 15 April 1896, CO 96/272, PRO.

21. Ibid.

22. Ibid. The governor even hoped that as a result of this new arrangement the colony would be able to do away with the Police Force. In general, he felt that there was "too much reliance on the Departmental idea" in the colony.

23. Ibid.

24. He divided the chiefs of the colony and the protectorate into three classes by order of importance: 1. *omanhin,* or ruler of country; 2. *ohin,* or ruler of a district; 3. *safuhin,* war chiefs, chiefs of towns.

25. *Gold Coast Aborigines,* 4 June 1898.

26. District Commissioner of Cape Coast's report, 1 October 1896. Enclosed in the Governor's dispatch to the Secretary of State, 16 January 1897, CO 96/288, PRO.

27. *Gold Coast Aborigines,* 9 April 1898.

28. Governor Maxwell to the Secretary of State, 9 June 1897, CO 96/294, PRO.

29. He died at sea on 14 December 1897. He was on his way back to England for leave. It should be noted that Governor Maxwell did not use the term indirect rule. Instead, he was critical of what he felt was the "over centralization" of the

colony's government which, he felt, depended too much on the "department idea."

30. Administrator Colonel Harley had deported King Kobina Gyan to Sierra Leone in 1873 during the period of warfare with the Asante that followed the sale of the Dutch castles and forts to the British. Crooks, *Records,* 411.

31. The District Commissioner to the Colonial Secretary, 30 January 1896, Elmina Native Affairs, ADM 11/1/1111, NAG, Accra.

32. Governor Maxwell to the Secretary of State, 28 April 1896, CO 96/275, PRO.

33. Case in the District Commissioner's Court, 30 November 1896, SNA 11/1108, NAG, Accra.

34. Kojo Mbra was unable to pay the fine and had "his hair clipped, and made to don prison clothes." J. E. Casely Hayford, *Gold Coast Native Institutions* (London, 1903), 260.

35. Case in the Cape Coast Divisional Court, 1 March 1897, SNA 11/1108, NAG, Accra. The stool family retained one of the leading Accra barristers, T. Hutton-Mills, to conduct the appeal, but it was the young Casely Hayford who actually conducted the appeal. Casely Hayford, *Gold Coast Native Institutions,* 285-287.

36. Telegram from the Governor, 14 May 1897, SNA 11/1109, NAG, Accra.

37. Colonial Secretary to the District Commissioner of Cape Coast, 7 October 1898, SNA 11/1109, NAG, Accra.

38. Ibid.

39. There was no love lost between Eminsang and Gyan. According to the district commissioner, it was well known in Elmina that the bullet that had hit and killed the Dutch officer in 1873 at the time of the town's transfer had been intended for Eminsang, and had been fired "with the secret knowledge and approval of the King." District Commissioner of Elmina to the Colonial Secretary, 5 July 1895, ADM 11/1/1111, NAG, Accra.

40. Kobina Gyan died first on 12 March 1896, George Eminsang next on 17 April and Quacoe Andoh sometime in 1898 or early 1899. Gyan's supporters accused Andoh of having murdered (poisoned?) Gyan, and they even hired a Cape Coast lawyer, G. H. Savage, to bring an action against Andoh. There was insufficient evidence to prove this charge. District Commissioner to the Colonial Secretary, 27 July 1896, ADM 11/1/1111, NAG, Accra.

41. District Commissioner to the Colonial Secretary, 4 January 1899, ADM 11/1/1111, NAG, Accra.

42. *Gold Coast Leader,* 10 July 1915.

43. Ibid.

44. Nana Ankwandah III's private manuscript of the stool history of Winneba. Cited in Hagan, "Aspects of Social Change Among the Effutu," 303-304.

45. District Record Book—Winneba Classification No. 25/5/2, NAG, Accra. Cited in Hagan, "Aspects of Social Change Among the Effutu," 315.

46. The Colonial Secretary's minute on the notes of a meeting between King Taki Tawia and the Governor, 21 October 1892, ADM 11/1086, NAG, Accra.

47. Parker, "Ga State and Society," 314.

48. *Gold Coast Independent,* 25 December 1928.

49. Obituary for Kojo Ababio IV, *Gold Coast Independent,* 30 April 1938. King Taki Tawia was actually prosecuted in the district commissioner's court for failure to supply carriers, but the decision in the Cape Coast Divisional Court came at this time and indicated that the government was unlikely to be successful in securing a conviction.

50. The Governor to the Secretary of State, 4 July 1898, CO 96/310, PRO. He refused to take his seat along with the two other Africans who had been nominated. The town council was far too unpopular in Accra for any African to have associated himself with it then. See Kimble, *A Political History of Ghana,* 418-426.

51. District Commissioner to the Colonial Secretary, 12 January 1895, SNA 11/1108, NAG, Accra.

52. Cape Coast Native Tribunal Records, 16 January 1911, ADM 71/1/1/1, NAG, Cape Coast. When the government finally recognized chiefly courts in the coastal towns, "Native Tribunals" was the name that was given to them to distinguish them from courts in the interior that initially were not affected by this legislation. This nomenclature also served to distinguish these courts from those of the British Supreme Court. Anthony K. Mensah-Brown, "The Traditional Courts and Their Successors in Ghana's Legal History, 1800-1914" (Ph.D. diss., University of London, 1970), 365.

53. For a detailed treatment of this protest see Kimble, *A Political History of Ghana,* 330-356.

54. *Gold Coast Aborigines,* 22 April 1899.

55. For example, the case of an "attempted seduction in Kojo Mbra's prison" (The District Commissioner to the Colonial Secretary, 15 October 1897, SNA 11/1108, NAG, Accra), and the "Case Involving King Tackie's Prison," in which a woman was kept without food for three days (The Colonial Secretary to the District Commissioner, 29 January 1890, ADM 1089, NAG, Accra). Such cases often also involved sexual misconduct.

56. This practice consisted of a "person in embarrassed circumstances" who wanted "to obtain a loan" doing so by placing "one or more of his family or slaves in temporary bondage to another." Sarbah, *Fanti Customary Laws,* 10. Antislavery organizations saw it as little different from slavery.

57. Raymond E. Dumett and Marion Johnson, "Britain and the Suppression of Slavery in the Gold Coast Colony, Ashanti, and the Northern Territories," in *The End of Slavery in Africa,* ed. Susan Miers and Richard Roberts (Madison, Wis., 1988), 94.

58. Ibid.

59. Ibid., 95.

60. Sarbah, *Fanti Customary Laws,* 85.

61. The Cape Coast Paramount Chief's Tribunal, 10 September 1909 to January 1931, ADM 71/1/1/17, NAG, Cape Coast.

62. *Gold Coast Leader,* 7 March 1903.

63. Terence J. Johnson, "Protest, Tradition and Change: An Analysis of Southern Gold Coast Riots, 1890-1920," *Economy and Society* 1, no. 2 (May 1972):167.

64. A. B. Ellis, *The Tshi Speaking Peoples of the Gold Coast of West Africa* (London, 1887), 280. This was hardly a departure from "the original scheme." For example, there were times in the eighteenth century when the *asafos* in Elmina were a source of constant disruptive behavior. See Feinberg, *Africans and Europeans in West Africa,* 108. Ellis spent six of the eight years that he stayed in the Gold Coast as a major with the First West India Regiment. For a discussion of his "Africanist credentials" see Ray G. Jenkins, "Confrontations with A. B. Ellis, a Participant in the Scramble for Gold Coast Africana, 1874-1894," *Paideuma* 33 (1987):313-335.

65. Two years later there were several letters to the editor of the London-based monthly *African Times* about this affair: 20 January, 1 February, 24 March and 1 June 1886. Prince Attah was probably too young to succeed to the stool before this time.

66. Governor W. Brandford Griffith to the Acting Colonial Secretary, 19 January 1887, Elmina Native Affairs, ADM 11/1/1111, NAG, Accra

67. Interview with John Anquandah, Elmina historian, 3 December 1988. He was supposed to have been a generous distributor of gold dust to help pay for funerals. It is not clear where this wealth came from. According to my informant, he "had a big mouth, and could persuade people to follow him." Andoh clearly must have made money from his labor-contracting operations, and perhaps "wealth" followed rather then preceded his rise in Elmina.

68. District Commissioner to the Colonial Secretary, 23 February 1906, ADM 1089, NAG, Accra.

69. Announcement from the Colonial Secretary, 18 July 1902, ADM 1089, NAG, Accra.

70. Letter from J. Vanderpuye to the Secretary of Native Affairs, n.d. (1903-1904?), ADM 1089, NAG, Accra.

71. Letter in his support from the Chief Justice, 16 November 1906, ADM 1089, NAG, Accra. At this point he was "blind and deserted by his people." The Legislative Council awarded him eighteen pounds as a gratuity for his services to the government.

72. Hagan, "Aspects of Social Change Among the Effutu of Winneba," 75.

73. Governor Hodgson to the Secretary of State, 21 April 1898, CO 96/314, PRO.

74. *Gold Coast Aborigines,* 16 July 1898.

75. Arthur ffoulkes, "The Company System in Cape Coast Castle," *Journal of the African Society* 7, no. 27 (April 1908):270.

76. The figures he cites for the numbers of riots in the southern Gold Coast from 1890 to 1929 are: 1890-1899—18, 1900-1909—52, 1910-1919—44, 1920-1929—12. Johnson, "Protest, Tradition and Change," 166.

77. *Gold Coast Leader*, 12-22 April 1916.

78. Cruickshank, *Eighteen Years on the Gold Coast of Africa*, 1:245-251. On the other hand, J. Barbot, in writing about the coast in the 1730s, describes young men who were then known as the *manceroes*, and seem to have been the counterparts to the *asafobii* of colonial times as having the "greatest sway" in matters concerning the whole state. J. Barbot, "Description of the Coast of North and South Guinea," in A. Churchill, *A Collection of Voyages and Travels* (London, 1732), 5:299. Cited in A. K. Datta and R. Porter, "The *Asafo* System in Historical Perspective: An Inquiry into the Origin and Development of a Ghanaian Institution," *Journal of African History* 12, no. 2 (1971):289.

79. J. C. de Graft Johnson, "The Fanti *Asafu*," *Africa* 5, no. 3 (July 1932):317.

80. For a description of this affair see, Johnson, "Protest, Tradition and Change," 186-187.

81. See Metcalfe, *Great Britain and Ghana*, 521-525.

82. Governor Rodger to the Secretary of State, 16 December 1904, CO 96/421, PRO. Kwamina Faibiu had come into conflict with the district commissioner over clearing the roads in his district. He had created a disturbance in the district commissioner's court and had been fined, but he refused to pay and had been arrested. It was this history of noncooperation that led to the government removing him from his chiefly position.

83. Ibid.

84. Kimble, *A Political History of Ghana*, 467.

85. Governor Nathan to the Secretary of State, 6 February 1904, CO 96/416, PRO.

86. Report by the GCARPS on titles to the Governor, 18 December 1903, CO 96/416, PRO.

87. There was still a great deal of variation in the spelling of these terms and "correct" Akan orthography continues to be contested.

88. The Governor to the Secretary of State, 2 February 1904, CO 96/416, PRO.

89. The Colonial Secretary to the Governor, 19 September 1892, ADM 11/1/1086, NAG, Accra.

90. First report of the Native Affairs Department, 1903. Enclosed in the Governor's dispatch to the Secretary of State, 27 April 1904, CO 96/417, PRO.

91. Ibid.

92. Sir Matthew Nathan, on the other hand, had come from Sierra Leone, where he had been administrator from 1899 to 1900. Before that he had been the secretary of the Colonial Defense Committee, having risen to that position after a career in the British army. Obituary, *Times* (London), 19 April 1939.

93. Governor Rodger to the Secretary of State, 7 June 1904, CO 96/418, PRO.

94. Secretary of State to Governor Rodger, 27 July 1905, CO 96/421, PRO.

95. The term "indirect rule" was not officially used in the Gold Coast until the governorship of Sir Ransford Slater (1927-1932).

96. Governor Rodger to the Secretary of State, A Report on the Native Affairs Department, 27 April 1904, CO 96/417, PRO.

97. Governor Rodger to the Secretary of State, 28 November 1904, CO 96/420, PRO.

98. For a discussion of this issue see Crabbe, *John Mensah Sarbah, 1864-1910*, 55-58.

99. Sarbah, *Fanti Customary Laws*, ix.

100. J. M. Sarbah's other important works were *Fanti Law Reports* (1904) and *Fanti National Constitution* (1906). In addition there was J. E. Casely Hayford's *Gold Coast Native Institutions* (1903) and A. B. Quartey-Papafio's "Law of Succession Among the Akras or the Ga Tribes Proper of the Gold Coast," *Journal of the African Society* 10, no. 27 (October 1910):65-72, and "The Native Tribunals of the Akras of the Gold Coast," parts 1 and 2, *Journal of the African Society* 10 (1910-1911):320-330, 434-446; 11 (1911-1912):75-94.

101. J. P. Brown, President of the GCARPS, to the Governor, 18 December 1903, CO 96/416, PRO.

102. Ironically, it was some of the chief justice's last important decisions that helped pave the way for the passage of new native jurisdiction legislation. In the cases of *Mutchi v. Kobina Annan, Kobina Inketsia* and *Mutchi v. Kudu* in 1907 he had ruled that the Annexation and Extension Orders in Council of 1901 had not abolished the jurisdiction of native courts in the Gold Coast. For the full text of these judgments see Brandford Griffith, "The Status of Native Courts in the Gold Coast Colony," 167-179. It was hardly surprising that his seemingly contradictory opposition to native jurisdiction became less and less influential.

103. This was not surprising since they were technically barred from appearing before the district commissioner's court.

104. *An Ordinance to Facilitate and Regulate the Exercise of Certain Powers and Jurisdiction by Native Authorities*, chapter 29.

105. Legislative Council Minutes, 2 and 4 July 1910. Cited in Kimble, *A Political History of Ghana*, 469. John Mensah Sarbah and T. Hutton Mills were then the African members of the Legislative Council.

106. Stone, "Colonial Administration and Rural Politics in South Central Ghana," 1. He takes this terminology from Michael Crowder, *West Africa under Colonial Rule* (Evanston, Ill., 1968), 217-221.

107. *The Native Jurisdiction Ordinance* (Accra, 1910), chapter 5.

108. As Crowder has pointed out, "The importance of the chief as a source of by-laws was a negative one: he could not introduce laws that the administration might feel necessary, but which would be unpopular with his people. No provision was made in such circumstances for the administration to enact by-laws as they felt desirable but which chiefs would not pass." *West Africa under Colonial Rule,* 222.

109. According to Crowder, in Northern Nigeria there was "little motive for innovation and little outside interference." Ibid., 219.

110. Stone, "Colonial Administration and Rural Politics in South Central Ghana," 2. This was to become most pronounced in the 1930s and 1940s when the Lugardian theory of indirect rule was adopted by Gold Coast administrators, particularly Governor Sir Ransford Slater.

111. The belief that a large part of the coastal population was "detribalized and even denationalized" was given currency by the Parliamentary undersecretary of state for the colonies, the Honorable W. G. A. Ormsby-Gore, M.P., after his visit to the Gold Coast in 1926. *Report by the Hon. W. G. A. Ormsby-Gore, M. P. on His Visit to West Africa During the Year 1926* (London, 1926). There was heated objection to this assertion in the Gold Coast press. For example, see the *Gold Coast Independent,* 28 August 1926 and the *Gold Coast Leader,* 2 October 1926.

112. The most extensive history of municipal government in the colony is to be found in Kimble's *A Political History of Ghana,* 360-361, 418-426.

113. Governor Hodgson to the Secretary of State, 4 July 1898, CO 96/318, PRO.

114. Letter from F. C. Grant and others to Administrator White, 18 May 1887. Enclosed in the Governor's dispatch to the Secretary of State, 5 July 1887, CO 96/182, PRO.

115. This was how Governor Nathan described King Taki Tawia shortly before his death in 1902. The Governor's confidential dispatch to the Secretary of State, 10 March 1901, ADM 11/1086, NAG, Accra.

116. Governor Hodgson to the Secretary of State, 4 July 1898, CO 96/318, PRO.

117. Chief John Vanderpuije was also one of the African members on the Legislative Council. The government had appointed him to this position in 1894.

118. Parker, "Ga State and Society," 193.

119. Kimble, *A Political History of Ghana,* 428.

120. Chief Johnfia to the Colonial Secretary, 21 February 1903, Sekondi Native Affairs, SNA 11/1131, NAG, Accra.

121. Petition to the Governor from those opposed to Chief Johnfia, 16 September 1904, SNA 11/1131, NAG, Accra.

122. Peter Awooner Renner was originally from Sierra Leone and had moved from Cape Coast in the early 1880s, but he had been attracted to Sekondi after it became one of the locations of the Concessions Court. Interview with his son,

P. C. F. Renner, Cape Coast, 13 July 1974. J. E. Casely Hayford had also established himself in the Western Province, with Sekondi as one of his bases of operation.

123. There was a Sekondi Town Committee that did send a formal protest to the governor. Town Councils file, 23 September 1904, 118/1965, NAG, Cape Coast. Significantly, however, there was no local section of the GCARPS as there was in nearby Axim, the other center of the concessions business in the Western Province.

124. Census reports, 1901 and 1910. Cited in Kimble, *A Political History of Ghana,* 144.

125. *Gold Coast Leader,* 7-14 February 1903. In 1900 thirty-six ships called at Cape Coast, but in 1904 there were only nine. *Gold Coast Colony Blue Book,* 1900 and 1904.

126. Letter from the *Oman* of Cape Coast to Governor Rodger, 1 November 1904, GCARPS file, "Town Councils, 1904-1921," 118/65, NAG, Cape Coast. Sarbah summarizes these demands in *Fanti National Constitution,* 150.

127. The reply of the Acting Governor to the *Omanhen* of Cape Coast, 16 December 1905. Cited in *Cape Coast Municipal Council, 1906-1956* (Cape Coast, 1957), 7.

128. In passing through one another's territories to get to the sites of such public works, the *asafos* would have to pass through one another's quarters and this could easily lead to fighting. The Provincial Commissioner to Kojo Mbra, 21 October 1904, ADM 21/1/1, NAG, Cape Coast.

129. For example, they wanted the society to take up the controversial issue of Christian marriage. *Gold Coast Aborigines,* 18 January 1902.

130. Obituary for J. P. H. Brown, *Gold Coast Leader,* 6-13 December 1919.

131. Governor Rodger to the Secretary of State, 23 July 1906, CO 96/444, PRO.

132. According to the *Gold Coast Leader,* 17 March 1905, "The *Omanhen* had gotten tired of waiting for the GCARPS to do something." The secretary of state granted Asaam an interview, but he won no concessions.

133. This club was really the Axim branch of the GCARPS.

134. Letter from the Secretary of the GCARPS to the *Omanhen* of Cape Coast, 1 February 1906, GCARPS file "Town Councils," 1965/118, NAG, Cape Coast.

135. Ibid. According to the provincial commissioner, when he left for England he did so without consulting with the society and did not leave with their consent. The Provincial Commissioner to the Colonial Secretary, 28 April 1906, ADM 23/1/1, NAG, Cape Coast.

136. Letter from the President of the GCARPS to Kojo Mbra, 7 February 1906, GCARPS file, "Town Councils, 1904-1921," 1965/118, NAG, Cape Coast.

137. He replaced the European who had initially held this position. Dr. Savage was one of the younger members of the GCARPS and originally from Nigeria. As far as the assessment was concerned, the rates remained at 5 percent. Not until 1910, when the economic condition of the town was as its worst, did the Town Council agree to lower the house rates to 3 percent. B. Pachai, "An Outline History of Municipal Government at Cape Coast," *Transactions of the Historical Society of Ghana* 8 (1965):143.

138. The Provincial Commissioner to the Colonial Secretary, 23 November 1905, ADM 23/1/1108, NAG, Cape Coast. They consisted of C. A. Barnes, a local surveyor who was to be the council's consulting engineer, and Dr. E. J. Hayford, a popular local doctor, who was to be the consulting medical officer.

139. Significantly, the government had also tried to diffuse the *omanhen's* antagonism to the council by nominating a chief as one of its nonofficial members. The nominees were: E. J. P. Brown and J. M. Sarbah (both barristers), Chief John Sackey and W. J. Hooper, who was an *asafo* representative. When they failed to take their seats, the Town Council's membership consisted of the district commissioner, its president, the European officer in charge of public works in the town, another European official and J. L. Minnow, who was the African comptroller of customs in Cape Coast.

140. In 1904 the government divided the colony into enlarged divisions which were called provinces. Initially there were two of them: the Eastern Province and the Western Province. Their administrative centers were Accra and Cape Coast. The chief administrative officer was the provincial commissioner, who was in charge of the district commissioners, who in turn administered the various districts that made up an individual province.

141. They were E. J. P. Brown, the society's president and the town's senior barrister, T. F. E. Jones, J. D. Abrahams and J. W. de Graft Johnson, merchants. "The Upcoming Town Council Election," *Gold Coast Leader*, 5-12 March 1910. This editorial contained a brief history of the body.

142. *Gold Coast Leader,* 20 March 1909.

143. There were also a few deaths in other areas of the colony. See the "Outbreak of Yellow Fever" file, ADM 5/3/14, NAG, Cape Coast.

144. *Gold Coast Leader,* 11 June 1910.

145. See Dr. Duff's report to the League of Nations Regional Health Conference, "A Note on Yellow Fever Control in the Gold Coast and the Present Situation," Cape Town, November 1932, ADM 23/1/632, NAG, Cape Coast.

146. The government tried to make this more appealing by paying this new official's salary and saving the council this expense. Pachai, "An Outline History of Municipal Government at Cape Coast," 142.

147. Ibid.

148. *Gold Coast Leader,* 10 July 1910.

149. Ibid.

150. *Gold Coast Leader,* 11 June 1910.

151. Instead, the government resorted to "nominating" the outgoing members to a further two years. This compromise was enough to ensure that there would be African representation. *The Cape Coast Municipal Council, 1906-1956*, 7.

152. Six candidates stood for four positions, and only one incumbent, E. J. P. Brown, was reelected. The newcomers were G. H. Savage, a barrister from Nigeria and Dr. R. Savage's brother, G. Amissah, a local merchant, and W. S. Johnston, who was the secretary of the GCARPS. Ibid.

153. Town Council meeting, 11 July 1917. Cited in Pachai, "An Outline History of Municipal Government at Cape Coast," 146.

154. For example, the editor of the *Gold Coast Leader* complained in 1914 that the government intended to spend £390,000 on Sekondi and a "paltry" £4,000 on Cape Coast. *Gold Coast Leader*, 13 February 1913.

155. At this time Moore claimed to be the *tufuhen* of Cape Coast, but he was bitterly opposed by a large section of what was then referred to as the native state. I will discuss this in greater detail in chapter 7.

156. *Gold Coast Leader*, 15-22 April 1916.

157. Sir John Pickersgill Rodger, "The Gold Coast Today," *Journal of the African Society* 9, no. 33 (October 1909):16. This is the text of an address that he delivered before the society on 1 July 1909.

158. Quartey-Papafio, "The Native Tribunals of the Akras of the Gold Coast," 87.

159. *Gold Coast Independent*, 27 July 1918.

160. "Obituary for the Late Chief W. Z. Coker, *Tufuhene* of Ogwaa," *Gold Coast Independent*, 23 April 1932.

161. Stone, "Colonial Administration and Rural Politics in South Central Ghana," 42-46. He takes this terminology from F. G. Bailey, *Stratagems and Spoils: A Social Anthropology of Politics* (Oxford, 1969), 38-42, 76-79.

162. The *ahenfie* was the chief's "palace." Given the poverty of most coastal stools, few of these buildings were particularly palatial.

Chapter 6

Competition for Traditional Office

The enhanced status that indirect rule imparted to the native order rapidly precipitated competition for traditional office from a new generation of the educated elite. In contrast to their predecessors in the late nineteenth century, who had usually been wealthy merchants, these newcomers were financially less successful. One of the best indications of this in Accra was the career of Christopher Benjamin Nettey, who claimed that he had been "proclaimed" captain in the Gbese quarter in 1866, after the death of his father, but did not "perform as *Asafoatse*" until the Asante Expedition of 1895-1896, when he provided carriers for the government.[1] In 1903 he went to England, like a number of enterprising Africans, to sell gold mining concessions. To enhance his credibility he had claimed that he was a "Chief in the Gbese quarter." The secretary of state had sought to verify this by seeking confirmation from Accra, but on making inquiries in Accra the colonial government had been told that Nettey had no standing in traditional society and was a "nobody."[2] This humiliating revelation effectively "spoiled" Nettey's business endeavors.[3]

On his return to the Gold Coast, he quickly sought a recognized position in the native order, and in 1907, when he was forty-two years old, he was formally installed as a "senior *Asafoatse* of Gbese quarter."[4] In court testimony he provided in 1928, he maintained that he had inherited this position patrilineally from his father, who had inherited his position from his maternal uncle. He argued that "the sword in [his] house

C. B. Nettey in his thirties. Source: S. T. Nettey (son).

[could go] both ways," but the defensiveness with which he maintained this position seemed to indicate that his claim to his traditional position was less than convincing. Apart from owning fishing canoes, Nettey also had inherited slaves and cocoa lands from his father up-country in the Asamangkese division, and sometime after his formal installation he was conducting a Native Tribunal for Ga farmers in this region. There were fees involved, and Nettey came into conflict with Kojo Ababio IV, the James Town *mantse,* over the distribution of this money and seems to have been fined for his activities.[5] Later on he was in conflict with *Mantse* Taki Obili of Ussher Town over much the same issue, which eventually became so serious that in conjunction with others who opposed Taki Obili's sale of stool lands in Accra, Nettey was able to engineer the *mantse*'s destoolment in 1918.[6]

Similarly attracted to a position in the Accra native order was the retired trader James Robert Meyers, who beginning in 1910 waged a long and bitter struggle to control the Akanmaji stool.[7] Like Nettey, he had been educated at the Wesleyan Methodist school in Accra. For a while he had been a tailor, but eventually he had gone to Old Calabar as a "trader" and had stayed for many years in Nigeria.[8] When he returned to Accra, he claimed that he had been the Akanmaji stool's custodian ever since its last occupant had died in 1879, but "as a Wesleyan could not carry out sacrifices" and had not been enstooled himself.[9] In 1915 he was able to win the Divisional Court's agreement that he was indeed the caretaker of the Akanmaji stool. But like many of these judicial decisions, it turned out be an ambiguous victory, since the court did not rule on whether he was entitled to enstool anyone.[10] To make matters even worse, the Full Court reversed the lower court's judgment and the struggle was still going on when Meyers died in 1922. Once again, control of a Native Tribunal's revenues was at the heart of this dispute, with Meyer's rival claiming that his opponent was "chopping all" this courts's money.[11]

The decentralized nature of the Accra political system ensured that there would also be bitter disputes between the many different quarters that made up the traditional state. Which stools the government would recognize as under the Native Jurisdiction Bill of 1910, and the concomitant prize of a recognized Native Tribunal and a prison, was guaranteed to heighten tensions, more so since it was a relatively arbitrary decision, as the Native Jurisdiction Bill did not make a distinction between chiefs. One indication of this were struggles over juridical jurisdiction as different Native Tribunals competed with one another to try the same cases. There were also bitter struggles to prevent enstoolments of subordinate chiefs that would result in the strengthening of one stool quarter relative to its rivals. In 1911 the government tried to bring some order to this chaos by finally applying the Native Jurisdiction Bill to Accra, but rather than producing order it promoted even more intense struggles on the part of those quarters that the bill did not grant recognized courts. It was the highly parochial quality of these struggles that contributed so much to preserving what John Parker has described as "the existing configuration of 'traditional' Ga Politics," even as Accra, the colony's capital, was going through important economic and demographic changes in the twentieth century.[12] Ironically, as land became more valuable, courtroom struggles to assert traditional authority and the closely related issue of control over land became the most visible indications of just how contested the structure of the native order had become.[13]

The situation in Cape Coast during the first decade of non-interventionist indirect rule was significantly different. With the important exception of W. Z. Coker, there were no other really well-educated members of the intelligentsia who sought traditional office as directly as he had done. Other members of this elite did hold traditional positions. John Mensah Sarbah, for example, had been installed as a *safuhen* in his father's *asafo* in Anomabu in 1898.[14] In contrast, however, to Coker, his position was clearly more ceremonial than active since Anomabu was twelve miles away from Cape Coast, where he lived.[15] Joseph Peter Brown, who was one of the African members of the Legislative Council from 1904 to 1909, was the leader of Number Six *Asafo* (Akrampa). His involvement in the day-to-day affairs of the Cape Coast traditional order was much more extensive as the leader of this *asafo*, but significantly this was the "mulatto company," which was also known as the Cape Coast Volunteers and was least like a traditional *asafo*. He did not have to participate in "heathen customs," which as a pillar of the local Methodist Church he would have been loathe to do.

In general the Cape Coast native order was much more attenuated than its Accra counterpart, which made it possible for one powerful personality like Coker to control its most important operations. He effectively dominated the affairs of the one Native Tribunal in the town which the government did not officially recognize until 1916. Rather than competing with their counterparts from other quarters, which was the case in Accra, the few important chiefs and *asafo* leaders in the town were members of this body. As a result there were no other chiefly tribunals to control which might have attracted the interest of other members of the intelligentsia. Neither was the government acquiring land for public purposes, as was the case in Accra. Indeed, ever since the opening of the railway line from Sekondi, first to Tarkwa in 1901 and then to Obuasi in 1903, there had been a spectacular decline in Cape Coast's fortunes, so that rather than land being in demand by either the government or the firms there had been an exodus of commerce from the town. Instead, the only really significant challenge to the status quo in the native order came from the underlying tensions in the town between the Brempong Kojo and the Aggrey stool families and their associated followers, whose rivalry to control the paramount stool of Cape Coast extended back to the eighteenth century. However, in contrast to the Accra native order, nearly all these potential challengers were illiterate and could offer only limited opposition to the wily *tufuhen*.

This was graphically evident after Kojo Mbra died in 1911. Immediately there were disputes between the various branches of the two stool families, the Aggrey and the Ebiradzi (Brempong Kojo's family) families, as well as the bodyguard sections of these families, over the choice of a successor.[16] The Aggrey faction wanted to return to patrilineal succession, and they got the support of a section of Number Four *Asafo*, Nkum, which in the past had been the *gyase* (bodyguard) for the Aggrey family stool holder. Kojo Mbra's bodyguard, however, actually had the stool and other paraphernalia in their possession, and when they disagreed with the Ebiradzi family's choice, there was then a faction within a faction. The *wirempe*, as they were called, were in a position to prevent the installment of a successor, and for over four years this tangled affair continued. These predominantly transactional disputes, superimposed upon a struggle over different succession principles, indicated just how fragmented and factious the Cape Coast native order was. There were no lack of political opportunities for enterprising "scholars" to exploit, as they were later on to realize.

Initially, however, Coker's control over the native order hardly suffered. Along with his right-hand man, Chief Sackey, who acted as regent for the state, he remained firmly in control of the tribunal. Finally, when the secretary of native affairs conducted an inquiry in Cape Coast in 1916, it was Coker's candidate whom the government approved as the legitimate successor. F. S. Bilson, who became Mbra II, was a grandnephew of the previous *omanhen*, which served to establish firmly the matrilineal principle in Cape Coast. In contrast to his predecessor, neither educational attainments nor character suitability seem to have been decisive factors, as there were clearly candidates from the Aggrey family who seem to have been similarly qualified. According to Coker, they "had decided that the descent should be in the female family line."[17]

This enstoolment can be seen as representing the final triumph of the long process of Fante/Akan political acculturation that had been going on in this originally Effutu area. Francis Crowther, the secretary of native affairs, who conducted a similar stool succession dispute in Winneba three years before, had noticed a corresponding process in that town where the original Effutu culture was much better preserved than in Cape Coast. Particularly in the latter case, he felt that the type of government that had evolved had been profoundly affected by the "Fanti element in the town [which had]...influenced all other native constitutions it had come in contact with."[18] It was a process that obviously linked both political and social practice, for it coincided with the increasing importance of the

matrilineage even among the intelligentsia. Legal legislation had unwittingly strengthened the position of the latter, while increasingly
interventionist indirect rule directed at producing a homogeneous native
order was to facilitate even further the spread of a political and
institutional culture dominated by Akan ideals.

The enstoolment was also important in that it did begin to stimulate an
increased interest in the affairs of the traditional order on the part of the
town's scholar class. The new *omanhen* was an important indication of
this. Nana Mbra II, unlike his predecessor, Kojo Mbra, was semiliterate
and obviously much more determined to control the affairs of the native
state.[19] His first concern was to exercise more control over the Native
Tribunal, whose revenue he wanted to use to discharge some of the
personal debts he had accumulated from his activities as a trader in his
private life before.[20] Not surprisingly, he rapidly came into conflict with
Coker, who was the main beneficiary of this revenue, which amounted to
some fifty to seventy pounds a month.[21] With so much money at stake it
was hardly surprising that the *tufuhen* was soon threatening the dissatisfied
omanhen with destoolment.

In addition, Mbra II further jeopardized his position by not attending
a durbar of the colony's chiefs that the GCARPS had convened in Cape
Coast in 1916. The main purpose of this gathering was to obtain a vote
from the colony's chiefs against Governor Clifford's plans to appoint an
omanhen from each province of the colony to the Legislative Council.
This addition to the ranks of the council's unofficial membership was part
of the governor's intention to make the "tribal system" part of the natural
machinery of administration.[22] When he had taken up the governorship of
the Gold Coast in 1913, he had been shocked at the minor role Africans
in general played in the administration of their own country. His
experience in Ceylon as colonial secretary (1907-1912), and as the British
resident in Penang (1896-1903), had made him an enthusiastic advocate of
indirect rule, and in addition to giving chiefs more representation on his
expanded Legislative Council, he also planned fundamental changes in the
1910 Native Jurisdiction Bill.[23]

It was clear enough to Mbra II, and to a number of his coastal counterparts, that the governor was determined to strengthen and upgrade the
position of chiefs in the colony and that they would benefit. As a result,
not only did the *omanhen* absent himself from the society's durbar, but he
also did not sign the society's petition protesting what it considered the
"unconstitutionality of chiefs sitting on the Legislative Council."[24] The
society's president, E. J. P. Brown, was furious and warned him "not to
meddle in the affairs of the Aborigines."[25] In contrast to his predecessor,
Kojo Mbra, who had sided with the GCARPS in 1897 and received crucial
support from them in his struggle with Coker, Mbra II was clearly trying
to strike out on his own by angling for one of the three appointments that

the government was offering to chiefs.[26] It was most unlikely that the government would have appointed someone as young and as untested as himself, and instead he was soon faced with a formidable array of opponents who wanted to get rid of him for different reasons.

The ease with which he was finally destooled, a scant ten months after his enstoolment, was an indication of how many people in Cape Coast benefited from the status quo that he had threatened to upset. Nevertheless, the importance of the native order, and particularly the tribunal, had inevitably begun to attract the attention of those who were not part of its arrangements, and who, like Mbra II, resented the way in which it functioned. Undoubtedly the most important representative of this trend was J. P. H. Brown, the editor of the *Gold Coast Leader*.[27] Initially, when Coker set in motion the process for destooling Mbra II, Brown maintained that he "held no brief for either side."[28] However, he had been critical of the GCARPS, whose old guard were deeply involved in Mbra II's destoolment. Whether or not he was indeed nonpartisan, as he claimed, is moot, since he had shortly before challenged the society over the issue of chiefly participation on the Legislative Council. Instead, he had argued that the "chiefs" were "quite capable of putting forward themselves," and that he was "not able to recognize the right of any body to set themselves up as spokesmen or controllers of the chiefs."[29]

With such strong feelings about the rights of chiefs, it was perhaps not surprising that he rapidly passed from being supposedly neutral to castigating Coker and his "entourage" for this "most disgraceful and wicked affair."[30] He quickly realized that the main issue was control of the tribunal's revenue, and accused Coker of "having his hands too deeply in the pie."[31] Mbra II's destoolment, he maintained, was neither unanimous nor in accordance with customary practice, and he sought to rally support among the *asafos* and Mbra II's illiterate family members. Even together, however, they were no match for the determined *tufuhen*. They hoped that they could draw the secretary of native affairs into yet another enquiry, but here they failed. The provincial commissioner, before whom the matter came, was less than satisfied with how the tribunal functioned, but nevertheless he accepted the wishes of the "majority," who in reality were the most articulate, and without further investigation he recommended to the secretary of native affairs that Mbra II's destoolment be accepted.[32]

Coker, on the other hand, felt so secure in his position that shortly afterward he left Cape Coast with a contingent of Gold Coast troops to serve in the East African campaign of the First World War. Chief Sackey was once again appointed regent, and it seemed as though little had changed. Indeed, when Coker returned to Cape Coast as a war hero in 1918, he felt that he could take advantage of his increased stature and tried to have himself enstooled as the town's *omanhen!* J .P. H. Brown, on this occasion, realized that more than an exposé of how "the handsome revenue which the Native Tribunal generated ended up in Coker's control" was necessary if he was going to effectively challenge the crafty *tufuhen*.[33] Instead, he tried to undermine Coker's support among the *asafos* by "reorganizing" a traditional body known as the *Ogua Basafu*. This organization was to consist of three members from each of the town's seven *asafos,* and with such a "strong representative body," Brown felt that the "treacherous practices that had been infesting the town could be checked."[34]

His commitment, however, to *asafo* politics was still ambiguous and unrealistic, as his response to an outburst of violent *asafo* rioting in the nearby town of Anomabu indicated. Most unsympathetically, he had called upon the government to "prosecute the rioters for murder" and impracticably suggested that "to have the companies serve a more useful purpose...[they should] be merged with the Boy Scouts."[35] Coker's advantage over such rivals was that he had a much more realistic understanding of the native order, but nevertheless he was still not able to realize his goal of becoming the town's *omanhen*. Undoubtedly the main reason for this lay in the increasing participation in the native order by other members of the intelligentsia. Brown had noticed this shortly after he had "reorganized" the *Ogua Basafu,* and had remarked in his paper on the numbers of new "self-made chiefs," as he described them, that were appearing in Cape Coast at that time.[36]

Among the first of these newcomers to the native order was Sam E. Amissah, who in 1918 announced that he had been "placed on the stool of his ancestors."[37] Amissah, like Brown, was a "standard seven boy" who had gone into carpentry and then trading on leaving school. His predecessor, Chief J. B. Hagan, had died in 1905, and it was not until thirteen years later that the family was able to enstool his nephew, Samuel Emmanuel Amissah, as his successor.[38] Initially it had been difficult to get Amissah to accept this position, since he was loath to "occupy the stool since he was a Methodist." [39] As indirect rule became better established, he obviously got over his religious scruples, and he turned his attention away from his trading activities to "chiefly affairs."[40] Less than a year later Kwamina Tandoh, a peripatetic entrepreneur who had spent twenty years of his life in Europe and the United States, followed Amissah's example. He "allowed himself to be installed as Chief Kofi Amoah III on his family's ancestral stool."[41] The position had been vacant since 1910, and we can speculate that Tandoh, like Nettey in Accra, had also come to appreciate the advantages of chiefly status to promote his business deals abroad.[42] As an indication of the increasing importance of traditional office, the family rapidly asserted their stool's importance, claiming that Amoah III was the *ohen* of Cape Coast. He was the chief who carried the "foot of the state" and was second only in importance to the *omanhen* "who carried the head."[43] To J. P. H. Brown

> it was a welcome sight that a member of the educated classes of the Gold Coast, who had been so successful in his remarkable business enterprises, should demonstrate that people like himself formed an integral and substantial part of the Gold Coast body politic.[44]

Positions in the Cape Coast chiefly order had never been the monopoly of any particular "aristocratic" group, and neither were educated classes able to dominate its ranks at this time. Apart from these enstoolments, other chiefs began to appear on the Cape Coast scene who had not been mentioned previously in government correspondence or in the local newspapers. We can assume that some were part of the proliferation of self-made chiefs that Brown had referred to. For example, shortly after Chief Sackey died in 1920, the *Gold Coast Leader* mentioned that Chiefs Tutu Dadzie and Kweku Arhin, along with J. P. Brown and W. Z. Coker, had been "fumbling" among the deceased regent's papers for documents referring to tribunal money "lying" in the Bank of British West Africa.[45] Neither seemed to have sat as members on the Native Tribunal, even though its membership seemed to have been increasing.[46] Both chiefs were illiterate, but in general there was a significant difference between these newcomers to the native order and similarly illiterate chiefs in the past.[47] They were not willing to be faceless people who Coker could manipulate. If they themselves were not literate, they could get advisers who were, and with such help they enhanced their visibility by communicating with the colonial government.

The competition for native office in Cape Coast was still not as intense as it was in Accra, but nevertheless it was indicative of how much it was changing that Coker's attempt to become the town's *omanhen* failed dismally. Instead, when Regent Sackey died in 1920, a number of the prominent members of the GCARPS were instrumental in selecting G. A. Mends, a brother of Kojo Mbra, to be enstooled as Mbra III. Like Bilson, he, too, was educated. Before his enstoolment, he had been employed as a primary school teacher in the nearby town of Saltpond.[48] Coker's unchallenged role as *omanhen*-maker had been eclipsed, though he was still able to continue as the tribunal's recorder. He was also lucky that his arch opponent, J. P. H. Brown, had died suddenly shortly before in 1919.[49] The new editor (Kwamina Sakyiama) of the *Gold Coast Leader* also continued to attack Coker and the operation of the tribunal, but lacked Brown's acerbity, and anyway more important events were unfolding in Cape Coast that took the spotlight from Coker and the Native Tribunal.[50]

In nearby Elmina the competition for traditional office that indirect rule stimulated was from much earlier more heated than in Cape Coast or even Accra. The native order was distinctly better preserved than in Cape Coast, while in contrast to decentralized Accra all the action was focused on one paramount position and its Native Tribunal. Secondly, more of the town's scholars were from a much earlier period attracted to positions in the ranks of this section of their society. Elmina offered such people a much more limited range of political or social options than either Cape Coast or Accra. Also, the social distance between Elmina's scholars and traditional officeholders was smaller. In addition, the recent past played a more critical role in effecting the development of indirect rule politics. In 1873, when the British had finally taken possession of all the remaining Dutch forts and castles on the coast, the educated classes, primarily represented by Eminsang, had been much more willing to come to terms with the new colonial order than the "illiterates," who had sided with Kobina Gyan.[51] Even after the British deported Gyan, this hostility had remained, and Gyan's return in 1894 rekindled a smoldering antagonism that was to influence Elmina's political life in the early twentieth century.

The continual turnover in paramount rulers that the town went through in the first two decades of the twentieth century was the most obvious indication of this unrest. Between Gyan's death in 1896 and 1918, when factional disputes became so intense that it was impossible to enstool any *omanhen*, the paramount stool changed hands four times. Three of these stool holders were scholars. Significantly, however, their tenure on the stool was brief. Kobina Condua II, who followed Kobina Gyan, lasted only three years (1896-1899); Barend Annan, who was really only a regent, served in this position for two years (1912-1914); while Kodwo Condua III, perhaps the best educated of these "scholar" *amanhin*, did no better than his predecessor, spending only three years on the stool (1915-1918).[52] In contrast, the one illiterate *omanhen* of this period, Kwesi Mensah, spent nine years on the stool (1903-1912), but he too was finally destooled, ironically, primarily at the instigation of his literate councillors.[53]

Influencing this disparity in the length of enstoolments were the relative sizes, importance and interests of the scholar faction as opposed to the fishermen who comprised the main support for the illiterates.[54] The latter dominated the town's *asafos* and were by far the larger faction numerically. Their interests were often diametrically opposed to those of the scholars. Apart from the typical struggles to control the revenue of the Native Tribunal for personal benefit, there were also more principled differences of opinion between these factions as to how the state's revenue should be used. For example, the scholars wanted to use some of this money to build a new courthouse, as well as an appropriate residence for the *omanhen*.[55] Politically they wanted to support the GCARPS' campaign against the government's Forest Bill, while later on during the First World War they were in favor of African recruitment for service in East Africa.[56] Most of these "progressive" ideals required money which, given the nature of the town's economy, could really only come from taxing the fishing community. Along with monopolizing the income of the Native Tribunal, and selling stool lands privately, it was attempts to raise revenue from the fishing community that contributed to the downfall of scholar *amanhin* who were most predisposed to introduce such taxation.

In addition, there were disputes over the use of purse-type fishing nets (the Ali net), the use of Christian versus traditional symbols in enstool-ment ceremonies (the Bible versus salt) and the use of English instead of Fante in the proceedings of the town's Native Tribunal. The disputants tended to divide along "scholar" and "illiterate" lines, and an attempt to navigate between the Scylla of scholar concerns and the Charybdis of *asafo* interests made any *omanhen* vulnerable. This was what happened to the scholar *omanhen*, Condua III, who, according to his opponents, in July 1918 finally "bent to the weight of popular opinion to go."[57] Neither did the brief show of unity between the town's factions which resulted in the selection of an illiterate carpenter as regent last long. By this time there were too many scholars who realized that there were opportunities for them on both sides. Chief C. R. Cathline, who was in many respects Elmina's counterpart to Coker and Nettey, sought to control the "regent."[58] His main opponent was another scholar, J. C. Smith, who tried to promote himself as the town's regent.[59] Finally both factions ended up enstooling their own *amanhin*. The Cathline faction enstooled their regent as Ntakudzi II, and the Smith faction reenstooled the ex-*omanhen* as Condua III.

By the 1930s, as the dispute dragged on, it was clear that neither faction was "exclusively composed of the element popularly assigned to it."[60] The commissioner of the Central Province was to observe that "each [faction had] a sprinkling of adherents from either category (scholars and illiterates)," though he still felt that the overwhelming majority of the two factions (95 percent) did consist of the adherents publicly associated with them.[61] More importantly, it was the scholar element in both factions who provided the leadership. The signatures on the plethora of petitions, memoranda and letters that passed between the two factions and the government's political officers indicate in graphic fashion how important scholars were in both camps. On the other hand, by looking at these long compilations of signatures and "X's," it is fairly clear that there were more scholars in the Condua faction than among the Ntakudzi supporters.

A number of these scholars had taken advantage of *asafo* links to advance themselves into the native order. This was so particularly for scholars who belonged to Akrampa Asafo, the mulatto *asafo*, which contributed to undermining the once dominant role that the prominent *asafos,* like Enyampa and Wombir, had enjoyed in Elmina's affairs.[62] At least as important in affecting the balance of power in the native order was the overall expansion of what came to be known as the *Oman,* or State Council. In the nineteenth century these councillors had consisted primarily of the *Besonfu,* which had expanded to fourteen in the mid-nineteenth century. By 1928, however, there were twenty-eight people who were involved in drawing up the state's first written constitution, and who considered themselves its councillors.[63] Neither were these all the people who felt that they were part of the State Council. According to the district commissioner, the constitution indicated that there were altogether fifty-nine members of this body!

Reflective of this development, the far more inclusive Akan term *Oman* became the accepted terminology in Elmina for describing those who participated in the affairs of state. Significantly, it included the *Besonfu,* which made up only a small portion of its membership. As was happening in many of the coastal towns, where the traditional state had a long history of being "confused and perplexed," Elmina was also incorporating aspects of state organization from the more structured inland Akan kingdoms. The use of the term *Oman* was one indication of this. Equally indicative of Akanization, the town's main chiefs began styling themselves divisional chiefs, which was another borrowing from the inland states where such chiefs actually presided over large territories. One of Ntakudzi's main supporters was Kweku Ewusi, who was the *ohen* of a small outlying village of Simew, but who came to be known as the *adontehen,* or also somewhat less pretentiously as the *simiwhen.* In a similar fashion, Cathline's right-hand man, Herbert Krakrue, another scholar, styled himself the *besonhen*—which, according to his opponents, was only indicative of his membership in "a private society and not part of any state creation."[64]

The Condua faction also had its scholar divisional chiefs. J. Chas Garhin was the *nifahin,* and also the *supi* of Number Nine *Asafo* (Maworefo), while Alfred Mensah was the *futursanyi* and *Oman* treasurer. Whether or not these titles were innovations is very hard to determine, but what does seem likely from a comparison with other coastal communities was that what may have existed as little more than family headships, or as a local chieftaincy, were enhanced by these more impressive-sounding titles.[65] It was clearly a way for those who in the past would have had little status vis-à-vis the important *asafo* leaders to acquire equality in the affairs of the state. Linked to this emergence of divisional chiefs was the increase in the number of outlying villages that were part of the Elmina state. In 1866 there were around sixteen that were considered to be part of the state, but in 1928 this number had increased to twenty-five.[66] These villages came to be important components of the various divisions that made up the state, and as the struggle to control its institutions increased winning their support was crucial. As an indication of how much larger the Elmina political world had become, by the 1920s it was publicly referred to as the Edina State, which encompassed a significantly larger area than the town alone.

As indirect rule developed there was competition from other towns that wanted to establish jurisdictional control over Edina's outlying villages to enhance the earnings of their native tribunals. Such struggles increased the importance of even relatively insignificant "bush" villages, and added an urban-rural dimension to the already chaotic affairs of the larger coastal towns. This kind of tension had been evident in Elmina from as early as 1908, when a struggle developed with Eguafo (ten miles northwest of Elmina) to exercise jurisdiction over the inland village of Berase and the coastal fishing villages of Ampeni, Brainu, Ankinim and Dutch Komenda.[67] In contrast to Effutu, which had been almost completely overwhelmed by Cape Coast, Eguafo had survived even the turmoil of the Asante invasions of the nineteenth century, and indirect rule gave Kofi Eutra, its *omanhen,* the opportunity to pursue in a substantially different manner the age-old struggle for supremacy between the original inland capital and its far more successful coastal offshoot.

At this time, however, the provincial commissioner was less than sympathetic to Kofi Eutra's claims since the latter had shortly before been charged "with having sex with one of his female debtors in his prison."[68] Even without this blot on his record, it would have been extremely unlikely for officialdom to have recognized what in effect would have been the extension of Eguafo's authority into an area where a district commissioner had his court. Berase, finally, ended up under the control of neither Elmina nor Eguafo, but as part of the paramountcy of Abrem. With hindsight we can see that the long-term significance of such struggles transcended immediate jurisdictional questions. Instead, the more important result of this close connection between town and countryside was that it facilitated the continuing penetration of Akan ideas into coastal towns like Elmina that possessed a political culture that was atypical of Akan communities.

Apart from borrowed terminology and titles, one of the best indications of this political acculturation was the attempt to replace patrilineal succession to the paramount stool of Elmina with the more typical Akan system of matrilineal succession. As early as 1915, seven of the ten *asafos* had petitioned the government in favor of abandoning patrilineal succession in favor of matrilineal because under the former system all *amanhen* were chosen from Enyampa *Asafo* (Number Seven).[69] Nothing had come of this suggestion at that time, but the district commissioner's suggestion in 1928 that the two factions put aside their candidates and select one that was mutually acceptable gave the proponents of matrilineal succession another opportunity to build support for matriliny. There was still, however, an overwhelming majority in the town against such a change, and nothing was resolved. In the early 1940s, when the stool succession dispute in Elmina had become linked to colony-wide opposition to interventionist indirect rule policies, the advocates of matrilineal succession gained sufficient ground to launch a major attempt to win the town to their position.[70] Significantly, their main leader was Chief Kweku Ewusi, the *adontehen* of Elmina, and the *ohen* of the outlying village of Simew.

As an indication of just how contentious this struggle became and how much seemed to be at stake, Kweku Ewusi and four of his supporters were eventually charged with a brutal "ritual murder" of a ten-year-old girl whose body parts were supposedly used "to make juju" to help them win a forgery case in which they were defendants. According to their opponents, the five had forged the names of those they claimed supported a switch in the town's succession for its paramount chief from patrilineal to matrilineal succession, and in 1945 a case against the latter was pending before the District Magistrate's Court in Swedru.[71] According to the prosecution the five had resorted to murdering the ten-year-old girl to make "medicine" with her body parts to ensure that they would win this forgery case.

The Bridge House murder, as it came to be known (after the name of the house where it was committed), was one of the most bizarre examples of how contentious stool politics could become in the Gold Coast. The case was concurrent with the far more celebrated Kibi murder case that followed the death of Nana Sir Ofori Attah, the *okyenhene* of Akyem Abuakwa, and to Sir Alan Burns, the colony's governor, they were an indication that "in spite of centuries of contact with European ideas, in spite of the spread of Christianity and the high standard of education reached by some of the people of the Gold Coast...[one could still] find in the Colony the grossest forms of superstition and savagery."[72] Not surprisingly, the colonial courts found the five accused guilty, and in contrast to the Kibi murder case they quickly exhausted their appeal options. Less than a year after the murder was committed, they were all hanged.[73]

The impact of indirect rule on Winneba was similar in many respects to Accra, Cape Coast and Elmina, but was complicated by the much more lively struggle between Akan and Effutu political systems than was the case elsewhere. In the early part of the twentieth century the town underwent only modest growth, and like Elmina there were relatively few political outlets for its scholar class.[74] As an indication of this, in 1904 a number of them formed a Town Scholars Association, and in keeping with the increasing interest in the Native Tribunals, they had applied unsuccessfully to the district commissioner for a judicial role.[75] Nevertheless, a "scholar" versus "illiterate" division did not come to characterize stool politics in this town to the extent that it did in Elmina. Instead, the struggle between the matrilineal Ayirebe Acquah and the patrilineal Ghartey families to enstool their respective candidates as the town's *omanhen* provided the main focus around which much of Winneba's indirect rule politics revolved. It reflected on a political level the long-standing struggle between this coastal enclave of indigenous Effutu culture and the dominant Fante/Akan culture of the region around.

The existence of only two *asafos* in Winneba clearly had an important influence on the way in which indirect rule politics developed in that town. In Elmina the *asafo* order had been expanding during the nineteenth century, and in the early twentieth century had continued to undergo important changes. This was not so in Winneba. In contrast, Winneba retained only two *asafos*, known either as Number One, or Tuafo, and Number Two, or Dentsefo.[76] They were divided into subsections, but there was still far less fragmentation than existed in the coastal communities where contact with Europeans had been much more extensive.[77] The two *asafos* were not territorially located, since Winneba's rather unique residence rules ensured that males, regardless of the *asafo* they belonged to, lived in the same compounds. Their membership tended to be more homogeneous, consisting mainly of fishermen, than was the case in other coastal towns with their mulatto, craftsmen and ex-company slave *asafos*. It meant that both scholars and illiterates who wanted to participate in stool politics were constrained to do so within the context of a narrower range of local organizations. Winneba was clearly predisposed to develop a political life that revolved around competition between its two *asafos*.

This became extremely obvious soon after the government recognized Acquah II's destoolment in 1907. The Ghartey family tried to enstool their candidate, Robert J. Ghartey, but the disunity among the town's two *asafos* prevented this from happening. Eventually, under pressure from the disputants, the government appointed Francis Crowther, the secretary of native affairs, to conduct an enquiry in 1913. He quickly discovered that the *asafos* had taken sides. Number One was staunchly in favor of the Ghartey candidate while Number Two supported the Ayirebe Acquah family. Crowther felt that this was a recent development, which he traced back to Ghartey IV, who had assigned the town's four subchiefs to be the patrons of the town's two *asafos*. In this fashion he had effectively divided the town into two factions. A bloody inter-*asafo* riot in 1885 had exacerbated this division, particularly since Ghartey IV had done nothing to stop the atrocities which Number One had committed on Number Two, and it had left Dentsefo with a smoldering antagonism to the Ghartey family in general. As a result, they had sided with the Ayirebe Acquah family and had supported their candidate in 1897 when Ghartey IV died.

It was an anomalous situation since both *asafos* customarily adhered to patrilineal succession within their own ranks. Crowther saw this development as an indication of the spreading influence of Fante customs in this originally Effutu enclave, rather than something that had taken place as a result of the direct intervention of the *asafos* themselves. He felt that it had gone so far that the town had basically accepted the idea that succession to the stool should alternate between the two families, and this belief clearly influenced his decision. He recommended to the government that Acquah II be recognized and allowed to complete the Ayirebe Acquah family's cycle on the stool. His doing so, however, would be "without prejudice" to the claims of the Ghartey family which, when Acquah II died, would have the right to enstool its candidate. In this fashion, Crowther unwittingly added official sanction to what had already become the bipartisan division of Winneba's political life.

Nevertheless, when Acquah died in 1916 both the Ghartey and Ayirebe Acquah families nominated candidates for the vacant stool. Significantly, it was the *akyeamehen* of Goma Assin and the *omanhen* of Goma Adjumako who advised the Ayirebe Acquah family to nominate a candidate to the stool "according to the practice in Akan states to supervise over the funeral ceremony."[78] Both these towns lie a short distance inland from Winneba and in an area that is to all intents and purposes thoroughly Fante, even though Goma Adjumako was the original inland capital of the Winneba region. The candidate they selected, Albert Mould Sackey, was a nephew in the female line of Acquah II. He had been educated at Mfantsipim, and before his enstoolment was a Methodist schoolteacher in Nyakrom.[79] The Ghartey family rallied around Robert J. Ghartey and got the support of Number One *Asafo,* while Sackey got the support of Number Two *Asafo.*

The contending parties were able to get the government to appoint local chiefs as arbitrators, but as was typical of these arbitrations there was little of substance they could agree on, and finally the government had to convene yet another commission of enquiry. The secretary of native affairs, J. T. Furley, and the commissioner of the Central Province, Colonel T. Harding, who conducted this enquiry, discovered, as Crowther had before, that the electors were almost equally divided in favor of the two families' candidates.[80] In contrast to Crowther, however, Furley and Harding looked at the manner in which the various substools in Winneba had been filled, and found that most of these stool holders had been selected matrilineally.[81] Indeed, even important *asafo* positions, like that of the *tufuhen,* which was also vacant, were being contested by both maternal nephews and agnatically.[82]

It was enough to convince these officers that in general Winneba was moving ineluctably in the direction of matrilineal succession, and in conjunction with the slight edge in support that the Ayirebe Acquah family seemed to enjoy among the *asafos,* they recommended Sackey's nomination. They recognized, however, that the switch to matrilineal succession was not complete, and somewhat ingenuously suggested that Sackey's enstoolment as Acquah III should still be "without prejudice to the claims of the Ghartey family in the future," and that it did not represent "the abandonment of the system of alternation."[83]

Ghartey's supporters were hardly satisfied by this decision, and it was merely a matter of time before they would seek to destool Acquah III. He clearly realized how precarious his position was, and astutely sought to increase his support by getting the allegiance of the newly enstooled subchiefs, who in keeping with the colony-wide trend, were occupying positions that had previously been vacant.[84] Acquah III also courted the support of the upper echelons of the town's scholar class, a number of whom were strangers to Winneba, and had been attracted to the town as it had grown in the early twentieth century. A significant number of them were married to his relatives, while others were his creditors and close friends.[85] In addition, for a while he sought colony-wide recognition by supporting Casely Hayford's National Congress of British West Africa, to the point of sending a cablegram to *West Africa* indicating his support for the NCBWA and his opposition to Nana Ofori Atta's campaign to discredit this organization.[86] Finally, he tried to upgrade his position from that of merely *ohen* of Winneba to *omandefe* (the Effutu term for a paramount chief), or in keeping with the Akanization of the region, to *omanhen*.

Acquah III was undoubtedly among the more capable of the coastal paramount chiefs, but juggling all the demands of office severely tested his abilities. Like other *amanhin* of this period, his sources of revenue did not keep up with his expenses. Most of all this was so because, like many of his counterparts, he was involved in expensive litigation over the ownership of disputed stool lands in the town and in outlying areas. Such disputes were inevitable given the increased commercial value of the region and the long history of contested possession of such lands.[87] The ability of his tribunal to generate the necessary revenue to pay lawyers was limited, and encouraged him to engage in questionable activities that brought him into conflict with the ever-hostile members of Number One *Asafo* and also the government.[88] By 1921, according to the district commissioner, he was "running heavily into debt and selling stool lands" to meet his obligations.[89] Faced with this financial crisis, he tried to "levy taxes" on his people, which so inflamed feelings that his enemies felt that they had enough support to destool him.

Skillfully, however, Acquah III was able to get a panel of his scholar supporters to arbitrate the matter, and survived by paying "pacification" to the *Oman* for his "unlawful" acts.[90] Ironically, as Number Two *Asafo* had become dissatisfied with the *omanhen*, Number One, his traditional enemies, had begun to side with Acquah III, so unwilling were they to unite with their rivals! Undoubtedly, part of the reason for this volte-face lay in the emergence of scholar leadership in Number Two *Asafo*. In 1920, Robert Frederick Ocran had finally managed to overcome his rivals and have himself enstooled as the *tufuhen* of Winneba with the stool name of Kweku Siripi. This once again represented a victory for Fante matrilineal succession since he was the grandnephew of the previous *tufuhen*, who had died in 1914. According to a contemporary informant, "he was found to be more energetic" than his rivals who claimed the position patrilineally, and the "stool" passed out of patrilineal control.[91]

Kweku Siripi's claim to a stool position was itself an innovation, since traditionally the *tufuhen* does not seem to have been a chief. He was selected by the *Oman* in conjunction with the *asafos,* and by convention he was to be a member of Number Two *Asafo*. The whip, rather than the stool, was the symbol of his office.[92] Siripi was clearly seeking to transform himself into a senior chief by claiming a stool and appropriating the paraphernalia and symbols of such office. It was in keeping with the trend all over the Fante coastal region as the military function of *tufuhens* declined. Undoubtedly the most spectacular example of this development was Coker in Cape Coast, who tried on two occasions to become the town's *omanhen*. Kweku Siripi was never able to aspire to such heights, but from the 1920s onward he was to be one of Acquah III's main opponents. It was not until 1927, however, when the government's highly controversial Native Administration Ordinance divided the upper echelons of the colony's intelligentsia, that he was able to mount his most serious attack on Acquah III, with the support of those members of the elite who refused to cooperate with this legislation.

In addition to the competition for office that indirect rule stimulated within towns, it also produced a number of intense struggles between coastal towns that wanted to be independent of inland capitals that considered the former part of their paramountcies. The bitter conflict between Komenda and Saltpond with the *omanhen* of the Nkusukum, their putative paramount ruler in the inland village of Yamoransa, was an excellent example of this. In this context, indirect rule was clearly the continuation of a long process on the part of wealthier and increasingly more assertive coastal populations to control their own destinies. Of all the towns that I have described, this process was least advanced in Winneba, which, up until 1927, in spite of Acquah III's attempts to upgrade the town's status, remained officially part of the paramountcy of Goma Adjumako. In contrast, however, to the *omanhen* of Goma Adjumako, who made no effort to assert political claims over Winneba, the *omanhen* of Nkusukum tried in 1909 to assert his control over the people of Komenda.[93] Eventually the government convened two commissions, one in 1913 and the other in 1917, to investigate this question, and finally decided in favor of the Komendas, elevating the town to a paramount stool equal to Nkusukum.

The trend towards a more interventionist indirect rule policy, which had become evident from as early as Sir Hugh Clifford's governorship (1912-1919), clearly contributed to the increasing contentiousness of the native order. By the 1920s there were almost six times as many destoolments as there had been in the first decade of the century.[94] *Asafo* unrest also remained high, and it seemed to both Africans and Europeans that the native state had changed considerably from how it had been in the past. To the editor of the *Gold Coast Independent* this change was reflected in the major difference he perceived between chiefs "in the olden days," when "there were no rewards attached to office," and those of "today," who were continually "pushing themselves forward, plotting, intriguing and devising all sorts of mean tricks to win the favor of political officers."[95] Even colonial officials conceded that there had been changes, but defended them as necessary signs of vitality and growth. They were necessary, as Governor Gordon Guggisberg was to argue, if "native customs and constitutions" were to survive "the disintegrating waves of Western civilization."[96]

Sir Hugh Clifford's appointment in 1916 of three chiefs to the expanded Legislative Council had been one of the first indications of how much the government was willing to strengthen the position of the chiefs. This was followed in 1919 by the governor's attempt to overhaul radically the 1910 Native Jurisdiction Bill. In legislation that he submitted to the Legislative Council, the governor sought to define more clearly the relationship between paramount chiefs and their subordinates, and at the same time give political officers more control over the operations of native tribunals. There was, however, so much protest on the part of the intelligentsia at this attempt to make "ignorant chiefs...become pawns and puppets in the hands of Provincial and District Commissioners [skilled] in the deft art of the so-called indirect rule" that the bill had finally been withdrawn.[97]

Sir Gordon Guggisberg, who succeeded Sir Hugh Clifford in 1919, was equally committed to supporting "the chiefs and Tribal Authorities in the proper exercise of their powers."[98] One indication of this was that soon after he arrived in the Gold Coast he sought to decentralize the colony's government so that both local political officers and chiefs would have more independence and be allowed greater initiative in helping to develop the colony.[99] He also realized that in order to incorporate the native order into colonial government, much more had to be known about its functioning. He called for systematic research into local customs and indigenous institutions. District commissioners were encouraged to write essays on local history and customs.[100] And on an even more practical level, the secretary of native affairs tried to collect written constitutions of the coastal states. However, by this time there was so much factionalism in these communities that those efforts were seldom successful.

Nevertheless, as an indication of how important the government then considered research, in 1921 it established an Anthropology Department for Asante under the direction of Captain R. S. Rattray, who was to produce the most extensive and important work of this era on an Akan people.

In 1922 Guggisberg sought to give legislative expression to these initiatives when he tried to steer a modified version of Clifford's Native Jurisdiction Bill through the colony's Legislative Council. He met much the same opposition as his predecessor, and he, too, had temporarily to abandon this project. His next approach was to allow the chiefs themselves to frame an ordinance. They moved slowly in this "unaccustomed world," and not until 1927 was the government able to gazette the new Native Administration Ordinance, which was to usher in what Robert Stone has described as a "fully interventionist indirect rule policy."[101] There were major limits as to how successful this policy was in incorporating the chiefs, as Governor Slater was to describe it, into a "living part of the machinery of government."[102] What was more obvious, as Robert Stone has pointed out, was that the government's interventionist actions to strengthen the chiefly order provoked more stubborn opposition to these policies, which in turn resulted in an even more interventionist government policy.[103]

However, the belief that the past had been far more ordered and structured than the present, even though hardly accurate, has had a powerful appeal. For example, Margaret Field, from her study of Ga social organization in the 1930s, felt that the stool succession disputes that were the "curse of Ga politics...would almost cease if agitators were certain that Government was acquainted with genuine native custom and resolved to see it was followed."[104] As a result of inappropriate indirect rule policies, the Ga state and society had degenerated into a morass of internecine conflict between self-serving, cynical political factions. Indeed, by the 1930s this had become official orthodoxy. As one official in the Colonial Office expressed it, "the native politics of Accra...are in an unholy mess...a crumbling fabric of Native Administration which is hastening towards complete disintegration."[105] It was a convenient assumption, especially for those who were critical of indirect rule. In reality, however, not even the "variegated succession principles" of the early twentieth century were "anomalous" in the sense of being simply a result of the colonial government's intervention in traditional state. Instead, as David Henige has suggested, they were "intrinsic to the nature of the Akan system."[106] Undoubtedly there was a great deal of continuity and change in the new order, and a partial answer to this conundrum lies in recognizing that even in the later part of the nineteenth century, when British authority was expanding, some degree of "state crystallization" paradoxically was continuing even in those communities where government intervention was considerable.

For example, James Sanders has shown that in Anomabu, the quintessential Fante coastal paramountcy, four of the present nine divisional chiefs originated in the second half of the nineteenth century.[107] He argues, however, that since the early occupants of these offices invariably "were distinguished participants in various wars," and that subsequently many of these positions were to experience long vacancies, "officials of the paramountcy constituted, in Weberian terms, an honor-status group rather than a formal bureaucracy."[108] These "offices," he suggests, "appear to have been used as rewards instead of functioning as essential parts of the paramountcy's administration."[109] Given, however, the close link between chieftaincy and adjudication, these newly created "officials" moved to occupy positions in the state's judicial system.

The establishment of formal British colonial rule obviously radically altered how this crystallization could continue, but at the same time we can see the indirect rule policies of the twentieth century as providing an opportunity for this process to continue in a new and albeit circumscribed fashion. By the 1920s, obviously, no states had emerged to rival the colonial bureaucracy, but from the stool politics that I have described we can see that at least an important link between traditional office and regular monetary reward had been established. In addition, even though the new order eliminated many of the functions that traditional office-holders had discharged, as indirect rule became increasingly more interventionist the government created new bureaucratic responsibilities for the chiefly order, and sought to structure a more formal hierarchy.

Indirect rule also resulted in an important shift in the skills necessary to pursue and maintain traditional office. In the eighteenth and nineteenth centuries these had been primarily religious and martial, but in keeping with the more bureaucratized nature of the traditional state in the twentieth century it was literacy and the ability to communicate with officialdom that became increasingly important. Both European and African investigations into the nature of the native state, as well as the more ad hoc attempts to adjudicate disputes, provided those who could participate in these inquiries with opportunities to manipulate the information that resulted for their own benefit. The importance of literacy was also reflected in the heated debates in the local press over issues regarding "proper native custom." This was partially a reaction on the part of the intelligentsia to charges that they had become "detribalized."[110] Of more immediate importance, they provided yet another opportunity to challenge the validity of an opponent's claims to offices that were in dispute.

Up until the 1920s many of the Western-educated people who were involved in these disputes were from the lower echelons of the colony's

Western-educated elite, and often less than successful in whatever career they had followed. However, by the end of the decade more interventionist indirect rule policies inadvertently broke down the barrier that the government had tried to erect between traditional society and the Western-style municipal councils of the major coastal towns. The result was that even those who had held aloof from the messy disputes of the native order, but had political ambitions, were inexorably drawn into the parochial world of local stool politics as active participants. It was to link trans-actional factionalism to the anticolonialism of the interwar years.

Notes

1. In 1928 Nettey sued the editor of the *Gold Coast Independent* for slander in the Divisional Court. The *Gold Coast Independent* carried verbatim reports of this case. This information comes from the 2 June 1928 issue.

2. *Gold Coast Independent*, 12 May 1928. Nettey claimed that "his people had let him down."

3. *Gold Coast Independent*, 2 June 1928.

4. Ibid.

5. *Gold Coast Independent*, 23 June 1928.

6. *Gold Coast Independent*, 26 May 1928.

7. Akanmaji was one of the nine quarters of Accra. It was located in James Town, or Nleshi.

8. Obituary for J. R. Meyers, *Gold Coast Independent*, 10 June 1922.

9. Notes of a meeting at Secretary of Native Affairs office, 1 December 1910, ADM 11/1086, NAG, Accra.

10. *J. R. Meyers v. Abossey Okai*, 29 March 1915, Judgment Book Accra, SCT 2/6/5, NAG, Accra.

11. The Secretary of Native Affairs to the Colonial Secretary, 17 May 1916, ADM 11/1086. NAG, Accra.

12. Parker, "Ga State and Society," 296.

13. Some of the most important of these cases were: the "Harbour Blockyard Case" (1907); *Tetteh Kwaku v. Kpakpo Brown* (1910) and the *Land for Accra Water Works* case (1918). For descriptions of these court cases see Parker, "Ga State and Society," 264-267, 302-305, 308-310.

14. *Gold Coast Aborigines*, 20-27 August 1898.

15. This was a much greater distance than it would be today since roads were terrible. It was easier at that time to travel by canoe.

16. The most detailed description of the tangled disputes that followed his death is to be found in Casely-Hayford, "A Genealogical Study of Cape Coast Stool Families," 259-271. There are different spellings for Ebiradzi (Abradie-Crowther Enquiry: Abiradzi-Faud Enquiry). Ebiradzi was the spelling used in the 1920s.

17. Coker's evidence before the Crowther enquiry, SNA 11/1109, NAG, Accra. Coker had a vested interest in matrilineal succession, since this was how he had succeeded to the position of *tufuhen*.

18. Crowther Report, 1916, Cape Coast Native Affairs, ADM 23/1/883, NAG, Cape Coast.

19. According to an informant in Cape Coast, he was "well educated at Wesley College in Cape Coast and had taken a job with one of the big European firms." Interview with Napoleon Forson, Cape Coast, 8 June 1974.

20. The *oman* had paid his debts when he had been enstooled, but he had not disclosed all of his financial obligations and continued to trade and amassed new debts after he had been enstooled. *Gold Coast Leader*, 9 December 1916.

21. This was the estimate of the editor of the *Gold Coast Leader*, 5 July 1919.

22. *Legislative Council Debates*, 3 October 1913. Cited in Kimble, *A Political History of Ghana*, 469.

23. The precedent had been already established in 1911 when Governor Thorburn had appointed Nene Mate Kole, the paramount chief of Manya Krobo, to the Legislative Council. Sir James Thorborn, like his predecessor, Sir John Pickersgill Rodger, and his successor, Sir Hugh Clifford, had also served in Britain's far eastern empire (Ceylon).

24. *Gold Coast Leader*, 15-22 April 1916.

25. Petition from F. S. Bilson to His Excellency, 8 May 1917, Cape Coast Native Affairs, ADM 11/640, NAG, Cape Coast.

26. The governor finally appointed Nana Amonoo V, paramount chief of Anomabu and one of the senior chiefs of the Central Province, to represent the Fante-speaking people in the Legislative Council. Nana Ofori Atta represented the Twi speakers and Togbui Sri II the Ewe speakers.

27. At that time it was the only regular newspaper in Cape Coast. Apart from being the joint editor of the *Gold Coast Aborigines*, and later on the *Gold Coast Leader*, Brown had also been an agent for Millers in Cape Coast, but his outspoken editorials had eventually resulted in his losing this position. James Mercer's obituary for Herbert Brown, *Gold Coast Leader*, 6-13 December 1919.

28. *Gold Coast Leader*, 4 November 1916.

29. *Gold Coast Leader*, 15-22 April 1916.

30. *Gold Coast Leader*, 11 November 1916.

31. Ibid. He later on realized that members of the GCARPS were also "receiving the Tribunal's funds from a safe distance." *Gold Coast Leader*, 11-18 January 1919.

32. The Provincial Commissioner to the Secretary of Native Affairs, 24 November 1916, Cape Coast Native Affairs, ADM 11/640, NAG, Cape Coast.

33. *Gold Coast Leader*, 11-18 January 1919.

34. *Gold Coast Leader*, 31 May-7 June, 1919.

35. *Gold Coast Leader*, 23 April 1919.

36. *Gold Coast Leader*, 24-31 July 1919.

37. Letter from J. B. Hagan to the District Commissioner of Cape Coast, 22 August 1918, ADM 23/1/280, NAG, Cape Coast.

38. Information from J. S. Watts Amissah, Chief Sam Amissah's son, Cape Coast, 3 August 1991.

39. Ibid.

40. Ibid.

41. *Gold Coast Leader,* 31 May-7 June 1919.

42. For a description of these endeavors see Baron Holmes, "Economic and Political Organizations in the Gold Coast, 1920-1945" (Ph.D. diss., University of Chicago, 1972), 116-119.

43. *Gold Coast Leader,* 31 May-7 June 1919.

44. Ibid.

45. *Gold Coast Leader,* 7 August 1919.

46. The tribunal kept a record of all those who sat as judges in its deliberations.

47. We know that these chiefs were illiterate because they signed various petitions that they were involved in sending to the government with an "X."

48. J. P. H. Brown and most of all J. W. de Graft Johnson, who was a prominent member of the society and much involved in using the tribunal to collect debts owed him, had been instrumental in approving Mbra III. Information from a one-page biography of J. W. de Graft Johnson's life given to me by his son, Hector de Graft Johnson, Cape Coast, 19 August 1974.

49. He died in December 1919. Obituary for J. P. H. Brown, *Gold Coast Leader,* 6-13 December 1919.

50. Governor Guggisberg's plans to construct a deepwater harbor at Takoradi, and also a railroad through the Central Province (of which Cape Coast was the administrative center), threatened the town's commercial future, and in the face of this danger the town's warring factions came together. For a description of this project see David Meredith, "The Construction of Takoradi Harbour in the Gold Coast, 1919 to 1930: A Case Study in Colonial Development and Administration," *Transafrican Journal of History 5,* no. 1 (1976):134-149.

51. A large part of the reason for this was due to the way that long-standing trading and military alliances with the Asante would be upset. Rene Baesjou, ed., *An Asante Embassy on the Gold Coast: The Mission of Akyempon Yaw to Elmina, 1869-1872* (Leiden, 1979), 17-52.

52. Both Annan and Condua were government pensioners. The latter had been the stationmaster at the Sekondi railway station.

53. One of the ringleaders in this affair was J. C. Smith, who claimed to be the linguist for Number Ten *Asafo,* Akrampa. There was a three-year interregnum between 1899 and 1903, which was not uncommon in coastal stool successions. Annan was the only ruler not to be destooled. He died in office in 1914. *Gold Coast Leader,* 28 November 1914.

54. Handing over notes on the Elmina State, 7 January 1945, Edina Native Affairs, ADM 23/1/749, NAG, Cape Coast. There was a long history of the town's stool disputes in this report.

55. Notes of an enquiry on a reported destoolment of Kwesi Mensah, 27 June 1912, Elmina Native Affairs, ADM 23/1/303, NAG, Cape Coast.

56. Ibid., and Notes of a meeting with the Commissioner of the Central Province, 16 July 1918, Elmina Native Affairs, ADM 23/1/303, NAG, Cape Coast.

57. Letter from the Companies of Elmina to the Provincial Commissioner, 29 July 1918, Elmina Native Affairs, ADM 23/1/303, NAG, Cape Coast.

58. Cathline had also been to prison like Coker, and like Nettey he had tried his hand at the gold mining concession business. Information from a letter from E. P. Dontoh, *Oman* Secretary, to the District Commissioner, 20 March 1922, Elmina Native Affairs, ADM 23/1/438, NAG, Cape Coast.

59. Ibid., and the District Commissioner to J. C. Smith, 19 December 1922, Elmina Native Affairs, ADM 23/1/438, NAG, Cape Coast. Smith was the *supi* and linguist for Number Ten *Asafo* (Akrampa, the mulatto *asafo*). The district commissioner refused to accept this.

60. The Provincial Commissioner to the Secretary of Native Affairs, 3 May 1934, Edina Native Affairs, ADM 23/1/749, NAG, Accra.

61. Ibid.

62. Enyampa elected the *omanhen* and Wombir selected the *tufuhen*, or the *ekuwessonhen* as he was called in Elmina.

63. The constitution was drawn up at the request of District Commissioner Duncan Johnstone so as to have a written document of this nature to help solve the succession crisis in the town. The Elmina Constitution and History of the Edina State, 4 September 1928, ADM 23/1/861, NAG, Cape Coast.

64. Petition from J. J. C. Smith and others to His Excellency, 27 February 1930, Elmina Native Affairs, SNA 11/1074, NAG, Accra.

65. Harvey Feinberg has pointed out that in the detailed descriptions of the fighting in Elmina in 1873, at the time of the final Dutch-British exchange of forts, there was no mention of divisional chiefs. "Elmina, Ghana: A History of Its Development and Relationship with the Dutch in the Eighteenth Century" (Ph.D. diss., Boston University, 1969), 76.

66. Ibid., 80.

67. Provincial Commissioner to the Secretary of Native Affairs, 17 October 1908, Elmina Native Affairs, ADM 11/1/1111, NAG, Accra. Berase is about two miles northeast of Eguafo. It is much closer to the latter than to Elmina.

68. Provincial Commissioner to the Colonial Secretary, 7 November 1906, Elmina Native Affairs, ADM 11/1/1111, NAG, Accra.

69. Memorial of the *Supis* of the seven of the ten Elmina *Asafos* to the Governor (?), 6 June 1915, Elmina Native Affairs, ADM 11/1/1111, NAG, Accra. Cited in Henige, "The Problem of Feedback in Oral Tradition: Four

Examples from the Fante Coastlands," 226. Only nine *asafos* were approached.

70. The nearby town of Shama (twenty miles to the west of Elmina) also acted as a stimulus to Elmina. In the 1930s the town's *tufuhen* was in favor of a change from patrilineal to matrilineal succession but there was strong opposition from the *asafos*. Eventually in 1942, under strong pressure from both factions, the colonial government appointed the provincial commissioner of the Eastern Province to conduct a commission of inquiry. However, his best efforts failed to resolve this conflict. A. Duncan-Johnstone, "Shama Stool Dispute," 18 May 1942, MSS.Afr.593 5\10, RH (Rhodes House), Oxford.

71. Governor Burns to the Secretary of State summarizing the case, 23 July 1945, ADM 12/3/81, NAG, Accra.

72. Alan Burns, *Colonial Civil Servant* (London, 1949), 179.

73. The case was much more clear-cut than the Kibi murder since the Crown actually had a witness to the killing. Also, the defendants lacked the family connections of their counterparts in Akyem Abuakwa, which made it possible for the latter to get Labor politicians who were opposed to the death penalty to intervene with the secretary of state and raise the issue in Parliament. For an extensive description of this case, which dragged on for over three years, see Richard Rathbone, *Murder and Politics in Colonial Ghana* (New Haven, Conn. and London, 1993).

74. In the 1901 census the town had a population of 5,578, and in 1911 it was 5,842. Cited in Kimble, *A Political History of Ghana*, 144.

75. District Commissioner to the Secretary of Native Affairs, 20 May 1905, Winneba Native Affairs, SNA 11/1135, NAG, Accra.

76. These are their names in Fante. In Effutu they are Tuawo and Dentewo.

77. It had been in contact with Europeans for more or less the same amount of time as most other such settlements on the coast since the English had built a fort there in 1694. From 1812, however, when the British blew up this fort to avenge the murder of its commandant, Henry Meredith, to sometime in the 1850s, there was no fort in this location. Lawrence, *Trade Castles and Forts of West Africa*, 68.

78. Nana Ankwandoh III's private manuscript, cited in Hagan, "Aspects of Social Change Among the Effutu of Winneba," 306.

79. Nyakrom is about twenty-five miles north of Winneba. Information from Mr. S. A. D. Arkhurst, Winneba, 17 December 1988.

80. Hagan, "Aspects of Social Change Among the Effutu of Winneba," 307.

81. J. T. Furley, "Report on the Winneba Stool Dispute," 1919, Winneba Native Affairs, ADM 11/1135, NAG, Accra.

82. Ibid.

83. Ibid., 15. Cited in Hagan, "Aspects of Social Change Among the Effutu of Winneba," 308.

84. The Acting Provincial Commissioner to the Secretary of Native Affairs, 16 March 1920, Winneba Native Affairs, ADM 11/1135, NAG, Accra.

85. Number One *Asafo* to the Secretary of Native Affairs, 11 October 1922, Winneba Native Affairs, ADM 11/1135, NAG, Accra. With the help of these friends he had acquired a motorcar.

86. The District Commissioner to the Provincial Commissioner, 2 August 1921, Winneba Native Affairs, ADM 11/1135, NAG, Accra. For a description of the struggle between the NCBWA and Nana Sir Ofori Atta, see Kimble, *A Political History of Ghana*, 389-403.

87. This was so because in the 1920s the town underwent significant expansion. In the 1931 census the town's population was 10,529. Cited in Kimble, *A Political History of Ghana*, 144. However, conflicts over the ownership of land extended back at least as far as to Acquah II. For example, in 1901 he had tried to lease supposedly auriferous lands to an English company, which had nearly resulted in a riot. As a result the lease had not been formalized. District Commissioner to the Governor, 31 January 1901, Winneba Native Affairs, ADM 11/1136, NAG, Accra.

88. For example, the representatives of the nearby village of Attaitu accused him of "misappropriating" money that the government had given for road clearing, and there was enough substance in this charge for the police to take action. District Commissioner to the Provincial Commissioner, 14 November 1921, Winneba Native Affairs, ADM 11/1135, NAG, Accra. Shortly after the police magistrate found him guilty of "unlawfully imprisoning in a place not recognized as a prison," which represented an attempt to upgrade the authority, and hence the revenues, of his court. Provincial Commissioner to the Secretary of Native Affairs, 29 December 1921, Winneba Native Affairs, ADM 11/1135, NAG, Accra.

89. The District Commissioner to the Secretary of Native Affairs, 9 November 1921, Winneba Native Affairs, ADM 11/1135, NAG, Accra. One of these cases that indirectly involved Acquah III had gone all the way to the Full Court. *Number Two Company of Winneba v. R. J. Ghartey*, 20 April 1921, Cape Coast Judgment Book, SCT 5/6/2, NAG, Accra.

90. Petition from Kweku Siripi, *Tufuhen* of Winneba and others to His Excellency the Governor, Sir Shenton Whitelegge Thomas, 1927, Winneba Native Affairs, ADM 11/1135, NAG, Accra.

91. Interview with Mr. S. A. D. Arkhurst, Winneba, 17 December 1988. This did not remain permanently so. Instead, alternation between patrilineal and matrilineal succession also developed for this office.

92. Hagan, "Aspects of Social Change Among the Effutu of Winneba," 254.

93. "Minutes of a meeting held in the Court House, Saltpond, of the Inkusukum Chiefs and people," 9 March 1909, ADM 23/1/122, NAG, Cape Coast. Cited in Sanders, "The Political Development of the Fante in the Eighteenth and Nineteenth Centuries," 159.

94. According to the government's statistics destoolments had increased in the following fashion: 1904-1908: 7; 1909-1913: 23; 1914-1918: 38; and 1919-1924: 41. Cited in Kimble, *A Political History of Ghana*, 490.

95. *Gold Coast Independent*, 5 July 1924.

96. Cited in R. E. Wraith, *Guggisberg* (London 1967), 179.

97. *Gold Coast Independent*, 19 April 1919.

98. Legislative Council Address, 13 October 1919, cited in Wraith, *Guggisberg*, 191. Unlike many of his predecessors, Guggisberg did not serve in an administrative capacity in Britain's Far Eastern empire. He did, however, spend four years in Nigeria (1910-1914) in charge of surveys when Sir Frederick Lugard, the leading advocate of indirect rule in Britains's West African empire, was governor of the colony. Guggisberg had also spent eight years doing similar survey work in the Gold Coast (1902-1910), where he had already been influenced by his extensive contact with indigenous society to appreciate its weaknesses and strengths.

99. Stone, "Colonial Administration and Rural Politics in South Central Ghana," 81-85.

100. One of the earliest examples of this work is that of Assistant Secretary of Native Affairs J. C. de Graft Johnson on "The Etsi People," an Akan subgroup north of the Fante (December 1921, ADM 11/1/813, NAG, Accra). A number of other officials also produced work on local people. For example, C.W. Welman (the secretary of native affairs) published *The Native States of the Gold Coast: Vol. 1, Peki* (London, 1925), and *The Native States of the Gold Coast: Vol. 2, Ahanta* (London, 1930).

101. Stone, "Colonial Administration and Rural Politics in South Central Ghana ," 95.

102. Sir A. R. Slater, *Native Administration in the Gold Coast and Its Dependencies* (Accra, 1930).

103. Stone "Colonial Administration and Rural Politics in South Central Ghana," 2.

104. Field, *Social Organization of the Ga People*, 51.

105. Minute by J. Flood, 10 June 1930, CO 96/692/6581, PRO. Cited in Parker, "Ga State and Society," 288.

106. Henige, "Akan Stool Succession Under Colonial Rule: Continuity or Change?" 300-301.

107. Sanders, "The Political Development of the Fante in the Eighteenth and Nineteenth Centuries," 307-308.

108. Ibid., 314.

109. Ibid.

110. The most controversial assertion of this opinion was made by the Honorable W. G. A. Ormsby-Gore, M.P., the Parliamentary under-secretary of state for the colonies, after he toured West Africa in 1926. *Gold Coast Leader*, 2 September 1926.

Chapter 7

Linking Two Political Cultures

Studies of the nascent anticolonialism of the 1920s and 1930s, or what Thomas Hodgkin described as "embryonic nationalism," continue to be based on the assumption that there were rigid divisions between the groups that made up colonial society. This has been especially seen as the case in the "new towns" where the "ideas of African nationalism [were] born and [grew] to maturity."[1] In these urban environments the possibilities for greater liberty accentuated the divisions between the putative three poles of African society: commoners, chiefs and the Western-educated elite.[2] For example, Dominic Fortescue, in his recent study of opposition to Governor Guggisberg's municipal council reforms of 1924-1925, focuses on the Accra *asafos* as the "organizational and ideological mouthpiece of commoner interests."[3] He argues that ranged against this anticolonial "Third Estate" were both the educated elite who "fully supported the ordinance's passage through the Legislative Council" and the chiefs whose "increasingly integral role in the British system of government removed them from the traditional checks and balances of popular support."[4]

His description of this "effective...direct anti-colonial protest by the urban poor" presents a picture of Accra as a rigidly compartmentalized society with a "basic cleavage between commoner and chief and elder."[5] Kathryn Firmin-Sellers, in her even more recent study of the transformation of property rights in the Gold Coast, continues in much this vein, but rather than emphasizing "pre-colonial commoner consciousness" clashing with "derived notions of constitutional advance held by the elite," [6] she sees the conflict as essentially a struggle between the elite and the *Manbii* (the people)" over defining a system of property rights.[7]

Clearly, by the 1920s Accra, the colony's capital, had acquired the attributes of the "colonial city," and seemed to reflect best of all the pace of social change away from what David Apter has characterized as "tribal society."[8] Yet as John Parker has astutely pointed out in his detailed study of the town up until the 1920s,

> the description of Accra as a "colonial" city shaped by the requirements of a "capitalist" economy is problematic. Accra was indeed the colonial capital and, until the opening of the harbor at Sekondi-Takoradi in 1928, the Gold Coast's principal port, but it remained very much an "African"—and essentially Ga—town in character.[9]

The town's inner core remained divided into its original *majii* in spite of several government attempts to redevelop these congested areas. Even Cape Coast, a much smaller area also subjected to urban renewal, remained largely unchanged and very much divided into its traditional *asafo* quarters. In general, coastal towns retained their inner spatial configurations with growth taking place on their peripheries on land over which the town's competing traditional rulers bitterly contested ownership. Most of all this was the case in Accra, where both the government and private firms sought to acquire land for public and commercial reasons.[10] These disputes accentuated local rivalries and fueled debates over identity and disputed histories. By the second decade of the twentieth century the political scene in Accra was every bit as contested as it was in other coastal communities, but rather than dividing this society into easily discernible groups, disputes over land ownership brought together a cast of participants that spanned the socially diverse ranks of this community.

Colonial policies in the 1920s and 1930s also played a major role in bringing commoners, chiefs and the intelligentsia ever more closely into the same political arena by creating a link between stool and municipal politics. This was to add an important new dimension to the political life of the colony's most important coastal towns, and ensured that transactional factionalism fused with anticolonialism and a still embryonic nationalism. The most important of these new polices were Governor Guggisberg's municipal council reforms of 1924, which were designed to give "certain populous municipalities a voice," but also contributed to linking these Western-style institutions and the native order.[11] He felt that the "detribalized natives" in the main towns could not be ruled through chiefs, but would have to be granted true municipal corporations with an elected town council majority and an African mayor.[12] In exchange for these concessions, however, it was evident that the new municipalities would have to increase property rates, and take on more potentially unpopular administrative roles. Political advancement would not be without its costs. This dilemma created disagreements within the African population, and political opportunities for enterprising individuals to exploit.

First of all this was so in Accra, where the Town Council was even more unpopular than usual. It had recently introduced more stringent sanitary bylaws, and even more controversial had been the council's removal of the town's main market to a new site and an increase in the rents for stalls that market women paid.[13] Nevertheless, neither the Ga *mantse*, Taki Yaoboi, nor the leading figures among the town's intelligentsia were in a position to provide effective opposition to this legislation. Casely Hayford, who had recently organized the National Congress of British West Africa (NCBWA) and was the leading politician in the colony, had initially welcomed the bill as "practically" conferring on the people of the Gold Coast the "privilege of self-government...[and] the substance rather than the shadow of self-government."[14] On the other hand, Taki Yaoboi was one of the chiefs who had sided with the NCBWA in its struggle with Nana Ofori Atta, and had been elected the president of the Accra branch.[15] There was clearly self-interest in this since he had been able to get legal help from the Accra lawyers who were members of the Congress's executive in his bitter struggle with the Asere and Sempe *akutsei* over the right to lease Kole Lagoon, which included an unsuccessful attempt in 1920-1921 to destool the Ga *mantse*.[16]

However, in 1924 it was not just the *asafobii* of Asere and their allies the Sempes who were opposed to Taki Yaoboi on account of his inability to challenge effectively the Municipal Corporations Ordinance. Instead, leading the opposition was C. B. Nettey and his right-hand man, J. D. Garshong, both Gbese *asafoatsemei*. Fortescue uncritically accepts them simply as *asafoatsemei* defending commoner interests. But by the standards of the 1920s both of them would have been considered members of the intelligentsia. Garshong's grandfather had been a Danish trader of Jewish background; his father had been a successful enough trader in Accra to send his son to Fourah Bay College in Sierra Leone; the younger Garshong was a member of the Anglican Church's executive board and apart from owning three stores in Accra, he was also a well-known auctioneer.[17] Nettey, as I have already mentioned, was a businessman who had gone to England to sell concessions in 1907. He was a standard seven graduate and a "staunch Methodist"; from 1909 to 1911 he had been a member of the Accra Town Council (a street in Accra had been named after him); and in 1911 he played a key role in the establishment of one

J. D. Garshong (on the left) with his family, c. 1920s. Source: H. A. Garshong (son).

of Accra's first soccer clubs, Accra Heart's of Oak.[18] In 1913 he had formed the Gbese Scholars Union.[19]

Neither can we really explain their conflict with the Ga *mantse* as generational, as was the tendency in colonial times, which students of "embryonic nationalism" have once again rather uncritically accepted. Nettey was fifty-nine years old in 1924 and Garshong was in his forties, while the Ga *mantse* was forty-five. Similarly, Coker, in Cape Coast, was sixty years old when he used his *asafo* base to angle for the position of *omanhen* in 1919, and Nana Mbra III was only in his twenties at his enstoolment in 1920. The term "young men," which Assistant Secretary of Native Affairs J. C. de Graft Johnson was to associate with the *asafos*, or Third Estate, referred to commoner males, without royal office, who were not elders.[20] In reality, however, even this definition was imprecise as the term "young men" came to be appropriated by those who felt, whatever their status, that they were "progressive."

Like many other young men at that time, Nettey and Garshong's involvement in stool politics was hardly disinterested. Particularly in the case of Nettey there had been a long history of conflict between him and Ga *mantses* over the exercise of adjudicative functions, and it had been this issue that had prompted him to engineer the destoolment of Taki Obili in 1918. A similar conflict had developed with Taki Yaoboi, and there was considerable opportunism on his part when he took advantage of the Ga *mantse's* lackluster opposition to the proposed ordinance to press for the latter's destoolment.[21] Bjorn Edsman has observed from his study of Accra politics that the many efforts to destool the Ga *mantse* that followed were "nearly always [to coincide] with acute grievances conditioned by government policies."[22] He recognized the close connection between "modern" and "traditional" politics in Accra and how they interacted with one another. Yet at the same time he remained "somewhat mystified by the interior architecture of Accra," and particularly the intricacies of stool politics.[23] There is little understanding of the underlying transactional issues, and how much the elite became drawn into these affairs and in turn became dependent on support in the "traditional order."

In addition to the many divisions within the ranks of Accra's traditional order, there was also developing an important split within the ranks of the colony's elite over Guggisberg's reforms that had the long-term effect of stimulating politicians from among the elite to seek support from what initially had been transactional factions. Casely Hayford, after wavering in his initial support of the Municipal Corporation Ordinance, finally decided that though it was "not perfect [it was] a distinct advance upon anything that had preceded it in British West Africa."[24] Quickly he was able to convince most of the membership of the NCBWA to "accept the idea of municipal practice versus central government."[25]The main opponent became the Cape Coast lawyer W. E. G. Sekyi, or Kobina Sekyi as he was known in the Gold Coast, who was able to take over the Cape Coast–based GCARPS and became increasingly more opposed to any compromise with the government.[26] The Nettey faction turned to this latter group for support. Initially, however, the "Compromisers" enjoyed substantially more effectiveness than their opponents.[27] In February 1925 they demonstrated this by successfully supporting Taki Yaoboi in a case he brought before the Divisional Court in which he claimed £500 in damages for a "false and malicious speech" in which Nettey and Garshong had proclaimed that he was no longer Ga *mantse*.[28] He did not actually win any damages, but Nettey and Ayi Bente, the Gbese *mantse*, ended up being fined and subjected to short terms of imprisonment.[29] In addition, through the medium of the *Gold Coast Independent,* Taki Yaoboi's supporters subjected Nettey to a series of blistering ad hominem attacks that also contributed to putting him on the defensive.[30]

Nevertheless, this trial gave Taki Yaoboi's opponents an opportunity to advance what the judge in the case, Chief Justice P. C. Smyly, considered a "novel" idea about who had the power to destool the Ga *mantse.* They had argued that this power lay with the *mambii* rather than with specific members of the native order. It hardly seemed in accordance with what colonial officials considered "correct" native customary practice, but as Nettey and company must have realized, officialdom was itself not adverse to resolving disputes in the native order on the basis of majority rule.[31] Smyly, the presiding judge, maintained that "*mambii* was a word that he had heard for the first time after being in the Colony for nearly fourteen years and studying native law."[32] It had undoubtedly been around long before, but from here onward the notion that there was an all-embracing political constituency that determined the structure of the native order was particularly useful to members of the intelligentsia who lacked a recognized position in its ranks, but wanted to control its institutions.

Apart from benefiting from the newspaper offensive against Nettey, Taki Yaoboi and his supporters had also shifted their position on the controversial question of the Town Council's future. In 1925 Governor Guggisberg had introduced a new constitution that had linked participation on the part of the coastal towns in the new Legislative Council with acceptance of the 1924 Municipal Council Ordinance. As part of this new constitution, the governor had also created three Provincial Councils for the colony's chiefs.[33] In the expanded Legislative Council, which was to come into being, the chiefs gained at the expense of the intelligentsia. Their number went from three to six, while the number of positions for the latter remained constant at three.[34]

The result was that any willingness the intelligentsia who dominated the NCBWA might have had for implementing the Municipal Council Ordinance evaporated. Instead, along with the Ga *mantse,* the leading members of the NCBWA were soon in the forefront of leading the protest against the new rate evaluation that was coupled with the ordinance and seemed imminent. Not surprisingly, they were also determined that Taki Yaoboi should not participate in the Eastern Provincial Council of Chiefs, and he continued with this opposition even after Governor Guggisberg reluctantly abandoned making acceptance of the new municipality obligatory for participation in the new Legislative Council. The result was that neither Taki Yaoboi nor a representative of the stool was present when the first meeting of the Eastern Provincial Council of Chiefs took place in 1926.[35]

Ironically, however, by taking this antigovernment position, Taki Yaoboi once again placed himself in an exposed position vis-à-vis his opposition in the native order, and they were quick to exploit it. The *mantsemei* of Gbese, Asere, Sempe and Akanmaji, who were all part of the Ga *mantse*'s main opposition in the native order, rapidly executed a volte-face, and from being opponents of government policies in 1924, they instead began to attack the Ga *mantse* for leaving Accra unrepresented on the Eastern Provincial Council![36] Equally opportunistic, A. W. Kojo Thompson, who had represented Nettey in a libel suit against the *Gold Coast Independent*, broke ranks with his fellow members of the intelligentsia, who opposed any compromise with the government, and took advantage of his connections to the Nettey faction to have them put him up as the municipal councillor for Accra.[37] Since there were no other candidates, the governor, not above some opportunism himself, nominated Thompson to this position.

In return for this support, Thompson sought to "assure" his supporters that now that he enjoyed the government's favor "the destoolment of the Ga *Mantse* would follow."[38] It obviously inspired Taki Yaoboi's opponents to pursue more vigorously their long-standing vendetta with him. In October 1926 they were once again leveling charges against him and proclaiming his destoolment.[39] According to the *Gold Coast Independent*, the "real strength of the opposition" seemed more "formidable" than it really was since it consisted of people who carried no "great weight."[40] It was hardly an objective appraisal since a number of the younger generation among the intelligentsia also identified with what had become the antiestablishment party. In addition to Kojo Thompson, there were his fellow barristers K. Quartey-Papafio and J. K. T. Orgle, who was particularly important since he was the proprietor and editor of the fortnightly newspaper *Vox Populi*.[41] It meant that the destooling party had their own organ, and the benefit of elite support that Taki Yaoboi had enjoyed before was no longer as one-sided.[42]

This became the case even more in 1927 when the feud that had been simmering between those who supported Casely Hayford and those who supported Sekyi exploded again out in the open.[43] After Casely Hayford returned at the end of 1926 from an unsuccessful one-man deputation to London to protest the 1925 constitution, he had quickly realized that further protest was useless, and that if he and his associates did not stand for election other Africans would. As a result, in July 1927, as elections to the Legislative Council once again drew near, he, along with his prominent supporters in Accra, organized a Ratepayer Association. This organization then nominated J. Glover-Addo, the most senior member of the Accra bar, to contest the election.[44] Sekyi, who by this time had become the driving force behind the Cape Coast– based GCARPS, refused to go along with this change in position. Indeed, his opposition to colonial policies had hardened. Shortly before, the government, in conjunction with the chiefs in the Legislative Council, had introduced a new Native Administration Ordinance that confirmed the intelligentsia's worst fears that the chiefs would abuse the new powers the government had given them.[45] Casely Hayford's call for compromise under such circumstances reflected what Seyki considered his "servile habit of mind."[46]

However, Sekyi was not able to prevent his counterparts in Accra from participating in the election to select a municipal councillor. The link between the factions within the native order and the rival sections of the intelligentsia was too well established for either camp to concede to its opponents the advantage of controlling the town's representation on the Legislative Council. Kojo Thompson, who had emerged as the de facto leader of the anti–Ga *mantse* party, decided to challenge the Ratepayers, and transformed the *mambii* into the Mambii Party with himself as its candidate for the position of Municipal Council representative. As an indication of the factiousness within the native order, however, Thompson's fellow barrister K. Quartey-Papafio refused to support his candidacy and created his own party, based on his supporters in the Asere quarter, called the Asere Kowulu Party.[47]

Of the 765 people who voted out of an electorate of 1,816 potential voters, 380 did so for Glover-Addo, 238 for Thompson and 147 for Quartey-Papafio.[48] According to the governor, Sir Ransford Slater, 60 percent of those who had voted were illiterate and few of the intelligentsia had actually taken part.[49] As Bjorn Edsman has observed, it was not surprising that the illiterate turnout was so high since the new rating system that the Municipal Ordinance of 1924 had proposed would have hit hardest the lower-income group and the wealthiest, and "gave excellent reason for [them] to join."[50] This schedule had not been enforced when the ordinance was abandoned in 1926. Nevertheless, the fear of its reintroduction was obviously enough to fuel the growth of the Mambii and Asere Kowulu Parties, the main parties of the illiterates, around lawyers like Thompson and Quartey-Papafio.

Glover-Addo's victory indicated that the older and more established section of the intelligentsia was still in control of municipal politics. At that time they also controlled three of the four seats on the Town Council.[51] Their grip, however, was not as firm as it had been as both Quartey-Papafio and Thompson were able to use their local political support to win election to this body in 1928. It was an indication also of how closely linked municipal politics and stool affairs in the town had become that Taki Yaoboi's opponents were able to take advantage of support from their town councillor supporters, for in February 1929 they were able finally to destool the Ga *mantse,* who had now become their implacable enemy.[52] Contributing to this development were important shifts in alignment in the native order. The new Native Administration Bill of 1927 elevated the Asere *mantse* to a "Divisional Stool" and prompted the *akutso* to put aside its old hostility to the James Town *mantse,* Kojo Ababio, who in turn withdrew his support for Taki Yaoboi.[53] The new bill elevated the status of paramount chiefs, and at this point Taki Yaoboi seemed more of a challenge to *both mantses* than he had been useful to Kojo Ababio in his conflicts with the Aseres and the Alatas.[54] Factional considerations had obviously become intimately linked with municipal politics.

Apart from indicating to factions in the native order the advantages of linking transactional feuds to colony-wide political issues, this successful challenge to Taki Yaoboi also demonstrated to the fringe members of the intelligentsia that they could profit politically from such alliances themselves. They were likely to be younger members of the intelligentsia who were not attracted to supporting Casely Hayford and the NCBWA, which had become the establishment party in the colony. They had little to gain by compromising with the colonial government, and were likely to gravitate towards the town's antiestablishment party. Kojo Thompson's rapid rise to prominence was the best indication of how advantageous this could be. As his Ratepayer opponents took every occasion to point out, up until 1924 he had "stood aloof" and taken "no active interest" in the colony's political life.[55] He had not been involved in the NCBWA, and it was clear that his fellow barristers did not consider him a leading member of the bar.[56]

Nevertheless, he was able with the support of the Mambii Party to establish himself as a major force in Accra's municipal affairs. In 1931 he again unsuccessfully challenged the Ratepayers for the position of Accra's representative on the Legislative Council. Their candidate this time was the proprietor of the *Gold Coast Independent,* Dr. F. V. Nanka-Bruce.[57] In 1935, however, he challenged again, and by this time he was a far more threatening contender. The Great Depression had caused considerable discontent, and the concomitant increase in public opposition to colonial policies benefited Thompson far more than it did Nanka-Bruce. The latter's ineffective opposition in the Legislative Council to unpopular colonial policies had seriously undermined his standing.[58] As an indication of this, he had only the support of his own newspaper, the *Gold Coast Independent,* and the halfhearted support of J. B. Danquah's *Times of West Africa.* The other local newspapers—the *Vox Populi,* the *Gold Coast Spectator,* the *Provincial Pioneer* and most importantly the daily that Nnandi Azikwie edited, the *African Morning Post*—supported Thompson to varying degrees.[59] Equally important, the Mambii Party's base in the native order had become much more solid. In 1933 it had been finally able to reenstool Taki Obili as the Ga *mantse,* so that in 1935 the party controlled what had become the most important body in the native order, the Ga State Council.[60] Significantly, Kojo Thompson was one of the "main props" of its executive.[61]

The Native Administration Ordinance of 1927 had made these State Councils the body before which succession disputes should come, and not surprisingly the Ga State Council had ruled in favor of contenders that supported the Mambii Party.[62] This was particularly important in the newly enfranchised areas of Labardi and Christiansborg, which voted overwhelmingly for Thompson. In addition, the Ga *mantse* beat "gonggong" on the eve of the election to tell his subjects to vote for Thompson, while "young roughs" who supported the Mambii Party, but were not ratepayers and hence ineligible to vote, effectively intimidated Nanka-Bruce's older and more feeble supporters by blocking access to the narrow alleyways in which the voting took place.[63] So blatant, however, was the interference of the Mambii Party's supporters in the electoral process that after Nanka-Bruce lost by a close margin, he successfully appealed the outcome of the election in the Accra Divisional Court.[64] It was to no avail, however, for in the new election that followed, Thompson was still able to win by a slightly larger margin.[65] Municipal politics in Accra were clearly no longer the preserve of the upper echelons of the educated elite.[66]

Baron Holmes, in what remains the most detailed study of the economic and political organizations of the interwar years in the Gold Coast, concludes that to describe the protest of this period as nationalist or even protonationalist is "misleading, despite the real elements of insight" this terminology offers.[67] Instead, he argues that "the events of this period need to be looked at in terms of interest articulation" partly because of the presence of what he considers "the influence of societal differentiation (i.e. class attitudes)."[68] His emphasis is on the social cleavages in this colonial society that divided people on class, occupational and residential lines.[69] It was only after their often conflicting interests were "aggregated," after the Second World War, that it was possible for a successful nationalist movement to begin. Most of all this meant the creation of new organizations, like Nkrumah's Convention People's Party, that understood "the dynamics of mass organization."[70] He offers a necessary corrective to those who have overemphasized the role of nationalism in the interwar

years, but at the same time veers in the direction of being overly
dismissive of the important role that the political organizations of this
period played in the parochial world of indirect rule politics. Much of the
reason for this also stems from his excessively rigid compartmentalization
of colonial society.

This is so particularly in regards to the GCARPS, which he scathingly
dismisses as "an essentially irrelevant irritant in its Cape Coast bastion."[71]
As far as building a nationalist movement was concerned, the society,
under the leadership of Kobina Sekyi, did fail to exploit the "real potential
for [developing an] anti-colonial movement" and weakened whatever
united front Gold Coast politicians might have presented against the
colonial government.[72] Nevertheless, more than in any other coastal
setting, the GCARPS, through its opposition to colonial policies, drew
members of the upper elite (like Kobina Sekyi) and also a host of fringe
members of the intelligentsia into the parochial world of indirect rule
politics. John Parker has characterized the political activity in Accra in the
1920s as the "politics of anxiety."[73] At least as much if not more anxiety-
ridden was the political scene in Cape Coast, where the precariousness of
traditional office was particularly acute. Most of all this was so because
the fringe members of the intelligentsia effectively took advantage of links
that they established with the native order to pursue careers in municipal
politics. The Cape Coast "rump" of the GCARPS facilitated this entry into
local politics by becoming the party of "non-cooperation."[74]

There were several reasons why this was so. In the 1920s, when
noncooperators were establishing themselves in the native order, they
could take advantage of its poorly preserved and chaotic condition to
manipulate this ill-defined section of their society to their own advantage.
Also of importance was the well-developed antigovernment feeling in the
town that its history of being superseded as the most important town on
the coast had left as a legacy. Ever since the government had moved the
colony's capital to Accra in 1878, and then at the turn of the century had
decided to make Sekondi the main port for the western portion of the
colony, people in Cape Coast had come to feel that the colonial
government was the town's "unmitigated enemy."[75] Cynically, they felt
that it was the price that the town's "wide-awake population" had paid for
leading the successful protest against the unpopular Lands Bill of 1897. It
was easy for the lower strata of the elite to see their own often
unsuccessful careers paralleling that of the town itself, and to take
advantage of the suspicion toward the colonial government, particularly
when unpopular colonial policies heightened these feelings.

The government's decision in 1921 to build a deepwater harbor at
Takoradi, some sixty miles to the west of Cape Coast, did much to bring
these tensions to the surface. The harbor, and the new Central Province
Railroad that was to be part of this development, undoubtedly represented

The Cape Coast Bar Association in 1923. *Left to right (back)*: A. J. E. Bucknor, W. Ward Brew, G. H. Savage, W. Renner, W. E. G. Sekyi, D. Myles Abadoo; *(front)*: A. F. E. Fieldgate (DC), C. Harding (PC), Justice Hall, C. E. Woolhouse Bannerman (PM) and E. J. P. Brown. Courtesy of NAG, Cape Coast.

a major threat to the town's economy. It was enough to bring together even those who had been mortal enemies in the past, and was also reflected by the town's more unified opposition to the Guggisberg legislative reforms than was the case in either Accra or Sekondi.[76] Even in 1927, when the intelligentsia in Accra and Sekondi decided that further opposition to the New Constitution was pointless, Cape Coast refused to go along. On the surface the town remained even more united against the new constitution on account of the Native Administration Ordinance, which seemed designed to destroy the Cape Coast–based GCARPS.

At the same time, however, there had always been an underlying concern that the reflexive opposition to colonial polices for which the town was well known had itself been responsible for the official disfavor from which it seemed to suffer. By playing on this apprehensiveness the government was able to break the opposition to the New Constitution. Not surprisingly, it was the upper echelons of the intelligentsia—barristers like A. K. Korsah and W. Ward Brew and prominent businessmen like H. Van Hein and W. R. Phillips—who took the lead. In their own careers they had more to gain from cooperation than unwavering opposition to colonial policies. Korsah, for example, represented the large metropolitan firms in cases before the colony's courts. As a die-hard opponent of colonial legislation, he would have had difficulty obtaining these lucrative retainers. With Casely Hayford's assistance, this elite established a Cape Coast Ratepayers Association in 1928, and Korsah ran unopposed for the position of municipal representative on the Legislative Council.

Given the strong feelings that existed in Cape Coast about cooperating with the colonial government, it was not surprising that the decision to form a Ratepayers Association split the town into two opposing camps.[77] Members of the upper echelons of the elite were on both sides, but significant numbers of the Non-Cooperators, as they came to be known in Cape Coast, came from the lower, less successful strata of the town's educated elite. For example, Kwamina Sakyiama, who was the "Founder, Proprietor and Managing Editor" of the *Gold Coast Times,* had originally worked as a bookkeeper for the African and Eastern Trading Corporation in Kumasi, but had fallen out with his superiors and resigned in 1918.[78] He had returned to Cape Coast and had become the assistant editor of the *Gold Coast Leader,* eventually taking over as editor when J. P. H. Brown died in 1919.[79] Initially, when Casely Hayford took control of the *Gold Coast Leader* in the early twenties, the two had worked closely together in promoting the ideas of the National Congress of British West Africa.[80] By 1923, however, he was shifting his alliance to Sekyi, and together they established a competing newspaper in Cape Coast, the *Gold Coast Times.*

Chief Sam Amissah, who had been entsooled in 1918, was also an important member of the Non-Cooperators' inner council. Like Sakyiama, he too was a "standard seven boy."[81] Apart from being a carpenter in Cape

Coast, he was also involved in trading and must have well appreciated the vagaries of the colony's economy for the small operator.[82] His important contribution to the Non-Cooperators was his close link to the *omanhen*, Mbra III.[83] He had become one of his councillors, and as a result of this connection the Non-Cooperators were able to obtain the support of the *omanhen*, who refused to attend the Central Province's Provincial Council of Chiefs. As a result of this alliance, the Non-Cooperators described themselves as the "Oman Party," since they monopolized the *omanhen's oman*, or body of councillors, and this was how they came to be referred to in Cape Coast in the 1930s.

Also seeking to function as a controlling force in the affairs of the Ebiradzi stool family was John Mensah Cooke. He was the "only educated member" of this family, and though he was not a "blood relative" but a "domestic," he sought to promote himself as the head of the family.[84] It seems as though it was more his need for support to win acknowledgment of his claim to this position than ideological considerations that brought him into the Non-Cooperators camp. During the 1920s he was in contention with his main opponent, Kofi Ebu, the *gyasihen*, to control the *ahenfie* and stool paraphernalia, and it was not surprising that as "Sekyi's Cowboys" were also interested in controlling Nana Mbra III that they should have come together as allies.[85] This joining of transactional and ideological interests preshadowed how much of Cape Coast's political life was to develop in the 1930s.

Finally there was George E. Moore. His earlier career in business, like Sakyiama's, had also been less than successful. Up until the early twenties he had been a cocoa broker in the Eastern Province, but in the unpredictable economy of the 1920s he had eventually gone bankrupt and in addition seems to have served a short jail sentence.[86] The result was that in the early twenties he returned to Cape Coast "bitter towards Europeans," and joined the GCARPS, where he became Sekyi's good friend.[87] Like many other standard seven boys, Moore also sought office in the ranks of the native order. In a similar fashion to Coker, he took advantage of the incorporative nature of the Akan matrilineal family. Even though his father had been a West Indian soldier stationed in Cape Coast in the 1880s, and consequently an outsider, Moore was able to claim a position in the native order through his mother's matrilineage. In 1925 he was "elected" a *safuhen* in Number Four (or Nkum) *Asafo*.[88]

Moore and Sekyi were to become the main forces behind the Non-Cooperators in Cape Coast, with Moore the party's public standard-bearer. They first of all tried to challenge the validity of Korsah's election as the town's municipal representative in the Cape Coast Police Magistrate's Court, but were unsuccessful.[89] More importantly, they quickly realized that effective opposition to the Native Administration Ordinance depended on more than controlling the *omanhen*. This was so particularly with regard to the important position of *tufuhen*. When the town had split over the issue of electing a municipal member for the Legislative Council, Coker had sided with the Ratepayers. He must have assumed that the Ratepayers represented the dominant party in the town, and had allowed himself to be elected the president of this organization. In a similar fashion to Taki Yaoboi, however, he overestimated how much support this alliance would bring him. Instead, it gave the Non-Cooperators an opportunity to wrest control of this important traditional position.

In contrast to J. P. H. Brown's attacks on Coker in the past, Sekyi and Moore realized that to destool the wily *tufuhen* they needed to undermine his base in the *asafos* by actively participating in the day-to-day affairs of these organizations. Sekyi did so by defending in court the right of individual *asafos* to parade with their flags in town. These displays had always been a source of potential violence, and as competition for traditional office had increased in the 1920s, and as *asafo* affairs had become potentially more violent, district commissioners had tried to forbid these parades.[90] Moore, on the other hand, supported the smaller *asafos* against Coker's *asafo*, Bentsir, over the right to use various musical instruments.[91] Coker was also very vulnerable on the controversial issue of tolls collected from stranger fishermen in Cape Coast. He clearly benefited from these payments, but at the same time, in a similar fashion to Elmina, these outsiders were Ali net users, and there was ongoing hostility between them and the *asafos* to which the Cape Coast fishermen belonged.

Eventually, Moore felt that he had gathered enough support among the *asafos* to proclaim himself the *tufuhen* of Cape Coast. It clearly was a radical challenge to traditional principles of legitimacy, and was rather anomalous coming as it did from someone who opposed the Provincial Councils on the grounds that they violated the proper constitutional practices of the native state! Moore could establish neither a patrilineal nor a matrilineal claim to this office, and instead advanced the novel argument that there was more to asserting a successful claim to this position than family connections. The candidate's bravery was far more important, and though he had no evidence to show that he was particularly suited in this regard, he and his supporters attacked Coker's record in the East African campaign during the First World War to show that he was unfit.[92]

In a similar fashion to what had happened in Accra, where the Ga *mantse* had counterattacked by seeking to destool his enemies, Coker did likewise in Cape Coast. He took advantage of the long-standing conflict in the stool family to encourage the *gyasefu* to serve charges against Mbra III that brought to the surface all the hostility within the Ebiradzi family over the sale of family land and a host of other more personal issues.[93] The

Tufuhen G. E. Moore in the 1940s. Source: G. S. Moore (son).

result was that political affairs in the town also rapidly came to take on a bipolar aspect with basically transactional factions seeking the support of what were now the two major political camps in the town. In contrast to the past, it was impossible for the political officers to settle these disputes by following the advice of an articulate member of the educated elite since there were such people on opposite sides of these disputes. The existence of the major dispute ensured that transactional disputes would also remain unsolved, while vice versa the struggles to control stool positions contributed to preserving the division between the feuding sections of the intelligentsia.

In addition, one of the ironies of interventionist indirect rule was that in exchange for incorporating native states into the system of colonial rule, the government had given them the responsibility for resolving their own internal disputes.[94] However, in situations where there was as much conflict as there was in Cape Coast, far too much division existed within the institutions of the native state for their members to resolve disputes in which they were themselves involved. Neither were official inquiries much use in resolving these matters. The native state was in such a condition of flux that there was no constitutional model to which the officers who conducted these investigations could turn.[95] Nor did they have the statutory authority to enforce their decisions. Instead, as the forces ranged against one another became more skillful in exploiting the weaknesses of the Native Administration Ordinance, political officials found themselves having to be more and more impartial, which contributed to contradictory decisions that prolonged the life of local stool disputes.

For example, when the government finally agreed in 1929 to hold an inquiry into the *tufuhen* dispute in Cape Coast, Deputy Secretary of Native Affairs Hugh Thomas, who spent one month in Cape Coast investigating, decided on the basis of majority opinion that Coker had indeed been "deposed from his office as *Tufuhen* with the full approval of all the Companies."[96] He concluded, however, that the position was hereditary and was governed by the native law of succession, which effectively barred Moore from succeeding since he was obviously not a member of Coker's maternal family.[97] The contradiction of juxtaposing majority rule and matrilineal principles of inheritance was not lost on Governor Slater, who refused to accept his secretary of native affairs' rulings. Left without any direction from their superiors, local political officers tended to side with Coker, and on the occasion of the acting governor's visit to Cape Coast in 1930 they even tried to force the *omanhen* to recognize him as the *tufuhen* of Cape Coast.[98]

It was an indication of how much the struggle to be the *tufuhen* of Cape Coast had come to involve more than just the two contestants for office that a few months after Coker died in March 1932, there was a major inter-*asafo* riot in the town which left six persons dead and twenty-eight wounded.[99] Moore, who had led the parade that had resulted in this riot, was arrested, convicted for having provoked and participated in a riot, and sentenced to a one-year imprisonment. But rather than undermining his status in Cape Coast, the *Oman* greeted him with an ovation when he was released from prison in 1933. His supporters maintained that his "bravery under fire" was an indication of how suitable he was to be the *tufuhen*.[100]

Secondly, the chaos that this struggle to control the native order created allowed a new generation of office seekers to emerge. Competition for these positions was definitely more intense than it had been in the past, as contestants for office could now seek support from the town's two main political factions. The most important of these newcomers was W. S. K. Johnston (Kwesi Johnston), who had spent the first twenty-five years of his life in Sierra Leone, where he had received an excellent secondary education.[101] When he returned to the Gold Coast in 1919-1920, he became active in journalism in Accra and Cape Coast. It was not a particularly remunerative career, and he eventually followed in his father's footsteps and entered politics. The way in which he did this, however, was quite different from his father. The latter had done so by being the secretary of the GCARPS, and with this organization's support had sat on the Town Council from 1914 until his death in 1928.[102]

Instead, Kwesi Johnston's entry into politics was an excellent indication of how people like himself in Cape Coast had come to realize that a base in the native order was the sine qua non for success in the town's political life in general. Fortuitously, his maternal uncle was Kwamina Tandoh, who had been enstooled as Chief Amoah III in 1919. Initially, Johnston took advantage of Tandoh's long absences from the colony on business and sought to promote himself as his uncle's official representative. Significantly, however, he had strong competition from another of Tandoh's educated maternal nephews, and in 1929, when Tandoh succumbed to "general paralysis" while on business in New York, the struggle to succeed to the latter's position became even more heated.[103]

Kwesi Johnston's desire to become a town councillor predisposed him to side with the Ratepayers. It meant that his opponent, Charles Wharton, had to turn to the Non-Cooperators, or the Oman Party, as they had taken to calling themselves, for support. Apart from having what may have been a better matrilineal claim to his uncle's office, Johnston more importantly used his superior education and understanding of how the colonial government functioned to good advantage. He quickly replaced the old and ailing Coker as the main representative of cooperation with the government in the native order. In 1933 he took advantage of his base in the native order and his position in the Ratepayer's Association to win a seat on the Town Council. Once again as an indication of how closely stool affairs and municipal politics had become intertwined, he was able to take advantage of his enhanced status as a town councillor to strengthen

Kwesi Johnston as Chief Amoah IV, c. 1960s. Source: K. W. S. Johnston.

his hold on his traditional position, and in 1935 he felt secure enough politically to have himself "officially" enstooled as Amoah IV.[104]

The career of H. Bart Plange, who in 1934 proclaimed that he was Kweki Gyepi II, was reflective of a third important development in the native order.[105] Like many of this new generation of traditional office seekers, he claimed a special position for himself in the native order which he described as that of the *akyempizhin*.[106] Thomas had noticed this development during his inquiry in 1929 into the *tufuhen* dispute, when he had observed that the Cape Coast chiefs had taken to styling themselves "wing chiefs" and that the *asafos* had taken "wing positions."[107] In 1930, Kwesi Johnston, who was in danger of being overshadowed by these wing chiefs, maintained that "these wing positions were of recent growth."[108] Five years later, when wing chiefs were even more established in Cape Coast, a contributor to the *Gold Coast Independent* went even further and maintained that "these titles were purely Akan in origin and were applicable only in the pure Akan states where chiefs ruled over large territorial divisions."[109]

As the colonial government's conception of chieftaincy had become patterned on what existed in the more centralized and better preserved states of the interior, contestants for chiefly office in the coastal communities realized that they needed more elaborate titles and functions. Gyepi had obviously come on the scene too late to claim a wing chief position. Instead, he maintained that his position allowed him to "punish in the stocks," which would have undoubtedly guaranteed him a position on the Native Tribunal, and even more fortuitously to be the "Oman Treasurer."[110] From which, if any, inland state Gyepi received inspiration is hard to determine. He claimed that his predecessor had died in 1879, and since the mystified district commissioner could find no reference in the town's records to any previous *akyempizhin* there was little that he could do but add Gyepi's name to the Chief's List.[111]

Gyepi's interest in asserting his right to be treasurer is not hard to ascertain. Sir Ransford Slater, who succeeded Sir Gordon Guggisberg in 1928, was even more determined than his predecessor to give the "Native Authority" a major role in promoting the colony's development.[112] Spurred on by the colony's declining economic condition in the 1930s, he tried to introduce a Native Administration Revenue Bill along with a general Income Tax Bill. Coming as this did during the height of the depression, it was not surprising that there was widespread opposition to these measures, and by 1932 the government was forced to withdraw both bills. Nevertheless, the issue of creating stool treasuries had remained central to the colonial government's policy of indirect rule. The relatively successful stool treasury system that the administration had established in Asante since 1927 continued to be the goal for the colony, as well. Consequently, to someone like Gyepi, who had been trained in accountancy, it obviously made excellent sense to establish a position in the native order that would give him "traditional" legitimacy to claim a dominant role in the operation of future stool treasuries.[113]

Important local events, such as Mbra III's sudden death in December 1933, also played an important role in stimulating competition for chiefly office as well as changes in the structure of the traditional state. Both factions nominated candidates for the paramount stool by taking advantage of the rival sections within the stool family. The Oman Party nominated a young boy, Kofi Kakraba, as their candidate, clearly wanting to make sure that they would be able to control his actions, while their opponents turned to F. S. Bilson, who had been destooled in 1916. There were also bitter struggles over who had the right to perform the deceased *omanhen*'s funeral custom, which was interpreted as a sign of legitimacy. Given the increasing importance that the government had come to attach to majority opinion, to strengthen the claims of the Oman's candidate, Sekyi was instrumental in incorporating what were basically family chiefs from villages surrounding Cape Coast into the structure of the traditional state. In this fashion he also sought to formalize the already existing links between Cape Coast's *asafos* and these outlying villages, which were their rural sections.

With the increasing importance of the traditional state, the *asafos* were themselves undergoing significant changes and the competition to control them was also increasing. "Standard seven boys" with no claims to chiefly office were turning to them as a source of traditional office to pursue political careers in Cape Coast. This development obviously conflicted with the interests of the wing chiefs who wanted these organizations to be part of their wing divisions. It meant that within the ranks of individual *asafos* the potential for conflict increased, as now there were invariably disputes over who actually was in charge of the *asafo*. Individual situations within the *asafo* determined which of the two main parties in the town contestants turned to for support. Neither did these alliances have to remain constant, as the career of Napoleon Forson indicated. When he became a *safuhen* in Number Two *Asafo* in 1930, he was the law clerk for local barrister A. J. E. Bucknor, and used his legal knowledge to become the "firebrand" of the *asafo*.[114] As such he was no doubt predisposed to side with the Oman Party, but when the regular *supi* who was allied with the *asafo*'s putative wing chief, an Oman Party supporter, returned from a long illness and challenged Forson's position in the *asafo*, the latter switched his support to the Ratepayers.

Switching sides in this fashion was indicative of the underlying transactional issues that were at the heart of most of the disputes in the Cape Coast native order. In general, however, during the 1930s it was the Oman Party that increased its strength at the expense of its opposition. Sekyi's and Moore's immediate involvement in the affairs of the native order was clearly a major factor in contributing to the success of the Oman Party. In addition, their spirited opposition to unpopular government polices during the depression enhanced their standing in Cape Coast at the expense of those who favored cooperation. The Ratepayer Association's representatives, on the other hand, were placed at a distinct disadvantage. However much they tried to distance themselves from unpopular colonial legislation, they were still associated with the government. As a minority on both the Legislative and Municipal Councils, they could only voice feeble protests which the government's representatives easily ignored.

The best example of the Ratepayer's dilemma was their opposition to Governor Slater's attempt in 1931 to introduce an income tax for all males who made in excess of forty pounds per annum.[115] Nanka-Bruce and A. K. Korsah bitterly attacked this legislation in the Legislative Council, and the local press also kept up a barrage of criticism.[116] In contrast, however, and consistent with its more active opposition to unpopular colonial policies, the Non-Cooperators were prominent in organizing popular protest in Cape Coast which ended in rioting. Along with more spontaneous rioting in Sekondi, it was this protest that pressured the government into withdrawing the bill. The result was that the GCARPS, which by this time was thoroughly under the control of the Non-Cooperators, took a great deal of credit for the defeat of the income tax measure. Coming in conjunction with the society's heightened campaign to prevent the implementation of the Native Administration Ordinance, it was more than enough to destroy what little was left of the relationship that had existed between the society and the government. Its effectiveness as a colony-wide political force was seriously weakened, but this was hardly so in Cape Coast.

The outcome of the income tax protest indicated to a wide spectrum of the town's population that the noncooperative approach to government policies could be far more effective than working within the system. It reinforced the already existing animosity to the colonial government, and was more than enough to ensure that the GCARPS would continue to be a major force in the town's political life. Local merchants, for example, continued to be attracted to the society, while their support for the local Chamber of Commerce declined to the point that by the early thirties they had deserted its ranks and the organization was no longer meeting.[117] In the 1930s schoolteachers, barristers and even civil servants were also attracted to membership in the society, and it was from the ranks of this elite that its leadership came. Paradoxically, even though the society was eclipsed in importance on a colony-wide level it was far from "moribund" in Cape Coast, as Baron Holmes has suggested, and demonstrated this by attracting more than just an "aged membership."[118]

The society and the Oman Party were hard to distinguish apart because of their dual concern with native affairs and opposition to colonial policies. As a result both organizations could expand their bases in the native order and among the town's small population of ratepayers. Korsah and Ward Brew, the Ratepayer Association's leading lights, did not provide the same kind of legal help that Sekyi did for Oman Party supporters. Indeed, Korsah acquired the reputation in Cape Coast of being a "recluse who lived in a well-defended castle."[119] Nor did the Ratepayers do much for homeowners who defaulted in paying their house rates and were in danger of having the Town Council sell these buildings. This was a particularly acute problem during the difficult years of the depression, and once again it was Sekyi who was active in challenging the legality of these actions.[120] Market women, who were opposed to paying for hawker's licenses, and those affected by higher motor vehicle taxes and gasoline prices also gravitated towards the Non-Cooperators. The GCARPS's very active involvement in the cocoa holdups of 1931 and 1937-1938 also helped.[121] In the 1937-1938 holdup, the Ratepayers in Cape Coast were at a serious disadvantage since the man who had become their most important spokesman, Kofi Bentsi-Enchill, was the senior representative for the United Africa Company (UAC), the main target of the holdup action.[122]

The result was that by 1936 the Non-Cooperators began to increase their strength among the Cape Coast municipal electorate, as well as in the native order. In that year C. F. Hayfron-Benjamin, a local barrister, and J. P. Allotey-Hammond, a teacher at Adisadel High School, who were both active members of the GCARPS, won election to the town council. The highest voter turnout ever indicated that the Cape Coast electorate recognized the significance of this development, which brought to an end the unchallenged monopoly that the Ratepayers had enjoyed of the four seats for Africans on the town council since 1928.[123] Undoubtedly the most important Ratepayer casualty was Kwesi Johnston. Since 1933 he had been one of the most vocal African town councillors, but as the Ratepayer's position in the native order had weakened so, too, had Johnston's. It was his situation that best of all indicated how important the link between support in the native order and success at the level of municipal politics had become.

Significantly, the two remaining Ratepayers, El Hadji Mohammed El Amin and Kofi Bentsi-Enchill, got their support from different sections of the Cape Coast community. The latter could rely on an important section of the Muslim community which supported the Hausa headman, Chief Smyla, who in turn depended upon the Ratepayers to uphold his position in this "stranger" community. On the other hand, Bentsi-Enchill represented a new generation of cooperators in Cape Coast. He had successfully worked his way up in the United Africa Company, and in 1936 he was the firm's district manager, the first African to hold such a senior position. His support in Cape Coast came from people like himself who also worked for the large metropolitan firms or for the government.[124] With his far greater managerial experience than either Allotey-Hammond or Hayfron-Benjamin, he could make practical suggestions as to how the council should conduct its affairs, in contrast to the provocative challenges of his colleagues which were easily outvoted by the European majority.[125]

In 1937, as an indication of the increasing interest in municipal politics, the Non-Cooperators established their own party, which they called the Independent Party to indicate that it was neither under the control of the government nor the large metropolitan firms.[126] The inaugural meeting of the party was held at Sekyi's home, and all the prominent Non-Cooperators were there.[127] Moore became the party's standard-bearer in the elections that followed in 1938, and along with Allotey-Hammond and Hayfron-Benjamin won election to the town council. The only Ratepayer to survive was Bentsi-Enchill, and even this was close. The election coincided with the cocoa holdup of 1937-1938, which the Independents were very active in supporting. It clearly contributed to their popularity in Cape Coast, and significantly there were some important defections from the Ratepayer camp at this time. Kwesi Johnston gave up his support for F. S. Bilson, the Ratepayer's candidate for *omanhen,* and so too did Chief Kweku Arhin, the *akomfudzihin.* Only Chief Gyepi II, who had shifted his support from Kofi Kakraba to Bilson, and a section of the stool family remained loyal to the ex-*omanhen.*

"Looking whitemen in the eye," as Moore later described his activities on the town council, clearly proved more appealing to the Cape Coast electorate than the passivity that the Ratepayers had demonstrated.[128] The best indication of this was their sweep of all four seats on the town council in the 1940 election.[129] Significantly, among their ranks was Kwesi Johnston, who in 1939 had switched from the discredited Ratepayers Association to become an active supporter of the Oman Party. Apart from the emotional satisfaction that came from seeing Africans "standing up" to colonial officials, the Independents were able to expand the range of issues that they forced the council into considering.[130] There were important parallels between their activities on the Town Council and in the native order. In both venues of local politics they were able to put government officials on the defensive by confronting them with issues for which there were no guiding precedents.

They increased their ability to do this even more in 1941 when Korsah resigned as the town's municipal representative on the Legislative Council, and Moore took his place unopposed. He used his new position on the Legislative Council to pressure the government into holding an investigation into the stool dispute in Cape Coast even though local officials tried to oppose this. The Sierra Leonean High Court judge, Justice Mustapha Faud Bey, who conducted this inquiry, could not help but be impressed by the overwhelming support that the Oman Party enjoyed in the native order, and recommended that the government recognize Kofi Kakraba as *omanhen* of Cape Coast. It was such a politically embarrassing recommendation to the government that officials went to great pains to keep the report confidential, which the Oman Party naturally interpreted as a victory for their candidate. Also, the Independents launched an unprecedented attack on the integrity of some of the European officials on the Town Council. In the past it had only been African employees who had been subject to such charges, and when the government tacitly acknowledged that there had been at least slackness on the part of some of the council's officials and replaced the ones most compromised, the Independents could claim this as another major victory.[131] To the provincial commissioner, A. F. E. Fieldgate, who was also the president of the Town Council, it was clear that the GCARPS was directly responsible for bringing the Cape Coast Town Council to what he considered to be "its present condition" of impasse.[132]

By 1942 the Independents in Cape Coast were near the height of their power. The electorate returned them unopposed to the town council, and all that escaped them for a clean sweep of the cape Coast political scene was government recognition of their candidate for *omanhen*. Ironically, however, the political success of uncompromising noncooperation brought to the surface once again the disquieting fear that in the long run the town would not benefit from these tactics. It was obvious that after the war there were going to be substantial changes in the structure of colonial rule, and the need for a middle passage between Korsah's excessive passivity and Moore's confrontational style seemed particularly appropriate.

To S. R. Wood, the editor/proprietor of the *Star of West Africa*, the "new world order" that was going to follow the end of the Second World War would require different strategies if Cape Coast was to benefit from these changes.[133] Initially, he had been a strong supporter of the GCARPS. Along with Moore, he had gone as one of the society's two delegates to England in 1934 to protest unpopular legislation. It had been through the society's help that in 1939 he had set up in Cape Coast his newspaper, the *Star of West Africa*.[134] His editorial attacks on Korsah had contributed to making him resign from the Legislative Council, but by 1944 he was publicly disappointed with Moore's "exertions" on this body which had led to "aggravating misunderstandings and ill feelings and the widening of the breach in the political affairs of Cape Coast."[135]

There were others who also began to feel this way. The most important was Kwesi Johnston, who once again shifted his loyalties.[136] As an indication of how important a base in the native order had become, in 1943 he took advantage of the provincial commissioner's suggestion that both parties should put aside their candidates for *omanhen* and select someone mutually acceptable. The recent death of one of the main contenders for the position of stool mother among the five branches of the stool family made this easier than otherwise might have been the case, but even so the Oman Party refused to go along. On this occasion, however, the government was able to outmaneuver the opposition by referring the legitimacy of this selection to the Central Provincial Council. Since the candidate agreed to attend Provincial Council meetings, it was a foregone conclusion that the Central Provincial Council would find in his favor, and in 1944 he was formerly recognized as Mbra IV.

This meant that when in 1944 the government passed the Cape Coast Town Council Ordinance, which expanded the size of the Town Council, and the Native Authority (Colony) Ordinance, which gave the native authority two seats on this expanded Town Council, there was a great deal of incentive to challenge the Independents for the control of the town's political life. Initially, Kwesi Johnston, S. R. Wood and A. B. Josiah, the *supi* of Number Two *Asafo* and who had also been an Independent supporter, tried to take advantage of these new opportunities to organize a third party, but it soon became obvious that they lacked the resources to do so.[137] Instead, it was Bentsi-Enchill, who had replaced Korsah as the leading Ratepayer, who profited.[138] Mends Cann, the young man who had become Mbra IV, had even before his enstoolment been Bentsi-Enchill's ward while he was a student at Adisadel, the Anglican High School in Cape Coast.[139] After his enstoolment, Bentsi-Enchill had provided him with an *ahenfie*, and not surprisingly was one of his most important councillors.[140] The result was that in 1944, when Bentsi-Enchill decided to contest the Cape Coast seat on the Legislative Council, he did so with a strong base in the native order, and he was clearly Moore's most important competition.[141]

Nevertheless, Bentsi-Enchill lost to Moore in a hard-fought election campaign that involved far more than the small number of ratepayers who were actually qualified to vote.[142] In a similar fashion to Accra, where Kojo Thompson had used "young roughs," both contestants used *asafo* members who were not eligible to vote. Their role consisted of collecting voters and bringing them to the polls, as well as intimidating the supporters of the opposing party. Since both parties engaged in these practices, there was no court challenge to the outcome of the election as there had been in Accra in 1935. Bentsi-Enchill's supporters, however, felt that they had suffered most of all from the police's inability to check the particularly blatant harassment of Ratepayer voters that their opponents practiced.[143]

The election also indicated that the winds of change were going to blow much more in the direction of confrontation than cooperation. This was not immediately obvious since Bentsi-Enchill and his supporters were able to maintain an important role in Cape Coast's affairs. They controlled the Oguaa Native State, as it was now called, and as a result had two seats on the expanded Town Council as well.[144] Bentsi-Enchill was also able to salvage a role for himself on the Town Council as the representative of the

Cape Coast Chamber of Commerce, which had been revived in 1937. In general the expanded responsibilities of the Town Council made its African members, who were now in a majority, less inclined to be confrontational, and anyway many of the issues that the Independents had fought for before the war the government had conceded.[145]

The boycott campaign of 1948, however, radically upset this relative harmony.[146] One of its main targets was the UAC, which put Bensti-Enchill on the defensive and in turn made Mbra IV vulnerable. Even though the Independents had not initiated the campaign in Cape Coast, they took advantage of the popular support that it received to move for Mbra IV's destoolment.[147] At the height of the campaign, Bentsi-Enchill died. Left without his most important mentor, the young *omanhen* had no choice but to abdicate on 2 March 1948.[148] In the colony's radically altered political climate, no longer could the government refuse to allow Kofi Kakraba's enstoolment as Mbra V, and at this point the Non-Cooperators emerged in complete control of the Cape Coast political scene. They seized control of the State Council. Josiah and Johnston lost their positions on the Native Court as well as on the Town Council, and the *omanhen* moved to a new residence. Indicative of these political successes, Sekyi, who had been content to be the éminence grise of the GCARPS, finally in 1945 allowed himself to be elected president of the society.[149] He was never to run for any public office himself, but in Cape Coast there was no doubt about his pivotal role in the town's political life. The traditionalism that he stood for and that made the society less and less effective as a national organization had proven very successful at the local level as indirect rule had given political affairs in the colony an increasingly parochial focus.

Cape Coast undoubtedly represented the best case of how successful noncooperation based on controlling the native order was in the colony's political life in the decades leading up to independence. To varying degrees it was also the case in the two other coastal towns with municipalities, with the similarities between Cape Coast and Accra the greatest. In the late 1930s and early 1940s, the Mambii Party, with its strong base in the many traditional quarters of Accra, was able to maintain Kojo Thompson in his position as the municipal representative on the Legislative Council from 1936 to 1944.[150] The party, however, had much more trouble capturing seats on the Town Council. In 1938, for example, when the Independents were sweeping all the seats for Africans on the Cape Coast Town Council, the Ratepayer candidates in Accra easily defeated the Mambii Party candidates.[151]

Not until 1942 were the latter finally able to add control of the Accra Town Council to their political laurels. Clearly, the deeply etched hostility towards the colonial government on the part of the intelligentsia that existed in Cape Coast was missing in Accra, and it was harder for an anti-establishment message to find acceptance among the town's elite. Instead, they were more attracted to the responsible government that the Ratepayers promised, while the Mambii Party clearly lacked the quality of leadership that their Cape Coast counterparts enjoyed. Kojo Thompson had neither Sekyi's legal brilliance nor Moore's public presence, and the GCARPS had never been able to establish itself effectively in Accra.[152]

Undoubtedly what also made Accra different from Cape Coast was its larger and more heterogeneous population. With its many distinct quarters, each with its own Native Tribunal, it was impossible to control the native order and use it to challenge colonial policies in quite the manner that Sekyi and his supporters did in Cape Coast. For example, the James Town *mantse*, Nii Kojo Ababio IV, remained a loyal Ratepayer supporter until his death in 1938. Even Taki Obili, who was the Mambii Party's candidate for the position of Ga *mantse*, had used the provisions of the Native Administration Ordinance to outmaneuver his opponent, Taki Yaoboi. In 1932-1933 he had submitted the dispute over the paramountcy of Accra to the Eastern Provincial Council of Chiefs to arbitrate, something that the Oman Party would never have agreed to let the Central Provincial Council of Chiefs do for the Cape Coast dispute.[153]

Also, the capital's larger population and more developed economic infrastructure meant that there were both more skilled and unskilled workers than was the case in Cape Coast. The result was that there was more potential for labor militancy, which the depression exacerbated. It contributed to making Accra one of the most lively political environments in West Africa during the 1930s. It was here the Sierra Leonean I. T. A. Wallace-Johnson established his West African Youth League (WAYL) in 1933, and quickly became involved in labor organizing.[154] In addition, Nnamdi Azikiwe's "new journalism" rapidly made the *African Morning Post* an important voice of protest against colonial rule.[155] Wallace-Johnson was avowedly socialist while Azikiwe was mostly an African nationalist. As such they both represented a much more truly anticolonial position than the Mambii Party.[156] It meant that unlike the Independents in Cape Coast who monopolized the left in that town, the Mambii Party often found themselves trailing behind the lead that Azikiwe and the WAYL established.

The younger, more radical generation that was attracted to this brand of anticolonialism tended also to be cynical about the value of belonging to an organization like a town council. Wallace-Johnson "claimed responsibility for exposing the fraudulent activities of the city officials" of the Freetown Municipal Council.[157] Membership on the Legislative Council at least gave the opportunity to voice opposition to major aspects of colonial policy. On the Town Council one was much more likely to become mired down in conservancy issues or in merely approving council expenditure.[158] In this climate of opinion, as Samuel Quarcoopome has observed, it was not surprising that the Mambii Party did not put all their energies into contesting Town Council elections.[159] Instead, during the 1930s antiestablishment politics had begun to move out of the indirect rule mold that the Native Administration Ordinance of 1927 had done so much to shape. Accra, which had pioneered the way into linking municipal politics with the affairs of the native order, by the end of the 1930s was indicating the next direction that political developments in the colony were to take.

Politically more quiescent Sekondi, the third town with a municipal council in the colony, also shared more in common with Accra than with Cape Coast. G. J. Christian, a West Indian from Dominica, was able to monopolize the position of municipal representative on the Legislative Council from 1930 to his death in 1940. In the contest, however, that followed for his seat it was the local barrister R. S. Blay, an Nzima, who was easily able to defeat his opponent and fellow barrister, F. Awooner Williams. Like Sekyi, Blay had been active in stool politics while his opponent held elitist views that he made no attempt to conceal from the masses.[160] But perhaps more importantly, Blay also benefited from the support that he got from railway union members in Sekondi, a small number of whom would have been able to vote in municipal elections.

What this indicated was that by the late 1930s, Sekondi's politics were also beginning to register significant differences from that of Cape Coast's. As the center of the colony's railway network, there was a considerable wage-earning class that as early as the second decade of the twentieth century had begun to form labor associations and engage in strike action.[161] The depressed conditions of the 1930s had discouraged industrial action, but by the end of the decade the then renamed Gold Coast Railway African Workers Union had become much more militant and in 1939 had staged a partially successful strike for better wages and official union recognition.[162] R. S. Blay had been drawn into this affair and had represented in court many of the strikers who had been charged with criminal actions. It had clearly contributed to his popularity. In 1941, when another railway union strike had spread to other wage laborers in the Sekondi-Takoradi area, Blay was even more prominently involved in seeking to negotiate a settlement with the railway's general manager.[163] By this time, however, the leadership of the railway union had become considerably more militant than Blay was prepared to be, and they rejected his arbitrating role since he seemed too ready to make concessions to management.

It was symbolic of the changes that were going to take place in the colony's political life. Noncooperation was soon to be replaced by Kwame Nkrumah's search for the political kingdom. Nevertheless, the messy, drawn-out parochial struggles of indirect rule were the foundations upon which a more radical generation of postwar politicians were able to build what Baron Holmes has described as the "aggregated" anticolonial movement.[164] The scholars and members of the intelligentsia of the interwar years who had played the vitally important role of straddling the realms of stool politics and municipal affairs had their counterparts during the era of mass nationalism in the Convention People's Party organizers, who were similarly underachieving and underemployed school leavers.

Notes

1. Thomas Hodgkin, *Nationalism in Colonial Africa* (New York, 1957), 18.

2. Ibid., 63.

3. Dominc Fortescue, "The Accra Crowd, the *Asafo,* and the Opposition to the Municipal Corporations Ordinance, 1924-25," *Canadian Journal of African Studies* 24, no. 3 (1990):348.

4. Ibid., 352, 353.

5. Ibid., 361.

6. Ibid., 352, 364.

7. Kathryn Firmin-Sellers, *The Transformation of Property Rights in the Gold Coast: An Empirical Analysis Applying Rational Choice Theory* (Cambridge, 1996), 45.

8. David Apter, *Ghana in Transition* (1955; reprint, New York, 1963), 12.

9. Parker, "Ga State and Society," 290.

10. Some of the most important of these disputes were the *Harbor Blockyard Case* of 1907 in which the Alata stool contested with the Sempes for ownership of land that the government acquired to extend the Accra harbor (SCT 2/4/41, NAG, Accra), the *Tetteh Kwaku v. Kpakpo Brown* case of 1910 (ADM 11/1/641, NAG, Accra) and the *Land for Accra Water Works* case of 1917-1918 (SCT 2/4/66, SCT 2/4/67 and SCT 2/4/68, NAG, Accra).

11. Cited in Wraith, *Guggisberg,* 179.

12. *Legislative Council Debates,* Annual Address, 6 March 1924, cited in Kimble, *A Political History of Ghana,* 446.

13. *Report on the Objections Lodged with the Colonial Secretary Against the Application of the Municipal Corporation Ordinance 1924* (Accra, 1925), SNA 11/1086, NAG, Accra.

14. *Gold Coast Leader,* 26 April 1924. It was hardly surprising that he was enthusiastic. He had been one of the four Africans on the committee of inquiry that Governor Guggisberg had appointed in 1921 to investigate and make recommendations on how municipal government should function in the colony. Wraith, *Guggisberg,* 209.

15. For a description of the activities of the congress and its bitter struggle with Nana Ofori Atta, the paramount chief of Akyem Abuakwa, see Kimble, *A Political History of Ghana,* 374-403.

16. Taki Yaoboi had succeeded the deposed Taki Obili as Ga *mantse* in 1919. He was literate and progressive, but given the bitterness surrounding the destoolment of his predecessor his position was easily open to challenge. In 1920 a British businessman, W. J. Blacker, sought to lease the Korle lagoon from the *mantse* and his councillors to turn it into a harbor. There was immediate protest against this "selling" of the sacred lagoon and some of the *asafobii* of Asere and Sempe tried unsuccessfully to destool Taki Yaoboi. Petition to Churchill, Secretary of State, August 1921, ADM 11/1086, NAG, Accra.

17. Interview with H. A. Garshong, one of J. D. Garshong's sons, Accra, 25 July 1994.

18. Interview with S. T. Nettey, one of C. B. Nettey's sons, Accra, 17 July 1994.

19. Parker, "Ga State and Society," 317.

20. De Graft Johnson, "The Fanti Asafu," 308.

21. Nettey and Garshong had suggested that the Ga *mantse,* his fellow *mantsemei* and the town's *asafoatsemei* should send a telegram and a petition to the secretary of state protesting the proposed ordinance. Casely Hayford opposed this since he felt it would upset the chances of getting the government to agree to changes in the legislation. *Report of an Inquiry Held by the Honorable C. W. Welman* (Accra, 1924), 5, ADM 11/1086, NAG, Accra.

22. Edsman, *Lawyers in Gold Coast Politics,* 97.

23. Parker, "Ga State and Society," 323.

24. *Gold Coast Leader,* 11 October 1924. By this time Casely Hayford had taken over this Cape Coast-based paper and was its editor. The visit of His Royal Highness the Prince of Wales to the Gold Coast in April 1925 added to this dissension. Sekyi and a number of his Cape Coast supporters accused Hayford and the leadership of the NCBWA of being "defective leaders" who had been too easily caught up in this official event at a time when the colonial government was proposing threatening legislation. This dispute had become public when the editor of the *Gold Coast Times,* Kobina Sakyiama, one of Sekyi's main supporters in Cape Coast, had published an editorial entitled "The Defection of the Leaders" in the 28 March 1925 issue of this weekly newspaper.

25. *Gold Coast Leader,* 11 October 1924.

26. For a description of how this happened see D. K. Baku, "An Intellectual in Nationalist Politics: The Contribution of Kobina Sekyi to the Evolution of Ghanaian National Consciousness" (Ph.D. diss., University of Sussex, 1987).

27. They came to be known locally by this name.

28. Counsel for Taki Yaoboi consisted of Frans Dove, H. F. Ribeiro, A. W. Sawyer and R. S. Sackey, most of whom were prominent supporters of the NCBWA. Appearing for Nettey and Garshong were A. B. Quartey-Papafio and his brother H. K. Quartey-Papafio, Kojo Thompson and Kobina Sekyi.

29. *Gold Coast Independent*, 28 February 1925. Nettey was fined thirty pounds and Ayi Bente twenty-five. They both received six months imprisonment. They were found guilty of illegally collecting money from the public without any accounting of how this money was spent.

30. Dr. Nanka-Bruce was proprietor and editor of this paper as well as the secretary of the NCBWA.

31. For example, majority opinion had played an important role in "settling" the Winneba stool dispute in 1917.

32. *Gold Coast Independent*, 28 February 1925.

33. They were the Eastern, Central and Western Provincial Council of Chiefs, and coincided with the colony's three provinces.

34. Even the number of unofficial Europeans representing the commercial and mining operations in the colony was larger (five). For a more detailed description of this new constitution see Kimble, *A Political History of Ghana*, 441-448.

35. *The Gold Coast Independent*, 11 September 1926.

36. Ibid.

37. *Gold Coast Independent*, 6 August 1927.

38. *Gold Coast Independent*, 6 November 1926.

39. *Gold Coast Independent*, 30 October 1926.

40. *Gold Coast Independent*, 6 November 1926.

41. Thompson had been called to the Bar in 1914, Kwesi Orgle in 1915 and Quartey-Papafio in 1916.

42. Orgle's support was not entirely unqualified. For example, he was in favor of a direct tax and also a supporter of the New Constitution.

43. There was also some coolness between Casely Hayford and his fellow NCBWA members as a result of the Strickler-Laing cocoa swindle in 1924. Nanka-Bruce, for example, felt that Casely Hayford was partly to blame for this disaster, which had cost Gold Coast cocoa farmers about £300,000. For a description of this affair see Holmes, "Economic and Political Organizations in the Gold Coast," 103-111.

44. *Gold Coast Independent*, 23 July 1927.

45. For example, the bill gave state councils more control over customary law, created a hierarchy among chiefs and in some instances extended their judicial powers. Kimble, *A Political History of Ghana*, 492-500.

46. *Gold Coast Times*, 30 April 1927.

47. *Gold Coast Independent*, 13 August 1927. The Quartey-Papafios considered themselves members of the Asere quarter's "royal" family, and hence it was not surprising that Kwatei Quartey-Papafio could get the support of this quarter.

48. The town's total population was over 40,000 at this time, but only males over twenty years of age who owned or rented property with an annual ratable value of two pounds or more could vote.

49. The Governor to the Secretary of State, 3 September 1927, ADM 1/622, NAG, Accra. Cited in Kimble, *A Political History of Ghana,* 452.

50. Edsman, *Lawyers in Gold Coast Politics,* 80.

51. Apart from Glover-Addo, the two other Ratepayers were T. Hutton Mills and E. C. Quist, both of whom were barristers. K. Quartey-Papafio was the other town councillor.

52. Fueling this hatred was Nettey's unsuccessful attempt to win a libel suit against the proprietors of the *Gold Coast Independent* in 1928. The court case had once again ranged representatives of the two hostile political camps among the town's intelligentsia against one another. *Gold Coast Independent,* 18 August 1928.

53. *Gold Coast Independent,* 26 March 1926. According to the secretary of native affairs the Aseres had become "tired of maintaining an intransigence which [had] brought them nothing but worry and expense." The Secretary of Native Affairs to the Colonial Secretary, 9 April 1927, ADM 11/1/1089, NAG, Accra. Cited in Parker, "Ga State and Society." 341.

54. The Native Administration Ordinance made divisional chiefs subordinate to paramount chiefs and specifically made it impossible to "claim independence from a Paramount Stool." *An Ordinance to Define and to Regulate the Exercise of Certain Powers and Jurisdictions by Native Authorities* (Accra, 1927), part 4, chapter 33.

55. *Gold Coast Independent,* 25 July 1931.

56. Up until his entry into municipal politics, he was best known in the Gold Coast for his prowess as a cricketer.

57. On this occasion Nanka-Bruce received 806 votes; Kojo Thompson, 558; and E. C. Quist, a barrister and town councillor, 343. *Gold Coast Independent,* 19 September 1931.

58. Undoubtedly the best indication of this was his role in the ill-starred delegation to London in 1934 to protest the "Obnoxious Ordinances," (the Waterworks Ordinance, the Newspaper, Books and Printing Presses Ordinance and the Criminal Code [Amendment] Ordinance). Even before the secretary of state rejected the arguments of the Central National Committee that Nanka-Bruce was part of, the delegation's twelve members had become involved in unseemly squabbling. For a description of this protest see: Chin Sheng-Pao, *The Gold Coast Delegations to Britain in 1934: The Political Background* (Taipei, Taiwan, 1970), and Stanley Shallof, "Press Controls and Sedition Proceedings in the Gold Coast, 1933-1939," *African Affairs* 71, no. 284 (July, 1972):241-263.

59. For a more detailed description of these alignments see Stanley Shallof, "The Press and Politics in Accra: The Accra Legislative Council Election of 1935," *Societas* 1, no. 3 (Summer 1971):213-219. Nnandi Azikiwe was originally from Nigeria. After studying in the United States and obtaining an M.A. and an M.S. from the University of Pennsylvania, he came to the Gold Coast in 1934 and became the editor of the Accra-based newspaper *African Morning Post,* the

colony's first daily. Nnamdi Azikiwe, *My Odyssey: An Autobiography* (London, 1970).

60. Obili had been destooled in 1918.

61. *Gold Coast Independent,* 24 June 1933.

62. *Gold Coast Independent,* 13 January 1934.

63. *Gold Coast Independent,* 12 October 1935. Even the *African Morning Post* admitted that "it [was] possible that not all of the voters of the Ratepayers Association and the Asere Kowulu Party might have voted" (10 October 1936). The turnout indicated this also. In contrast to the 1931 election where 69 percent of the electorate voted, only 48 percent voted in 1935. The Acting Governor to the Colonial Secretary, 26 October 1935, 535/35. Cited in S. S. Quarcoopome, "Political Activities in Accra: 1924-1945" (M.A. thesis, Institute of African Studies, University of Ghana, 1980), 144.

64. *Gold Coast Independent,* 7 March 1936.

65. The results in 1935 were 1,030 for Thompson and 926 for Nanka-Bruce. In 1936 they were 1,022 for Thompson and 867 for Nanka-Bruce.

66. The support that Thompson got from I. T. A. Wallace-Johnson and his West African Youth League was also important and has been described by Stanley Shallof, "The Press and Politics in Accra," 213-219, and Leo Spitzer and LaRay Denzer, "I. T. A. Wallace-Johnson and the West African Youth League," *International Journal of African Historical Studies* 6, no. 3 (1973):413-452.

67. Baron Holmes, "What was the 'Nationalism' of the 1930's in Ghana?" *Mitteilungen Der Basler Afrika Bibliographien* 12 (February 1975):13. A more extensive work is his "Economic and Political Organizations in the Gold Coast, 1920-45" (Ph.D. diss. University of Chicago, 1972).

68. Holmes, "What Was the 'Nationalism' of the 1930s in Ghana?" 13.

69. Ibid., 16.

70. Holmes, "Economic and Political Organizations in the Gold Coast," 813.

71. Ibid., 533.

72. Holmes, "What was the 'Nationalism' of the 1930s?" 24. One of the best examples of how much the Aborigines undermined a united front against colonial policies was their dispatch in 1934 of a competing delegation (made up of G. E. Moore and S. R. Wood) to London to protest the "Obnoxious Ordinances." It exacerbated the bitter feelings between the Cape Coast–based GCARPS and the Accra–based Central National Committee led by Dr. Nanka-Bruce. For a description of these two delegations see: Chin Sheng-Pao, *The Gold Coast Delegations to Britain in 1934,* and Shallof, "Press Controls and Sedition Proceedings in the Gold Coast," 241-263.

73. Parker, "Ga State and Society," 319.

74. The 1928 dispute over contesting municipal elections split the GCARPS with the rump of the society becoming the Cape Coast branch. The terminology comes from Stone, "Colonial Administration and Rural Politics in South Central Ghana," 111.

75. *Gold Coast Leader,* 7-14 February 1903.

76. Coker, for example, who had been under bitter attack in the *Gold Coast Leader,* was accepted back into the fold. He even became one of the town's main public spokesmen against the harbor scheme. He had been around for so long that he had an unrivaled knowledge of promises that previous governors had made in respect to helping the town's economy, and much to Governor Guggisberg's annoyance, he could point out when the latter was quoting from the wrong speech. *Gold Coast Leader,* 4 November 1922.

77. Apart from the hostility to the Takoradi scheme, there was also a great deal of bitterness toward the government in the town over the decision to charge water rates for the newly installed pipe-borne water system. The *omanhen* of Cape Coast had given the land on which the reservoir for this project had been built, and his subjects had also given a considerable amount of free labor. Yet as soon as the project was completed, the government announced its intention to charge a water rate. The people in Accra and Sekondi, who had received pipe-borne water since 1914 and 1916, had not had to pay water rates for more than a decade, even though they had not given anything free for their systems. It seemed manifestly unfair to the people of Cape Coast. Memo to Governor Slater from the people of Cape Coast, 31 August 1927, ADM 23/1/661, NAG, Cape Coast.

78. Information from an interview with his son, Father K. Sakyiama, Cape Coast, 24 September 1974.

79. Ibid.

80. *Gold Coast Leader,* 11 August 1925. With Casely Hayford's endorsement he had become the secretary of the GCARPS.

81. Standard seven represented the end of primary education. In those days it was a substantial achievement, and represented a considerably higher level of educational achievement that it would today.

82. Interview with Mr. Joseph S. W. Amissah, Cape Coast, 3 August 1991.

83. For example, in 1924 he was very much involved, along with Sekyi, in advising the *omanhen* not to part with lands, which the government wanted to build a post office on in Cape Coast, for "a drink or a dash." The Provincial Commissioner to Sekyi, 7 October 1924, ADM 23/1/519, NAG, Cape Coast.

84. Interview with Napoleon Forson, Cape Coast letter writer, Cape Coast, 23 June 1974.

85. Interview between the Provincial Commissioner and the *Omanhen* and the *Oman,* 15 February 1921, ADM 23/1/364, NAG, Cape Coast. Sekyi and the inner circle of the Oman Party were facetiously referred to in Cape Coast as the "Cowboys."

86. Interview with Mrs. Agnes King, Moore's daughter, Cape Coast, 19 June 1974.

87. Ibid.

88. According to the *Gold Coast Leader,* his great-granduncle, Nana Tobee, had fought in the Appolonian War of 1849. *Gold Coast Leader,* 22 April 1925.

89. The case came before C. E. Woolhouse Bannerman, who in 1919 had been the first African to be appointed a police magistrate. Sekyi and A. J. E. Bucknor represented the petitioners, who were *Omanhen* Mbra III and his councillors. Woolhouse Bannerman ruled that the case was "frivolous and vexatious" and should never have been brought to his court. Cited in Kimble, *A Political History of Ghana*, 455.

90. The District Commissioner's Confidential Diary, September 1929, ADM 23/1/716, NAG, Cape Coast.

91. Ibid.

92. The *Gold Coast Leader* tried to defend "this truly great man" (Coker), and "lamented that it was being sought to cover the gallant *Tufuhen* with infamy" (13 July 1929). There must have been a hollow ring to this defense, coming as it did from a newspaper that up until 1923 had been attacking the *tufuhen* as a rascal. I have discussed this attempt to destool Coker in "Indirect Rule in the Gold Coast: Competition for Office and the Invention of Tradition," *Canadian Journal of African History* 28, no. 3 (1994):421-446.

93. For example, he was also accused of seducing a niece of Chief Sam Amissah's "to the disgrace of the Stool of Cape Coast." W. Z. Coker to the Acting District Commissioner, 7 June 1929, R 65, NAG, Cape Coast. Cited in Cawson, "Local Politics and Indirect Rule in Cape Coast," 57.

94. The Native Administration Ordinance had given the Provincial Councils the right to hear stool disputes. In turn these decisions could be appealed in the colony's Joint Provincial Council of Chiefs.

95. After trying for several years, they had failed to get a complete constitution for Cape Coast. What the GCARPS had finally submitted in 1924 was an "unsatisfactory memo which was mainly portions from different official inquires." District Commissioner to the Provincial Commissioner of the Central Province, March 1924, ADM 23/1/364, NAG, Cape Coast.

96. Report of the Thomas Commission, November 1929, ADM 11/1759, NAG, Accra.

97. Ibid. Significantly, by this time succession to the position of *tufuhen* in Cape Coast was no longer considered to be patrilineally determined.

98. As a result, Mbra III refused to attend the durbar that was held in the governor's honor, and the government saw this as a major insult to "the King's representative." There was eventually a long investigation which resulted in the provincial commissioner being censured for being partial. It meant that from then onward local officials were determined to be as "impartial" as possible, which made it even harder for the dispute to be resolved. For a description of this affair see Cawson, "Local Politics and Indirect Rule in Cape Coast," 73-79.

99. Acting Governor Northcote to the Secretary of State, 14 October 1932, ADM 1/2/199, NAG, Accra. Cited in Stanley Shallof, "The Cape Coast *Asafo* Company Riot of 1932," *International Journal of African Historical Studies* 7, no. 4 (1974):602.

100. *Gold Coast Times,* 23 November 1933. Coker's family challenged this and enstooled their own successor, who, given the Akanization of Cape Coast, was W. Z. Coker's maternal nephew. Significantly, he took the stool name Coker II. *Gold Coast Independent,* 8 September 1934.

101. Information from an interview with K. W. S. Johnston, Cape Coast, 3 July 1974. As a result of this long period away from the Gold Coast, he did not speak Fante fluently. His opponents in Cape Coast used this to discredit his Fanteness. *Ashanti Pioneer,* 25 August 1934. Johnston's use of his Akan name, Kwesi (it meant that he was born on a Sunday), was an attempt on his part to combat this criticism.

102. *Gold Coast Leader,* 9 May 1928.

103. This was a "chronic, progressive disease of the brain." Memorandum of the British Consulate General on K. E. Tandoh, 13 December 1929, FO 371/14288/583. Cited in Holmes, "Economic and Political Organizations in the Gold Coast," 129. As the *ohen* of the Cape Coast state, Amoah III was also entitled to sit on the Native Tribunal. The financial reward that derived from this position obviously contributed to making the competition to take over even more intense.

104. Letter from Mrs. Lize Johnston [undoubtedly written by her son] to the Provincial Commissioner, 15 August 1935, ADM 23/1/883, NAG, Cape Coast.

105. Plange finished six years of high school and had also studied accounting. He had worked for several years as an agent for various European firms in the colony before being enstooled. Interview with Chief Gyepi II, Cape Coast, 13 February 1974.

106. Gyepi II's personal papers; interview with Chief Gyepi II, Cape Coast, 14 February 1974.

107. The Thomas Inquiry, SNA 11/1109, NAG, Accra.

108. Kwesi Johnston to the District Commissioner, 19 August 1930, 23/1/364, NAG, Cape Coast.

109. *Gold Coast Independent,* 9 February 1935.

110. Gyepi II to the District Commissioner of Cape Coast, 11 May 1934; Gyepi's personal records.

111. The long interregnum was indicative of how much "educated" people sought to avoid office in the late nineteenth and early twentieth century. Gyepi's father, a commercial agent, had tried to make sure that his son would not succeed to traditional office by taking him away from Cape Coast. Instead, he wanted his son to follow in his footsteps. Interview with Chief Gyepi II, Cape Coast, 13 February 1974.

112. Stone, "Colonial Administration and Rural Politics in South Central Ghana," 96-98.

113. After receiving his elementary education in Cape Coast and six years of high school education in Lagos, Gyepi had taught in the Wesley Boys Elementary School in Cape Coast. Like many of his generation, he had soon abandoned

teaching for a more lucrative career in the "commercial field," and had received training in accountancy while a junior agent in Winneba. Chief Gyepi II interview, 13 February 1974.

114. The District Commissioner's Confidential Diary, 4 November 1930, ADM 23/1/716, NAG, Cape Coast.

115. Legislative Council Debates, 24 September 1931.

116. For a detailed description of this affair, see Stanley Shallof, "The Income Tax, Indirect Rule, and the Depression: The Gold Coast Riots of 1931," *Cahiers d'Etudes Africaines* 54, XIV-2:359-375.

117. V. P. Brey [the president?] to the Provincial Commissioner, 9 June 1933, Cape Coast Chamber of Commerce file, ADM 23/1/255, NAG, Cape Coast.

118. Holmes, "Economic and Political Organizations in the Gold Coast," 515.

119. *Star of West Africa,* 29 April 1939. Both Brew and Korsah lived in large, impressive mansions with the former living the furthest away from the center of the town. Wardbrew, as his house was called, was several miles away from Cape Coast. Sekyi, on the other hand, lived near the main fishing beach, ironically in Bentsir *Asafo*'s quarter, which exposed him to a great deal of harassment from his main *asafo* opponents.

120. The Cape Coast Town Council Minutes, 15 September 1933, ADM 23/1/668, NAG, Cape Coast.

121. For a description of Sekyi's role in organizing cocoa-buying schemes as an alternative to those that the large metropolitan firms offered, see Samuel Rhodie, "The Gold Coast Aborigines Abroad," *Journal of African History* 6, no. 3 (1965):389-411, and Samuel Rhodie, "The Gold Coast Cocoa Hold Up of 1930-31," *Transactions of the Historical Society of Ghana* 9 (1968):105-118.

122. Report of the Bailiff to the District Commissioner, 15 February 1938, ADM 23/1/798, NAG, Cape Coast. For a detailed account of these holdups see Holmes, "Economic and Political Organizations in the Gold Coast," 140-184, 210-301.

123.*Gold Coast Times,* 15 February 1936.

124. Interview with his brother, Kodwo Bentsi-Enchill, Cape Coast, 23 April 1974.

125. For example, he suggested that the council set up a depreciation fund for its vehicles, which the council eventually did. The Cape Coast Town Council Minutes, 9 August 1937, ADM 23/1/858, NAG, Cape Coast.

126. Interview with J. O. Eshun, former secretary of the party, Cape Coast, 21 July 1974.

127. Ibid.

128. GCARPS file no. 5, 25 January 1945, 1964/77, NAG, Cape Coast.

129. Bentsi-Enchill had disastrously undermined his popularity in Cape Coast by voting with the officials to empower the council to take legal action against people who did not pay their water rate. *Gold Coast Spectator,* 17 September 1938. Sekyi, much to the government's dismay, was soon involved in defending

people prosecuted in this fashion. *Gold Coast Independent*, 5 November 1938.

130. For example, they called for emergency meetings, sent petitions to the governor, threatened legal action against the council's bylaws, and demanded representation on all the council's committees.

131.Their main target had been the European building inspector, a controversial official member of the council since it was his job to approve or condemn buildings in Cape Coast. He had allowed council employees to take "unwanted" Town Council building materials. His entry into wartime service provided a convenient way of getting rid of him. Report of a Meeting held at Hamilton Hall, 16 January 1942, in Cape Coast Town Council Minutes, ADM 23/1/1010, NAG, Cape Coast.

132. A. F. E. Fieldgate note on Town Council minutes, 18 September 1941, Cape Coast Town Council File, ADM 23/1/1010, NAG, Cape Coast. One of the African councillors, Allotey Hammond, had publicly called the European building inspector a thief, and then, in protest over how the council's minutes were being corrected, all four of the African councillors boycotted Town Council meetings.

133. *Gold Coast Observer*, 25 August 1944.

134. Obituary for S. R. Wood, *West African Monitor*, 4 May 1948. Toward the end of the war he also became the editor of the *Gold Coast Observer*, another Cape Coast weekly. Ephson, *Gallery of Gold Coast Celebrities*, 102.

135. *Gold Coast Observer*, 1 September 1944.

136. His relationship with the Independents had always been precarious partly due to his claims to chiefly office. As Amoah IV, he claimed to be the *ohen* of Cape Coast, the town's second most important chief, which put him in competition with the *adontehen*, an Oman Party supporter, who also claimed to be the second most important local chief. When he joined the Independents, Johnston solved this conflict by describing himself as the *mankrado*. It was undoubtedly a borrowing from the Akan states of the interior where the holder of this position was second after a chief of a town, and clearly inferior to the *adontehen*. However, in Cape Coast, where town and state were basically synonymous, the *mankrado's* position was far more ambiguous.

137. Their most innovative attempt to do so was by holding a centenary celebration for the Bond of 1844. Significantly, neither the leading figures from the Ratepayer Party nor the Independent Party attended this event. *Gold Coast Observer*, 30 June 1944.

138. Bentsi-Enchill was obviously also planning on taking advantage of the "new order," and reentering Cape Coast's political life. In 1943 he had become vice president of an organization called the Cape Coast Club, which according to the organization's secretary "was a body of gentlemen who wished to study the Colony's needs and to take such steps [as they considered necessary] from time to time with others like-minded." Victor Delaquis [Bentsi-Enchill's secretary at the UAC] to the Provincial Commissioner, 25 November 1943, ADM 21/1/298, NAG, Cape Coast.

139. Interview with Kodwo Bentsi-Echill, Cape Coast, 19 July 1974.

140. Ibid. Among the many disputes in Cape Coast was that between the different sections of the stool family over who owned the *ahenfie*. Bentsi-Enchill, who at this time was one of the wealthiest men in Cape Coast, was able to provide Mbra IV with a residence at Prospect Hill, some distance from the *ahenfie*, which served the valuable purpose of insulating him from the factiousness within the stool family.

141. For example, his faction controlled what had been renamed a B Grade Native Court. A. B. Josiah became its president.

142. The vote was 298 for Moore and 232 for Bentsi-Enchill.

143. Interview with Kodwo Bentsi-Enchill, Cape Coast, 23 August 1974.

144. These were held by A. B. Josiah and Kwesi Johnston, both of whom had abandoned the "middle passage."

145. One of the most controversial had been their objection to the Town Council employing non-Cape Coasters. Even the controversial position of European building inspector was Africanized, and after 1944 this officer became simply the building inspector.

146. The Accra chief Nii Boone initiated this campaign to protest the high cost of imported goods. For his own description of this campaign see Nii K. Boone, *Milestones in the History of the Gold Coast* (Ashford-in-Middlesex, U.K., 1953); See also Dennis Austin, *Politics in Ghana, 1946-1960* (London, 1964), 70-74.

147. The boycott had begun fairly spontaneously in Cape Coast.

148. *West African Monitor*, 2 March 1948.

149. *Gold Coast Observer*, 16 November 1945.

150. It was through his own indiscretions that he lost this seat. He clumsily tried to get the general manager of the British firm, G. B. Ollivant, who was also the chairman of the Association of West African Merchants (AWAM), to pay him £25,000 for not making a speech against AWAM in the Legislative Council. The government clearly helped to set this up since the CID planted microphones to record incriminating evidence. The case that followed was a cause célèbre in the Gold Coast press. It was carried verbatim in the *Gold Coast Independent* on 20 and 27 May 1944. Thompson was found guilty, lost his appeal to the West African Court of Appeal, was fined £200 with one day in jail, and this ended his political career. As it was he was in poor health. He eventually died on 26 February 1950.

151. *Gold Coast Spectator*, 5 March 1938.

152. His greatest asset, as S. K. B. Asante suggests, was his "willingness to insult the colonial regime." *Pan-African Protest: West Africa and the Italo-Ethiopian Crisis* (Accra, 1975), 113.

153. It would have been tantamount to recognizing the legitimacy of this body, to which the Oman Party and the Sekyi-led GCARPS were totally opposed.

154. For a description of his activities in the Gold Coast see Spitzer and Denzer, "I. T. A. Wallace-Johnson and the West African Youth League," 413-452. The organization ostensibly appealed to a younger generation, hence its name.

There was also clearly a class appeal. It attracted members of the lower strata of the intelligentsia.

155. J. B. Danquah was supposedly the first to use this term in the Gold Coast (*Gold Coast Independent*, 9 March 1935), but Azikiwe clearly brought a more hard-hitting American-style journalism to the colony. It was reflected in the fivefold increase in *African Morning Post* circulation (2,000 to 10,000 issues) during his two years as editor. Azikiwe, *My Odyssey*, 259.

156. Apart from attempts to organize lorry drivers in Accra and taking up the case of forty miners who lost their lives in a Prestea mine disaster, Wallace-Johnson was also active in supporting such international causes as the Scotsboro Boys' case and the defense of Ethiopia after the Italians invaded this still-independent country in 1935. Asante, *Pan-African Protest*, 108-130. Many people in the Gold Coast thought that Governor S. W. Thomas had introduced the Criminal Code Amendment Bill in 1934 (known as the Sedition Bill) largely as a result of Wallace-Johnson's activities in the colony. Not surprisingly, he played a leading role in organizing opposition to this attempt to "muzzle the press." For a discussion of this see Shallof, "Press Controls and Sedition Proceedings in the Gold Coast," 241-263. Significantly, Wallace-Johnson was later prosecuted under the Sedition Bill for an article ("Has the African a God?") which appeared in the *African Morning Post* on 15 May 1936.

157. Spitzer and Denzer, "I. T. A. Wallace-Johnson and the West African Youth League," 417.

158. "Conservancy" was the euphemism that the colonial government used for referring to the disposal of human waste. Before the introduction of waterborne sewage, it was one of the most unpleasant of the council's responsibilities.

159. Quarcoopome, "Political Activities in Accra: 1924-1945," 149.

160. Interview with J. C. Vandyck, 5 June 1971, cited in Jeffries, *Class, Power and Ideology in Ghana*, 32.

161. Their first recorded strike was in 1918. Ibid., 28-29.

162. Ibid., 33.

163. An account of this strike is given in Governor Burns to the Secretary of State, 30 April 1943, CO 96/774/31312, PRO.

164. Holmes, "What Was the 'Nationalism' of the 1930s in Ghana?, " 17.

Chapter 8

Linking Different Judicial Traditions

The link that developed in the 1920s and 1930s between the transactional affairs of the native order and municipal politics was paralleled by a similar development in the colony's judicial system which resulted in an intermingling of traditional and British legal ideas.[1] Here, too, it was an unanticipated result since initially the colonial government assumed that traditional or customary law was separate and distinct from the English common law that the British courts administered. In reality, however, it was even harder to maintain a division between these two different legal traditions than it was between the colony's different political systems. With increasing frequency many of the cases that came before the courts involved issues in which customary law and English common law were in competition with one another, and it seemed as though one legal system had to supersede the other. In reality, however, what resulted was that over time the jurisprudential system that emerged was an amalgam of both judicial influences.

Both African reactions to European attitudes toward African culture and indirect rule played a vital role in shaping this development. Initially the "racial and racist, imperial and imperialist ideologies" that sought to render Africans "invisible" in their own history "prompted the small, close-knit community of coastal intellectuals to provide alternative interpretations of their 'Gold Coast pasts.'"[2] In the "literary exuberance" that followed they also wanted to attack the main ideological premise of their imperialist opponents, who uncritically assumed that British rule represented civil-

ization and progress while anything African represented the barbarism of
the past. Rapidly, defining and defending customary law became an integral part of what the Cape Coast clergyman Reverend Attoh Ahuma came
to popularize as the "gone Fantee" movement.[3] The colony's small but influential group of British-trained lawyers were particularly attracted to
these concerns, and it was their work that was to leave the most important
legacy.

Among the first of these defenders of customary law was John Mensah
Sarbah, who returned from England to the Gold Coast in 1887 as the first
Gold Coast African to qualify for the Bar. Shortly after his return, at the
suggestion of the Mfantsi Anambuhu Fékuw, he wrote a series of articles
based on his study of Cape Coast court records, which he later expanded
into a full-scale work, *Fanti Customary Laws*.[4] Undoubtedly he had a
didactic purpose in mind, especially as far as "newly arrived European
officials" were concerned. In the work's preface he emphasizes how
important "reduc[ing] into writing the Customary Laws and Usages of the
Fanti and other Akan inhabitants of the Gold Coast" had become to correct
the view held by many of these newcomers that "there were no Customary
Laws."[5] The "wholly unexpected" acceptance that the work met with
indicated that by 1903, when a second edition appeared, there was
developing, even at this early stage in the colony's history, considerable
common ground between these European outsiders, increasingly converts
to indirect rule and upholding native law, and the cultural nationalists of
the colony's coastal communities.[6]

Ironically, also, the government's contradictory policies toward native
custom during the 1890s contributed to expanding the concern with
customary law. Undoubtedly the most important in this regard was the
Lands Bill legislation of 1894 and 1897, since this legislation challenged
what the educated elite considered was the colony's unique form of
traditional land tenure and their own financial interest in preserving it. The
protest that followed stimulated even more interest in defining and
codifying native customary law on the part of the colony's small but grow-
ing numbers of African lawyers. Very much the result of this agitation was
Casely Hayford's *Gold Coast Native Institutions,* published in 1903,
which was the first comprehensive attempt to describe more than just the
indigenous legal system of the Gold Coast. The major inspiration for
writing this book came from work that Casely Hayford had done in
helping to prepare the GCARPS's case against the Lands Bill. In doing
this he had collected a wealth of material about Gold Coast "native
society," and after the bill was defeated he decided to present his material
in a fashion which would be useful to "the aborigines anxious to know the
constitutional history of their country, and also to [officials] seeking
precedents to guide [their] conduct."[7]

However, most importantly, he continued the conflation of Fante customs and practices with those of the larger Akan world that Sarbah in *Fanti Customary Laws* had already set in motion.[8] Even though they began from opposite directions, the end result was much the same, for in reality both men drew heavily upon their Fante backgrounds. Nevertheless, indicative of how important these works were, their basic assumption was to leave a lasting legacy to later phases of the colonial jurisprudential tradition. Fante/Akan customary law came to influence how British courts interpreted customary law in the Akan area, but led to the tendency to apply it to other ethnic groups like the Ga and the Ewe as well. The long-term result was that "native law was regarded as being more or less uniform in the Gold Coast."[9] In addition, Casely Hayford's descriptions of the many cases involving coastal chiefs, which had been decided in colonial courts, indicated how inextricably interwoven with the British judicial system the affairs of the native states had become.

The colonial government's expansion of indirect rule to the coastal areas of the colony in the first decade of the twentieth century provided the impetus for a much more detailed and specific study of the native state. In 1906 John Mensah Sarbah published what was to be the most important work on this subject until the 1920s. *Fanti National Constitution* was a far more sophisticated attempt to describe the complexity of Akan government than Casely Hayford's *Gold Coast Native Institutions* had been. Sarbah did not attempt to generalize beyond the area of the colony. Instead, he recognized that Casely Hayford's assumed homogeneity of the native states of the Gold Coast did not exist. The similarities between the Fante and the Asante were at best superficial. Indeed, he recognized important differences between even the coastal Fante states and those inland. He cautioned his readers "not to be misled by what they saw on the coast, since government here was a variation of the general system due to the frequent intercourse between these areas and Europeans."[10] He had obviously been affected by some of the astute criticisms that had been made of his earlier work.

Instead, he selected the inland kingdom of Wassaw in the Akim Sefwih district as a closer approximation of the original Fante state.[11] As a result, in contrast to Casely Hayford, he was able to present a much more accurate picture of how the traditional native state functioned. The work, however, still reflected the predominantly Fante focus that Sarbah's earlier researches had exhibited. In contrast to Reverend Carl Christian Reindorf's earlier *History of the Gold Coast and Asante,* which was intended as a "provisional national history," *Fanti National Constitution* underscored the basically Fante/Akan weltanschauung of its author and the Cape Coast–educated elite in general. Contributing to this focus was Sarbah's inherently legalistic aims. As Mary Kingsley noticed, subtly he

was attempting to make Fante customary law the basis for the administration of law in the colony's Native Tribunals, which was in fact
happening in the seaboard area of the colony.[12]

It was not surprising that this was so. Most of the legal matters that
came before the British courts concerning customary law involved
"natives" who were Fantes or at least Akans. In addition, lawyers like
Sarbah, who were involved in the process of codifying native law, also
tended to select cases from the Fante area where British justice had begun
and was still most extensive, and where most of his practice took place.
In general, the increasing collection of decided cases that a number of the
colony's lawyers in addition to Sarbah and Casely Hayford were compiling
clearly exhibited a Fante/Akan bias.[13] Moreover, for Sarbah, a member of
one of the most litigious of these coastal Fante communities as well as a
practicing lawyer, there were major benefits from this development. A
customary law that was heavily influenced by Fante jurisprudential ideas,
in which he was the recognized expert, gave him important advantages in
dealing with British judges before whom his cases came.

Already by the last decade of the nineteenth century most of these cases
had to do with property and inheritance. Over 70 percent of the decided
cases that Sarbah cites in *Fanti Customary Laws* are concerned with these
issues. They involved a wide spectrum of coastal society which, as was to
be the case with indirect rule politics, served to blur the boundaries
between the different "classes" that made up these communities. There
were few people who were not at some time party to such disputes and
litigants before the colony's courts. This included the leading advocates
of the "gone Fantee" movement. They were even willing to use their
private affairs to challenge what Sarbah later on was to describe as the
legally "demoralizing effects" of "European influences."[14]

In 1894, when Jacob Anaman challenged his brother's widow for the
possession of the dead man's property, the Wesleyan Methodists were in
the midst of an aggressive campaign to make Christian marriage the sine
qua non for full membership in the church. Even though Anaman was then
in training for a position in the Methodist ministry, it was an indication of
his commitment to the "gone Fantee" movement that he was willing to use
his own family affairs to challenge English common law, which the
missionaries had come to see as an important underpinning of Christian
marriage in the colony.[15] Sarbah was also willing to demonstrate such
commitment. To ensure that his property would remain in his
matrilineage, he appointed his mother and two sisters his executrices.[16]
When he finally married an "ordinance" wife in 1904, he only added a
minor codicil to the original will, which gave this wife and her children
only £250 pounds and 300 shares in an Asante gold mining company.
When he died suddenly in 1910, his wife unsuccessfully challenged the
validity of her husband's will. Compounding her problems, the gold

mining shares turned out to be worthless, and she was reduced to importuning the government to pay for her children's education.[17]

It is unlikely that Sarbah conceived of things working out quite so badly for his ordinance wife and her children. Instead, he probably wanted the same treatment for them that he describes in *Fanti Customary Laws* as the practice that had developed "in the early days of the missionaries...[in which at her husband's death] his children and widow took half of his moveable property, while his own family took the other half."[18] Perhaps he was seeking to build up his nuclear family's half, and the gold mining shares were part of this plan. His early and fairly sudden death (at forty-six) robbed him of the time he needed to complete this project. Nevertheless, the priority that he gave to his matrilineage is an indication of how attitudes to marriage and customary notions of inheritance were being rethought even among staunch Christians.[19] Sarbah's father, for example, had willed the bulk of his personal property to his nuclear family, and in contrast to his son had made relatively small bequests to his matrikin. Like members of his generation, he wanted to ensure that the bulk of his property passed to his nuclear family when he died in 1892.[20]

The emergence of an official policy of indirect rule in the early twentieth century also played an important role in the recognition of customary law. The new approach to incorporating the native state into the machinery of colonial government inevitably meant enhancing the status of customary law before the colony's courts. It inspired what S. K. B. Asante has aptly described as an attempt on the part of the colony's British courts to adopt a far more sympathetic attitude to "pure native law." As such it represented a reversal from an earlier more "socially realistic" phase in the colony's jurisprudential tradition which was best exemplified in the opinions of the long-serving chief justice, Sir William Brandford Griffith (1895-1909).[21] He had continued the tradition of "judicial activism" that Captain George Maclean, the Gold Coast's first judicial assessor, had established. Maclean had "looked upon the judiciary as a sub-division of the executive" and as a "major instrument for promoting civil change."[22]

By the early twentieth century the official acceptance of "pure native law" and an increasingly more articulate defense of African customs contributed to putting "pure" English common law much more on the defensive than been the case in the nineteenth century. Even "judicial activists" like Sir William Brandford Griffith had come to recognize that there were important limits as to how far the colony's customary system of land tenure had "ripened" into English freehold. The passage of the Native Jurisdiction Bill in 1910 was one indication of this new attitude to the traditional state and, by extension, customary law. Even though the bill was basically a reenactment of the 1883 legislation, it did provide more native courts for the colony. Appeal lay from these inferior courts to the colony's superior courts, with the result that a greater volume of cases involving customary law were likely to come before the judges of the Supreme Court. It contributed to creating a judicial climate that was far more sympathetic to customary law in general, and challenged what John Mensah Sarbah at that time still considered "the tendency of the Supreme Court...to deal with everything in the light of English law."[23]

Initially, however, it was in the area of land tenure that customary law achieved its most important victories. In the new climate of opinion the GCARPS was able to score a notable victory against the government's Forest Bill of 1911.[24] In 1912 the society was able get H. C. Belfield, the special commissioner that the secretary of state had sent to investigate land alienation in the colony, to condemn legislation like the Lands Bill of 1897, and to acknowledge publicly that "all land belongs to the people which has not been acquired by other parties."[25] To the executive of the GCARPS the important corollary that followed from this admission was that Gold Coast natives could dispose of this land, if they so desired, in any way they saw fit so long as this conformed to customary law.[26]

As Anne Phillips has pointed out, however, the members of the West African Lands Committee, which the Colonial Office convened in 1916 to formulate land policies for all the British West African colonies, were opposed to the commercialization of what they considered communal land. They felt the state should intervene "to halt the transition to individual tenure" which they realized was happening both as a result of sales to European concessionaires and because of the rapid expansion of the cocoa industry.[27] The committee's specific proposals as to how this should be done "sank virtually without a trace in the course of the First World War."[28] Nevertheless, the important result was that during the interwar years that followed colonial governments all over British West Africa came to assume that economic development should be based "on the activities of independent peasants" who had to be protected from the "destructive influences" of capitalism and "modern individualism" by preserving the precolonial institutions of which they were part.[29] Indirect rule acquired an economic rationale which inevitably required strengthening the power of chiefs. Legally both the government and the courts had to uphold their claims based on traditional custom to exercise usufructuary control over land.[30] The stream of ordinances that emerged from the colony's legislature during the interwar years dealing with the native states and their courts was an important indication of this.

In the coastal towns, where land alienation was already far advanced, the effect of this return to "pure native law" was much greater on conflicts that resulted from the different systems of inheritance in customary as opposed to ordinance marriages. In her recent work *The Transformation of Property Rights in the Gold Coast*, Kathryn Firmin-Sellers locates the struggle over "defining" property rights primarily in the colony's political arena.[31] Undoubtedly much of the parochial politics of the colonial period did involve struggles over property ownership in the colony's coastal towns, but the far more important venue for debating these issues was the colony's courts.[32] Here contests transcended the political arena as the range of participants spanned the diverse components of colonial society; individuals were pitted against one another, their families and lineages. Most of all this was so since in the colony's coastal communities Anglicization had gone too far to allow a return to exclusively customary marriage practices. Indeed, as Kobina Sekyi in his bitingly sarcastic play *The Blinkards* describes, by the second decade of the twentieth century "anglomania" had affected a wide spectrum of "blind" imitators of "undigested and indigestible foreign ideas" in coastal towns like Cape Coast who wanted to do things in the "English manner."[33] Ordinance marriage, and specifically the Christian version, was one of the most sought after of these "ideas," even if it meant violating time-tested Fante marriage customs. In his far more autobiographical work, published three years later in 1918 and suggestively entitled "The Anglo-Fanti," he recognizes how difficult it was even for people like himself to avoid conforming to the Anglicized norms that his society had adopted even when they recognized the damaging effects of European cultural imperialism.[34]

Apart from presenting unrelentingly bleak portrayals of Anglicized coastal society, these two fictional works can also be seen as symbolic of how the conflict between Christian and matrilineal Fante/Akan marriage customs became more acute as "pure native law" found increasing favor before the colony's courts. By recognizing pure native law, the colonial judiciary contributed to exacerbating the conflicts that already existed between the lineage and the conjugal family. In his 1916 play, Sekyi had recognized, with some degree of prescience, that there were important changes under way in the extent to which colonial courts were willing to uphold the supremacy of English common law when it came to matters regarding marriage. Indeed, his fictional judgment regarding the 1884 Marriage Ordinance in *The Blinkards,* which at the outset seems rather improbable, becomes more plausible when seen in conjunction with an important ruling that the Nigerian Full Court handed down in 1921 involving basically the same Marriage Ordinance.[35]

In this case, *Frederick Germanus Martins v. Emily Fowler,* the issue was inheritance of intestate property which had already passed through two generations in accordance with the principles of English common law when the respective owners had died intestate in 1873 and 1911. In 1921, the wife of the original owner tried to will property she considered she had inherited from her son, who had died intestate in 1911, to someone who was neither a member of her husband's maternal nor his paternal lineage. Her husband's surviving sister, however, challenged the devise and claimed the property herself on the basis of Yoruba customary practice.[36]

Kobina Sekyi wearing a Fante cloth. From *Negro: An Anthology,* collected and edited by Nancy Cunard, 1934. Copyright (c) by The Frederick Ungar Publishing Company. Reprinted by permission of the Continuum Publishing Company.

Initially the Lagos Divisional Court had upheld the validity of the wife's devise, but the Full Court overturned this decision on the grounds that the Marriage Ordinance of 1884 did not apply to the original marriage, which had taken place before 1884 and was recognized as already valid. As such the court did not feel that English common law principles of inheritance should apply. In 1926 the Privy Council concurred with this ruling, even though it recognized that in 1873 and 1911 the "law as to the devolution of real property in Lagos was similar to the law in force in England."[37]

It was a judgment that was indicative of how much more sympathetic colonial courts had become in upholding pure native law even to the extent of influencing the judges of the Privy Council in the metropole itself. The *Martins v. Fowler* ruling had important legal repercussions in the Gold Coast. Its influence on the long, drawn-out case of *Rebecca Carr v. Jemina Carr and Samuel Addaquay* that was finally settled in the Cape Coast Divisional Court in 1926 was a good indication of this.[38] Here the dispute was over inheriting the property of Thomas A. Carr, who had died intestate in 1907. Even though he had been legally married, the court had granted letters of administration to his mother and sister, since the man who claimed to be his son turned out to be illegitimate. The legal wife challenged this ruling, but it was not until 1926 that the court ruled in her favor on the bases of *Cole v. Cole*. On the surface this seemed a predictable enough decision, but clearly the court was influenced by the *Martins v. Fowler* ruling, which the presiding judge cited in the proceedings to see if it had any relevance to the case before him. He had finally decided that it did not, but the delay in handing down judgment was an indication of how much more uncertain British courts all over West Africa had become in settling inheritance disputes that arose from different marriage customs.

In general the increasingly more sympathetic attitude on the part of the British courts in the Gold Coast to customary law was responsible for stimulating lawyers to experiment with new ways of presenting old arguments that had initially been unsuccessful. For example, in this climate of judicial uncertainty towards the issue of inheritance it was hardly surprising that the controversial issue of nuncupative wills would once again resurface. In 1927 an important case of this nature appeared before the Accra Divisional Court involving the estate of a Ga man, Timothy Mensah Otoo.[39] It was very similar to the *In re Isaac Anaman* case of 1894. The difference, however, was that the dead man's two legitimate daughters were challenging his uterine sister's right to inherit property when he died intestate in 1927.[40] According to the defendant, who had cared for her brother during his final illness, on his deathbed he had supposedly made a testamentary disposition of his property with her as beneficiary.

His daughters, who even though they seemed to have done little for their father during his final illness, nevertheless, as the legitimate issue of the ordinance marriage that he had contracted in 1890, challenged the validity of this action. Apart from relying on the emotional appeal of the case, the sister's counsel tried to maintain that such testamentary dispositions were part of Ga native custom, but he had no more success than Sarbah in 1894, who had tried to argue that this was Akan custom. The judge in the case, Acting Chief Justice W. P. Michelin, refused to recognize any special status for Ga native law, and instead relied on previous judicial rulings that had been unequivocal on the matter of *saminsiw* in general. Indeed, he tried to put an end to this challenge to English common law by categorically stating that "when a person alters his legal status by contracting a marriage under the Marriage Ordinance of 1884, he is incapable of making such a will."[41]

It was hardly surprising that Justice Michelin turned back such a frontal attack on English common law principles of inheritance. To have made concessions to customary law in this matter would have seriously undermined the already scaled back ability of a woman who had made a statutory marriage to inherit the property of her husband, as well as of the children to inherit from their father. Undoubtedly, this uncompromising position that the court took on the issue of succession contributed to what was already the perception on the part of most members of the coastal intelligentsia that Western cultural norms were increasingly going to be in the ascendancy in the Gold Coast. This had been Sekyi's conclusion in "The Anglo-Fanti." He recognized, correctly enough, that Anglomania had penetrated deeply into coastal societies like Cape Coast and Accra, and to "revolutionary conservatives" like himself this "cankerous growth" represented a fundamental threat to the well-being of his society.[42]

However, to most members of the coastal elite this was hardly the case, and instead, as a contributor to the *Gold Coast Leader* expressed it, the colony was "handicapped in progress by evil customs."[43] Apart from condemning polygyny, which "degrad[ed] women," he also felt that one of the most harmful customs was the "expensive" and "degrading" system of customary marriage. Indeed, an editorial in the *Gold Coast Independent* went so far as to suggest that these "extravagant" and "expensive weddings" were the cause of "national poverty," and drove young men into the "arms of the money lender."[44] In addition, there was considerable public agreement among the members of this Western-educated community that the "primitive" and "monstrous" custom of matrilineal inheritance would be swept away by the advancing tide of "civilization."[45] The outcome of the highly charged debate over whether sons or nephews should inherit, which the Young Peoples Literary Club sponsored at the Rodger Club in Accra in 1932, was an excellent indication of this.[46] Everyone who was anyone in Accra was there. It was a matter that clearly concerned both Akans and

Gas, as was reflected in the ethnic diversity of the debaters, the judges and the audience.[47] Nevertheless, indicative of the majority sentiment among the audience, the judges—representing the bar, the pulpit and the traditional state—on this occasion had no difficulty rendering a unanimous decision in favor of the son. It was hardly a unique expression of this opinion. Most letters and editorials in the colony's press invariably supported this position.[48]

Public sentiment, however, did not necessarily reflect what even the most Westernized members of this community actually did when confronted with questions of ownership and inheritance in their own lives. Reality was far more complex than either the "revolutionary conservatives" or the "anglomaniacs" would have been willing to admit. This was well exemplified in debt litigation and the disputes over property ownership that were an integral part of such cases. By the 1920s suits arising out of indebtedness were among the most frequent form of litigation before the colony's civil courts. It was a reflection of the increasing commercialization of the colony's economy, which in turn had resulted in more and more people using property as security for loans and advances on trade goods. However, the unpredictability of the economy during these years resulted in large numbers of defaulters even before the depression of the 1930s.

Invariably creditors wanted to seize property that a defaulting debtor had mortgaged, but to do so usually resulted in interpleader actions in which a third party claimed that the property in question was not personal but family property and could not be seized in accordance with the provisions of English common law. Judges recognized that there was a great deal of collusion between debtors and family heads to avoid surrendering property that had been legitimately mortgaged. Nevertheless, since British judges in general were much more sympathetic to the rights of the extended family than had been the case during the phase of "judicial activism," these interpleader actions had a considerable chance of being successful. It was an indication of how much more respect for customary law had developed that judges were even willing to question the legitimacy of wills and deeds of conveyance that were presented to the court to prove ownership. In this judicial arena the competition between "pure native" law and English common law had clearly become much more even, and litigants in such cases were likely to resort to whichever body of law best served their interests.

Indicative of this was the case of *W. G. Quartey v. Mann Little and Co. Ltd.* that came before the Accra Divisional Court in 1924. Mann Little and Co. had lent £150 to a Sophia Adjüah with property that the latter claimed was hers as security. When she died without this debt being repaid, her creditor sought to seize the property in question. The family that was actually in residence (W. G. Quartey was the family head) challenged this move on the grounds that the property in dispute was theirs. Even though Adjuah had possessed a deed of conveyance, the judge ruled that this deed "had no value" since Ga customary law of succession ensured that the property could not be hers but belonged to the family, who had not been party to the mortgaging transaction.[49]

An indication of how opportunistic litigants in these property owner-ship disputes could be was the interpleader action that came before the Cape Coast Divisional Court in 1930. The case demonstrated that not only creditors relied on deeds of conveyance to establish ownership, but also illiterate claimants could try to base their claims to ownership on written testaments! Nevertheless, the judge was even more suspicious of the validity of the documentation that the claimant presented in this case than his counterpart in the case of *W. G. Quartey v. Mann Little and Company Ltd.* had been of Sophia Adjuah's deed of conveyance. The brief descrip-tion of the case in the Cape Coast Judgment Book gives no indication of why this was so, but he quickly decided that the deed of conveyance in this latter case was an outright forgery "made to defraud the creditors," and he ruled in favor of the creditor.[50]

This willingness on the part of a claimant to use English common law procedure was an indication that there was no guarantee that arguments based on customary law would always be successful. There were enough examples of this in the colony's courts to show the contrary.[51] Instead, what had happened was that the British courts had become a great deal more unpredictable when it came to establishing ownership than had been the case during the period of judicial activism. It was undoubtedly the most important reason why the outmoded system of imprisonment for debt continued in the colony until as late as 1934.[52] Even when the Supreme Court introduced rules to abolish imprisonment for debt, there still remained provisions for imprisoning "fraudulent" debtors.[53]

Of even greater long-term significance than extending the life of the obsolete common law practice of imprisonment for debt in the Gold Coast, the British court's sympathy to "pure native law" contributed to preserving matriliny even in the coastal communities where the increasing exposure to Western notions of individualism seemed likely to undermine this "outmoded" custom. Undoubtedly, some of the advantages that matriliny offered to people in rural areas were carried over into the coastal communities.[54] It offered a far wider range of people an opportunity to profit from the industriousness of individual family members than was the case for the nuclear family. Many were likely to be of the same generation or older than the deceased, and they could more easily marshal resources to defend their interests than their opponents. When it came to hiring a lawyer to undertake litigation, they could rely on the resources of the matrilineage itself. The wife, on the other hand, especially if her children were young, was much more isolated and financially dependent. This was particularly likely if her marriage had conformed to the ideal of the woman as homemaker which the Christian missions upheld.[55] Under these circumstances it was hardly surprising that the matrilineage, even in the "civilized" coastal communities, did not "retire into oblivion."[56]

Less obvious, but also adding to the attractiveness of the matrilineal system of inheritance, were the opportunities that it presented for a wide range of matrikin to succeed to family property. Particularly heated could be the competition between descendants of "domestics" and "blood" relatives for this right. For example, a few years after J. P. H. Brown, the editor of the Cape Coast newspaper *Gold Coast Leader,* died in 1919, there was such a dispute between a man who claimed to be his maternal nephew and a woman who maintained that she was the head of the family. According to her, the "nephew" was only a son of one of the descendants of J. P. H. Brown's father, and a "domestic" who was not entitled to inherit by Fante customary law. Behind this dispute was another educated domestic member of J. P. H. Brown's matrilineage who had initially tried to control the property by putting up a more compliant nephew. When this man died in 1926, the arrangement had collapsed and the only surviving maternal nephew had moved to assert his rights. This was how the court interpreted the case, and after determining that even though the maternal nephew was from a domestic background, he was nevertheless entitled to inherit his uncle's property.[57]

Taking advantage of the colony's different judicial principles could also produce some bizarre situations, as was the case involving the property of J. W. de Graft Johnson, a wealthy Cape Coast merchant who died in 1928. In this instance one of his sons by an ordinance wife, J. C. de Graft Johnson, who was then assistant secretary of native affairs, challenged one of his half-brothers over the right to inherit any of their father's property on the grounds that the latter's mother had been a slave. J. C. de Graft Johnson's counsel tried to maintain that the Emancipation Proclamation of 1874 had ended slavery in the colony, and consequently extinguished the rights of inheritance under customary law that slaves had enjoyed! In the climate of judicial sympathy for customary law then prevailing, it was a foregone conclusion that the court would rule against such an argument. Instead, the presiding judge could not help observing how much of a "spectacle" it was to see the assistant secretary of native affairs "arguing against" his own Fante customary law.[58]

In general the existence of a dualistic legal system was a lawyers' paradise, and preserving this situation was clearly in their interest. As far as disputes involving inheritance were concerned, it meant that they could base their arguments on either English common law or on customary practice depending on which better suited the interests of their clients. For example, in the 1927 attempt to get legal sanction for the validity of nuncupative wills, the counsel for the defendant was J. H. Coussey, who

Assistant Secretary of Native Affairs J. C. de Graft Johnson, c. 1920s.
Source: Rev. J. W. de Graft Johnson (son).

was from a well-known Cape Coast, Euro-African family. He was defending oral testamentary disposition. Appearing on behalf of the plaintiffs was K. Quartey-Papafio, who was related to the royal lineage of the Asere quarter in Accra, and was shortly afterward to use these connections to form the Asere Kowulu Party to contest the position for municipal member for Accra on the Legislative Council. Nevertheless, in this particular case he was arguing in favor of English common law!

In addition, there was clearly tremendous room for maneuver within the area of customary law itself, which in reality contained a plurality of legal traditions. The unwritten nature of this law gave lawyers opportunities to present their own interpretations of what was indeed customary among the different ethnic groups that made up the colony's population. Following in Sarbah's footsteps there were others who wrote about their own customary traditions, like the Accra barrister A. B. Quartey-Papafio, who sought to codify Ga native traditions. In a similar fashion to earlier students of customary law, he published much of this work in the metropole, where it was likely to find a wider distribution than in the colony alone.[59] His fellow Ga, J. M. Bruce-Myers, followed suit, though his emphasis was less on legal issues than on more general descriptions of Ga customs.[60] On a more local level, one of the first serials the Accra weekly *Gold Coast Independent* began publishing soon after its establishment in 1918 was on the Ga National Constitution.

Nevertheless, by this time Akan influence in this area was extensive. In 1910, when Quartey-Papafio wrote about the Native Tribunals in Accra, he acknowledged that seven of the nine tribunals applied what he considered Akan law or a mixture of Akan and Ga customary law.[61] Specifically what this meant was that the ostensibly patrilineal Ga were increasingly accepting Akan matrilineal principles of inheritance. Indeed, as far back 1868 the British court had come to this conclusion in the case of *Akosua v. Orbodie,* which had come before Judicial Assessor W. A. Parker. In conjunction with the chiefs of James Town, Ussher Town and Christiansborg, he had ruled that the customary law in Accra was that "a sister's son is the lawful heir of the uncle."[62] It is significant, however, that this was an appeal from a lower court ruling that had upheld the son's right to succeed to his father's property. There was clearly a great deal of confusion over what was indeed customary practice among the Ga in general, and the court's decisions could fluctuate from one extreme to the other.

For example, in 1908 Sir William Brandford Griffith, the chief justice, had "no alternative" but to rule in favor of patrilineal succession in the case *In the Matter of the Estate of Lomotey Nukpa (deceased), Lomotey Obesi (Caveator).* In passing judgment in this case, the chief justice acknowledged that "few customs are universal among the same people" and that in Nungua (five miles to the east of Accra) "the usual Ga custom...for the brother on the mother's side to succeed to personal property of a deceased person" was contradicted by "a mass of evidence" that he could not ignore.[63] In 1915, however, the pendulum swung in the opposite direction when land owned by the descendants of the Brazilians who had returned to the Gold Coast in the 1830s was in dispute. The Accra Divisional court ruled against succession in the male line, as was supposedly the case in Brazilian law, on the grounds that the original descendants had married Accra women, and since they had "long used Ga native courts" they were subject to "the Accra law of succession which was not in the male line."[64]

In a similar fashion in 1919 in the case of *Sackey v. Okantah,* the colony's then chief justice, Sir Crampton Smyly, when faced with conflicting evidence of customary practice among the Ga in relation to intestate succession, "granted letters of administration to the nephew of the deceased in the maternal line."[65] He considered that the written evidence available did not lay down clearly that "children of the deceased had an exclusive right to the property in question, but...that they might share in it together with the matrilineal family."[66] Neither was the evidence of expert witnesses more helpful, but seemed on balance to indicate that matrilineal inheritance was the norm. Accepting such general norms could sometimes have major disadvantages for non-Akan litigants. For example, in the case of *The Estate of Timothy Mensah Otto,* the British court's earlier decision versus the validity of nuncupative wills for Akans married in Western style was applied across the board to all Africans regardless of their ethnic background.

Recently, N. A. Ollennu has tried to resolve this question of what was truly the normative principle of succession among the Gas by arguing that by the beginning of the twentieth century most of the Accra Gas (Ga-Mashi) could no longer be considered representative of the traditional Ga. There had been a great deal of Akan immigration into the town that had profoundly affected its customary practices.[67] Instead, he argued that the Gas of Nungua and his own Labardi people represented the Ga proper, among whom patrilineal succession was the norm. He pointed out, however, that in spite of Sir William Brandford Griffith's ruling in *The Estate of Lomety Nukpa, Lomotey Obesi,* British judges continued to interpret the Ga law of succession as matrilineal.[68] By 1939 even the Ga *mantse*'s Tribunal in Accra had also accepted matrilineal succession, and had proclaimed this practice to be standard among the Ga in its ruling in the case of *Cole v. Okine and Okine and anor.*[69]

Given what Margaret Field recognized as the centuries old history of fission and fusion of the Ga coastal communities, Ollennu's search for normative Ga customary practice seems more chimerical than based on an appreciation of historical reality. Undoubtedly what made matrilineal inheritance attractive to Akans did so for Gas, also. A much wider range of people stood to benefit when property passed from one generation to the next, and invariably many of these people would have been from an older generation than a man's sons and could consequently marshal the resources to use the colonial legal apparatus to further their interests. In communities like Labardi and Nungua, which were still basically fishing villages with a less extensive history of interaction with European traders than Christiansborg, Ussher Town or James Town, the process of adapting customary law to new conditions was undoubtedly less advanced. Under these circumstances it was hardly surprising that the question of inheritance, as a reporter in the *Gold Coast Independent* pointed out in 1932, remained such "an unsettled or moot question" in "the Ga speaking community."[70]

Apart from offering a wide range of people opportunities to inherit, ironically, once this system of inheritance began to be "judicially noticed" the British court's emphasis on a "stringent doctrine of *stare decisis*" made it increasingly likely that matrilineal inheritance would become the accepted form of customary law.[71] It was an unanticipated development that seemed unlikely given the initial position that British judges had taken vis-à-vis customary law. The operative position in the late nineteenth and early twentieth century was that customary law was basically "on the same footing as foreign law, and [had to] be proved by the evidence of expert witnesses."[72] However, the Privy Council decision in the 1916 case of *Angu v. Atta* recognized that by this time the British courts had "judicially noticed" a considerable body of customary law, which as a result could hardly be considered "foreign law" any longer and did not need to be proved by experts.[73] It meant that "in deciding questions of native law and custom the Court [might] give effect to any book or manuscript recognized in the Colony as a legal authority."[74]

The result was to divide native customary law into two parts. There was "native law," which as a result of being judicially noticed had actually become part of what in essence was becoming the colony's own common law tradition. It was readily available in the numerous compilations of such rulings that had followed from Sarbah's pioneering work *Fanti Customary Laws*. On the other hand there were "customs," particularly those of non-Akan peoples, that had not been judicially noticed and still needed proof, but in the highly politicized communities of the late colonial period it became increasingly difficult to obtain such information. As the *Report of the Commission of Inquiry into the Expenses Incurred by Litigants in the Courts of the Gold Coast* pointed out in 1945, "evidence of so-called experts differ[ed] remarkably and usually according to their interests."[75] The result was, as the attorney general indicated, the courts often found themselves in the position that no side would make its case and the customary law in dispute remained "unilluminated."[76] It was basically the same dilemma that confronted political officers who sought to resolve succession disputes.

By default this contributed to strengthening the position of Akan matrilineal inheritance. So too did the colony-wide judicial reforms of the 1930s.[77] The legal dualism that developed as a result of the return to "pure native law" forced the colonial government into trying to define the relationship between British and customary law. The Courts Ordinance of 1935 "employed two different techniques for relating the different categories of legal norms" that existed in the colony.[78] The ordinance sought to order hierarchically the courts that administered the different bodies of law in the colony, and to assign "discrete areas of application to each set of norms in the system."[79] Maintaining a clear separation between what were seen as distinct bodies of laws was the approach that had underscored the judgment in the case *In the Matter of the Estate of Timothy Mensah Otto,* when the acting chief justice had categorically ruled against the validity of nuncupative wills for those married under the 1884 Marriage Ordinance.

By this time, however, such cases where English common law and customary practice seemed clearly distinct were the exception rather than the rule. Far more often British judges had to deal with cases that inextricably involved customary law, and they gravitated toward the judicially noticed native law with its Akan bias and its heavy emphasis on the rights of the matrilineage.[80] Ironically, it was an approach that could easily rob customary law of the very flexibility that anthropologists were coming to recognize was one of its essential characteristics.[81] Margaret Field, for example, had concluded from her studies of the Ga people that they had no really "rigid laws of inheritance."[82] Nevertheless, the colony's Supreme Court and the West African Court of Appeal in the 1940s and 1950s continued to rule in favor of matrilineal inheritance on the basis of previous court rulings.[83] By this time the British courts had accepted the principle that family property was indivisible. In its ruling in the case of *Wellington v. Papafio* in 1952, the West African Court of Appeal sought to go one stage further and lay down also as a principle that children in Ga society were limited to the right of support from the self-acquired property of their father. On his death, however, such property would become family property and could not be apportioned.[84]

By the 1940s the colony's courts had often come to the conclusion "that succession among some of the tribes [of the Southern Gold Coast] which [had] been regarded as patrilineal [was] in fact matrilineal."[85] Ollennu cites, for example, the Divisional Court ruling in the case of *Chapman v. C. F. A. O.,* confirmed by the West African Court of Appeal in 1943, which ruled that inheritance in an Anlo Ewe family was matrilineal.[86] This and other rulings, Ollennu argues, led Madeline Manoukian "to say that succession among the Anlos is matrilineal."[87] Significantly, however, she did not see this as the case for many of the other Ewe subgroups. Among the Ho, for example, she maintained that "individual property is transmitted patrilineally."[88] In general, the distinction is between coastal and inland peoples. Perhaps in a similar fashion to the Gas, those who were drawn into trade with Europeans and contact with the coast were more inspired to adopt Akan ideas of inheritance. Subsequent rulings in the Divisional Court, such as *Tamakloe & ors. v. Attipqoe* (1948) and *Tay, etc. v. Adamah* (1952), which held that inheritance was patrilineal, were graphic indications of how "moot" and "unsettled" this issue of inheritance was among the Ewes. Equally confusing was the situation among the Guans and the Adas of the Ga-Adangbe people who lived in predominantly fishing communities. For them court rulings in the late 1940s and early 1950s took the position that succession in their communities was a mixture of matrilineal and patrilineal principles![89]

With such a widespread dissemination of the matrilineal system of succession it was hardly surprising that this "unreasonable" and "unnatural" system of inheritance did not "disappear" even in areas where extensive "modernization" would have seemed to have undermined it. Kofi Busia, for example, in surveying the ethnically heterogeneous Sekondi-Takoradi in 1949, could not help noticing in this town, which was basically a colonial creation, how powerful a force matrilineal inheritance was even among the educated.[90] Even more recently, Christine Oppong, in her study of Akan senior civil servants in Accra, has also demonstrated the persistence of the matrilineal family among a strata of Ghanaian society that would seem to have been most likely to have adopted the Western-style conjugal family.[91] By the end of the colonial period the Akan model of statecraft, with its emphasis on matrilineal inheritance of office, had become the dominant political force in the relatively cosmopolitan communities of the coast. Equally important, and the opposite side of the same coin, was the pervasive role that Akan conceptions of property and inheritance had come to play in the colony's judicial system.

Clearly, however, the operation of matrilineal principles of inheritance hardly conformed to the monolithic, unilineal descent systems that structural functionalists erected to conceptualize African societies. On closer inspection, like all monoliths, these structures turned out to have cracks, intrusions and eroded edges. The result has been, as Martin Chanock has pointed out, that contemporary anthropologists now exhibit "a clear tendency towards an agnostic view of structures."[92] In the invariably highly disruptive colonial situation, he goes on to argue, "claims about custom" must be seen as "competitive rather than descriptive."[93] In such settings, in a similar fashion to more rural communities, values and customs become important weapons in an "armory of arguments to be deployed when fighting over the distribution" of both property and political power.[94] It was hardly surprising that those who were Western-educated and lived in communities where many new ideas competed enjoyed an important operational advantage.

By viewing "custom" as functioning in this fashion, we also have to face the intriguing question of how much theoretical discussions contributed to creating the paradigm. For example, the heatedly contested issue of *samansiw*, which John Mensah Sarbah had defended in 1894 as part of native customary law, was most likely of "modern growth," as Sarbah himself recognized.[95] He cites Brodie Cruickshank's description of "the ceremonies observed upon occasions of death" to show how common the ceremony of willmaking was as far back as the mid-nineteenth century.[96] Identifying assets and debts seem to have been one of the most important functions of these ceremonies, and Cruickshank points out these "death-bed declarations, made in the presence of responsible witnesses, [were] always received as evidence in the event of litigation afterwards."[97] Cape Coast society, by the time Cruickshank wrote about it, had been significantly influenced by long contact with European traders, and it is possible that the development of the customary ceremony of *samansiw* was very much the result of what Martin Chanock has described as "changes in material relations."[98]

Apart from commerce, religious sources may also have played a role in the development of this custom. Cruickshank saw great similarity between the *samansiw* ceremony in the Gold Coast and Old Testament accounts of patriarchs making similar deathbed declarations of their property.[99] By this time Christian missions were well established on the coast, and it is not unlikely that the Bible was more than just a source of what David Henige has described as "feedback" into oral tradition.[100] God's chosen people struggling to preserve their identity and faith among hostile and more populous communities was an image with great appeal to Gold Coast Christians. What better way to ensure their survival from generation to generation than by adopting similar customs to the Israelites of old, who also struggled to survive in a wilderness of nonbelievers? There is no way, as Henige has pointed out, of really identifying the "tortuous and often nearly imperceptible routes by which outside materials can be—and have been—absorbed into local historical lore once they become available for public consumption."[101] It would be even harder to do so with customs that by definition claim roots in a distant past.

What is more important, however, is to recognize how such customs gain increasing legitimacy over time, ironically by the actions of very nontraditional institutions. In the case of *samansiw*, the initially unsuccessful attempts to have the British courts accept this custom as so basic and fundamental that it should apply to all Africans regardless of how they were married, turned out to be only temporary reverses. Finally, in 1959, in the first flush of nationalist assertiveness, the Ghana Court of Appeal in the case of *Coleman v. Shang* overturned the previous decisions by British judges that had ruled against the validity of nuncupative wills for those married under the 1884 Marriage Ordinance. On this occasion the court officially sanctioned wills made "in accordance with customary law" as one of the two ways of legally devising property in Ghana.[102]

The result has been that in present-day Ghana the legal profession entertains few doubts about the pedigree of this custom. N. A. Ollennu, for example, discounts Sarbah's suggestion that *samansiw* was probably of "modern growth" on the grounds that it must have been "as old as the individual ownership of property."[103] Instead, he turns to Sir Henry Maine's *Ancient Law* for help in determining "the origin of the Ghana *Samansiw* and to trace the principles regulating it."[104] As a product of British legal training with its "unhistorical conception of the origin of common law" it is not surprising that Ollennu is more comfortable working in this essentially deductive tradition than dealing with the messy uncertainties of acculturation.[105] In general, contemporary Ghanaian legal scholars, who have devoted considerable attention to customary property law, have assumed a priori that it is either based on matrilineal or patrilineal principles of inheritance.[106]

Given the important legitimizing role that both colonial and Ghanaian courts have played as they have sought to return to "pure native law," we can understand why appeals to custom were more than merely opportunistic manipulations primarily by the Western-educated. Specifically, matrilineal descent systems and principles of succession to office and property acquired a judicially recognized existence that made them more than "a kind of vague notional ideal," as David Henige has suggested.[107] Undoubtedly, we are unlikely to settle the question of how truly normative matriliny was in Akan society, but it clearly came to be defined by a carefully stipulated set of rules in the colony's judicial system that has been passed on as a lasting and important legacy to independent Ghana. Administrative policies and academic theories share in common a mercurial quality. Particularly in times of ideological conflict, they can oscillate from one extreme to the next, and clearly the post–Second World War period has been one such time for Africa. Social processes, however, once set in motion, are more like the supertanker that once under way does not shift course easily. The interactive process that I have described in this chapter is an excellent example of how one important aspect of the judicial system in the Gold Coast Colony developed its own momentum, which often took it in most unpredictable directions that did not conform to assumed paradigms. By focusing exclusively on the political process and assuming discrete groups—the educated elite, divisional chiefs and commoners—Kathryn Firmin-Sellers misses the contradictory manner in which property rights developed in the Gold Coast.

However, the British courts also had a much more predictable impact on the overall development of the country's legal system. By the end of the colonial period it was clear that one court system was emerging that institutionally was going to combine what were known as the Native

Tribunals and the British courts of the colony's Supreme Court system. In the following chapter I will look at this process to show how much both customary forms of justice and their judicial principles were affected by the link that developed with the English common law system. Here, too, there were some unexpected surprises.

Notes

1. An earlier version of this chapter appeared as "Competing Systems of InheritanceBefore the Courts of the Gold Coast Colony," *International Journal of African Historical Studies* 23, no. 4 (1990):601-618.

2. Jenkins, "Gold Coast Historians," 95, 159.

3. Tenkorang, "John Mensah Sarbah," 77-78.

4. The Mfantsi Anambuhu Fékuw (literally, Fante Political Society) had been established in Cape Coast in 1889, and was one of the first public indications of how important the concern with upholding the value of African culture had become. The book was published in London in 1897.

5. *Fanti Customary Laws*, ix.

6. Indeed, both *Fanti Customary Laws* and Sarbah's later work, *Fanti National Constitution*, were to become standard issue for new political officers.

7. Casely Hayford, *Gold Coast Native Institutions*, xiii. Casely Hayford particularly had in mind Governor Frederic Hodgson's "ill-advised hunt" for the Golden Stool of the Asante in 1900. It had resulted in the governor's party being attacked and blockaded in Kumasi for several weeks. He was convinced that this "waste of money and blood would have been saved" if the government had been willing to take advice from the "representatives of the people." Ibid., 268.

8. According to Sarbah, "Fanti laws and customs appl[ied] to all Akans and Fanti, and to all persons whose mothers are of Akan or Fanti race." *Fanti Customary Laws*, 15.

9. Inez Sutton, "Law, Chieftaincy and Conflict in Colonial Ghana: The Ada Case," *African Affairs* 83, no. 330 (January 1984):48.

10. Sarbah, *Fanti National Constitution*, 15.

11. Ibid., 25.

12. For Kingsley's views on Sarbah see S. Gwynn, *The Life of Mary Kingsley* (London, 1932), 177.

13. Apart from Africans who were engaged in codifying customary law, there were a number of expatriate judges and political officers who also contributed to this process by their compilations of cases that had come before their courts. The overwhelming majority of such cases which involved customary law were in the Akan area of the colony. For example, see: H. W. Hayes Redwar, *Comments on the Ordinances of the Gold Coast Colony* (London, 1909); A. Earnshaw,

Judgments Delivered at Cape Coast Castle (1910; reprint, Accra-Tema, 1976); Peter Awooner Renner (originally from Sierra Leone), *Reports, Notes of Cases and Proceedings and Judgements in Appeals...Relating to the Gold Coast Colony and the Colony of Nigeria, 1861-1914,* 2 vols. (London, 1915); W. Brandford-Griffith, *A Digest of an Index to the Reports of Cases Decided in the Supreme Court of the Gold Coast Colony* (Accra, 1936). This work was the culmination of several compilations of such decided cases that Brandford Griffith had first begun collecting in 1887 when he was a district commissioner in the Gold Coast.

14. Sarbah, *Fanti National Constitution,* xvii.

15. The term "gone Fantee" was popularized by Reverend Attoh Ahuma. See Tenkorang, "John Mensah Sarbah," 77-78. For a discussion of the difficulties involved in "going Fantee," see Kimble, *A Political History of Ghana,* 518-520.

16. *J. M. Sarbah deceased Ekua Marian Sarbah Cavetrix,* 23 March 1911, Cape Coast Registrars Minute Book, SCT 5/9/22, NAG, Accra. Information about his will, which he made on 16 July 1903, comes from the records of this case.

17. The government, however, did not entertain her plea. And neither could the widow agree to her mother-in-law's offer to educate the children provided that they lived with her. Crabbe, *John Mensah Sarbah, 1864-1910,* 10.

18. Sarbah, *Fanti Customary Laws,* 44.

19. Sarbah was a staunch Wesleyan Methodist. He was an active member of the Cape Coast circuit, and in 1900 he presented to Wesley Chapel in Cape Coast "a magnificent Pipe-Organ in memory of his lamented father (d. 1892) and brother (d. 1892)." Sampson, *Makers of Modern Ghana,* 1:125.

20. John Sarbah's will, 31 August 1889. Cited in Kaplow, "Primitive Accumulation," 25.

21. S. K. B. Asante, "Interests in Land in the Customary Law of Ghana: A New Appraisal," *Yale Law Journal* 74 (April 1965):865.

22. Edsman, *Lawyers in Gold Coast Politics,* 23.

23. J. M. Sarbah, "Maclean and Gold Coast Judicial Assessors," *Journal of the African Society* 9, no. 36 (July 1910):358.

24. The government wanted to establish forest reserves.

25. H. C. Belfield, *Report on the Legislation Governing the Alienation of Native Lands in the Gold Coast Colony and Ashanti; With Some Observations on the "Forest Ordinance," 1911* (London, 1912), 8. Belfield was the British resident in Perak, which was part of the Federated Malay States, and like many other officials who had served in this area of the British Empire he was an advocate of indirect rule.

26. According to Casely Hayford, if chiefs, who held the land in trust, tried to sell land against the wishes of their subjects, the latter could always destool such offending rulers, and this power was sufficient to prevent any violation of custom. Casely Hayford to the West African Lands Committee, question 823, African West 1046, 1916. Cited in Anne Phillips, *The Enigma of Colonialism: British Policy in West Africa* (Bloomington, Ind., 1989), 84.

27. Ibid., 77.

28. Ibid., 78.

29. Ibid.

30. S. K. B. Asante cites the Privy Council decision of *Amodu Tijani v. Secretary, Southern Nigeria* in 1921 as the first major indication of this swing on the part of British justice to a more pro customary land tenure position. There were also a number of examples of this shift in the Gold Coast, such as *Kuma v. Kuma* and *Summnu v. Disu Raphael.* "Interests in Land in the Customary Law of Ghana," 868-870.

31. Firmin-Sellers, *The Transformation of Property Rights,* 2.

32. It is significant in this regard that she does not include the courts in her discussion of colonial institutions. As a result there is a serious gap in her analysis since it ignores the voluminous court records of this period.

33. *The Blinkards* (London, 1974), 139, 70. Sekyi wrote this play some time after he returned from England in 1915 after obtaining a first degree in philosophy from London University. R. Jenkins, "Sekyi's Formative Years," *West Africa* (6 September 1982):2270-2272.

34. It was serialized in the newly established London-based weekly, *West Africa,* and ran from 25 May to 18 September 1918.

35. For a description of the Nigerian 1884 Marriage Ordinance, see Mann, *Marrying Well,* 44. As a result, rulings in Nigerian courts regarding marriage established a judicial precedent for the Gold Coast as well. The case of *Cole v. Cole* in 1898 was an excellent example of this.

36. Unlike the Fante, the Yoruba, who made up the majority of Lagos' population in the 1920s, were patrilineal, and the lineage held "corporate rights to land and titles, although persons could acquire individual rights to other kinds of property." Mann, *Marrying Well,* 36. As such this would have given Smith's patrikin a strong customary claim to his real property.

37. *Martins v. Fowler,* 18 June 1926. *Law Reports of Appeal Cases* (London, 1926), 747-748. This period when English common law was in effect would correspond to the phase of "judicial realism" in the Gold Coast. It was inherently linked to what A. G. Hopkins has pointed out was the development of new ideas about property rights that the annexation of Lagos in 1861 brought into being, and consequently corresponded to the new social conditions that Sir William Brandford Griffith felt had come into being in the Gold Coast in the late nineteenth century. "Property Rights and Empire Building: Britain's Annexation of Lagos, 1861," *Journal of Ecomonic History* 40, no. 4 (December 1984):777-798.

38. *Rebecca Carr v. Jemina Carr and Samuel C. Addequay,* 29 October 1926, Cape Coast Judgment Book, SCT 5/6/1, NAG, Accra.

39. His middle name would seem to indicate that he probably also had Akan forebears.

40. *In the Matter of the Estate of Timothy Mensah Otoo,* 29 March 1927, Accra Divisional Court Judgment Record Book, SCT 2/6/12, NAG, Accra.

41. Ibid.

42. This is how J. Ayo Langley has described Sekyi to indicate that he wanted to see a radical return to precolonial Fante values and customs. "Modernization and Its Malcontents: Kobina Sekyi of Ghana and the Restatement of African Political Theory (1892-1956)," *Institute of African Studies Research Review* 6, no. 3 (1970):1.

43. J. A. Dodoo in the *Gold Coast Leader*, 16 April 1927.

44. *Gold Coast Independent*, 19 June 1926.

45. *Gold Coast Independent*, 23 July 1932.

46. In spite of its name, this society was not made up of "young people." Its membership consisted of Accra's intellectual elite. The growth of such organizations in the 1920s and 1930s was, as Yaw Twumasi has suggested, apart from being a social club, a response to the lack of opportunities for higher education in the colony. Y. Twumasi, "Aspects of Politics in Ghana: A Study of the Relationships Between Discontent and the Development of Nationalism" (Ph.D. diss., Oxford University, 1971), 188.

47. The debaters consisted of A. K. Q. Quartey, Attram (arguing for the sons) and Owusu and Richard Akwei (arguing for the nephews), while the judges were Dr. J. B. Danquah, an Akyem, Father E. D. Martinson, an Akwapim, and Nii Kojo Ababio IV, the James Town *mantse*, a Ga. According to the *Times of West Africa*, 23 July 1932, the audience "included all the talents."

48. For example, the *Gold Coast Leader*, 16 April 1927; *The Times of West Africa*, 23 April 1930, 26 May 1932, 29 July, 19 October 1933, 23 April 1934; and the *Gold Coast Observer*, 23 November 1944. It should be noted, however, that not everyone necessarily agreed with this "Anglomania." Kobina Kwaansa (a nom de plume, and very likely an Akan), writing in the 18 November 1933 issue of the *Gold Coast Independent*, defended the matrilineal system as "by far away better and more suitable than any other social system known." Also defending "African customs" was "Darl" in the *Gold Coast Spectator*, 19 February 1938.

49. Suspicion of the validity of wills could also extend to inheritance disputes as the case of *John Charles Vandyck and Others v. Joseph William Qyayson* that came before Full Court in Cape Coast on 22 April 1930 indicated. After Charles Vandyck died in 1925, there had been a fairly typical scramble for his property. But even though a written will existed, the Full Court ruled against its validity on the grounds that it "overrode native law of administration."

50. *W. A. Johnson Deceased v. Chief Amoah III with Maria Duncan Claimant*, 30 March 1930, Cape Coast Judgment Book, SCT 5/6/1, NAG, Accra.

51. For example, the two interpleader actions that came before the Accra Divisional Court on 5 December 1924 were won by litigants who had what the court considered valid deeds of conveyance. *J. W. Appiah v. K. Q. Aryeh with Daedaye Ankrah Claimant*, and *Dr. C. E. Reindorf v. Akuse Marman with Jacob J. Simmons Claimant*, Accra Judgment Book, SCT 2/6/10, NAG, Accra.

52. Periodically before this time there had been discussions about bringing Gold Coast laws into conformity with English law. In 1919, for example, the attorney general canvassed a wide range of officials for their views on this matter. The general opinion was that the "country was not ripe for bankruptcy laws." The District Commissioner of Saltpond to the Provincial Commissioner, 5 November 1919, ADM 23/1/328, NAG, Cape Coast.

53. *Times of West Africa,* 23 May 1934. In Sierra Leone imprisonment for debt had long since passed out of use with the passage in 1883 of *An Ordinance for the Abolition of Imprisonment for Debt and the Punishment of Fraudulent Debtors.* In Nigeria the practice had continued, but its judges had more "discretion" in dealing with debtors. Attorney General to the Colonial Secretary, 23 July 1933, CSO 4/1/169, NAG, Accra. In both colonies the notion of individual property was better developed. In neither colony did English common law have to compete with a customary law influenced by matrilineal cultures.

54. For example, Mary Douglas identifies some of these as matriliny's limited "demands on the loyalties of men," and the "scope" that it gives to "the enterprising individual to override ascribed roles." See "Is Matriliny Doomed in Africa?" in *Man in Africa,* ed. Mary Douglas and Phyllis Karberry (London, 1969), 128.

55. Even women who were married to leading members of coastal society could expect only limited success in the colony's courts. This was similar to the situation that Kristin Mann describes for Lagos. See *Marrying Well,* 84-85.

56. This had been what the reporter who covered the Rodger Club debate in Accra in 1932 for the *Times of West Africa* had predicted in the 29 July 1932 issue.

57. *George Fynn v. Arabah Inyinah and Arabella Brown,* 8 October 1926, Cape Coast Judgment Book, SCT 5/6/3, NAG, Accra.

58. *In the Matter of the Estate of J. W. de Graft Johnson Deceased,* 15 April 1930, Cape Coast Judgment Book, SCT 5/6/1, NAG, Accra.

59. His main source was the London-based Royal African Society's *Journal of the African Society:* "The Law of Succession Among the Akras or the Ga Tribes Proper of the Gold Coast," 10 (1910):65-72; "The Native Tribunals of the Akras of the Gold Coast," 10 (1910-1911):320-330, 434-446, and 11 (1911-1912):75-94; "The Use of Names Among the Gas or Accra People of the Gold Coast," 13 (1913):167-182; and "Apprenticeship Among the Gas," 13 (1913-1914):415-422.

60. For example, "The Connubial Institutions of the Gas," *Journal of the African Society* 30, no. 121 (October 1931):399-409, and "The Origin of the Gas," *Journal of the African Society* 27, no 105 (October 1927):69-76, and 27, no 106 (January 1928):167-193.

61. "The Native Tribunals of the Akras of the Gold Coast," 321-330, 434-438.

62. Cited in Sarbah, "Maclean and Gold Coast Judicial Assessors," 354.

63. Judgment delivered on 24 October 1908, unreported. Cited in N. A. Ollennu, *The Law of Testate and Intestate Succession in Ghana* (London, 1966), 191. He obviously did not feel that this "mass of evidence" was overwhelming enough on which to base his decision.

64. *Jemina Nassu and Others v. the Basel Mission*, 10 July 1915, Accra Judgment Book, SCT 2/6/5, NAG, Accra.

65. Cited in A. St. J. J. Hannigan, "The Impact of English Law upon the Existing Gold Coast Custom and the Possible Development of the Resulting System," *Journal of African Administration* 8, no. 3 (July 1956):129-130.

66. Ibid.

67. Ollennu, *The Law of Testate and Intestate Succession in Ghana*, 189. Ollennu began practicing in the colony in 1943.

68. He cites two cases to show this: *Sackey v. Okantah*, which came before Chief Justice Crampton Smyly in 1916, and *Aryeh and Others v. Dawuda and Others*, which finally came before the West African Court of Appeal in 1944. See *The Law of Testate and Intestate Succession in Ghana*, 191-192.

69. Ibid., 190.

70. *Gold Coast Independent*, 23 July 1932.

71. Asante, "Ghanaian Land Law," 849. For a more complete discussion of this question see his article "Stare Decisis in the Supreme Court of Ghana," *I. U Ghana Law Journal* 52 (1964).

72. For examples see the decision of Acting Judge Hayes Redwar in the 1891 case of *Eccuah Bimba v. Effuah Mansah* (Sarbah, *Fanti Customary Laws*, 137-142), and *Hughes v. Davies and another* before Judge Francis Smith in 1909 (cited in Crabbe, *John Mensah Sarbah, 1864-1910*, 57).

73. *Eccuah Bimba v. Effuah Mansah*, 25-26 November 1891. Cited in Sarbah, *Fanti Customary Laws*, 137.

74. Ibid., 58.

75. *Report of Commission of Inquiry*, 38.

76. Ibid.

77. The widely publicized trial in Asante of a European medical officer, Dr. Benjamin Knowles, for the murder of his wife in 1928 did much to raise interest both in Britain and the Gold Coast over what were seen as failures in the colony's judicial system. Indeed, a few years afterward the Colonial Office's legal adviser, H. G. Bushe, visited the Gold Coast to give advice on improving the colony's administration of justice. W. C. Ekow Daniels, *The Common Law in West Africa* (London, 1964), 48-49.

78. William Harvey, *A Value Analysis of Ghanaian Legal Development Since Independence* (Accra, 1963), 8.

79. Ibid.

80. The likelihood of this had increased with time since those who focused on the Akan tradition had continued to dominate the process of codifying customary law. The two most important contributors in this regard were J. B. Danquah, *Akan*

Laws and Customs and the Akim Abuakwa Constitution (London, 1928), and the government anthropologist R. S. Rattray, *Ashanti Law and Constitution* (London, 1929).

81. This was hardly restricted to the situation in the Gold Coast alone. It was particularly acute in colonial societies where the distance between European and customary law was great. For example, Elizabeth Colson, in analyzing the possible impact of the right to make wills among the Plateau Tonga of Northern Rhodesia, recognized how formal recognition of customary law ironically had the effect of slowing down change in the legal systems of traditional societies. See "Possible Repercussions of the Right to Make Wills upon the Plateau Tonga of Northern Rhodesia," *Journal of African Administration* 2, no. 1 (1950):24-34.

82. Field, *Social Organization of the Ga People,* 43.

83. The West African Court of Appeal was established in 1928 to hear appeals from the Supreme Courts of the four British West African colonies.

84. W. A. C. A., unreported, 4 April 1952. Cited in Hannigan, "The Impact of English Law upon the Existing Gold Coast Custom," 130.

85. Ollennu, *The Law of Testate and Intestate Succession in Ghana,* 175.

86. Ibid.

87. Ibid.

88. Madeline Manoukian, *The Ewe-Speaking People of Togoland and the Gold Coast* (London, 1952), 24. The Anlo Ewe are in the coastal section of this linguistically homogeneous area that extends from the Volta River to the border of the present-day country of Benin.

89. Ollennu, *The Law of Testate and Intestate Succession in Ghana,* 175-176.

90. Kofi Busia, *Report on a Social Survey of Sekondi-Takoradi* (London, 1950), 44-45.

91. Christine Oppong, *Marriage Among a Matrilineal Elite: A Family Study of Ghanaian Senior Civil Servants* (London, 1974). She did her fieldwork for this study in 1967-1968.

92. Martin Chanock, *Law, Custom and Social Order: The Colonial Experience in Malawi and Zambia* (Cambridge, U.K., 1985), 16. An example of this "agnostic" approach in the Ghanaian context is Michel Verdon, *The Abutia Ewe of West Africa: A Chiefdom that Never Was* (Berlin, 1983).

93. Chanock, *Law, Custom and Social Order,* 17.

94. R. Frankenburg, introduction to *Social Change and the Individual: A Study of the Social and Religious Responses to Innovation in a Zambian Rural Community,* by Norman Long (Manchester, 1968), viii.

95. Sarbah, *Fanti Customary Laws,* 97.

96. Cruickshank, *Eighteen Years on the Gold Coast of Africa,* 2:213.

97. Ibid., 214.

98. Martin Chanock, "A Peculiar Sharpness: An Essay on Property in the History of Customary Law in Colonial Africa," *Journal of African History* 32 (1991):65.

99. Cruickshank, *Eighteen Years on the Gold Coast of Africa*, 2:214.

100. David Henige, "Truths Yet Unborn? Oral Tradition as a Casualty of Culture Contact," *Journal of African History* 23, no. 3 (1982):395-412.

101. Ibid., 409.

102. *Ghana Law Review*, 390, 402-403. Cited in Crabbe, *John Mensah Sarbah, 1864-1910*, 33.

103. Ollennu, *The Law of Testate and Intestate Succession in Ghana*, 272. The most recent indication of how much a recognized part of Ghanaian law *samansiw* has become can be seen in the Provisional National Defense Council's 1985 Intestate Succession Law, which in chapter 18 specifically recognizes *samansiw* as a valid form of willmaking in Ghana.

104. Ibid., 270.

105. Chanock, *Law, Custom and Social Order*, 3.

106. For examples, see N. A. Ollennu, *Principles of Customary Law in Ghana* (London, 1962); K. Bentsi-Enchill, *Ghana Land Law: An Exposition, Analysis and Critique* (London, 1964); A. K. P. Kludze, *Ghana I: Ewe Law of Property* (London, 1973) and *Modern Law of Succession in Ghana* (Dordrecht, Holland, and Providence, R.I., 1988); S. K. B. Asante, *Property and Social Goals in Ghana, 1844-1966* (Accra, 1975); and Kofi Awusabo-Asare, "Matriliny and the New Intestate Succession Law of Ghana," *Canadian Journal of African Studies* 24, no. 1 (1990):1-16.

107. Henige, "Akan Stool Succession Under Colonial Rule: Continuity or Change?" 300.

Chapter 9

Linking Different Legal Systems

There was a converse side to the interaction between British and customary law in the Gold Coast.[1] The British judicial system had an increasingly important influence on how the Native Tribunals operated. Specifically, this was reflected in the procedure these courts followed, the makeup of their membership and, most importantly, in the nature of the customary law that they came to administer. In a similar fashion to the colony's political development, where Western-style municipal institutions affected the affairs of the native order, so too was there extensive bilateral borrowing between its different judicial systems. As the government's policy of indirect rule worked to enhance the importance of the native order, it was understandable that those who sought to benefit from this would copy aspects of the British judicial system to increase the standing of their most important institution, the Native Tribunal. Apart from social forces contributing to this process of amalgamation, in a similar fashion to political developments in the colony's main coastal towns, colonial policies also had a major impact on how British justice came to affect the operation of the Native Tribunals.

The influence of British administration and justice on native courts was evident as early as the mid-nineteenth century. Particularly in the coastal towns, these institutions had lost their right to try serious criminal cases.

The Bond of 1844 had given formal sanction to this development by stipulating that

> murders, robberies and other crimes and offences [were to] be tried and inquired into before the Queen's judicial officers and the chiefs of the district, moulding the customs of the country to the general principles of British law.[2]

The result was that by the 1850s the native courts in the coastal towns adjudicated predominantly civil matters. According to Brodie Cruickshank, most of these matters concerned property, and reflective of this Fante laws referred "principally to property."[3] In addition, he observed that these courts applied basically the same kind of punishment—fines of varying amounts—to nearly all the cases that they heard, and as a result Europeans in general concluded that there was no real distinction between tort and crime in customary law. There clearly was a self-fulfilling quality to this observation since especially after the British government established a Supreme Court in 1853, local chiefs who attempted to adjudicate more than "trivial [criminal] cases" invariably found themselves in conflict with both the chief magistrate and the governor. For example, one of the main reasons for the particularly hostile relations between King Aggrey of Cape Coast and Governors Pine and Conran in 1865-1866 resulted from the former's attempt to imprison his subjects without appeal to the British court and his intention to raise a "small police force."[4] Both clearly would have represented an encroachment on the British monopoly of criminal jurisdiction.

How much King Aggrey's determination to exercise criminal jurisdiction was due to the influence of the British court system in Cape Coast or a resurfacing of an intrinsic feature of customary law will probably remain as impossible to determine as the normative structure of the native state. Significantly, however, when the British government formally recognized the exercise of chiefly judicial power in the 1883 Native Jurisdiction Ordinance, the bill specifically delineated spheres of criminal and civil jurisdiction.[5] However, as far as the former were concerned, the "Commissioner of the district" was still to deal with all "serious offence[s] or crime[s] such as murder, robbery, slave-dealing, or any other serious crime."[6] The chiefs' role in the adjudication of serious criminal matters consisted only of "apprehending, detaining, and sending to the Commissioner of the district" those people who were suspected of such crimes.[7] As far as their own courts were concerned, they were restricted to dealing with petty assaults and thievery. As an indication of the role that the government wanted the chiefs to fulfill as indirect rulers, they were also given the power to punish those who violated the colony's sanitary ordinances. To uphold their authority, chiefs could also punish those who disobeyed their orders with short periods of imprisonment.

In seeking to introduce the distinction between criminal and civil matters, the ordinance made an important concession to African sensibilities by including "seduction," "slander," "fetishism" and "witchcraft" as criminal offenses that Native Tribunals could adjudicate. To Africans these were serious offenses—particularly fetishism and witchcraft, since the purpose was to injure or kill rivals and enemies.[8] In general these crimes were considerably different from what English common law considered defamation, the closest legal equivalent, since both slander and libel were by this time primarily civil actions in the British court system with the aggrieved party only entitled to damages.[9] As a result the British courts could not satisfactorily deal with what Europeans conceded could result in "horrible practices."[10] The evidence in such cases was too circumstantial to hold up in a jury trial. It was impossible to get witnesses to come forward, and in one particularly notorious case involving a woman accused of poisoning a child, even trying to get her committed as a "dangerous lunatic" failed.[11] By allowing native courts to prosecute such "horrible practices" as crimes came much closer to underscoring what to Africans was the seriousness of these offenses.

Initially, however, the Native Tribunals continued to adjudicate primarily civil matters. The Hutchinson Commission of 1895 indicated that most chiefs still sent "to the English Courts for trial all cases of a criminal nature which [were] in any degree serious."[12] Indeed, as John Mensah Sarbah pointed out in 1897, "in matters covered by English criminal law" customary laws had "in the protected territories ceased to exist with the Bond of 1844."[13] Customary laws that native courts adjudicated were almost exclusively concerned with civil matters. Significantly, in *Fanti Customary Laws,* Sarbah deals almost exclusively with matters like marriage, divorce, property, succession, inheritance and debt. There is only one very short section on slander, which occupied a rather unique position in the colony's judicial system. His treatment of seduction is not much more detailed, and significantly he does not deal with it as a crime, but as a civil action involving the return of bridewealth and/or the payment of damages.

Also contributing to the difficulty of formalizing the distinction between criminal and civil law was the colonial administration's unwillingness to grant Native Tribunals the power to enforce their decisions. Even after the Supreme Court's *Oppon v. Ackinie* ruling in 1887, Governor William Brandford Griffith considered chiefly courts in the coastal towns to be only venues of "family arbitration."[14] In these locations British officials were extremely reluctant to allow local rulers to have prisons. Not until the first decade of the twentieth century did they finally relent, and even then it was more due to decisions by local district commissioners than as a result of official policy. Under these circumstances it was not surprising that Native Tribunals were slow to develop a criminal adjudicative role. In 1905, when Chief Justice William Brandford Griffith investigated the functioning of native courts, he discovered that when "an offence" was "dealt with by the [Native] Court...in almost every case it only [came] out during the course of the civil matter."[15] As an indication of the ad hoc nature of these investigations, such criminal offenses were "dealt with summarily in the course of or after the civil case with the fine going to the *Omanhen*."[16]

Whether or not imprisonment in a specially constructed facility for this purpose also represented a major innovation in the exercise of traditional justice is difficult to determine. Placing offenders in stocks was an established practice among the Akan, and chiefly messengers did more than merely bring greetings from their masters. They were also empowered to carry out their wishes. In conjunction with the existence of government prisons, these customs no doubt influenced chiefs to create their own facilities in the late nineteenth century. Indicative, however, of official resistance to this development, it was not until 1910, in conjunction with the amended Native Jurisdiction Bill, that the government passed a Native Prisons Ordinance that sought to regulate the prisons that de facto existed. Even at this point the governor, James Thorburn, was "not convinced of the necessity for requiring chiefs to have registered prisons."[17] The colony's chiefs, however, were far more realistic as they had come to recognize that no court in the colony could function without a prison, and they were soon engaged in building a "large number of Native Prisons" on plans the government approved.[18]

In a similar fashion the chiefs recognized the need for a regular police force, and a number of enterprising chiefs took advantage of the formal recognition of their courts to establish "chiefs policemen" with uniforms closely patterned on those the colony's Escort Police wore.[19] However, the governor refused to recognize "agents" of the Native Tribunals as anything more than "messengers," and was adamant that they be prohibited from wearing any uniform that could be confused with those that the civil police wore.[20] Instead, the governor suggested that as far as a uniform was concerned, tribunal messengers should be easily distinguished from the civil police by wearing a yellow sash over their shoulders with a large brass plate with the words "Chief's Messenger" inscribed on it. The prosecutions for impersonating police officers that periodically came up in the colony's lower courts were an indication of how the Native Tribunal's officers recognized that they needed more than just messengers if their courts were to have any authority.[21] It was a contradictory situation, for this failure to win recognition from the government to have a bona fide police force ensured that the Native Tribunals would have considerable difficulty discharging even the limited criminal jurisdiction that the government envisaged.

Not surprisingly, even though the 1910 amendment to the Native Jurisdiction Bill described much more precisely the areas in which the native state could make bylaws and expanded the range of criminal jurisdiction for the Native Tribunals, their adjudicative role still remained primarily civil. The extant record for one of the oldest of the coastal Native Tribunals, that of Cape Coast, indicates that these bodies in the coastal areas continued to function primarily as courts of civil adjudication. Of the twenty-nine cases which make up this record from 1909 to 1912, only one concerns assault, one slander and one witchcraft while the rest deal with matters ranging from unpaid debts (ten), the return of brideprice (six), seduction (four), land trespass (three), wife support (one), paternity (one) and one chiefly deposition.[22] According to the colonial government's definition of what was a civil versus a criminal offense, roughly only 10 percent of this tribunal's activities dealt with the latter. In addition, the slander and witchcraft cases procedurally were more akin to civil than criminal cases, since the tribunal would have charged hearing fees as it would have in civil cases, and also assessed damages.

In 1920 the government officially began collecting half-yearly statistics of the criminal and civil cases heard before the colony's Native Tribunals, and from this source of information it is clear that there had been little change in the judicial activity of these courts. For example, in the first six months of 1922 the Cape Coast Native Tribunal heard 155 civil cases and only 23 of a criminal nature. Reflective of the town's importance as a commercial center, 45 percent of the civil cases had to do with debt while the rest concerned marriage issues and general claims for damages. On the other hand, in a town well known for its *asafo* rivalries, assault cases made up a surprisingly small proportion of the criminal cases that the tribunal heard. Understandably, prosecuting violators of the local sanitary bylaws was unattractive to native authorities whose positions were already precarious. Neither were there financial incentives, for in such court hearings there were no hearing fees, and in cases of incarceration the native state had to pay for the upkeep of prisoners at a standard rate set by the colonial government.

Instead, the British courts remained the main venue for dealing with criminal offenses in the coastal areas. After 1919 this was further reinforced when the government appointed police magistrates for the larger coastal towns like Accra, Cape Coast, Sekondi and later Winneba. They got considerably more civil and criminal jurisdiction than district commissioners, and also took over much of the latter's former task of prosecuting sanitary violations. As vehicular traffic increased in the towns, enforcing driving codes also became an important function of the district magistrates court. The result was that between about 40 and 60 percent of the district magistrate's caseload in Cape Coast in the 1920s dealt with what were considered criminal cases. Many of these cases were obviously settled with fines; interestingly enough, this court generated more revenue from this kind of activity than it did from civil cases.[23]

Significant was the proportionally large number of "fetish" cases the Native Tribunals heard. Not surprisingly, in the smaller towns this was more pronounced than, for example, in Cape Coast, but even in this "center of Christian civilization" such "superstitious practices" were still common. More important, however, was the increase in cases involving "slander" and "defamation." For example, out of thirty-nine cases selected at random that came before the Accra Native Tribunal in 1925, thirteen deal with "defamation." Often they involved people accusing one another of witchcraft or "fetishism." Others, however, were basically what the Blackall Commission of 1943 was to describe as "vulgar abuse." They might conceivably have become witchcraft accusations, but in general, as the Blackall Commission indicated, they were the primary contributors to the "frivolous litigation" that the Native Tribunals were accused of encouraging. In such cases "damages out of all proportion to the seriousness of the slander [were] frequently awarded."[24] It was not surprising that the Native Tribunals encouraged such litigation, for it obviously represented an important source of revenue, but this was hardly what colonial administrators had anticipated would be the "criminal" adjudicative activity of these courts.

As far as seeking to extend the criminal jurisdiction of the Native Tribunals was concerned, the next formal attempt to do so came with the 1927 Native Administration Ordinance. In contrast to the 1910 Native Jurisdiction Amendment Bill, this legislation emphasized the criminal rather than the civil jurisdiction of the Native Tribunals. In considerable detail it expanded the former, and also specified more precisely than had been the case in the past what the punishments for these offenses should be. The ordinance also underscored the tribunal's responsibility for enforcing the colony's health and sanitary bylaws. It also made disrespect and willful disobedience of Tribunal personnel criminal offenses, which was obviously designed to strengthen the position of native authorities who were to be "a living part of the machinery of government."[25]

In conjunction with the increased political power of the colony's chiefs, the ordinance clearly strengthened their judicial power, and it was hardly surprising that there was so much opposition to it in the colony. One indication of this was that not until 1931 was the government able to collect statistics on civil and criminal cases before the colony's Native Tribunals. By this time, however, there had been a dramatic increase in the number of criminal cases that they tried. In districts and small towns where there were no police magistrates or district commissioners, the number of civil and criminal cases were almost equal. Indeed, in the Saltpond district, to the east of Cape Coast, there were actually more criminal than civil cases.[26] Significantly, even in those places where there were both police magistrate and district commissioner courts, like Cape Coast and Winneba, there was still a considerable increase in criminal adjudication. Some of this was the result of court activity by Native Tribunals in the surrounding district. This was particularly so in Cape Coast, where the struggle to control the Native Tribunal severely affected its ability to function in the town itself.

Increasing criminal adjudication was clearly a long-term trend. When the Korsah Commission on Native Courts conducted its investigation of these institutions in 1951, 65 percent of the cases that came before them were criminal cases under Gold Coast ordinances. Significantly, 30 percent were cases involving assault, larceny and sanitary offenses. At the same time, however, in spite of the Blackall Commission's strictures against "frivolous defamation litigation," 17 percent of the types of cases heard in the colony's Native Courts were described as "miscellaneous cases under customary law," and many would have involved "vulgar abuse."[27] Customary conceptions of criminal activities had obviously been permanently amalgamated into a judicial system that was open to many influences. The accommodation that developed between African and European concepts of civil law regarding property was also to be mirrored, albeit, to a lesser extent, in the realm of criminal law.

Apart from extending the criminal adjudicative authority of the Native Tribunals, a more interventionist indirect rule policy also meant allowing chiefs to tax their subjects. Recourse to prosecution in the Native Tribunal became an important means of enforcing such payments, and in general upholding the authority of the chief. In addition, the government came to depend, especially in areas where there were no police magistrate courts, on the Native Tribunal to enforce the colony's sanitary regulations. By allowing these courts to charge fines, and hence generate revenue, the government made the adjudication of such criminal matters financially attractive to the Native Tribunals. The 1927 ordinance also specifically permitted paramount chiefs "to keep and maintain one or more registered prisons," and as a formal indication of their acceptance the secretary of native affairs was to register them in "a Register to be called the Register of Native State Prisons."[28] And most significantly, as a further indication of the changing function of these courts, in 1928 the government began to concede that the Native Tribunals needed "Native Police" rather than "messengers" if they were to function as effective criminal courts.

This resulted through the initiative of the commissioner of the Central Province, A. C. Duncan-Johnstone, who in 1928 introduced a training course for the Central Province's Native Police. It was under the supervision of the commissioner of police, who "lectured on the criminal and civil jurisdiction of the Native Tribunals."[29] Indicative of the government's intention to use the native states to help enforce the colony's sanitary regulation, "parties [of trainees] followed the European Sanitary

Tribunal Police in Cape Coast in 1928 at the beginning of their two-week training period. Source: NAG, Accra.

Inspector" on his rounds. They were given a Service Record Book, a standard wage with a specified per diem, and by the following year there was even talk of gratuities for specified periods of service. In the previously sensitive matter of uniform, the unappealing sash and brass plate were replaced with a khaki outfit, a deep blue cummerbund and a black fez, which altogether made this uniform very similar to that of the colony's Escort Police. Finally, in 1945, with the passage of the Native Authority Colony Police Amendment, what by then were called the Native Administration Police were absorbed into the colony's general police force.

To see these changes in the functioning of the Native Tribunal, as Jarle Simensen has argued, as simply "provid[ing] the traditional elite with a new opportunity to exploit their judicial power through corrupt practices and extortive fees and fines" is to ignore an important feature of British justice. Lower courts in the British legal system invariably discharge an important petty, criminal judicial role, and in this sense we can see the Native Tribunals operating in this fashion as an important coming into line with well-established British judicial practice. In addition, what should also be taken into consideration was the actual composition of these Native Tribunals. Just as their judicial activities during the early twentieth century were undergoing important changes, so, too, did their membership. Especially in the coastal areas, by the 1930s no simple distinction between chiefs and commoners really applied when it came to who actually controlled the native state and its institutions. The composition of the Native Tribunals best illustrated how much this was so, and not surprisingly changes in personnel were reflected also in the changing procedures these courts adopted and the customary law these courts applied. In contrast to the important role that the government played in expanding the criminal adjudicative activities of the Native Tribunal, here there was much more African initiative.[30]

Changes in the manner in which native courts operated were already apparent enough in 1905 for Chief Justice William Brandford Griffith to take notice of them. In describing specifically the operation of the court of the *omanhen* of Akwapim, but recognizing that what happened in the colony's other "Native Courts" differed only in "details," he pointed out that the earlier procedure of instituting legal proceedings in these courts by swearing an oath had been replaced with a practice similar to that followed in the English courts.[31] An applicant now had to pay a fee to the *omanhen's* court before it would issue a summons.[32] In addition, litigants had to appear before the court with a surety who had to swear to pay any fines or settle any damages that the court might decide on in the event of the guilty party absconding. In the past, obedience to such decisions would have been enforced through the "barbarous custom" of *panyarring*.[33] Instead, seizing the property of a debtor, or even of a surety who refused

Tribunal Police after two-week training period with Duncan-Johnstone on the right. J. E. Casely Hayford (in dark suit) is to the left of the traditional rulers dressed in cloths. Source: NAG, Accra.

to pay, had become "an innovation copied from the British Courts."[34]

A more formal questioning of witnesses, patterned after British judicial procedure, had also begun to replace the "appearance of debate" that Brodie Cruickshank had described in 1853 as characteristic of even the native courts in the principal towns.[35] Indeed, in some instances the procedure for hearing evidence then followed what Brandford Griffith described as the typical procedure in the British courts. Rather than the defendant giving his statement, "he [was] merely asked for his witnesses, his evidence being taken after the plaintiff's witnesses [had] been heard."[36] As a concession to the increasing Christian population, particularly in the coastal towns, by the early twentieth century litigants and witnesses could chose to swear either on a local fetish or on the Bible. Technical language taken from the British courts had also been incorporated into the proceedings of the Native Tribunals in places where literacy was high. For example, the records of the Cape Coast Native Tribunal are replete with references to "subpoenaed witnesses," cases being adjourned "sine die," "interlocutory" proceedings and judgments with "costs and no costs allowed."

The personnel who dominated the affairs of the coastal tribunals were also undergoing important changes. Chief Justice William Brandford Griffith recognized that the educated classes had been able "to make some capital out of [the Tribunals]," as they presented "so many openings...to a clever educated native."[37] The rise to prominence of people like W. Z. Coker in Cape Coast, C. B. Nettey in Accra and C. R. Cathline in Elmina was graphic evidence of how much this was so. The 1894 Hutchinson Commission, which reported on the colony's native courts, had recommended against native courts keeping "any written records."[38] However, the 1910 Native Jurisdiction Ordinance made literate chiefs responsible for keeping a written record of their tribunal's activities. Illiterate chiefs had to inform the district commissioner of their tribunal's monthly activities, which were then recorded in a special book for that purpose. In areas of extensive literacy, such as the coastal towns, this innovation clearly enhanced the importance of tribunal registrars. It was hardly surprising, as a result, that succession disputes in these towns invariably involved educated natives seeking to take over the position of tribunal registrar, and to win positions as counselors (judges).

In addition to enterprising educated natives seeking positions on the Native Tribunal, the colony's lawyers were attracted to participating in its judicial affairs. As far as the colonial government was concerned, they were barred from its proceedings to ensure that the justice these courts offered would be as cheap as possible, but maintaining this ban became harder and harder to enforce. In especially important cases, African lawyers won entry into the Native Tribunals' proceedings by standing "surety" for litigants, or by having themselves subpoenaed to appear as witnesses. Judging from the records of the Cape Coast Native Tribunal, this development was clearly under way by the second decade of the twentieth century. In general, since a great deal of the litigation that ended up in the colony's Divisional Courts originated in the Native Tribunals, lawyers had a vested interest in being able to participate in the affairs of what were in essence lower courts.[39]

Indeed, it was difficult for the political officers in whose areas these tribunals operated to do much about preventing African lawyers from circumventing the ban on their participation in the colony's lower courts in general, since these officials were themselves compromised. From as early as 1906, the commissioner of the Central Province, from whose court lawyers were also supposedly barred, was informing the secretary of native affairs "that it was customary for native chiefs to have a lawyer...[and that it was] difficult to ignore or refuse to allow him to be present at palavers." Indeed, the commissioner pointed out that in general the "practice of refusing to hear lawyers when both sides in a case were illiterate was tacitly ignored by the majority of judges and commissioners."[40] Part of the reason for this willingness to turn a blind eye to African lawyers participating in the colony's lower courts was that it made the work of the invariably overburdened district and provincial commissioners who presided over them easier. They could rely on African lawyers who understood local languages to sort through the often contradictory and confusing evidence before the court and simplify the judge's task.[41]

By the early twentieth century lawyers had become an inseparable fixture particularly of coastal society, and most litigants wanted to appear in court with some kind of legal representation. The amended Native Jurisdiction Ordinance of 1910, in a concession to the demand for at least support in pleading cases before Native Tribunals, had allowed husbands, wives, family members, guardians, servants, masters or any inmate of a household who could give satisfactory proof that he had the authority to do so to appear for plaintiffs or defendants.[42] It was a concession that was obviously easily abused and helped to create what officials disparagingly referred to as a "race of bush-lawyers."[43] Nevertheless, the 1927 Native Administration Ordinance further compromised the policy of excluding professional pleaders from the Native Tribunals by including the proviso that legal professionals could be "granted leave" to participate in civil cases "wherein all parties desire[d] to be legally represented."[44] It was clearly a lesser evil than a proliferation of bush-lawyers, and a belated recognition that, like King Croesus, the colonial government could no more hold back the tide of educated natives who saw opportunities for themselves in the Native Tribunals.

What resulted, however, from this deep involvement in the affairs of the Native Tribunal was that lawyers were positioned to be some of the most unrelenting critics of what Cape Coast lawyer Kobina Sekyi was later to describe as these "queer courts."[45] The way many of these tribunals worked invited invidious comparison with the British courts in which African lawyers conducted most of their legal work. Counselors in the Native Tribunal were usually totally dependent on the fees and fines the tribunal collected for their livelihood, and they consequently had great incentive to draw out cases and maximize the payments they received. The Hutchinson Commission of 1895 had sought to establish a uniform scale of fees and fines, and subsequent native administration bills had included measures to enforce such schedules. In addition, the colonial government published this information, but Native Tribunals got around this by multiplying the number of such charges, and equally infuriating they were notorious for adjourning cases and charging "adjournment fees."

The result was that justice in these tribunals could often be more expensive than in the British courts, and not only were lawyers often dissatisfied with their judgments, but members of the Western-educated elite found it doubly infuriating to have to come before a body, most of whose members were illiterate, and at the same time be subjected to a host of fees that had no counterpart in the British courts. It was hardly surprising, as a result, that the colony's press was filled with criticisms of these "incompetent" and "tyrannical" courts that "enriched" the chiefs and made the "people suffer hardship."[46] Indeed, these criticisms echoed much of what Sir William Brandford Griffith had objected to in 1904 when he produced his minority report against the expansion of the role of native courts. It meant that African lawyers were in an ambiguous position vis-à-vis these institutions. On one hand, they were publicly staunch upholders of the customary law that the Native Tribunals putatively adjudicated, but at the same time they were highly critical of how these institutions functioned.

Undoubtedly one of the most bitter of these critics was Cape Coast barrister Kobina Sekyi. In the 1920s, when he became one of the most unrelenting of indirect rule's critics, the Native Tribunal that played such an important role in the overall system was his particular bête noire. He castigated official policy that, after "first destroying the soul of the African and his institutions," had in a "sudden somersault" sought to re-create indigenous institutions by appointing chiefs "without previous training," and had surrounded them with "councillors, advisors and sub-chiefs, just as ill qualified for their positions."[47] To make matters worse, the government had placed these courts under the control of the executive rather than the judiciary. The result was that political officers had more power to restrict or allow the right of appeal from these tribunals to the colony's British courts than judges of the Supreme Court, even though such officers might "be as ignorant of law as the man in the moon."[48] Neither could African lawyers do much for a "client, broken in soul by experiences in

some Native Tribunal," since he also was officially barred from representing clients in its deliberations.[49]

There were clearly some very anomalous aspects to how the Native
Tribunals functioned that contributed to putting African lawyers on the
same side as British judges. As Bjorn Edsman has pointed out, both were
opposed to administrative control over any courts in the colony.[50] It was
criticism that contributed to the colonial government's recognition that the
standard of justice in the Native Tribunals needed considerable upgrading,
and coincided with more interventionist indirect rule policies of the 1920s.
One important indication of this concern was the government's attempt in
1922 to provide formal training for people who were now styled "Tribunal
Registrars." However, most of the young men who received such training
in district commissioner's offices did not remain in the service of the
native states. They "sought employment elsewhere simply because the conditions of service in the Native Administration were regarded by them as
not being good or attractive enough."[51] In the colony's then expanding
economy there were obviously better opportunities elsewhere, and the
quality of personnel who administered the affairs of the Native Tribunals
continued to be a major concern to the colonial government. Apart from
their susceptibility to corruption, there was also the problem of them
understanding and conforming to the technical rules regulating appeal to
higher courts.

Not until 1929 did the government try once again to provide training
for tribunal registrars, which from then onward became an annual two-
week course in which potential registrars attended lectures on evidence
giving, simple agriculture, English composition, character training, police
duties, office routine and native history, law and custom. The colony's
tribunal registrars also formed an association (the Tribunal Registrars
Association) with its headquarters in Cape Coast.[52] With the onset of the
depression and employment opportunities shrinking, the number of people
seeking registrar positions soon became much larger than the number of
positions available. By "stiffening" the requirements for the course in
1932, the government sought to reduce the number of qualified registrars.[53] The result was that the failure rate, which was already high,
increased so that by 1935 only one candidate out of thirty-eight passed the
final exam.[54] It did not, however, mean that the general quality of tribunal
registrars improved. According to the 1943 *Report of the Native Tribunals
Committee of Enquiry* the "majority of registrars [were] semi-educated
persons whose only qualification is that they [were] one-eyed rulers in the
country of the blind."[55]

Nevertheless, for the more important tribunals this selectivity contributed to a further enhancement of the position of the tribunal registrar.
Indeed, by the 1930s the responsibilities and authority of important tribunal registrars extended considerably beyond that of their counterparts in

the British court. As one such official aptly observed, while looking back on his career, he had been "the first public servant in the Native Administration after the Chief."[56] The position combined both judicial and administrative tasks, and in this respect was like the role that the colony's political officers discharged. They, too, operated as both administrators and judges. In retrospect it was ironic that as the Native Tribunals evolved under the influence of British justice, they copied what was one of the most anomalous features of British colonial justice. Indeed, in some respects the registrar's powers even went beyond that of the political officer. Apart from their duties as court scribes and administrators, they were the chief's main legal counselors, and the complex interplay between customary law and English common law in the colony often required that they act as law "modifiers" and "ammenders."[57]

W. Z. Coker, undoubtedly one of the most important of these court registrars, well exemplified how "responsive to the needs of the people" in a "rapidly changing social order" such officials could be.[58] He allowed litigants to appear before the Cape Coast Native Tribunal as though they were married couples, but who had not paid *itsir nsa*.[59] In the past, men and women living in what would have been considered "concubinage" would not have been entitled to bring their disputes before the elders. In essence, he was sanctioning an alternative to native marriage, which at that time had become increasingly more expensive as the cost of brideprice escalated.[60] Coker's "innovation" must have been particularly appealing to young *asafo* members who would have been hard-pressed to find mates if they conformed to customary practice.[61] In addition to being *tufuhen,* a major labor recruiter and the tribunal registrar (or recorder, as Coker described this position), he was also an important law "modifier." Under these circumstances it was hardly surprising that he enjoyed as much power and influence as he did in Cape Coast.

Apart from the procedural, compositional and jurisdictional changes that were taking place as a result of contact with British justice, the Native Tribunals were also under increasing pressure to apply judicial standards that existed in the British courts. Undoubtedly one of the most controversial was the matter of inheritance in cases of intestacy. As early as 1916 the Paramount Tribunal in Akyem Abuakwa had "consented" to recognizing "the so-called Christian [system] of succession" in the case of *Frempoma & ors v. Buxton.* Even though the wife had been married in native fashion, she received one-third of her deceased husband's property while the nephew, his maternal successor, received two-thirds.[62] This apparently was the "custom" that had come into operation as a result of the influence of the Basel Mission, the most successful Christian denomination in this area of the colony. When the children, however, under the advice of their pastor, demanded a one-third share of the estate, the tribunal ruled against this because there had "been no breach of faith" on the part of the of the uncle, who had agreed "to keep and look after the deceased's children."[63]

Nevertheless, this partial recognition of "Christian succession" was an important indication that native marriage could be made to move in the direction of the full Christian practice. It was clearly an imperfect solution, since it had no statutory base. Like the practice of "blessing" native marriages that the churches had introduced as a way of putting moral pressure on those so married to be monogamous and accept that divorce was possible only in cases of adultery, "Christian succession" depended on voluntary compliance.[64] Significantly, neither were Africans entirely satisfied with what had emerged. They continued to exhibit much the same ambiguity that had characterized their initial reaction to the 1884 Marriage Ordinance. Some continued to agitate for more recognition of native marriage since, as an editorial in the *Gold Coast Leader* expressed it, "there is nothing wrong in our system of marriage, provided one man is married to one woman."[65] Others, like Magnus Sampson, who had returned as a qualified barrister to the colony in 1922 and had become the secretary for the paramount chief of Akyem Abuakwa (Ofori Atta), were critical of what they felt were the "disadvantages" that native marriage offered.[66]

However, it was not until the 1930s that some of the native states were well enough established to consider formal initiatives that would amend important aspects of native customary law pertaining to marriage. In 1933 Reverend Issac Sackey, the superintendent pastor of the A. M. E. Zion Mission at Winneba, suggested at the Central Province Provincial Council meeting in Saltpond that widows and children of men who died intestate should have the same protection offered to those married under the 1884 ordinance, even though the marriage had been a customary one.[67] This suggestion to bring native marriage into alignment with "foreign marriage" was too radical for the Provincial Council to act on without the "support of the majority of [the] people."[68] As was typical of such controversial issues, the Provincial Council avoided making a decision by referring the matter to the province's "different states."[69] This effectively killed any likelihood of the Provincial Council as a body effecting any changes in the customary law of inheritance.

It was clear, however, that some of the chiefs in attendance were in favor of bringing customary law into agreement with "natural justice." The Winneba State Council actually passed a "resolution...which recommended that one-third of the property of a male intestate should go to his wife and children together."[70] In 1938 the Joint Provincial Council also passed a "recommendation...that one quarter of the property of a man dying intestate should go to his children."[71] The Akyem Abuakwa State Council in 1939 proposed as a bylaw "that one-third of a man's estate should descend to his children in equal shares."[72] None of these initiatives were actually legally binding since they never received the approval of the governor-in-council, as was required by the Native Administration Ordinance of 1927. It was hardly likely that they would have received this approval, either, since this would have undoubtedly generated protest at a time when the government was already under fire for introducing the highly controversial Native Administration Treasuries Ordinance.

Nevertheless, in their day-to-day operations tribunals had clearly begun to adjudicate issues that represented innovations in customary inheritance practice. As early as 1925, for example, the Ga *mantse's* tribunal in Accra was dealing with cases that involved wills that stipulated who was entitled to reside in the testator's property.[73] From the evidence in some of these cases, it seems as if these were even in written form, though clearly this was a judicial venue that would have accepted nuncupative wills. In addition, by the time the Blackall Commission investigated the operations of the Native Tribunals in 1943, they had taken on the task of determining who should have custody of children in disputes between couples who were not married under the Marriage Ordinance, but whose monogamous marriages Christian ministers had "blessed." There was some concern on the part of church authorities to this practice since they feared that the tribunal "might give the custody of the children to persons who would not look after them in a Christian way."[74]

Apart from the role that the Christian church and court registrars played in bringing pressure to modify and amend customary law in accordance with British justice, women also exerted considerable pressures of their own. Wives clearly had a great deal to gain from amendments to customary laws concerning inheritance. It is not hard to detect their presence in suits involving inheritance. They also had an interest in seeing modifications of customary practice concerning divorce, which according to customary law was a right that was "marital only."[75] Here also British justice offered important inspiration, particularly after the Matrimonial Causes Act of 1923 enabled a wife to seek divorce simply on the grounds of her husband's adultery.[76] A number of well-reported cases in the colony's press played the important role of publicizing this new development. In some instances these cases were reported verbatim, and were graphic indication of how much easier it had become for women married under the 1884 ordinance to obtain a divorce.[77] It seems fair to assume that this publicity stimulated both "frock" and "cloth" women to be more assertive in demanding marital fidelity

One of the most iconoclastic indications of how this new climate of opinion could result in a challenge to customary law regarding adultery was the case reported in the *Times of West Africa* in 1933. In a letter to Marjorie Mensah, the putatively female editor of the paper's "Ladies Column," a woman in Accra reported a case that had come before the Awunu Eire headman's court in which a woman had sued another woman for damages because the latter had an affair with the former's husband.[78] The headman had felt unable to proceed with this highly unusual and charged case and had referred the matter to the Ga *mantse's* court, where the case became a two-way contest with the wife suing her rival and the latter's husband suing the former's husband! As such the case represented a combination of what was customary practice, the aggrieved husband suing the man who had "tampered" with his wife, and a partial application of British law, which allowed the aggrieved wife to take action against her adulterous husband.

It was clearly not a complete application of English common law since the aggrieved wife was not directly confronting her adulterous husband. Nevertheless, for Marjorie Mensah, an advocate of more equality for women, establishing even this innovation in customary law would have been most welcome since it would "be an authority for women to go after their husbands," and would contribute to making "our men chaste."[79] Judging from some of her other editorials, she obviously felt that male sexual profligacy was contributing to a breakdown in "harmony" in the African home.[80] Rectifying this situation was going to depend on more than eliminating the evils of polygyny and prostitution, which she also inveighed against. It was at least going to mean giving women the legal power to challenge "husband-stealers" in the Native Tribunals.

As was typical of such controversial cases, the matter must have been settled privately, since there was no further mention of it even though Marjorie Mensah indicated her determination to follow the case through the Ga *mantse's* court. Unlike the changes in customary practice concerning inheritance, this case failed to set a precedent. Nevertheless, it was indicative of the increasing assertiveness of women before the Native Tribunals in general. In theory wives were supposed to rely on their kin to bring pressure on husbands who misconducted themselves. In reality, however, wives on their own behalf were bringing their husbands before the tribunal on charges of assault, desertion or failure to provide financial support for themselves and their children. Women brought at least a third of the cases before the Ga *mantse's* tribunal and the Cape Coast Native Tribunal. Most of them had to do with debt, which reflected the important role of women in the colony's retail trade, but a significant number were obviously family disputes with the wife seeking to use the court to discipline unsatisfactory husbands.

Clearly, a variety of changing social conditions were operating to alter the structure of the native courts as well as the nature of the customary law they administered. They were also caught up in the parochial politics of indirect rule that characterized the interwar period in the colony, and this, too, had an important impact on their development. As the most attractive prize for local factions to win control over as well as useful tools for intimidating opponents, these tribunals invariably became embroiled in highly politicized cases with scandalous consequences that contributed to undermining their reputations. In 1933, for example, the struggle between *Omanhen* Mbra III and members of the stool family, led by J. M. Cooke, had resulted in a slander case before the Cape Coast Native Tribunal.[81] At that time Mbra III and his supporters controlled this court, and not surprisingly it had ruled in the *omanhen*'s favor. On appeal the Divisional Court had overturned this ruling and had awarded Cooke damages and costs. The tribunal, however, was in no position to pay, and for a while was in danger of having its furniture sold to pay the eighty pounds involved![82]

Even worse, in particularly politicized towns like Cape Coast and Elmina where there were unresolved and bitter succession struggles during the interwar period, the native state became so disorganized that there was no operating tribunal. For example, during the height of the struggle between Coker and Moore over the *tufuhen*'s position in Cape Coast, the town's tribunal did not function at all. On a number of occasions colonial officials even closed tribunals to force warring factions to compromise. It was a strategy, however, that could easily serve to highlight even further the politicized nature of these institutions. For example, when in 1935 the government decided to close the Cape Coast Native Tribunal, it quickly became apparent that the Native Administration Ordinance contained no adequate provisions for doing so. Instead, the government had to pass special legislation to deal with a situation that the already cumbersome ordinance had not anticipated.[83] In general this strategy of closing overly politicized tribunals could also backfire by contributing to the mushrooming of private courts of arbitration. These were beyond the control of local political officers, and from the government's perspective a thoroughly unsatisfactory development.

As it was the financial attractiveness, political usefulness and communal pressures contributed to a proliferation of Native Tribunals. By 1942 in the Central Province there were "122 Tribunals of which 51 [were] in the Winneba District."[84] In many "instances these Tribunals were concentrated in a small area near to one another." For example, "in the Ajumaku-Esiam area of Saltpond there [were] no less than four Paramount Courts and four of lower order, although the entire area would, in the view of the District Commissioner, [have been] adequately served by a single properly run tribunal."[85] In the large towns it was harder for this kind of proliferation in the numbers of courts to take place, but even in these locations there was pressure from stranger communities demanding their own institutions. The small but factious Muslim community in Cape Coast was a good example of this. As early as 1918 the Wangaras were in conflict with the Hausas over control of their respective communities.[86] Inevitably this became a struggle over operating their own tribunals.[87] By the 1930s, when the Cape Coast Muslim community also consisted of substantial numbers of Moshis, Fulanis, Walas, Zabarimas, Grunshis, Gonjas and Bambalas, struggles to control or set up separate judicial (and religious) institutions became even more intense.[88]

By being so much at the center of the parochial politics that indirect rule produced, the Native Tribunal found itself in the limelight of public scrutiny that served to magnify its shortcomings. Litigants who had lost cases could easily claim political bias. If they were strangers they could claim that the tribunal was hostile to their community, and in addition applied a law that was not their customary law. Lawyers resented both their exclusion from the tribunals and administrative attempts to improve the operation of these courts. Sekyi, for example, was publicly critical of the Tribunal Registrars Training Course, which he saw as yet another misguided attempt to sustain what he felt was the disastrous policy of indirect rule.[89] Tribunals' "devot[ion] to the extortion of money" embarrassed district commissioners whose task it was to inspect periodically their operations.[90] At times even the colony's chief justice could be scathingly critical of what he saw as the incompetence of the tribunals' personnel.[91]

It is hard, however, not to escape the feeling that there was a hyperbolical quality to much of this criticism. In reality, the tribunals performed an important role in the colony's judicial system. When they were closed, even district commissioners who were critical of how these bodies functioned were quick to complain that their courts were swamped with cases as a result. Significantly, also, official investigations into the "grave irregularities" that these tribunals were accused of produced more innuendo than "chapter and verse." Both the Blackall and the Havers commissions of inquiry seemed to indicate that the worst situations were in rural areas where states had not yet established native treasuries. In addition, the worst irregularities had to do with land cases, but as the Havers Commission pointed out, it was a situation that was as much influenced by the volume and nature of such litigation as it was by the tribunals themselves. The uncertainty of boundaries and title to land, along with the "variability of native customary law," and "the absence of proper facilities for credit" guaranteed that litigation arising out of these matters would be expensive and easily corrupted.[92]

Nevertheless, the perception gained ground during the 1940s that Native Tribunals had to "be adapted to meet modern conditions and the changing needs of this progressive Colony."[93] As such it was part of a wider concern that the colonial administration in general was in need of major reforms if the colony was to survive successfully in the postwar "New World Order." The result was that in the 1940s there were two major official investigations into the operations of the Native Tribunals, which contributed to the pressure on the government to reform these institutions. In 1942 the Legislative Council appointed a committee of enquiry under the chairmanship of the attorney general, H. W. B. Blackall, to "report on the necessity for reforms in administration of justice in native tribunals."[94] In 1945 Justice C. R. Havers headed a one-man commission of inquiry into expenses and indebtedness incurred by litigants in the colony's court, with special reference to Native Tribunals.

According to Lord Hailey, the Blackall report "presented to the public a convincing picture of the defects of the existing system," but undoubtedly more important were the number of far-reaching recommendations that it made, most of which were incorporated into the Native Courts Ordinance of 1944. The most important was that the government finally rejected "the claim that the Chiefs or any other Stoolholders possessed any right of inherent jurisdiction," and the now-styled "Native Courts" were "specifically declared to be constituted by a Government Order in Council."[95] It meant that their members could be appointed ex officio, though initially no one was appointed without consulting the Native Authority. Rather than the "sharing" of fees and fines that had been the situation before, the court's members were to be paid a regular salary from the Native Authority Treasury. There were to be four grades of courts, with jurisdictions that varied from those that could only deal with personal suits (Grade D Courts) that did not exceed ten pounds to Grade A courts that had jurisdiction in land cases of unlimited amounts.

On the other hand, apart from identifying a link between expensive litigation and the colony's confused land tenure situation, the Havers Commission added little that was really new. It supported the need for native treasuries that would pay a fixed honorarium for Native Court members.[96] It recommended abolishing the various hearing fees, judgment fees and fees for viewing land that Native Tribunals charged, and instead establishing a uniform scale of fees that they could charge.[97] Both of these recommendations were also incorporated into an ordinance, the Native Courts (Colony) Procedure Regulation, which in addition established a uniform method of procedure that tribunals should follow, modeled on that of the Supreme Court.

The commitment was clearly still very much to indirect rule and preserving the judicial role of the chieftaincy. The Blackall Commission concluded that in spite of the "strong feeling that there [was] urgent need for reform, there [was] no general demand for the abolition of a system which is indigenous to the country and familiar to the people."[98] The reforms, however, that the commission set in motion clearly represented a major concession to the tradition of "judicial realism" as represented by George Maclean and Sir William Brandford Griffith. Henceforth the Supreme Court was to exercise much more direct control over the Native Courts. The most important indication of this was the appointment of a judicial adviser whose role was "to advise native authorities in regard to the improvement of the administration of justice in their courts," as well

as providing advice on ways of modifying native customs.[99] He did not
have the same power as the judicial assessor of the nineteenth century,
who functioned more as a judge than as an adviser, but this new official
did have the power to review cases that came before Native Courts in
conjunction with the district commissioner.

The Native Courts still remained, however, separate and distinct parts
of the colony's judicial system, but it was clear in what direction change
was heading. As Inez Sutton has pointed out, as the procedure that they
followed and the content of the law that they applied became more and
influenced by "English practices and legalities...eventually there was little
to distinguish...native court[s] from the district or magistrate's court
which was meant to apply English law."[100] The resulting blurring of the
boundaries between the two made the need for different court systems less
and less defensible, but it was not until after 1948, as Richard Crook
suggests, when support for indirect rule really began to wane, that their
final incorporation into a uniform, colony-wide judicial system took place.
The colonial government, he argues, "faced [with] what appeared to be
united opposition of farmers, urban dwellers and chiefs," recognized the
"unreliability and lack of cooperation of the chieftaincy" and set about
"looking for alternatives" to indirect rule.[101] And since "the apparatus of
Indirect Rule [was] both judicial and political," it was inevitable that in
this new conjuncture the role of distinct Native Courts should come into
question.[102]

In 1951 the Korsah Commission on Native Courts finally completed the
process of dissociating the native authorities from any judicial functions.
It recommended "that the executive should be separate from the judiciary,"
and that "the Chief Justice should have complete control" over what were
now to be called "local courts."[103] In spite of the advantages that chiefs
offered, the commission recommended that "no chief who is the hereditary
territorial ruler of an area, however small, should be appointed a member
of a local court." The same applied also for state councillors, and instead
the commission recommended that the "District" and "Area" courts, the
two subdivisions into which Local Courts were to be divided, should be
presided over by either professional, stipendiary magistrates or honorary
lay magistrates rather like the justices of the peace in England. Neither
was their jurisdiction to coincide with the territorial boundaries of specific
native states, but instead were, "as a general rule," to coincide "with the
boundaries of local authority areas."[104] What this meant in practice was
that the number of courts could be reduced considerably "without
appreciably reducing the judicial facilities at the same time."[105] These
courts were also "to have jurisdiction over all persons, without distinction
of race or origin." The time had come for "special courts for particular
classes of inhabitants [to] give way to general courts for all manner of
men."[106] The new system would also replace the old district and provincial

commissioners' courts and would thus bring to an end the anomalous situation of political officers exercising both administrative and judicial responsibilities.

It was not possible to move at quite the pace that the Korsah Commission envisaged. Cost, more than anything else, prevented a full-scale implementation of its recommendations, but the information that the inquiry produced on how the colony's Native Court system worked graphically indicated how similar its operations were to the British courts. For example, even though the commission recognized that customary law could not "easily be fitted into the classification of 'civil' and 'criminal' law...no difficulty [was] experienced in practice."[107] Indeed, the percentage of criminal cases as opposed to civil cases that these courts adjudicated was very similar to that of the police magistrates' courts.[108] Significantly, also, the criminal offenses had become much like those dealt with in the British courts, since the "trend" in customary crimes was towards "the reduction of the number of these offences."[109] As far as personnel were concerned, chiefs were making up less and less of the membership of the Native Courts.[110] In Cape Coast, for example, the first president of the town's Native Court was A. B. Josiah, who was the *supi* of Number Three *Asafo* (Ntsin) and also a public letter writer.

In contrast, however, to earlier phases of colonial rule in which reforms in how the Native Tribunals operated came about in a gradual fashion, the changes of the 1950s were much more rapid and abrupt. In the increasingly politicized world leading up to independence, as William Harvey has observed, the "chiefs and other traditional officials, whose primary qualification was familiarity with the customary law, [were] replaced by political appointees."[111] Neither was there much success in improving the educational level of the magistrates in these courts, which ironically was one of the stated aims of these judicial reforms. According to the minister of justice in Ghana's first independent government, "the incumbent Magistrates were non-educable."[112] The result was that the cure was worse than the disease. Justifiably, "suspicions of bribery and corruption" came to be associated with these Local Courts, and this more recent reality has done much to color our views of their predecessors.[113]

In writing about the "textbook illustration of the employment of law as instrument and as ideology in serving the interests of the ruling class" in Britain in the eighteenth century, E. P. Thompson has come to the "paradoxical" conclusion that English common law had to be more than "partial and unjust" if it were to serve to legitimate the ruling class's hegemony.[114] The colonial legal system, in its many forms, had to serve in much the same fashion in a colony that had moved well beyond the stage of pacification. Particularly in the coastal areas of the Gold Coast Colony, the Native Tribunals had evolved through a process of cultural interaction, the most important feature of which was that neither the government nor any one section of the local communities were able to dominate their activity. Clearly, the Native Tribunals did not live up to some ideal standard of the rule of law, but perhaps their most important contribution to "legitimizing" the hegemony of the colonial state was that they institutionalized recourse to a legal system increasingly influenced by British judicial ideas.

Notes

1. An earlier version of this chapter appeared as "British Justice and the Native Tribunals of the Southern Gold Coast Colony," *Journal of African History* 34, no. 1 (1993):93-113.

2. Crooks, *Records,* 296.

3. Cruickshank, *Eighteen Years on the Gold Coast of Africa,* 1:270. This included property in people.

4. King Aggrey to Governor Pine, 16 March 1865, and Aggrey to Blackall mentioned in Governor Conran's dispatch to the Secretary of State, 24 April 1866, CO 96/67 and 71, PRO.

5. These courts were "officially christened Native Tribunals to distinguish them from the courts in non-affected areas." Mensah-Brown, "The Traditional Courts and Their Successors in Ghana's Legal History, 1800-1914," 86-87.

6. *An Ordinance to Facilitate and Regulate the Exercise of Certain Powers and Jurisdiction by Native Authorities* (Accra, 1883), 26, c.

7. Ibid.

8. In the past these charges would have resulted in purgation ordeals, but such methods were clearly ruled out as repugnant to natural justice and the principles of the law of England.

9. Also, with the development of the print media, libel had become the more common action, which served to separate even more the situation in the Gold Coast from the metropole.

10. The District Commissioner of Cape Coast to the Queen's Advocate, 1 January 1894, SNA, ADM 111/1/1382, NAG, Accra.

11. Queen's Advocate to the Colonial Secretary, 3 March 1894, SNA, ADM 111/1/1382, NAG, Accra.

12. Ibid.

13. Sarbah, *Fanti Customary Laws,* 24.

14. Governor Brandford Griffith to the Secretary of State, 10 April 1888, CO 96/190, PRO.

15. W. Brandford Griffith, "The Native Courts of the Gold Coast," *Journal of the the Society of Comparative Legislation* 6, no. 2 (1905):513.

16. Ibid.

17. Governor Thorburn to the Secretary of Native Affairs, 27 October 1912, ADM 11/1/423, NAG, Accra.

18. The Commissioner of the Western Province to the Secretary of Native Affairs, 16 October 1912, ADM 11/1/1261, NAG, Accra.

19. The Escort Police were the lowest section of the colony's civil police force. They were illiterates who were entrusted with the simplest police functions. Many were Hausas or from northern areas of the Gold Coast.

20. Governor Thorburn to the Secretary of Native Affairs, 1 November 1911, ADM 11/1/342, NAG, Accra.

21. Acting Commissioner of the Central Province to the Commissioner of Police, 31 August 1911, ADM 11/1/342, NAG, Accra.

22. The Cape Coast Native Tribunal Civil Record Book, September 1909-2 September 1912, ADM 71/1/1/1, NAG, Cape Coast. Seduction was technically a criminal offense, but in reality the court treated it as a civil offense. Also, there was no provision for such cases to be tried before British courts.

23. "Annual Reports of the Cape Coast District," 1921-1928, ADM 23/1/392, NAG, Cape Coast. In 1926, for example, this court generated £844..3..6d in fines and £682..12..1d from hearing civil cases.

24. *The Report of the Native Tribunals Committee of Enquiry* (Accra, 1943), 13.

25. This was Governor Slater's description of how he felt that the policy of indirect rule should develop. *Native Administration in the Gold Coast and its Dependencies* (Accra, 1931), 3.

26. There were 2,931 criminal cases to 2,658 civil cases. Civil and Criminal Cases Returns, ADM 11/1/1286, NAG, Accra.

27. *Report of Commission on Native Courts* (Accra, 1951), 11.

28. *An Ordinance to Define and to Regulate the Exercise of Certain Powers and Jurisdictions by Native Authorities, and to Assign Certain Functions to the Provincial Councils, and for Purposes Connected Therewith* (Accra, 1927), part 12.

29. A. C. Duncan-Johnstone, "Report of Training of Native Administration Police," September 1928, ADM 11/1/1019, NAG, Accra.

30. Simensen, "Rural Mass Action in the Context of Anti-Colonial Protest," 29.

31. Brandford Griffith, "The Native Courts of the Gold Coast," 507.

32. These fees could vary from as little as two and sixpence in a subchief's court to four pounds in a head chief's court. "Report of the Commission appointed by the Governor on the 1st of August, 1894, to enquire into various matters relating to Native Courts," enclosed in the Governor's dispatch to the Secretary of State, 15 April 1896, CO 96/272, PRO.

33. *Panyarring,* the seizure of the debtor, a relative or even an unrelated stranger, and holding them as a slave until the debt was paid, was outlawed by the Bond of 1844. Crooks, *Records,* 296. It was also specifically outlawed in the

Native Jurisdiction Ordinance of 1883. It was linked with the theft of property.

34. Brandford Griffith, "The Native Courts of the Gold Coast," 510.

35. Cruickshank, *Eighteen Years on the Gold Coast of Africa*, 1:284.

36. Brandford Griffith, "The Native Courts of the Gold Coast," 508.

37. Brandford Griffith's minority report on the Native Tribunals of the Gold Coast in 1905. Cited in the *Report of the Commission on Native Courts*, 5.

38. *Report of the Commission Appointed by the Governor on the 1st of August 1894 to Enquire into Various Matters Relating to Native Courts*, 8, CO 96/272, PRO.

39. A few important land cases that began in the Native Tribunals were appealed all the way to the Privy Council. For example: *R. J. Ghartey v. No 2 Company of Winneba per Kwesi Attaidzi and others*, 22 December 1924; *Abakah Nibah subs. for Kweku Kaigh v. Anguah Bennieh subs. for Kweku Ackah*, 23 October 1930; and *James Johnson subs. for Chief Kwamina Sakyiama v. J. M. Cooke*, 1931. Cited in *Judgments of the Judicial Committee of the Privy Council* (London, 1924, 1930 and 1931).

40. The Commissioner of the Central Province to the Secretary of Native Affairs, December 1906, SNA, ADM 11/1/6, NAG, Accra.

41. However, there was a disadvantage. As the provincial commissioner of Cape Coast pointed out, cases with barristers appearing for clients invariably took longer to complete. The Provincial Commissioner to the Colonial Secretary, 19 June 1919, ADM 23/1/324, NAG, Cape Coast.

42. *An Ordinance to Amend The Gold Coast Native Jurisdiction Ordinance, 1883* (Accra, 1910), chapter 19, 18.

43. *Report of the Native Tribunals Committee of Enquiry*, 14.

44. Chapter 57.

45. W. E. G. Sekyi to A. F. E. Fieldgate, Commissioner of the Central Province, 8 September 1939, Sekyi Files: Correspondence with Officials, 322/1964, NAG, Cape Coast.

46. *Gold Coast Independent*, 10 August and 23 November 1918.

47. W. E. G. Sekyi, "Our White Friends," unpublished manuscript dated 29 July 1943, 12. Sekyi Papers 400/64, NAG, Cape Coast. This work was first serialized in the *Gold Coast Leader* in 1921-1922.

48. Ibid, 99.

49. Ibid., 19.

50. Edsman, *Lawyers in Gold Coast Politics*, 22.

51. *Gold Coast Independent*, 16 July 1932.

52. *Gold Coast Independent*, 6 May 1933.

53. *Times of West Africa*, 21 May 1932. The number of subjects was also increased.

54. *Gold Coast Independent*, 5 January 1935. In contrast, in 1931 nine out of thirty-eight tribunal registrars obtained certificates after undergoing tribunal registrar's courses. *Gold Coast Independent*, 14 March 1931.

55. *Report of the Native Tribunals Committee of Enquiry, 5.*

56. A. M. Kojo-Aboagye, "The Tribunal Registrar," *Gold Coast Observer,* 2 July 1943. He was the tribunal registrar for the Asiakwa Native Tribunal in Akyem Abuakwa.

57. Ibid.

58. Ibid.

59. Or *etsir nsa-nkredzi,* as J. M. Sarbah spells it, which means literally "tokens or price of the head." *Fanti Customary Laws,* 47.

60. In some instances the bridegroom was even supposed to supply a Singer sewing machine as part of the brideprice. J. W. A. Amoo, "The Effect of Western Influence on Akan Marriage," *Africa* 16, no. 4 (1946):230.

61. W. E. G. Sekyi to A. F. E. Fieldgate (CCP), criticizing how Coker had conducted his "queer tribunal," 8 September 1939, Sekyi Files: Correspondence with Officials, 332/1964, NAG, Cape Coast. Not only were Native Tribunals under pressure to do something about brideprice, but also the churches. In 1926, for example, the Wesleyan Methodist Synod ordered its church members to charge no more than £30 for brideprice at a time when "cloth ladies" were commanding £85-150 and "frock ladies" £180-250. *Gold Coast Independent,* 5 February 1927.

62. Cited in Ollennu, *The Law of Testate and Intestate Succession in Ghana,* 148.

63. Ibid., 148-149.

64. By 1917 the Wesleyan Methodists had formally recognized "the validity of native marriage." Synod Minutes, Gold Coast District, January 1917. For a description of this kind of marriage, see Amoo, "The Effect of Western Influence on Akan Marriage," 235.

65. *Gold Coast Leader,* 26 August 1922.

66. *Gold Coast Leader,* 10 November 1922.

67. Native Marriage File, 6 April 1930, ADM 23/1/446, NAG, Cape Coast. Not only Akan customary inheritance was under attack, but also the confused Ga practice. According to "Lobster" in the *Times of West Africa,* the time had come for "overhauling" these customs, and instead of dealing with "nauseating stool disputes" this was what he felt the State Council should do. 23 April 1934.

68. Letter from Bannerman Martin, Secretary of the Central Provincial Council, to the *Gold Coast Independent,* 29 November 1933, published on 9 December 1933.

69. Ibid.

70. 14 November 1933, cited in Ollennu, *The Law of Testate and Intestate Succession in Ghana,* 144.

71. Ibid.

72. Ibid.

73. The Ga *mantse*'s Native Tribunal Book, 1925. I would like to thank Nii Amugi II, the present Ga *mantse,* for permission to look at these records.

74. *Report of the Native Tribunals Committee of Enquiry,* 15.

75. Sarbah, *Fanti Customary Laws,* 52.

76. From 1859 divorce laws in the colony followed those laid out in the Matrimonial Causes Act of 1857. Divorce *a vinculo* (a dissolution of a marriage) was only possible on the grounds of adultery. However, in contrast to men who only had to prove that their wives had committed adultery, women had to prove adultery compounded with incest, rape, sodomy, desertion or cruelty.

77. For example, there was such a case in 1926 that the *Gold Coast Independent* followed in great detail from 6 March to 22 May, and one in 1927 that the paper once again covered verbatim from 26 March to 16 April.

78. There was heated debate in Accra over whether Marjorie Mensah was really a man or a woman. There were many who felt that no woman had yet reached the educational level necessary to be a contributing editor to a local newspaper. In 1934, however, there was a messy court case in which a former male editor of the *Times of West Africa* claimed royalties from a book of earlier Marjorie Mensah editorials on the grounds that he had actually written them. It turned out, however, that along with himself a number of women (among whom was J. B. Danquah's wife, the former Mabel Dove) had also contributed to this column. *Times of West Africa,* 11 May 1934.

79. *Times of West Africa,* 22 May 1933. However, in many respects Marjorie Mensah was quite conservative in her views on women. For example, she opposed the use of makeup, the latest in European dress styles, advocated separate education for boys and girls, and was not above criticizing women for being "too full of complaints." *Times of West Africa,* 23 May 1932.

80. *Times of West Africa,* 26 May 1932 and 9 August 1934.

81. At this time Cooke was a well-known Ratepayer supporter.

82. *Gold Coast Independent,* 9 September and 7 October 1933. Finally, the richest man in Cape Coast, Chief Biney, had to come to the tribunal's assistance and paid enough of the money in question to prevent the bailiff from serving a writ of *fi fa.*

83. Cawson, "Local Politics and Indirect Rule in Cape Coast," 96-97.

84. This was for a total population of approximately 166,000 people. *Report of the Native Tribunals Committee of Enquiry,* 21.

85. Ibid., 4. Altogether there were 324 Native Tribunals in the colony at this time.

86. An increasing number were actually Yoruba Muslims, primarily from the Lagos area and often confusingly referred to as Lagosians.

87. This court was not an officially recognized tribunal, but neither was it simply an informal "arbitration." In a similar fashion to the way in which political officers recognized that local chiefs needed judicial power over their people in Cape Coast in the 1890s, so, too, did they recognize that there was a similar role for Muslim chiefs as their populations increased. From as early as 1914 the Cape Coast district commissioner was cooperating judicially with the chief of the Hausa

community by sending cases to one another's "courts." The District Commissioner of Cape Coast to the Provincial Commissioner, 29 October 1914, ADM 23/1/449, NAG, Cape Coast.

88. "Hausa Zongo Cape Coast," ADM 23/1/375, NAG, Cape Coast. They were also drawn into Cape Coast's factional municipal politics.

89. *Gold Coast Spectator,* April-May 1933.

90. The District Commissioner's Confidential Diary entry for 19 May 1939, DAO 625, NAG, Cape Coast. Cited in Stone, "Colonial Administration," 125.

91. *Gold Coast Independent,* 18 November 1933.

92. *Report of the Commission of Inquiry into Expenses Incurred by Litigants in the Courts of the Gold Coast and Indebtedness Caused Thereby,* 35.

93. "Chairman's Broadcast Address," *Report of the Native Tribunals Committee of Enquiry,* appendix A, 18.

94. *Gold Coast Independent,* 1 July 1944. Five of its seven members were Africans.

95. Lord Hailey, *Native Administration in the British African Territories* (London, 1951), 211.

96. The Native Administration Treasuries Ordinance of 1939 had already tried to introduce this change.

97. *Report of the Commission of Inquiry into Expenses Incurred by Litigants in the Courts of the Gold Coast and Indebtedness Caused Thereby,* 11. As far back as 1895 the Hutchinson Commission had wrestled with this question.

98. *Report of the Native Tribunals Committee of Enquiry,* 17.

99. Ibid., 6.

100. Sutton, "Law, Chieftaincy and Conflict in Colonial Ghana," 43.

101. Richard C. Crook, "Decolonization, the Colonial State, and Chieftaincy in the Gold Coast," *African Affairs* 85, no. 338 (January 1986):99.

102. Ibid., 103.

103. *Report of Commission on Native Courts,* 24.

104. Ibid., 27.

105. Ibid.

106. Ibid., 24.

107. Ibid., 17.

108. Thirty-four percent of the cases were civil and 65 percent were criminal. Ibid., 11.

109. Ibid., 18.

110. According to the commission 45 percent of their membership consisted of nonchiefs. Ibid., 11.

111. William B. Harvey, *Law and Social Change in Ghana* (Princeton, N.J., 1966), 237.

112. Ibid., 238.

113. Ibid.

114. E. P. Thompson, *Whigs and Hunters: The Origin of the Black Act* (New York, 1975), 263, 269.

Conclusion

During the struggle for independence it was not surprising that the complex interplay of facing two ways, especially during the interwar years, stimulated limited interest on the part of most observers. For the politicians who led Ghana to independence, this was a past that belonged more to their rivals than themselves. Nkrumah, for example, in his autobiography dismisses the interwar years as a period of "political vacuum." Africans, like his main political rival, Dr. J. B. Danquah, who participated in its politics, had been "seduced into scrambling for seats" on the white controlled legislature.[1] To the first generation of postcolonial historians it was a similarly uninspiring period. It was one that Europeans had dominated. There seemed limited opportunities to "recover African initiatives," which became the raison d'être for much of the new nationalist history of this era.[2] The "imperial balance sheet" accounting of colonial rule's achievements by those who were the main ideological opponents of the nationalist historians merely contributed to increasing the disinterest of the latter in the more recent colonial past.[3]

I have also implicitly and explicitly criticized a number of contemporary historians for taking an excessively reductionist approach to colonial society by compartmentalizing it into rigidly defined groups. Seeing especially urban coastal society as strictly divided into commoners, chiefs and educated elite is perhaps one of the most enduring legacies of nationalist historiography. It was a convenient way of analyzing the development of nationalism that derived its momentum from conflict with colonial administrators as well as with what the West Indian revolutionary George Padmore disparagingly described as "pro-British stooges."[4] However, on closer inspection it becomes much harder to accept such facile divisions. As I have tried to show, urban colonial society was far too much in a state of flux for there to be a rigid compartmentalization between groups. To demonstrate this I have sought to fill "discredited" gaps in this past as well as shift the focus in Ghanaian colonial historiography away from either celebrating African political initiatives or colonial apologetics to looking at the cultural interaction between African and European societies, as well as within the many African societies that made up the social mosaic of the southern Gold Coast.

This has meant distinguishing between the stated aims of the policies of the colonial state as well as other important European institutions and their actual impact on the colony's subject people. Even more importantly, I have tried to avoid seeing resistance to these policies, or even challenges to what John Mensah Sarbah described as "the demoralizing effects of certain European influences," as necessarily normative behavior. This approach is far too selective for treating the wide range of issues to which facing two ways gave rise. Indeed, all too easily making resistance the dominant reality has played into what Richard Rathbone has recently described as the "post-colonial liberal conscience." It has led to an unwillingness to look critically at both European and African activities, and this "position" has "neither aid[ed] understanding nor in the long run help[ed] the continent and its inhabitants."[5]

Indeed, much of Ghana's recent history is an unfortunate indication of the long-term dangers of collective amnesia and excessive advocacy. On many levels it has contributed to denying the new nation the opportunity to learn from the full range of experiences that shaped the immediate past. Much of the institutional debris that has accumulated from the efforts of eight governments since independence to "restructure," "rehabilitate," "redeploy" or "recover" from the mistakes of its predecessors has resulted from unwitting returns to policies, practices and approaches that were tried, improved on, or discredited and discarded during the colonial period. The price of not retaining this "past experience" has all too often meant that "infancy [has been] perpetual."[6] Ghana today continually seems to be starting anew to rebuild what already existed, but with little sense of how déjà vu these new beginnings are.

For example, the Provisional National Defence Council's (PNDC) creation in 1982 of Public Tribunals to operate supposedly "in parallel" with the "regular" courts inherited from the British, but to administer "revolutionary justice," was not unlike the situation that existed between the British courts and the Native Tribunals during colonial rule.[7] A major difference, however, was that these colonial courts operated in tandem, with appeal from the Native Tribunals to the superior courts well defined. Until 1984 there was no appeal possible from judgments of Public Tribunals, but as a result of national and international pressure the PNDC announced that appeals were going to be possible from "community to district tribunals to regional tribunals and thence to the National Tribunal."[8] In addition, not unlike the Native Tribunals of the past, what happened was that the Public Tribunals operated more and more in keeping with what was often confusingly referred to as the "traditional" judicial system.[9] The voluminous collection of laws that the PNDC promulgated was another indication that the "natural justice" that the Public Tribunals supposedly were to apply was no more satisfactory in guiding their operations than it was for the Native Tribunals of the colonial period.

For anyone familiar with the past, this was hardly surprising. Like the wheel, there is really only one shape possible for the Ghanaian judicial system. The PNDC interlude with its "revolutionary" courts represented yet another diversion in the process of providing Ghanaians with a single judicial system. It clearly, however, has been a costly experience that the country could ill afford. Moreover, those responsible for the unavoidable task of amalgamating the country's judicial systems face the difficult challenge of paring down what had become still another bloated and underfinanced section of the civil service, and trying not to exacerbate the tensions that already exist within the Ghanaian judiciary.[10] But with so little retention of past experience, there is no guarantee that some future revolutionary government might not once again become dissatisfied with what the Chief Justice Phillip Archer has recently described as "the present chaos in [the country's] courts," and reach out for a far more radical solution than the system of arbitration that he favors to relieve "the courts of their heavy workload."[11]

Finding an acceptable and useful place in Ghanaian society for the country's hereditary chieftaincy has also been affected by an inability to build on past experiences. In spite of many concerted attacks on its existence since independence, this institution has displayed a remarkable resiliency. The elections in 1989 for nonparty, district assemblies were a graphic indication of this. As far as voter participation was concerned, they were far more successful in the rural areas than in the large towns, largely due to the important role that the chiefs played in mobilizing support for the exercise.[12] It is clear, however, that these elections were no more successful than the Supreme Military Council's (SMC) last-ditch attempt to save itself by creating nonparty, union government in 1978.[13] What is of more historical interest, however, is the degree to which this election underscored how much any form of local government in Ghana must involve the chiefs. The colonial government's policy of indirect rule was an attempt to take this into account. The messy process of "state crystallization" that took place during the interventionist phase of indirect rule will undoubtedly have to be continued if some kind of stable, representative government is ever to emerge in Ghana. In this context one must wonder how realistic the provisions are in the new constitution for the Fourth Republic that bar chiefs from being involved in party politics and taking part in presidential elections.

As Donald Ray has recently pointed out, the issue of "divided sovereignty" remains a critical one in Ghana today. The constitution of the Fourth Republic represents a return to the earlier "hands-off" policy "with regard to state determination of who is a chief," but at the same time has "effectively removed [chiefs] from being actors in the legislative and top executive spheres of the state."[14] As the conveners of the Conference on the Contribution of Traditional Authority to Development, Democracy and Human Rights held in Ghana in 1994 recognized, "the current opportunities for democratic participation and good governance in most African states [seem] unprecedented, yet the possibilities of failure [are] starkly looming on the horizon" if the "relationships between the contemporary state and the traditional chiefs" is overlooked. In spite of the many attacks on the institution of the chieftaincy, it still "[acts] as a unique linkage between the contemporary state and civil society in many African countries in the areas of democratization, development, human rights (including gender) and environmental protection."[15]

However, at the same time, chieftaincy disputes can still be extremely destabilizing, as was the recent conflict between the Nanumbas and the Konkombas that resulted in the deaths of many thousands in Northern Ghana in 1994.[16] As was the case in the colonial past, there was "a sense of frustration" on the part of the state at "the inability of traditional authority to control its own sphere of responsibility."[17] Rather than preventing or stopping the violence, chiefly rivalries had been a major contributing factor. Nevertheless, with little sense of how futile this had been in solving chiefly disputes in the colonial era, there were calls for "fresh efforts to collect information for documentation of genealogies of stools and skins of the 1870 traditional councils in the country."[18] Clearly, this did not work during the era of indirect rule, since the colony's chiefly order was too much in a state of crystallization for there to be firm genealogies. Among the northern peoples of Ghana, many of whom were acephalous, the chieftaincy was a creation of indirect rule, and as Sean Hawkins has recently argued for the LoDagaa, very much the "victims of invented traditions."[19]

The election of 1989 also brought to the surface the controversial question of local taxation, as the newly constituted assemblies sought in many cases to increase dramatically local revenue to pay for unrealistically ambitious programs. The onerous nature of many of these exactions prompted comparisons with Governor Hill's unsuccessful attempt in 1852 to impose a poll tax on equally "poverty stricken people," which "had to be abandoned because of massive opposition."[20] Once again, however, as far as the present situation is concerned, there is much more to be learned from the colonial government's attempts to fund municipal government during the difficult years of the depression than from the gunboat-government era of the 1850s. Determining how much communities could realistically pay in local taxes and establishing ways of enforcing payment were issues with which the colonial government wrestled, with mixed success. Nevertheless, continuing this search is clearly of vital importance today if Ghana is to maintain its recently "rehabilitated" infrastructure.

Reversing Ghana's decline will be difficult, and will require the contributions of many people with special skills and inspirations. There is clearly an important role for historians in this process. In Ghana, this challenge has been compounded by what Adu Boahan has described as the "culture of silence," one of the important by-products of so many years of military rule.[21] Judging from past experience, it will undoubtedly be easier to restore civilian rule than to stimulate a truly spirited inquiry into Ghana's past that does not fall quickly into the ruts of nationalist historiography or an excessive concern with advocacy. Swinging back and forth from soldiers to politicians has recently become all too much established tradition. These about-faces have made it difficult to appreciate just how much Ghana's colonial past continues to influence the present.

"Every wise man knows where he is going, but only the fool does not know where he is coming from" is the exhortation and admonition of the Sankofa bird. With its head turned backward and its body facing forward, this legendary creature from Akan mythology also faces two ways, like the Roman god Janus, and underscores the need for people to learn from and build on the past as they face the future. Yet when it comes to learning from the immediate colonial past, it seems as though Ghanaians, as well as those who have studied the country's past, have all too often allowed this advice to go unheeded.

Notes

1. Kwame Nkrumah, *The Autobiography of Kwame Nkrumah* (Edinburgh, 1957), viii.

2. For the most extensive discussion of this trend in the East African context, see D. Denoon and A. Kuper, "Nationalist Historians in Search of a Nation: The 'New Historiography' in Dar Es Salaam," *African Affairs* 69, no. 277 (October 1970):329-349.

3. The best example of this approach to the colonial past is Lewis Gann's and Peter Duignan's *The Burden of Empire* (London, 1968).

4. George Padmore, *The Gold Coast Revolution: The Struggle of an African People from Slavery to Freedom* (London, 1953), 105.

5. Richard Rathbone, "African Studies: Africa since Independence," *West Africa,* 29 October 1984, 2173.

6. George Santayana, *The Life of Reason, or the Phases of Human Progress: Reason in Common Sense* (1905; reprint, New York, 1936), 284.

7. For a description of this "experiment," see Roger Gocking, "Ghana's Public Tribunals: An Experiment in Revolutionary Justice," *African Affairs* 95, no. 379 (April 1996):197-223.

8. Bortey Lamptey, "Beware of Politics," *West Africa*, 21 May 1984.

9. That is, the system inherited from the British.

10. For an indication of how bitter these feelings are, see "Bar, Bench and Rights," *West Africa*, 17-23 July 1989.

11. *West Africa*, 10-16 October 1994.

12. Kojo T-Vieta, "Mixed Results," *West Africa*, 27 March-2 April 1989.

13. For a description of this exercise see Naomi Chazan, *An Anatomy of Ghanaian Politics: Managing Political Recession, 1969-1982* (Boulder, Colo., 1983), 245-267.

14. Donald Ray, "Divided Sovereignty, Traditional Authority and the State in Ghana," *Journal of Legal Pluralism* 37-38 (1996):190, 193.

15. Donald Ray and E. Adriaan B. van Rouveroy van Nieuwaal, "The New Relevance of Traditional Authorities in Africa: Conference; Major Themes; Reflections on Chieftaincy in Africa; Future Directions," *Journal of Legal Pluralism* 37-38 (1996):1. The entire issue of this journal consisted of papers presented at this conference.

16. Initial reports were of 500 people dead and 30 villages destroyed (*West Africa*, 21-27 February 1994), but by the time the emergency that the government proclaimed was lifted in August the number of dead had been increased to 6,000 and the villages destroyed to 200 (*West Africa*, 24-30 October 1994).

17. Ray, "Divided Sovereignty," 196.

18. *Daily Graphic*, 29 July 1994.

19. Sean Hawkins, "Disguising Chiefs and God as History: Questions on the Acephalousness of LoDagaa Politics and Religion," *Africa* 66, no. 2 (1996):202.

20. Kofi Kasah, "Burdensome Taxes," *West Africa*, 4-10 September 1989.

21. *West Africa*, 28 March 1988.

Glossary

There are considerable differences in the spelling of Akan and Ga terms. This was so during the colonial period and continues to be the case today. In this work I have tried to use the most contemporary spellings, but sometimes, usually when quoting, I have used earlier spellings.

Abusua	An Akan matrilineal lineage
Abusuakuw	The larger totemic clan
Adontehen	A divisional chief
Ahenfie	An *omanhen*'s official residence
Akutsei	Quarters within a Ga town
Akutso	A single *akutsei*
Akwason	Court comprising members from all *akutsei*
Akyeamehen	Akan term for a paramount ruler in the Winneba area
Amanhin or *Amanhen*	Plural of *omanhen*
Asafo, or *Asafu*	The military companies into which males in Akan coastal towns are divided
Asafoatse	An individual *asafoatsemei*
Asafoatsemei	"Fathers" of the *asafo,* a Ga term
Asafobii	Ga term for members of an *asafo*
Asantehene	Ruler of the Asante people
Besonfu	A body of councillors in the Akan state
Besonhen	A divisional chief
Caboceers	Portuguese term for a "head man"
Consawment	Part of the bridewealth exchange

Destoolment	Removing a chief or other leader from his position
Dey	Ruler of the Effutu people
Ekuwessonhen	The Elmina term for *tufuhen*
Enstoolment	Placing an Akan ruler on a "stool"
Fie panyin	The head of the household
Futursanyi	The treasurer of an Akan state
Gyase	An Akan ruler's bodyguard
Itsir nsa	Fante term for brideprice
Kpabu	A prison
Majii	Ga towns or states
Man	A single town or state
Manbii	The people of a Ga town
Manceros	Portuguese term for *asafo* members
Mankrado or *mankralo*	An administrator of a town
Mantse or *manche*	A single *mantsemei*
Mantsemei	"Fathers" of Ga towns
Mashi	Original Ga
Mmusa	Plural of *abusua*
Nifahen or *nifahin*	A divisional chief
Odefey	Modern term for ruler of the Effutu people
Ogua Basafu	A Cape Coast body of councillors
Ohen, ohene or *ohin*	Ruler of a village and in a town below an *omanhen*
Okyenhene	The paramount chief of Akyem Abuakwa
Oman	The *omanhen*'s immediate body of advisers
Omandefe	Effutu term for a paramount chief (Winneba)
Omanhen or *omanhene*	The paramount chief of a Fante traditional state
Panyarring	Seizing a person for nonpayment of a debt
Safuhin	One of the captains of an *asafo*
Samansiw	An oral or nuncupative will
Simiwhen	The chief of the village of Simew
Supi	Chief officer of an individual *asafo*
Tufuhen, tufuhene or *tufuhin*	"Field marshal" of a town's *asafos*
We	Ga term for lineage or house
Wetse	Head of the lineage
Wirempe	The custodians of an Akan stool
Wulomei	A Ga priest

Selected Bibliography

INTERVIEWS

James Abakah, Cape Coast, January 1974
Joseph Amissah, Cape Coast, August 1991
J. A. Annobil, Cape Coast, July 1974
John Anquandah, Elmina, December 1988
S. A. D. Arkhurst, Winneba, December 1988
Eva Armah, Cape Coast, June 1974
Father E. M. Arthur, Cape Coast, January 1974
Kodwo Bentsi-Enchill, Cape Coast, July 1974
E. J. Blankson, Cape Coast, May 1974
Mary Blankson, Cape Coast, June 1974
Dr. Boison, Cape Coast, September 1974
E. A. P. Brown, Cape Coast, July 1974
T. R. Coker, Cape Coast, July 1974
Reverend Dr. Cole, Cape Coast, February 1974
Sam Decorsky, Cape Coast, September 1974
Dominic de Graft Aidoo, Cape Coast, January 1974
Hector de Graft Johnson, Cape Coast, August 1974
J. W. de Graft Johnson, Accra, July 1974
Dr. Duker, Cape Coast, September 1974
Father H. C. Elliot, Cape Coast, August 1974
J. O. Eshun, Cape Coast, July 1974
Napoleon Forson, Cape Coast, June 1974
Victor C. A. Fynn, Cape Coast, August 1974
H. A. Garshong, Accra, July 1994
Chief Gyepi II, Cape Coast, February 1974
J. P. Hammond, Cape Coast, August, 1974

E. Hansen, Cape Coast, January 1974
Reverend David Hudson, Cape Coast, December 1973
James Intsiful, Cape Coast, July 1974
Willie Johnson, Cape Coast, July 1974
K. W. S. Johnston, Cape Coast, July 1974
Agnes King, Cape Coast, June 1974
Amin Majoub, Cape Coast, August 1974
Richard Matheson, Cape Coast, January 1974
James A. Minneaux, Cape Coast, July 1974
Pastor Daniel Neizer, Cape Coast, February 1974
S. T. Nettey, Accra, July 1994
C. W. Newton, Cape Coast, July 1974
Father Martin Peters, Cape Coast, January 1974
L. Phillips, Cape Coast, June 1974
Mrs. Osam-Pinanko, Cape Coast, August 1974
P. C. F. Renner, Cape Coast, July 1974
George C. E. Ribeiro, Accra, July 1994
Dr. Mercier Ricketts, Cape Coast, June 1974
Kate Sagoe, Cape Coast, June 1974
Father K. Sakyiama, Cape Coast, September 1974
Anna Sam, Cape Coast, July 1974
T. Sam, Cape Coast, March 1974
Agnes Magnus Sampson, Cape Coast, July 1974
Said Sangari, Cape Coast, August 1974
S. Vroom, Elmina, March 1974
Reverend E. K. Yamoah, Cape Coast, March 1974

MANUSCRIPT SOURCES

Archives: United Kingdom

The Public Record Office, London
C.O. 96/31 to 96/448 and passim to 96/641
Gold Coast Colony Blue Book, 1846-1945

Rhodes House, Oxford
The Duncan-Johnstone Papers, the W. L. Hanschell Papers and the
William Beeton Papers

Methodist Mission Archives
School of Oriental and African Studies, London University
Minutes of the Methodist Synod, 1868-1911

United Society for the Propagation of the Gospel
USPG Library, London
Records of the English Church Mission in the Gold Coast

Archives: Ghana

National Archives of Ghana, Accra
SNA, ADM 11/1 series, SNA, ADM 111/1 series
SCT 2/6, 5/4 and 5/6 series

National Archives of Ghana, Cape Coast
ADM 21/1, 23/1 and 71/1 series
GCARPS files, 1964/77 and 1965/118
Sekyi Files: Correspondence with Officials, Sekyi Papers

Ga Mantse's Records
Native Tribunal Book, 1925-1926

NEWSPAPERS AND PERIODICALS

Gold Coast
Gold Coast Aborigines, 1898-1902 (weekly-gaps)
Gold Coast Chronicle, 1894-1901 (weekly-gaps)
Gold Coast Echo, 1888 (weekly-short run)
Gold Coast Free Press, 1899 (weekly-short run)
Gold Coast Express, 1897-1900 (weekly-gaps)
Gold Coast Independent, 1895 and 1898 (weekly-gaps)
Gold Coast Independent, 1918-1948 (weekly-regular for long periods)
Gold Coast Leader, 1902-1929 (weekly-gaps)
Gold Coast Methodist Times, 1897 (weekly-short run)
Gold Coast Observer, 1942-1947 (weekly-irregular)
Gold Coast Spectator, 1938 (weekly-short run)
Gold Coast Times, 1874-1885 (weekly-periods regular)
Gold Coast Times, 1930-1939 (weekly-mostly regular)
Times of West Africa, 1933-1935 (daily-regular)
Western Echo, 1885-1887 (weekly-mostly regular)

United Kingdom

African Times, 1862-1895 (monthly-regular)
Illustrated London News, 1846-1945 (weekly-regular)
West Africa, 1917-1996 (weekly-regular)

THESES

Baku, D. Kofi. "An Intellectual in Nationalist Politics: The Contribution of Kobina Sekyi to the Evolution of Ghanaian National Consciousness." Ph.D. diss., University of Sussex, 1987.

Casely-Hayford, Augustus L. "A Genealogical Study of Cape Coast Stool Families." Ph.D. diss., School of Oriental and African Studies, London University, 1992.

Cawson, Alan. "Local Politics and Indirect Rule in Cape Coast Ghana, 1928-57." Ph.D. diss., Oxford University, 1975.

Gocking, Roger S. "The Historic Akoto: A Social History of Cape Coast Ghana, 1848-1948." Ph.D. diss., Stanford University, 1981.

Hagan, George P. "Aspects of Social Change Among the Effutu of Winneba." Ph.D. diss., Oxford University, 1975.

Holmes, Baron A. "Economic and Political Organizations in the Gold Coast, 1920-1945." Ph.D. diss., University of Chicago, 1972.

Jenkins. Ray G. "Gold Coast Historians and Their Pursuit of the Gold Coast Pasts: 1892-1917." Ph.D. diss., University of Birmingham, 1985.

Kaplow, Susan B. "African Merchants of the Nineteenth Century Gold Coast." Ph.D. diss., Columbia University, 1975.

Mensah-Brown, A. Kodwo. "The Traditional Courts and Their Successors in Ghana's Legal History, 1800-1914." Ph.D. diss., University of London, 1970.

Parker, John. "Ga State and Society in Early Colonial Accra, 1860-1920s." Ph.D. diss., University of London, 1995.

Rowand, Evelyn. "Press and Opinion in British West Africa, 1855-1900: The Development of a Sense of Identity Among the Educated British West Africans in the Later Nineteenth Century." Ph.D. diss., University of Birmingham, 1972.

Sanders, James R. "The Political Development of the Fante in the Eighteenth and Nineteenth Centuries: A Study of a West African Merchant Society." Ph.D. diss., Northwestern University, 1980.

Stone, Robert. L. "Colonial Administration and Rural Politics in South Central Ghana, 1919-1951." Ph.D. diss., Cambridge University, 1975.

BOOKS

Agbodeka, Francis. *African Politics and British Policy in the Gold Coast.* Evanston, 1971.

Ahuma, Attoh, S. R. B. *The Gold Coast Nation and National Consciousness.* 1911. Reprint, London, 1971.

Akyeampong, Emmanuel. *Drink, Power and Cultural Change: A Social History of Alcohol in Ghana, c. 1800 to Recent Times.* Portsmouth, N.H., and Oxford, 1996.

Allot, A. N. *Essays in African Law, with Special Reference to the Law of Ghana.* London, 1960.

Anaman, Jacob B. *Simple Stories from Gold Coast History.* 2 vols. Vol. 1. Cape Coast, 1913 Vol. 2. Cape Coast, 1919.

Anquandah, James. *Rediscovering Ghana's Past.* London, 1982.

Arhin, Kwame. *West African Traders in Ghana in the Nineteenth and Twentieth Centuries.* London, 1979.

Asante, S. K. B. *Property and Law and Social Goals in Ghana, 1844-1966.* Accra, 1975.

Austin, Dennis. *Politics in Ghana, 1946-1960.* London, 1964.

Awooner, Kofi N. *Ghana: A Political History.* Accra, 1990.

Azikiwe, Nnamdi. *My Odyssey: An Autobiography.* London, 1970.

Baesjou, Rene, ed. *An Asante Embassy on the Gold Coast: The Mission of Akyempon Yaw to Elmina, 1869-1872.* Leiden, 1979.

Bailey, F. G. *Strategies and Spoils: A Social Anthropology of Politics.* Oxford, 1969.

Bardot, J. *A Description of the Coasts of North and South Guinea.* London, 1732.

Bartels, F. L. *The Roots of Ghana Methodism.* Cambridge, 1965.

Boahen, Adu A. *Mfantsipim and the Making of Ghana: A Centenary History.* Accra, 1996.

Bonne, Nii K. *Milestones in the History of the Gold Coast.* Ashford-in-Middlesex, U.K. 1953.

Bosman, William. *A New and Accurate Description of the Coast of Guinea.* 1704. Reprint, London, 1967.

Brandford Griffith, William. *The Far Horizon: Portrait of a Colonial Judge.* Ilfracombe, U.K. 1951.

292   Facing Two Ways

Brathwaite, Edward. *The Development of Creole Society in Jamaica, 1770-1820*. Oxford, 1971.
Brown, E. J. P. *Gold Coast and Ashanti Reader*. London, 1929.
Burton, Richard F. *Wanderings in West Africa from Liverpool to Fernando Po*. 2 vols. London, 1863.
Canny, N. and A. Pagden, eds. *Colonial Identity in the Atlantic World, 1500-1800*. London, 1987.
Casely Hayford, Joseph E. *Ethiopia Unbound: Studies in Race Emancipation*. London, 1911.
———. *Gold Coast Native Institutions*. London, 1903.
Chin Sheng-Pao. *The Gold Coast Delegations to Britain in 1934: The Political Background*. Taipei, Taiwan, 1970.
Christensen, James B. *Double Descent Among the Fanti*. New Haven, Conn., 1954.
Claridge, W. *A History of the Gold Coast and Ashanti*. 2 vols. 1915. Reprint, London, 1964.
Cohen, Abner. *The Politics of Elite Culture: Explorations in the Dramaturgy of Power in a Modern African Society*. Berkeley, Calif., 1981.
Crabbe, S. Azu. *John Mensah Sarbah, 1864-1910*. Accra, 1971.
Cromwell, Adelaide M. *An African Victorian Feminist: The Life and Times of Adelaide Smith Casely Hayford, 1868-1960*. London, 1986.
Crooks, J. J. *Records Relating to the Gold Coast Settlements, 1750-1874*. 1923. Reprint, London, 1973.
Crowder, Michael. *West Africa under Colonial Rule*. Evanston Ill., 1968.
Cruickshank, Brodie. *Eighteen Years on the Gold Coast of Africa*, 2 vols. 1853. Reprint, New York, 1966.
Cunard, Nancy. *Negro: An Anthology*. London, 1934.
Daaku, Kwame. *Trade and Politics on the Gold Coast, 1600-1720*. Oxford, 1970.
Daniels, W. C. Ekow, and G. R. Woodman, eds. *Essays in Ghanaian Law, 1876-1976: Supreme Court Centenary*. Legon, 1976.
Danquah, J. B. *Akan Laws and Customs and the Akim Abuakwa Constitution*. London, 1928.
de Graft Johnson, J. W. *Towards Nationhood in West Africa*. London, 1928.
Edsman, Bjorn M. *Lawyers in Gold Coast Politics, c. 1900-1940: From Mensah Sarbah to J. B. Danquah*. Uppsala, 1979.
Ellis, A. B. *A History of the Gold Coast of West Africa*. 1893. Reprint, New York, 1969.
Ephson, I. *Gallery of Gold Coast Celebrities*. Accra, 1969.
Feinberg, Harvey. *Africans and Europeans in West Africa: Elminans and Dutchmen on the Gold Coast During the Eighteenth Century*. New York, 1990.
Field, Margaret J. *Social Organization of the Ga People*. London, 1940.

Firmin-Sellers, Kathryn. *The Transformation of Property Rights in the Gold Coast: An Empirical Analysis Applying Rational Choice Theory.* Cambridge, U.K., 1996.

Hailey, William Malcolm. *An African Survey.* Rev. ed. London, 1957.

Harrell-Bond, Barbara E., Allen M. Howard, and David E. Skinner. *Community Leadership and the Transformation of Freetown, 1801-1976.* The Hague, 1978.

Harvey, William B. *Law and Social Change in Ghana.* Princeton, N.J., 1966.

Henige, David. *The Chronology of Oral Tradition: The Quest for a Chimera.* Oxford, 1974.

Hobsbawm, Eric, and Terrence Ranger, eds. *The Invention of Tradition.* Cambridge, 1983.

Hodgkin, Thomas. *Nationalism in Colonial Africa.* New York, 1957.

Horton, James A. *West African Countries and Peoples.* 1868. Reprint, Edinburgh, 1969.

Howard, Rhoda. *Colonialism and Underdevelopment in Ghana.* London, 1978.

Hutchison, C. F. *The Pen Pictures of Modern Africans and African Celebrities* Vol. 1. London, n.d.

Jones, Adam. *German Sources for West African History, 1680-1700.* Wiesbaden, 1985.

Jones-Quartey, K. A. B. *History, Politics and Early Press in Ghana: The Fictions and the Facts.* Accra, 1975.

Kea, Ray. *Settlements, Trade, and Politics in the Seventeenth-Century Gold Coast.* Baltimore and London, 1982.

Kemp, Dennis. *Nine Years at the Gold Coast.* London, 1898.

Kilson, Marion. *African Urban Kinsmen: The Ga of Central Accra.* London, 1974.

Kimble, David. *A Political History of Ghana: The Rise of Gold Coast Nationalism, 1850-1928.* London 1963.

Kingsley, Mary. *Travels in West Africa.* 2nd ed. London, 1898.

Kludze, Kodzo A. *Modern Law of Succession in Ghana.* Dordrecht, Holland, and Providence, R.I., 1988.

Kuczynski, R. R. *Demographic Survey of the British Colonial Empire.* Vol. 1. London, 1948.

Lawrence, A. W. *Trade Castles and Forts of West Africa.* London, 1963.

Lloyd, P. C. *Africa in Social Change.* London, 1967.

Lynch, Hollis. *Edward Wilmot Blyden: Pan Negro Patriot, 1832-1912.* London, 1967.

Mann, Kristin. *Marrying Well: Marriage, Status and Social Change Among the Educated Elite in Colonial Lagos.* Cambridge, U.K., 1985.

Mann, Kristin, and Richard Roberts, eds. *Law in Colonial Africa.* London, 1991.

McCarthy, Mary. *Social Change and the Growth of British Power in the Gold Coast: The Fante States, 1807-1874*. New York, 1983.

Metcalfe, G. E. *Great Britain and Ghana: Documents of Ghana History, 1807-1957*. London, 1964.

Miers, Suzanne. *Britain and the Ending of the Slave Trade*. New York, 1975.

Miers, Suzanne, and Richard Roberts, eds. *The End of Slavery in Africa*. Madison, Wis., 1988.

Ollennu, N. A. *The Law of Testate and Intestate Succession in Ghana*. London, 1966.

Oppong, Christine. *Marriage Among a Matrilineal Elite: A Family Study of Ghanaian Senior Civil Servants*. London, 1974.

Padmore, George. *The Gold Coast Revolution: The Struggle of an African People from Slavery to Freedom*. London, 1953.

Pfann, Helene. *A Short History of the Catholic Church in Ghana*. Cape Coast, 1965.

Phillips, Anne. *The Enigma of Colonialism: British Policy in West Africa*. Bloomington, Ind., 1989.

Priestley, Margaret. *West African Trade and Coast Society*. London, 1969.

Rathbone, Richard. *Murder and Politics in Colonial Ghana*. New Haven, Conn., and London, 1993.

Rattray, R. S. *Ashanti Law and Constitution*. London, 1929.

Reindorf, Carl C. *History of the Gold Coast and Asante*. Basel, 1895.

Reynolds, Edward. *Trade and Economic Change on the Gold Coast, 1807-1874*. London, 1974.

Roberts, Andrew D., ed. *The Colonial Moment in Africa: Essays on the Movement of Minds and Materials, 1900-1940*. Cambridge, U.K., 1990.

Sampson, Magnus J. *Makers of Modern Ghana*. Vol. 1, *From Phillip Quarcoo to Aggrey*. Accra, 1969.

Sarbah. John Mensah. *Fanti Customary Laws*. 1897. Reprint, London, 1968.

——— .*Fanti National Constitution*. 1906. Reprint, London, 1968.

Sekyi, W. E. G. *The Blinkards*. London, 1974.

Southon, Arthur E. *Gold Coast Methodism*. London, 1935.

Spitzer, Leo. *The Creoles of Sierra Leone: Responses to Colonialism, 1870-1945*. Madison, Wis., 1974.

Stone, Robert, and Addo Fenning, eds. *Akyem Abuakwa and the Politics of the Inter War Period in Ghana*. Basel, 1975.

Wraith, R. E. *Guggisberg*. London, 1967.

GOVERNMENT PUBLICATIONS

Report of an Inquiry Held by the Hon. C. W. Welman, SNA, On a Commission by His Excellency the Governor Issued Under the Commission of Inquiry Ordinance, 26 February 1925. Accra, 1925.

Report of Commission of Inquiry into Expenses Incurred by Litigants in the Courts of the Gold Coast and Indebtedness Caused Thereby. C. R. Havers, Accra, 1945.

Report of Commission on Native Courts. Accra, 1951.

Report of the Commission Appointed by the Governor on the 1st of August 1894 to Enquire into Various Matters Relating to Native Courts. Under the Chairmanship of Chief Justice J. T. Hutchinson. Accra, 1895.

Report of the Native Tribunals Committee of Enquiry. Accra, 1943.

ARTICLES

Aktia, J. M. "The Transfer of the Seat of Government from Cape Coast to Accra." *Gold Coast Teachers Journal* 1 (1956):42-47.

Akyeampong, Emmanuel. "What's in a Drink? Class Struggle, Popular Culture and the Politics of *Akpeteshie* (Local Gin) in Ghana, 1930-67." *Journal of African History* 37 (1996):215-236.

Allot, A. N. "Marriage and the Internal Conflict of Laws in Ghana." *Journal of African Law* 2, no. 3 (Autumn 1958):164-184.

———. "Native Tribunals in the Gold Coast, 1844-1927." *Journal of African Law* 1, no. 3 (1957):163-171.

Amoo, J. W. A. "The Effect of Western Influence on Akan Marriage." *Africa* 16, no. 4 (1946):228-237.

Anquandah, James. "State Formation Among the Akan of Ghana." *Sankofa* 2 (1976):47-57.

Arhin, Kwame."Diffuse Authority Among the Fanti Coastal Stools." *Ghana Notes and Queries* 9 (November 1966):66-70.

———. "Rank and Class Among the Asante and the Fanti in the Nineteenth Century." *Africa* 53, no. 1 (1983):34-52.

Asante, S. K. B., "Interests in Land in the Customary Law of Ghana-A New Appraisal." *Yale Law Journal* 74, no. 5 (April 1965):848:885.

Bevin, H. J. "The Gold Coast Economy About 1880." *Transactions of the Gold Coast and Togoland Historical Society* 2, no. 2 (1956):73-86.

Birmingham, David. "A Note on the Kingdom of Fetu." *Ghana Notes and Queries* 9 (November 1966):30-33.

Brandford Griffith, William. "The Native Courts of the Gold Coast." *Journal of the Society of Comparative Legislation* 6, no. 2 (1905):507-513.

———. "The Status of Native Courts in the Gold Coast Colony." *Journal of the Society of Comparative Legislation* 8 (1908):167-179.

Bruce-Myers, J. M. "The Origin of the Gas." Parts 1 and 2. *Journal of the African Society* 27, no. 105 (October 1927):69-76; 27, no. 106 (January 1928):167-193.

Buxton, T. F. V. "The Creole in West Africa." *Journal of the African Society* 12, no. 48 (July 1913):385-394.

Christensen, James B. "African Political Systems: Indirect Rule and Democratic Processes." *Phylon* 16 (1954):69-83.

Chukwukere, B. I. "Agnatic and Uterine Relations Among the Fante: Male/Female Dualism." *Africa* 52, no. 1:61-68.

———. "Perspective on the *Asafo* Institution in Southern Ghana." *Journal of African Studies* 7, no. 1:39-47.

Colson, Elizabeth. "Possible Reprecussions of the Right to Make Wills upon the Plateau Tonga of Northern Rhodesia." *Journal of African Administration* 2, no. 1 (January 1950):24-34.

Crook, Richard C. "Decolonization, the Colonial State, and Chieftaincy in the Gold Coast." *African Affairs* 85, no. 338 (1986):75-105.

Datta, A. K. "The Fante Asafo: A Reexamination." *Africa* 42, no. 4 (October 1972):305-315.

Datta, A. K., and R. Porter. "The *Asafu* System in Historical Perspective: An Inquiry into the Origin and Development of a Ghanaian Institution." *Journal of African History* 12, no. 2 (1971):279-299. de Graft Johnson, J. C. "The Fanti Asafu." *Africa* 5, no. 3 (July 1932):307-322.

Dumett, Raymond E. "African Merchants of the Gold Coast, 1800-1905: Dynamics of Indigenous Entrepreneurship." *Comparative Studies in Society and History* 25 (1983):661-693.

———. "John Sarbah the Elder and African Mercantile Entrepeneurship in the Gold Coast in the Nineteenth Century." *Journal of African History* 14, no. 4 (1973):653-679.

———. "The Campaign Against Malaria and the Expansion of Scientific Medicine and Sanitary Services in British West Africa." *African Historical Studies* 1 (1968):153-197.

———. "The Rubber Trade of the Gold Coast and Asante in the Nineteenth Century: African Innovation and Market Responsiveness." *Journal of African History* 12, no. 1 (1971):79-101.

Dumett, Raymond E., and Marion Johnson. "Britain and the Supression of Slavery in the Gold Coast Colony, Ashanti, and the Northern

Territories." In *The End of Slavery in Africa,* edited by S. Miers and Richard Roberts, 71-116. Madison, Wis., 1988.

Easmon, M. C. F. "Sierra Leone Doctors." *Sierra Leone Studies* 6 (June 1956):81-96.

Feinberg, Harvey M. "An Incident in Elmina-Dutch Relations, Gold Coast (Ghana), 1739-1740." *African Historical Studies* 3 (1970):359-372.

————. "There Was an Elmina Note, but..." *International Journal of African Historical Studies* 9 (1976):618-630.

ffoulkes, Arthur. "The Company System in Cape Coast Castle." *Journal of the Royal African Society* 7, no. 27 (April 1908):261-277.

————. "The Fanti Family System." *Journal of the African Society* 7, no. 28 (July 1908):348-409.

Fortescue, Dominic. "The Accra Crowd, the *Asafo* and the Opposition to the Municipal Corporations Ordinance, 1924-25." *Canadian Journal of African Studies* 24, no. 3 (1990):348-375.

Fynn, John K. "Nananompow of the Fante." *Sankofa* 2 (1976).

————. "The Pre-Borbor Fante States." *Sankofa* 2 (1976).

————. "Trade and Politics in Akanland." *Tarikh* 7, no. 2:23-24.

Gale, Thomas S. "The Struggle Against Disease in The Gold Coast: Early Attempts at Urban Sanitary Reform." *Transactions of the Historical Society of Ghana* 16, no. 2, New Series 1 (1995):184-203.

Gocking, Roger S. "British Justice and the Native Tribunals of the Southern Gold Coast Colony." *Journal of African History* 34, no. 1 (1993):93-113.

————. "Colonial Rule and the 'Legal Factor' in Ghana and Lesotho," *Africa* 67, no. 1 (1997):61-85.

————. "Competing Systems of Inheritance Before the British Courts of the Gold Coast Colony." *International Journal of African Historical Studies* 23, no. 4 (1990):601-618.

————. "Creole Society and the Revival of Traditional Culture in Cape Coast During the Colonial Period." *International Journal of African Historical Studies* 17, no. 4 (1984):601-622.

————. "Indirect Rule in the Gold Coast: Competition for Office and the Invention of Tradition." *Canadian Journal of African Studies* 28, no. 3 (1994):421-446.

Green, Jeffrey P. "Caribbean Influences in the Gold Coast Administration in the 1900s." *Ghana Studies Bulletin* 2 (December 1984):10-16.

Hannigan, A. St. J. J. "The Present System of Succession Amongst the Akan People of the Gold Coast." *Journal of African Administration* 6 (October 1954):166-171.

Henige, David. "Akan Stool Succession Under Colonial Rule: Continuity or Change?" *Journal of African History* 14, no. 2 (1975):285-301.

————. "John Kabes of Komenda: An early African Entrepreneur and Early State Builder." *Journal of African History* 17, no. 1 (1977):1-19.

———. "Kingship in Elmina Before 1869: A Study in Feedback and the Traditional Idealization of the Past." *Cahiers d'Etudes Africaines* 55, XIV-3:499-520.

———. "Truths Yet Unborn? Oral Traditions as a Casualty of Culture Contact." *Journal of African History* 23, no. 3 (1982):395-412.

Hyland, A. D. C. "The Architectural History of Cape Coast." *Transactions of the Historical Society of Ghana* 16, no. 2, New Series 1 (1995):163-184.

Jenkins, Ray G. "Confrontations with A. B. Ellis, a Participant in the Scramble for Gold Coast Africana, 1874-1894." *Paideuma* 33 (1987):313-335.

———. "Gold Coasters Overseas, 1880-1919: With Specific Reference to Their Activities in Britain." *Immigrants and Minorities* 4, no. 3 (1985):6-52.

———. "Impeachable Source? On the Use of the Second Edition of Reindorf's History as a Primary Source for the Study of Ghanaian History." *History in Africa* 1, no. 4 (1977):123-147.

———. "North American Scholarship and the 'Thaw' in the Historiography of Ghanaian Coastal Communities." *Ghana Studies Bulletin* 3 (1985):19-28.

Johnson. Terence J. "Protest, Tradition and Change: An Analysis of Southern Gold Coast Riots, 1880-1920." *Economy and Society* 1, no. 2 (May 1972):164-193.

Jones-Quartey, K. A. B. "Anglo-African Journals and Journalists in the Nineteenth and Early Twentieth Centuries." *Transactions of the Historical Society of Ghana* 4, no. 1 (1959):47-56

Kaplow, Susan B. "The Mudfish and the Crocodile: Underdevelopment of a West African Bourgeoise." *Science and Society* 41, no. 3 (1977):317-333.

———. "Primitive Accumulation and Traditional Social Relations on the Nineteenth Century Gold Coast." *Canadian Journal of African Studies* 12, no. 1 (1978):19-36.

Killingray, David. "Repercussions of World War I in the Gold Coast." *Journal of African History* 19, no. 1 (1978):39-59.

Kludze, A. K. P. "Evolution of the Different Regimes of Customary Law in Ghana within the Framework of the Principle of *Stare Decisis*." In *People's Law and State Law: The Bellagio Papers,* edited by Anthony Allot and Gordon Woodman, 97-103. Dordrecht, Holland, 1985.

Kortenaar, Neil ten. "Beyond Authenticity and Creolization: Reading Achebe Writing Culture." *PMLA* 110, no. 1 (January 1995):30-42.

Langley, J. Ayo. "Modernization and Its Malcontents: Kobina Sekyi of Ghana and the Restatement of African Political Theory (1892-1956)," *Institute of African Studies Research Review,* 6, no. 3 (1970):1-61.

Little, Kenneth. "The Significance of the West African Creole for

Africainst and Afro-American Studies." *African Studies* 49, no. 197 (October 1950):309-319.

Loveridge, A. J. "The Future of Native Courts." *Journal of African Administration* 1, no. 1 (January 1949):7-18.

———. "Wills and the Customary Law in the Gold Coast." *Journal of African Administration* 2, no. 4 (October 1950):24-28.

McSheffrey, Gerald M. "Slavery, Indentured Servitude, Legitimate Trade and the Impact of Abolition in the Gold Coast, 1874-1901: A Reappraisal." *Journal of African History* 24 (1983):349-368.

Meredith, David. "The Construction of Takoradi Harbour in the Gold Coast 1919 to 1930: A Case Study in Colonial Development and Administration." *Transafrican Journal of History* 5, no. 1 (1976):134-149.

Metcalfe, G. E. "After Maclean: Some Aspects of British Policy in the Mid-Nineteenth Century." *Journal of the Gold Coast and Togoland Historical Society* 1, no. 5 (1955):178-192.

Nadel, S. F. "The Concept of Social Elites." *International Social Sciences Bulletin* 3, no. 3 (1956):413-424.

Ollennu, N. M. "The Influence of English Law on West Africa." *Journal of African Law* 5, no. 1 (1961):21-35.

Pachai, B. "An Outline History of Municipal Government at Cape Coast." *Transactions of the Historical Society of Ghana* 8 (1965):130-160.

Patton, Adell. "Dr. John Farrell Easmon: Medical Professionalism in the Gold Coast, 1856-1900." *International Journal of African Historical Studies* 22, no. 4 (1989):601-636.

Phillip, Arthur. "The Legal Factor in a Changing Africa." *African Affairs* 54 (January 1955):280-287.

Porter, R. "The Cape Coast Conflict of 1803: A Crisis in Relations Between the African and European Communities." *Transactions of the Historical Society of Ghana* 11 (1970):27-82.

Priestley, Margaret. "The Emergence of an Elite: A Case Study of a West African Coast Family." In *The New Elites of Tropical Africa*, edited by P. C. Lloyd, 87-100. Cambridge, U.K., 1966.

———. "Richard Brew, an Eighteenth Century Trader at Anomabo." *Transactions of the Historical Society of Ghana* 4, no. 1 (1959):29-46.

Quartey-Papafio, A. B. "Law of Succession Among the Akras or the Ga Tribes Proper of the Gold Coast." *Journal of the African Society* 10, no. 27 (October 1910):65-72.

———. "The Native Tribunals of the Akans of the Gold Coast." Parts 1 and 2. *Journal of the African Society* 10 (1910-1911):320-330, 434-446; 11 (1911-1912):75-94.

Ranger, Terence. "The Invention of Tradition Revisited: The Case of Colonial Africa." In *Legitimacy and the State in Twentieth Century Africa: Essays in Honour of A. H. M. Kirk-Greene*, edited by Terence Ranger and Olufemi Vaughan, 62-111. London, 1993.

Reynolds, Edwards. "The Rise and Fall of the African Merchant Class on the Gold Coast, 1830-1874." *Cahiers d'Etudes Africaines* 54, XIV-2:253-264.

Rhodie, R. Samuel. "The Gold Coast Aborigines Abroad." *Journal of African History* 6, no. 3 (1965):389-411.

Robinson, R. E. "Why 'Indirect Rule' Has Been Replaced by 'Local Government' in the Nomenclature of British Native Administration." *Journal of African Administration* 2, no. 3 (July 1950):12-15.

Sanders, James. "The Expansion of the Fanti and the Emergence of the Asante in the Eighteenth Century." *Journal of African History* 20, no. 3 (1979):349-364.

———. "Village Settlement Among the Fante: A Study of the Anomabo Paramountcy." *Africa* 55, no. 2 (1985):174-185.

Sarbah, John Mensah. "Maclean and Gold Coast Judicial Assessors." *Journal of the African Society* 9, no. 36 (July 1910):349-359.

Sekyi, W. E. G. "The Anglo-Fanti." *West Africa*, 25 May–18 September 1918.

Shallof, Stanley. "The Cape Coast *Asafo* Company Riot of 1932." *International Journal of African Historical Studies* 7, no. 4 (1974):591-607.

———. "The Income Tax, Indirect Rule, and the Depression: The Gold Coast Riots of 1931." *Cahiers d'Etudes Africaines* 54, XIV-2:359-375.

———. "The Press and Politics in Accra: The Accra Legislative Council Election of 1935." *Societas* 1, no. 3 (Summer 1971):213-19.

Skinner, D., and Barbara Howell. "Misunderstandings Arising from the Use of the Term 'Creole' in the Literature of Sierra Leone." *Africa* 47, no. 3 (1977):305-319.

Stone, Lawrence. "The Revival of Narrative: Reflections on a New Old History," In *The Past and the Present,* by Lawrence Stone, 74-96. Boston, 1981.

Stone, Robert. "The Junior Administrative Officers' Petition of 1946." *Ghana Notes and Queries* 12 (June 1972):27-30.

Swanzy, Henry. "A Trading Family in the Nineteenth Century Gold Coast." *Transactions of the Gold Coast Historical Society* 2, no. 2 (1956):87-120.

Tenkorang, Samuel. "The Founding of Mfantsipim, 1905-1908." *Transactions of the Historical Society of Ghana* 15, no. 2 (1974):165-175.

Thomas, H. B. "Native Tribunals in the Gold Coast Colony." *Journal of Comparative Legislation and International Law Third Series* 26, parts 3 and 4 (1944):30-35.

Wilks, Ivor. "Akwamu and Otublohum: An Eighteenth Century Akan Marriage Arrangement." *Africa* 29, no. 4 (October 1959):391-404.

Woodman, Gordon R. "Customary Law, State Courts, and the Notion of Institutionalization of Norms in Ghana and Nigeria." In *People's Law and State Law: The Bellagio Papers,* edited by Anthony Allot and Gordon Woodman, 143-163. Dordrecht, Holland, 1985.

Wyse, A. J. G. "On Misunderstandings Arising from the Use of the Term 'Creole' in the Literature of Sierra Leone: A Rejoinder." *Africa* 49, no. 4 (1979):409-417.

Yarak, Larry. "Elmina and Greater Asante in the Nineteenth Century." *Africa* 56, no. 1 (1986):33-52.

Zabel, Shirley. "Legislative History of the Gold Coast and Lagos Marriage Ordinance: III." *Journal of African Law* 23, no. 1 (Spring 1979):10-36.

INDEX

Abora, 38
abusua, 67, 98, 102
Accra, 24, 34, 35; anticolonial
    feeling in, 204; disputes
    in, 151, 178; elections in,
    184, 186; Ratepayers
    Association, 184; state
    crystallization in, 39
Ackinie of Aikunfie, 114
Acquah II, 164
Acquah III (Albert Mould
    Sackey), 165-166
African identity, 73-74
African Times, 76n12
Afro-European, 6
Ahuma, Rev. Attoh, 220
Akanization: affects marriage,
    89-90; in Cape Coast, 196;
    in Elmina, 160; influence
    on coast, 3- 4, 14, 153-
    154, 160-161; in Winneba,
    163-166
Akosua v. Orbodie, 233
akutsei, (quarters of Accra), 35
Akwamu, Akan kingdom of,
    34-35

amanhen, 39, 161
Ameko v. Amevor, 101
Amissah, Chief Sam, 156, 189-
    190
Amoah IV, 215n136. *See also*
    Johnston, Kwesi
Anaman, Rev. Jacob B., 222
Andoh, Chief Quacoe, 118,
    121, 140n40
Anglicization, 4, 225
Anglo-Fantis, 6
Anomabu, 32, 38
Apter, David, 178
Asaam, Rev. Egyir, 13, 133
asafos: conflict with merchants,
    122; development of, 38;
    economic role of, 122;
    matrilineal succession in,
    33-34; in military cam-
    paigns, 121; opposition to
    chiefs, 123; sense of cor-
    porate identity, 123; source
    of disturbances, 121; source
    of positions, 197; as third
    estate, 123; in Winneba,
    118